The Soviet–East European Relationship in the Gorbachev Era

The Soviet–East European Relationship in the Gorbachev Era

The Prospects for Adaptation

EDITED BY
Aurel Braun

Westview Press
BOULDER, SAN FRANCISCO, & LONDON

Westview Special Studies on the Soviet Union and Eastern Europe

This Westview softcover edition is printed on acid-free paper and bound in library-quality, coated covers that carry the highest rating of the National Association of State Textbook Administrators, in consultation with the Association of American Publishers and the Book Manufacturers' Institute.

All rights reserved. No part of this publication may be reproduced or transmitted in any form or by any means, electronic or mechanical, including photocopy, recording, or any information storage and retrieval system, without permission in writing from the publishers.

Copyright © 1990 by Westview Press, Inc.

Published in 1990 in the United States of America by Westview Press, Inc., 5500 Central Avenue, Boulder, Colorado 80301, and in the United Kingdom by Westview Press, Inc., 13 Brunswick Centre, London WC1N 1AF, England

Library of Congress Cataloging-in-Publication Data
The Soviet-East European relationship in the Gorbachev era: the
  prospects for adaptation / edited by Aurel Braun.
    p. cm.—(Westview special studies on the Soviet Union and
Eastern Europe)
  Includes bibliographical references.
  ISBN 0-8133-7799-4
  1. Europe, Eastern—Relations—Soviet Union. 2. Soviet Union—
Relations—Europe, Eastern. 3. Soviet Union—Foreign
relations—1985-   I. Braun, Aurel. II. Series.
DJK45.S65S662 1990
327.47—dc20   89-29014
                                                              CIP

Printed and bound in the United States of America

∞ The paper used in this publication meets the requirements of the American National Standard for Permanence of Paper for Printed Library Materials Z39.48-1984.

10   9   8   7   6   5   4   3   2   1

To Julianna, David, and Daniel

Contents

Preface ix
Acknowledgments xi

Introduction, *Aurel Braun* 1

PART ONE
SOVIET PERSPECTIVES

1 Soviet Political and Ideological Perceptions and Policies Toward Eastern Europe, *Karen Dawisha* 9

2 Soviet Efforts to Restructure the CMEA: The Case of Regional Energy Relations, *Carl H. McMillan* 26

3 Soviet Military Concerns and Prospects in Eastern Europe, *Edward N. Luttwak* 47

PART TWO
EAST EUROPEAN CONCERNS

4 East European Political and Ideological Perceptions and Concerns, *Andrzej Korbonski* 65

5 Reforms in the USSR and Eastern Europe: Is There a Link? *Paul Marer* 84

6 The Lesser Allies' View: Eastern Europe and the Military Relationship with the Soviet Union, *Ivan Volgyes* 101

7 Lands In-Between: The Politics of Cultural
   Identity in Contemporary Eastern Europe,
   Melvin Croan 115

PART THREE
DILEMMAS AND PROSPECTS

8 On Reform, Perceptions, Misperceptions,
   Trends, and Tendencies, *Aurel Braun* 135

Epilogue, *Aurel Braun* 218

Bibliography 231
About the Editor and Contributors 243
Index 245

Preface

Shortly after he came to power, Mikhail Gorbachev declared that close ties with Eastern Europe would be his "first commandment." Although it is doubtful that he was suggesting a reorientation of Soviet foreign policy whereby the relationship with the East European states would occupy the center of Moscow's foreign policy concerns, he signalled that he recognized the need for change in that very important relationship. For just as Gorbachev apparently understands that the Soviet Union must modernize domestically in order to be able to ensure both the regime's survival and the position of the state as a superpower in the international system, so it seems he has concluded that Moscow must adapt its external relations to changing conditions.

Given that Gorbachev has been in power for less than five years, it may be too early to judge precisely the nature of changes in the Soviet-East European relationship, but one may be able to identify certain trends or at least tendencies. The contributors assess not only the nature of the relationship but also the possibilities for more "organic" linkages between Eastern Europe and the Soviet Union. There has been a diminution in the exercise of Soviet "petty dominance" over Eastern Europe, but are current changes more form than substance? Ultimately, how well are the parties adapting to changing conditions?

Beyond the actual policies pursued by the various states, the perception that they have of the relationship is particularly significant. Consequently, the analyses in the book involve an examination not only of policies but also of perceptions in a multidimensional approach. Thus, it is important that a broad range of expertise is brought to the issues. Four key areas are at the center of this study: political/ideological, economic, military, and sociocultural. And since the perceptions of the various parties play a vital role in the relationship, a double-entry system is employed that allows experts on Soviet policy on the one hand and those on Eastern Europe on the other to examine the same issues and thereby collectively provide a 360-degree analysis. In the concluding chapter the editor brings the various approaches together and examines trends and tendencies in Soviet-East European relations.

Aurel Braun
University of Toronto
June 1989

Acknowledgments

Collective works depend not only on scholarship but also on cooperation, management, and logistics. This book has greatly benefited thus not only from the wide-ranging expertise of the contributors but also from their readiness to cooperate, their willingness to make prompt revisions, and their patience in bringing this work together.

Many individuals have given us advice and comment on this work. I would like to thank Vernon Aspaturian, Morris Bornstein, Timothy Colton, Walter Connor, Richard Day, Mary Ellen Fischer, Charles Gati, Trond Gilberg, Marshall Goldman, Bennett Kovrig, Michael Mandelbaum, Robin Remington, Radoslav Selucky, H. Gordon Skilling, Joseph Skvorecky, and Jiri Valenta, who have all helped make this work more sharply focused and relevant. Of course I assume responsibility for errors and omissions.

Generous financial help has been provided for this project by the Centre for Russian and East European Studies at the University of Toronto and the Social Sciences and Humanities Research Council of Canada.

Several individuals have provided vital help in the preparation of this manuscript. I am especially grateful to Susan McEachern, a senior acquisitions editor at Westview Press, for her encouragement, suggestions, and patience. William Guest, Jr., Douglas Alderson, Jana Oldfield, and Joe Lim at University of Toronto have ably assisted us. And I would like to thank Brenda Samuels of Erindale College, University of Toronto, in particular for her patience and persistence in the preparation of several drafts of the manuscript. Her technical expertise and calm under the pressure of deadlines were most welcome.

My wife and children not only provided me with encouragement but graciously coped with a great deal of disruption.

A. B.

Introduction

Aurel Braun

Mikhail Gorbachev, at the time of this writing, has been in power a little longer than four years. This is certainly not long in comparison with some of his predecessors such as Stalin, Brezhnev or even Nikita Khrushchev. Such brevity, of course, does affect reasonable expectations of change, policy formulation, and implementation. Nevertheless, it is also noteworthy that Gorbachev has been in power somewhat longer than the combined rule of his two immediate predecessors, Yuri Andropov and Konstantin Chernenko. And, despite obvious differences in political systems, it is also worth remembering that Gorbachev has also exceeded in time the period during which John F. Kennedy held the presidency of the United States. Therefore, even in the case of a system that may be as difficult to change as the Soviet one, a period of over four years does afford opportunities for considerable movement. But perhaps even more important than the time factor is Gorbachev's often-declared intention to bring about "radical" reforms. If there is to be change at a certain stage, the shape of the process should become discernable. And, if it is not, then this may raise basic questions both regarding the analytic tools and the nature of the process.

There are intrinsic uncertainties in the analysis of any process of change, but there are particular difficulties in the case of the socialist systems. Different statistical and accounting systems and the frequent unavailability of data are only some of the impediments. These are not insurmountable but they do make the identification of trends and the prospects for prediction more difficult. In evaluating reform, whether it is within the Soviet Union itself or in the relationship between Moscow and the East European states (the focus of this work involves the six East European Council for Mutual Economic Assistance (CMEA) member states—the German Democratic Republic, Poland, Czechoslovakia, Hungary, Romania and Bulgaria) there are conceptual problems relating to reform and to crisis. There is also the difficulty of assessing the role of a single individual, in this case the General Secretary of the Communist Party of the Soviet Union in bringing about change in the Soviet system and in the relationship with Eastern Europe. It is not merely the problem of the single actor model that is evident in all political systems but also the specific conundrum of discerning the balance in roles that exists in socialism between the roles played by the individual leader and the system. Furthermore, there may be differences between the roles played by individual states and the manner in which a regional system operates. The paramount concern of this study is the nature of change in the interstate system in the Soviet bloc, focused on the Soviet–East European relationship. Yet this cannot be assessed without an examination of Gorbachev's policies and the nature of the changes he has proposed and so far has implemented.

Timing, as in all politics, is essential and may be crucial to Gorbachev's success. His initiatives certainly appear to be ambitious, and he has repeatedly emphasized the urgency of change. He has at the very least managed to effect a change in atmospherics, not only domestically but also in Soviet–East European relations. The psychology of change can generate a momentum of its own though the outcome may be quite unpredictable. The tremendous energy that Gorbachev has brought to the task that he has outlined for himself and the scope of his declared programs have raised both expectations and fears in the Soviet Union as well as in Eastern Europe. Karen Dawisha is probably quite correct in her contention (Chapter 1) that Gorbachev has already had a significant impact on Eastern Europe. Whether such impact will move development in a substantive way in the direction that Gorbachev hopes may be difficult to confirm. If there are no substantive changes in that direction three years after his rise to power, that in itself may be an important indicator of the nature of the process that Gorbachev has tried to set into motion. Still, the very change in atmospherics may in itself justify the labelling of Gorbachev's period in power as an era, though its duration may prove to be considerably shorter than that of the rule of such Soviet leaders as Stalin or Brezhnev.

The contributors to this volume do take into account the views of those scholars who believe that profound changes are or are about to take place and thus do not exclude the *possibility* of transformation. But conceptual clarification and probative analysis require that a series of basic questions should be asked. In politics, and particularly in international politics that involve the Soviet–East European relationship, there are no innocuous questions. Nevertheless, the scope of such a study requires a focus on a number of specifics where comprehensive analysis of all external developments together with the domestic motivating factors is not feasible. Though these questions are in themselves value-laden, the authors in this study have attempted to focus on those issues that are the chief driving forces in the Soviet–East European relationship.

On the one hand, Soviet–East European relations do not quite mirror the interchanges between sovereign states. On the other hand, it would be a mistake to think of the East European states as part of the Soviet in-state system, for their area of autonomy is clearly larger. It is not the case, then, that the Soviet Union alone determines the nature of significant developments within Eastern Europe and the very character of interstate relations within the region. Nevertheless, there are vital asymmetries that profoundly affect the nature of the Soviet-East European relationship. These involve asymmetries in power—political, economic, and military. In all these areas the Soviet Union alone is far stronger than all of the East European states combined. There is also an asymmetry in interest in that relationship. Whereas for the East European states the relationship with the Soviet Union is clearly their most important external link, the degree of interest on the Soviet part is far more difficult to assess. Shortly after he came to power Gorbachev declared that the strengthening of relations with East Europe would be his "first commandment"[1] and this combined with his advocacy of *novoe myshlenie* (new thinking) tends to indicate a strong interest in the region indeed. Nevertheless, this does not necessarily indicate that Eastern Europe is the primary focus of Soviet foreign policy— or at least not that it is consistently so. As a superpower with consequent global concerns, the Soviet Union needs to confront a series of external issues which can divert its interests from the region. There is, then, some disagreement among the authors as to the centrality of Eastern Europe in Gorbachev's foreign policy concerns with Karen Dawisha (Chapter 1) emphasizing, for instance, the centrality of Eastern Europe and Andrzej Korbonski suggesting that at certain times and in specific areas Gorbachev may have subjected the region to "benign neglect" (Chapter 4).

Other questions also arise out of the focus of this study. In a sense, regardless of the socio-economic system in particular states, all foreign policy starts at home. But, in the case of the Soviet Union and Eastern Europe, given the tenets of Marxism-Leninism and the asymmetrical relationship between the Soviet Union on the one hand and a diverse Eastern Europe on the other, Soviet domestic determinants of foreign policy, in particular, are crucial. And not only the nature of changes taking place in the Soviet Union but also the motives behind Gorbachev's decision to try to institute reforms become salient. His motives have already had an impact on the nature of the change taking place and are likely to help define the future course of developments. Several of the authors, but particularly economists Paul Marer (Chapter 5) and Carl McMillan (Chapter 2), analyze these motives.

Defining change may be at least as difficult. Perestroika (reconstruction, restructuring) may involve merely an attempt to reform the ineffective aspects of the system or may entail a systemic change. William E. Odom, who has asked whether Gorbachev's proposals constitute a systemic change, has laid out three criteria for gauging the nature of the current process in the Soviet Union.[2] These involve: a major shift to market pricing and allocation where the market exceeds central planning; the free flow of information to the degree required for effective market activity involving both domestic economic activity and international trade; and the assurance of the legal rights over the factors of production. Paul Marer (Chapter 5), takes a similar approach in the economic area, for it seems that in order for the Soviet Union to deal with fundamental economic problems it may indeed need to undergo a systemic change. Boris Meissner of Cologne University has also formulated the question in a rather stark fashion by asking whether Gorbachev's perestroika represents reform or revolution.[3] He contends that the reforms which Gorbachev has carried out so far are of a limited nature but that his perestroika envisions revolutionary changes. There are uncertainties, though, and a great many blank spots in Gorbachev's proposals, as is seen in the various assessments of it, both in this volume and elsewhere.

However, domestic developments in the Soviet Union, as noted, have a profound impact on the shape of the Soviet-East European relationship. And here another question arises as to what constitutes "normalcy." It should involve, one would think, a more "organic" relationship in the Hegelian sense between the Soviet Union on the one hand and the East European states on the other, where mutual interests and interdependence rather than the primary threat of force constitute the most important binding elements. In 1976 Helmut Sonnenfeldt and his boss, Henry Kissinger, tried to fine-tune a policy which would help foster such a development, a policy which came to be known as the "Sonnenfeldt Doctrine."[4] I would disagree with critics who contended that it meant the abandoning of the "captive nations" in Eastern Europe. Rather, it aimed for a "more autonomous existence" for the East Europeans. For such a relationship to develop, the East European regimes (as well as that of the Soviet Union) must become stable. But here Gorbachev would have to face the classic Soviet dilemma in the region of maintaining both cohesion and viability.[5] As Charles Gati said, Gorbachev realizes that "only profound reforms have a chance to make the region more stable but he had a problem because the price of stability is more independence from the Soviet Union."[6]

It is then particularly difficult for the Soviet Union and the East European states to adapt to changing conditions in such a way as to ensure that healthy, normal relations develop between them. It involves adaptation both at the national level in order to create internal stability and adaptation of the regional system to changing conditions. The states involved must be able to build and use power, authority, and policy instruments so as to employ available resources effectively in pursuit of such goals. Adaptation may be purposive (that is, deliberate, blatant, etc.) and/or situational (that is, passive, involuntary, flexible, etc.).

Successful adaptation, though, involves not only policies but especially perceptions—both in Eastern Europe and in the Soviet Union. The problems of perception played an important role in shaping the format of this volume. There are differences in perception between the masses and the elite and among the elite in the region. And there is, of course, considerable diversity in Eastern Europe. Even the source of advice to decision-makers is important in formulating perceptions (Marer, Chapter 5). Nevertheless, collectively we have tried to delineate the broad Soviet and East European perceptions. Consequently, we have employed a double-entry system where in a number of chapters specialists look at crucial issue areas from the Soviet perspective and try to analyse Soviet perceptions and goals, and other scholars examine the same or similar issue-areas in terms of East European perspectives. Moreover, we have found it useful not only to concentrate on the main issue areas such as political and ideological developments, economic imperatives, military strategic concerns, and political-cultural relations, but also to provide whenever possible a historical perspective to current developments, as Korbonski (Chapter 4) has done.

There is also the importance of selecting appropriate case studies to try to assess trends or at least tendencies. In the economic realm this is particularly vital since this is where the main thrust of Gorbachev's policies have taken place. From the Soviet perspective, energy policies within the CMEA should provide a good indication both of the direction and dilemmas of Gorbachev's policies and the impact on the Soviet-East European relationship. Furthermore, an analysis of economic development in Hungary under the New Economic Mechanism (NEM) should help illuminate the issues of reform throughout Eastern Europe and also in some important respects in the Soviet Union. Whereas there are differences in size between Hungary's economy and that of the Soviet Union and in the nature of external mechanisms of control, there are significant similarities in policies between NEM and Gorbachev's perestroika. Moreover, recent developments in Hungary, which have resulted in the removal of Janos Kadar from his position as General-Secretary and in wholesale changes in the Politburo, should provide some important clues as to possible directions that such reforms may take.

Political/ideological, economic, and military factors, though, do not give us a complete picture because perception is affected to a significant degree by cultural attitudes. In the first three chapters which deal with the Soviet perspective the authors do touch both in a direct and in an indirect fashion on Soviet attitudes as a superpower and as the regional hegemon toward the East European states. In the last section, in Chapter 7, Melvin Croan devotes his contribution to an examination of East European political culture and cultural attitudes towards the Soviet Union and the possible emergence of a regional cultural identity.

Throughout the region cautious developments have been combined with ambitious plans. We are examining a process rather than single events and there are bound to be blank spots which prevent accurate prediction. It is also quite possible that the decision-makers who are formulating and attempting to implement policies, including Gorbachev, do not have a master plan and they themselves cannot accurately predict the outcome. It is also conceivable that there will be a whole range of unexpected developments and unintended consequences. However, after more than four years of Gorbachev's rule and the energy and ambition that he brought to the task of rejuvenating, not only the domestic structure but also Soviet-East European relations, we should be able to discern certain trends or at least tendencies in that relationship.

Notes

1. *Pravda* (Moscow), 12 March 1985.
2. William E. Odom, "How Far Can Soviet Reform Go?" *Problems of Communism*, November-December 1987, Vol. XXXVI, pp. 23-5.
3. Boris Meissner, "Gorbachev's Perestroika, Reform or Revolution?" *Aussenpolitik*, Vol. 38, No. 3, 1987, pp. 211-30.
4. Aurel Braun, "Soviet Naval Policy in the Mediterranean, The Sonnenfeldt Doctrine and Yugoslavia," *Orbis* (Spring 1978), Vol. 22, No. 1, pp. 101-33.
5. See James F. Brown, "Relations Between the Soviet Union and Its East European Allies: A Survey" *Rand Report R-1742-PR*, 1975 passim.
6. *Newsweek*, May 9, 1988, p. 26.

PART ONE

Soviet Perspectives

1

Soviet Political and Ideological Perceptions and Policies Toward Eastern Europe

Karen Dawisha

Even though Soviet views of Eastern Europe and its relationship to the USSR have gone through a period of reappraisal since Mikhail Sergeevich Gorbachev was elected General Secretary of the Communist Party of the Soviet Union (CPSU) in March 1985, that reappraisal has done little to erode the firm Soviet commitment to Eastern Europe as a geographically contiguous entity, populated by peoples who share a long historical memory of relations with Russia, and governed by like-minded Communist leaders. Therefore, it was not surprising that Gorbachev, upon coming to power, should have chosen to emphasize that of all the issues on his foreign policy agenda, he would take as his "first commandment" the strengthening of relations with Eastern Europe.[1] Far from receding as US-Soviet arms control negotiations began to dominate international news, Gorbachev continued to underline the centrality of Eastern Europe, emphasizing at a Moscow meeting of bloc prime ministers and Party secretaries convened in October 1987 to discuss economic reform that the Soviet Union "views cooperation with socialist countries as the most important, priority direction of its policy."[2]

From the inception of the Gorbachev period, there was every reason to believe that Eastern Europe would occupy a central place on the Soviet policy agenda. Gorbachev reaffirmed during such occasions as the renewal of the Warsaw Treaty in April 1985 and the 27th Party Congress in March 1986 that the Soviet and East European people still share a "common historical destiny,"[3] emphasizing in the process the fact that he, like his predecessors, considers core Soviet strategic, ideological, and economic interests to be invested in Eastern Europe. His admission of Soviet culpability for mismanaging relations in the past and for failing, for example, to "avert crisis situations,"[4] underlined only his commitment to reappraise certain important aspects of the relationship, without suggesting for a moment that Moscow was considering allowing a situation to develop which would lead to the denunciation or overthrow of socialism in Eastern Europe or the demise of the Soviet alliance system in Eastern Europe. While admitting that the development of the socialist bloc has encountered a large number of problems, Gorbachev himself clearly sees the existence of the bloc as a major force in international politics. As Gorbachev himself wrote:

> Over the postwar decades socialism has become a strong international formation and a major factor in world politics. A socialist form of economy functions in a large group of countries. The foundations have been laid for an international division of labor. Multilateral organizations of socialist states have gained a varied experience of activity. Scientific and cultural exchanges have assumed large proportions. Of course, this does not mean that the development of world socialism always proceeded successfully.[5]

In attempting to discern the extent to which Soviet perceptions and policies toward Eastern Europe have changed since Gorbachev was elected General Secretary, the analyst is presented with several major difficulties. First of all there exists little agreement among scholars and policymakers in the West about the basic nature of Soviet policy in Eastern Europe *before* March 1985, when Gorbachev came to power. The field is riven by disagreements, many of them—particularly in the United States—coalescing around two opposite poles which suggest that Soviet preeminence in Eastern Europe is derived on the one hand from the imperative of maintaining a military posture in Eastern Europe for the forward defense of the Soviet heartland and on the other from Marxism-Leninism itself, whose very essence is seen by adherents to this second pole as thriving and depending upon external expansion to maintain its legitimacy as a world force.

These two poles which dominate American Sovietology are supplemented by other, but no less agreed, views emanating primarily from the spectrum of European public opinion. There the views are more extreme, stemming from closer geographical proximity and more direct experience in coping with Soviet power. The European right is even more convinced than its American counterpart that Soviet military power in central Europe is offensively oriented and not intended ultimately for the defense of Russia. This suspicion of Soviet motives is shared, for different reasons, by social democratic, communist, and emigre groups, all of whom see the Soviet position in Eastern Europe as stemming not from what they see as the humanist aspirations of Marxism, but from the despotic impulses of Stalinism.

These views are supplemented in Europe and the United States by a very strong centrist sentiment which at its roots believes that Soviet hegemony in Eastern Europe is not a sine qua non of Soviet power—that given thorough-going de-Stalinization and detente the bloc system created by Stalin and bolstered by the Cold War would also have to be fundamentally revised.

All of these views are echoed among unofficial circles in the Soviet Union and Eastern Europe, where dissident communities have been united in their condemnation of Soviet hegemony in Eastern Europe but disunited in their analysis of its sources. To these perspectives must, of course, be added the official Soviet and East European view of their mutual relationship—namely that the Red Army liberated these countries from fascism, creating the conditions for indigenous progressive and communist parties to flourish; but that in no way was socialism imposed from outside after the Second World War, and nor has it been maintained by force since. The community of socialist states to which the Soviet Union and the East European countries belong has traditionally been seen and portrayed as a voluntary association of countries who have allied themselves economically, politically and militarily for the defense and promotion of socialist ideals.

Because of continued disagreement over the root sources of Soviet policy in the region, considerable debate in both the West and throughout the Eastern bloc remains about the prospects of maintaining the current reform momentum in the long term, much less achieving fundamental structural changes in the bloc system which has dominated Europe for the past forty years. All of these views are, however, united in agreement that Eastern Europe is, and has always been, of the most fundamental importance to the Soviet Union. For this reason, it is also agreed that the most careful scrutiny must be given to Gorbachev's East European policies as they unfold; since success in Eastern Europe is the crucial litmus test for Gorbachev's power, skill, and determination.

There is universal agreement, too, on a third point: namely that Gorbachev has already had a significant impact on Soviet–East European relations. East European officials, dissidents and public opinion are universal in agreeing both that Gorbachev represents a major force for change in the region and that this force has already been unleashed, albeit with differing results. It is the progress made so far, both in words and in deeds, and less the still uncertain prospects for the future, that is the subject of this article.

Gorbachev's efforts in Eastern Europe have been directed along three lines:

1. *Pereotsenka* (or reappraisal) of certain core ideological and philosophical formulations which had shaped the broader world outlook of Soviet leaders and which consequently also had a crucial effect on the course of Soviet–East European relations in the past;
2. *Perestroika* (or restructuring) of the specific ideological basis governing Soviet–East European relations; and
3. *Perevyazka* (or bandaging) of old wounds which have been allowed to fester in the past, to the detriment of normal, healthy intra-bloc relations.

Pereotsenka

Recognition by Gorbachev that Soviet–East European relations require fundamental transformation has produced "new thinking" in all areas. This effort has benefitted first and foremost from the reappraisal of core ideological precepts which have guided Soviet policy for decades. Among these is (1) the changed view of the nature of the international system and the Soviet Union's place in it; and (2) a redefinition of the entire concept of correlation of forces.

The nature of the international system

Gorbachev and his closest advisors have rejected the traditional "two-camp" doctrine which posed the notion of implacable hostility between the socialist and capitalist worlds. This doctrine has been replaced with a more complex view of the international system which poses interdependence between socialism and capitalism as the new iron law. The ideological justification for this transformation was offered by Yevgeniy Primakov, Director of the USSR Academy of Sciences' Institute of World Economics and International Relations, in a September 1987 article in the CPSU's premier theoretical journal, *Kommunist*:

> In Party documents of the last two years, it has been repeatedly pointed out that the Soviet Union and socialism as a whole are influencing the course of global events under the conditions of the dialectical compatibility between the division of the world into two opposite sociopolitical systems and the preservation of its unity. This indicates the rejection of the previously unilateral approach, in which the first part of the formula of "unity and struggle of opposites" was if not ignored, at least clearly underestimated by Soviet social scientists in their study of historical developments. However, without a clear understanding of these dialectics we may draw the false conclusion that the past, present and future influence of socialism on the contemporary world is possible only through its confrontation with capitalism.[6]

This notion, that the historical dialectic between communism and capitalism can proceed both on a competitive and a cooperative plane, eliminates in a stroke much of the ideological objection which had previously been voiced to closer East-West relations in general and East European–West European relations in particular.

Redefinition of correlation of forces

It is aided by an equally new conception of how to measure the correlation of forces between capitalism and socialism. Lenin had once called the correlation of forces (*sootnosheniye sil*) "the main point in Marxism and Marxian tactics," further stating that "we, Marxists, have always been proud of the fact that by a strict calculation of the mass forces and mutual class relations we have determined the expediency of this or that form of struggle."[7] However, while the correlation of forces was meant to take into account the grand sum of a society's total capabilities in the social, economic, political, moral and military spheres, its calculation was increasingly distorted by the dual phenomena of on the one hand over-reliance on military power and quantitative economic indicators and on the other ritualistic assertions that the "correlation of forces is shifting in favor of socialism."

Both phenomena have now been rejected. More attention is being paid to qualitative indicators in the non-military fields, with the result that all Soviet leaders and theoreticians have become much more critical of the failings of Soviet-style socialism and much more accepting of certain inherent and long-term strengths of capitalism. Equally, it is by no means assumed that the correlation of forces will proceed to shift in favor of socialism without setbacks and uneven development between, for example, military strength and social factors. As Primakov states, in the article cited above, "change in the correlation of forces is . . . a lengthy process encompassing a number of spheres—political, economic, military—whose development proceeds unevenly."[8] Indeed, Primakov goes on to maintain:

> The study of the real correlation between the interests of social development, on the one hand, and class interests, on the other, is of the greatest possible significance in terms of the balance of forces between the two systems at the contemporary stage. V.I. Lenin considered that the interests of the development of society as a whole superseded those of the working class.[9]

The result of this reformulation has been extensive both in the Soviet Union and in Eastern Europe. In both, much more attention, as a result, has been given to the enhancement of an agenda for social reform, encompassing *glasnost,* multi-candidate elections, economic restructuring, and attention to legality and human rights, details of which are presented in the section on perevyazka below. It is important here to emphasize that such reforms stem from a fundamental shift in core Soviet ideological perspectives. It is precisely because they are the result of this deep reappraisal that both Soviet and East European leaders express optimism that they are irreversible.

Perestroika

The reformulation of ideological precepts has proceeded from the general process of pereotsenka to the specific reconstruction or perestroika of the ideological assumptions underlying Soviet-East European relations. These relations have been transformed by the following new formulations: (1) the rejection of the notion of a single universal "model" of socialism; (2) the redefinition of socialist internationalism; and (3) a broader conceptualization of Europe as "a common home".

Rejection of a single model of socialism

Gorbachev himself set the standard in revising these notions, beginning at the 27th Party Congress when he specifically emphasized "unconditional respect in international practice for the right of every people to choose the paths and forms of its development." In what appeared as almost a *mea culpa* for past Soviet practices, Gorbachev stated that "unity has nothing in common with uniformity, with a hierarchy."[10] Gorbachev was subsequently to outline in detail the source of previous problems:

> In the field of state building, too, the fraternal socialist states largely relied on the Soviet example. To an extent, this was inevitable. Assertions concerning the imposition of the "Soviet model" distort this objective necessity of that time [immediate post-war era]. . . .
> But it was not without losses, and rather serious ones at that. Drawing on the Soviet experience, some countries failed duly to consider their own specifics. Even worse, a stereotyped approach was given an ideological tint by some of our theoreticians and especially practical leaders who acted as almost the sole guardians of truth. Without taking into consideration the novelty of problems and the specific features of different socialist countries, they sometimes displayed suspicion toward those countries' approaches to certain problems.
> . . . Furthermore, negative accretions in these relations were not examined with a sufficient degree of frankness, which means that not everything obstructing their development and preventing them from entering a new, contemporary stage was identified.[11]

If this was the problem, the solution also appeared clear: Adopt new principles which eliminate the need for slavish adherence to a single model of socialism. Toward this end, Gorbachev enunciated the need for Parties to proceed according to principles which have at their root "absolute independence" of every socialist state. As Gorbachev made clear: "The independence of each Party, its sovereign right to decide the issues facing its country and its responsibility to its nation are the unquestionable principles."[12]

This view came to be shared by other leaders and top advisors. Politburo Secretary Yegor Ligachev, identified by some in the West as having a more conservative view of such matters, was at pains during a trip to Hungary in April 1987 to emphasize his agreement with this new approach. Speaking on Hungarian television, Ligachev stressed that "every country looks for solutions independently, not as in the past. It is not true that Moscow's conductor's baton, or Moscow's hand is in everything. . . . Every nation has a right to its own way."[13]

Redefinition of socialist internationalism

The changes that did take place could not have taken place, however, without the thorough-going revision in the definition of socialist internationalism (also sometimes referred to synonymously as proletarian internationalism, the Brezhnev doctrine, or the doctrine of limited sovereignty) which has occurred since Gorbachev came to power. Since the earliest days of the Comintern, Soviet leaders have espoused adherence to some form of socialist internationalism. However, the definition of the term has varied widely according to the prevailing political climate. The Soviets have long since rejected the Stalinist dictum that "he is an internationalist who steadfastly promotes the strengthening of the Soviet state" in favor of more subtle and less restrictive formulations.

After the invasion of Czechoslovakia in 1968, the definition once again became more restrictive. And until 1985, socialist internationalism came to mean the acknowledgement that the socialist bloc's greatest strength lay in its *class*-based unity. Sovereign states, therefore, had to subordinate their separate national interests to the historically more progressive interests of socialism. As the definitive *Pravda* editorial which announced the new definition maintained, "every communist party is responsible not only to its own people but also to all socialist countries" and "the sovereignty of individual socialist countries cannot be counterpoised to the [higher] interests of world socialism and the world revolutionary movement."[14] This new definition, applied with force by Soviet tanks, obviously was meant to limit the independence of the East Europeans far more than that of the Soviets.

After coming to power in March 1985, Gorbachev called several times for building intra-bloc relations on a new basis. On the whole he has shied away from using the term socialist internationalism, limiting his references to only the most important state occasions, like the renewal of the Warsaw Treaty. Meanwhile, theoreticians within the Soviet Union were engaged in an extremely intensive debate about the meaning of socialist internationalism in these new conditions. The first deputy head of the CPSU Central Committee Department for Liaison with Ruling Workers and Communist Parties (DLRWCP), Oleg Rakhmanin, published an article under the pseudonym O. Vladimirov, which laid down a direct challenge to reformist trends in this area:

> Anticommunist theoreticians and opportunists, slandering proletarian internationalism, declare it to be "outdated," try to pose as trailblazers of some new kind of "unity."[15]

In upholding a "hard-line" interpretation of socialist internationalism, Rakhmanin set himself against a growing number of high-ranking theoreticians who were indeed posing as "trailblazers of some new kind of 'unity.'" The "trailblazers" included such personages as Georgiy Shakhnazarov, another deputy head of the DLRWCP; Ivan Frolov, the new editor of *Kommunist*; Oleg Bogomolov, head of the Institute of the Economics of the World Socialist System; Aleksandr Bovin, the influential political commentator for *Izvestiya*; Nikolai Shishlin, head of sector in the Central Committee's Information Department; and Anatoliy Butenko, Yevgeniy Ambartsumov, and Yuriy Novopashin, all section heads in Bogomolov's institute. It goes without saying that the formulations contained in articles written by this group found almost universal appeal in Eastern Europe (an exception being the anti-reformist views expressed by Czechoslovak leaders before the ouster of Husak).

While Rakhmanin's point of view was certainly not without adherents in the Central Committee and elsewhere, opposition to it grew and gained preeminence. One of the most forceful, and earliest, enunciations of new thinking in the realm of socialist internationalism came from Yuriy Novopashin, who warned that there was "no magic wand, that could dispose of 'national egoism' on the one hand or of 'great-power ambitions' on the other."[16] He noted that, far from dying out, "national and state interests" of individual socialist states were increasingly being expressed and were often "contradictory." As a result, even though socialist states were by no means equal, each deserved to be treated as equal. This would involve renouncing "domineering" methods, "great-power ambitions," and "hegemonistic pretensions." Finally, Novopashin adamantly rejected unspecified "attempts" by theorists and practitioners alike—including, obviously, Rakhmanin—"to define the essence of socialist internationalism in terms of subordination or to suggest, for example, that, where the socialist countries are concerned, the principle of respect for national sovereignty could be subordinated to some higher principle governing their relations—namely that of unity."[17]

It was these views, rather than those of Rakhmanin (who also subsequently lost his post), which gained preeminence, leading intra-bloc relations to be defined as "mutual relations between sovereign and independent countries with their own national interests—yet, between countries that are socialist."[18] Therefore, while the sovereignty of every state and independence of every party came to be the touchstone of Soviet conceptions of intra-bloc relations, the fact that these countries were at the same time socialist was also stressed. Thus, Gorbachev emphasized:

> We are also firmly convinced that the socialist community will be successful only if every party and state cares for both its own and common interests, if it respects its friends and allies, heeds their interests and pays attention to the experience of others. Awareness of this relationship between domestic issues and the interests of world socialism is typical of the countries of the socialist community. We are united, in unity resides our strength, and from unity we draw our confidence that we will cope with the issues set forth by our time.[19]

Europe as a "common home"

Soviet views of Europe are complex and multifaceted. They arise from the historical Russian conflict between on the one hand the Slavophile rejection of Western culture's subversive and corrupting nature and on the other the Westernizers' embrace of the values of the Enlightenment and the objectives of economic development. These two strains continued into the post-1917 Soviet phase, with Soviet policy toward the West frequently influenced by one or other conflicting view.

The Gorbachev period is no exception. The goals of economic autarky and social isolationism are as alien to Gorbachev's reform plans as they were to the Westernizers who dominated the Russian court under Peter the Great. Gorbachev's conception relies on greater economic, political, and social interaction amongst the socialist and capitalist states of Europe with the aim of reducing both American hegemony and the rigid division of Europe. While NATO policymakers have rightly felt concern about the impact of such formulations on alliance cohesion, East European leaders without exception have welcomed the Soviet change of heart.

To many in Eastern Europe, Gorbachev appeared sincere when he labelled Europe a "common home" and declared that "Europe's historic chance and its future lies in peaceful cooperation between the states of that continent." This pan-European element of Gorbachev's outlook was first enunciated at the 27th Party Congress, and then further elaborated during his 1987 visit to Czechoslovakia and in his book *Perestroika*. He emphasized the broader philosophical, historical and cultural underpinnings of this view, stemming as they do from his own belief that: "We are Europeans. Old Russia was united with Europe by Christianity. . . . The history of Russia is an organic part of the great European history. . . . Europe 'from the Atlantic to the Urals' is a cultural-historical entity united by the common heritage of the Renaissance and the Enlightenment."[20]

In addition to the general concepts which lay behind this notion, Gorbachev also had specifically reconceptualized the entire notion of European security, bringing it more into line with the ideals embodied in the Helsinki Final Act. At the center of this new view of European security was an acceptance of detente, disarmament and peaceful coexistence within Europe as objectives separate from U.S.-Soviet relations. This formulation represented a victory for those East European leaders who had persistently argued since the early 1980s that European detente had to be protected from the deterioration in U.S.-Soviet relations. Thus, Gorbachev emphasized in the 27th Party Congress speech that "it is important . . . to move forward from the initial phase of detente to a more stable, mature detente; then to the creation of reliable security on the basis of the Helsinki process and radical cuts in nuclear and conventional arms."[21]

In line with this call for a more mature detente, Soviet leaders have also emphasized new formulations about security which could have a fundamental impact on Soviet-East European relations in the future. Deputy Foreign Minister Loginov, speaking in Hungary, characterized as a "new feature" of Soviet foreign policy the fact that Soviet leaders now believe that Soviet security could only be guaranteed if "we take into consideration other states' security." Loginov went on to stress that "the only possible solution to issues is one that is acceptable to our partners too."[22] This notion was taken up by many Soviet leaders, including Gorbachev, and has produced a marked invigoration in intra-bloc meetings, called for the purpose of reaching joint formulations and emphasizing common approaches. While clearly much remains to be done in the field of bloc security policy, even this modest beginning is note-worthy. Revisions in Soviet military doctrine governing Eastern Europe are dealt with in other chapters, but clearly it remains to be seen whether Soviet military doctrine could be revised sufficiently to allow for the total withdrawal of their forces from

Eastern Europe, surely a move that would indeed be "acceptable" to their partners.

This new conceptualization of Europe and European security is seen as having the most far-reaching possibilities for the future of Eastern Europe. In reaction to statements such as these, even the most skeptical East European intellectuals like Hungary's George Konrad have admitted the possibility of a "gradual, controlled transformation of the Soviet bloc into a looser community of nations capable of interacting with Western Europe on a partnership basis."[23] Moreover, Alexander Dubcek, the former General Secretary of the Czechoslovak Communist Party who has been in internal exile in Czechoslovakia for almost two decades, gave the rarest of illegal and illicit interviews to the Italian Communist paper, *L'Unita* in January 1988. In it he emphasized that "one of the main positive aspects of Gorbachev's visit to Prague was the idea of a 'new way of thinking' about Europe. This idea ought to be consistently affirmed in our country, to overcome the burden of the past and to set in motion Czechoslovak restructuring. To build a united process, we must first restore confidence among European nations and states. I see this as the only way in which we can have a future, given the present conditions."[24]

Perevyazka

The process of bandaging old wounds, perevyazka, is long over-due in Soviet-East European relations. The mere admission that there are wounds to bandage is in itself an example of glasnost, but beyond this, perevyazka has proceeded along the following lines: (1) the denunciation of formalism in intra-bloc relations; (2) the promotion of indigenous reforms in East European countries which are not a mere copy of Soviet efforts; (3) the recognition that multilateral bloc mechanisms require reform; and (4) the elimination of certain "blank spots" from the official histories of Soviet-East European relations.

The denunciation of formalism

Soviet leaders have come to recognize that their relations with their East European partners have in the past been based less on full and frank exchanges of views than on ritualistic and formalized rhetoric meant to conceal and suppress differences rather than promote the deepening of close relations. This recognition has gone hand in hand both with the marked increase in bilateral and multilateral meetings at all levels and in all spheres and with the Soviet admission that Moscow has no monopoly on the "best" way to construct socialism. To quote Gorbachev: ". . . we gain more from a critical and earnest evaluation of our moves and initiatives than from loud applause for just anything we have done. . . . [W]e do not claim we are the only ones to know the truth. Truth is sought in a joint quest and effort."[25]

It is to this end that joint communiques at the end of bilateral meetings very often have included references to the need to reject past approaches in intra-bloc relations, without foisting on each of the East European parties the current Soviet model of development. A good example in this regard was the final communique following Gorbachev's May 1987 visit to Romania. Clearly, a large number of outstanding conflicts exist between the two countries, ranging from Ceausescu's rejection of all Soviet-style political and economic reforms to the economic plight of Romania which serves as a burden to the other CMEA countries. And the final communique, while emphasizing the areas of coincidence of views between the two leaders (in primarily the foreign policy realm), did also openly portray the differences which separate the two sides. For example, the communique emphasized that the CPSU "attaches great significance to openness, to eliminating areas closed to criticism, and overcoming the tendency to make pronouncements for effect [deklarativnost], formalism, bureaucratic distortions, and methods of management by command and order." No support for these measures from Romania was forthcoming in the communique, however, with Ceausescu instead delivering his own view of the "system of workers' revolutionary democracy" which had been evolving for the last twenty years since he came to power. All the bilateral meetings in the bloc, whether or not amongst leaders in agreement over the path of reform, have thus been characterized by this decline in formalism, and concomitant increase in openness, stemming both from the reforms being implemented in the Soviet Union itself and from Gorbachev's acknowledgement, as discussed above, that there is no single model of socialism.

The promotion of indigenous reform

The abandonment of the notion of a single model of socialism has both legitimized existing differences and produced increased diversity between socialist states. All of these changes have taken place under the watchful eye of Soviet leaders and commentators, who, more often than not, have welcomed changes both as contributing to the new "treasure chest of socialist experiences" and as meeting the specific needs of individual countries. Particularly close attention has been paid to political, social, and economic reforms in Poland, Hungary, the GDR and Bulgaria, all of which have instituted the further reform of their systems with Soviet encouragement. Wholesale economic reforms have been implemented virtually without impediment from Moscow, and in fact, most East European economies have yet to deplete the potential for reform opened up by this new reform era.

Political reforms have traditionally been more difficult to introduce, both because of Moscow's sensitivities and due to the vested interests of the East European leaders themselves in maintaining the political status quo. Such reforms, however, where they have taken place have been accepted by Moscow as within the purview of legitimate East European actions.

In Bulgaria, for example, a decision was implemented in August 1987 to eliminate all unnecessary ceremonies, parades, and ostentatious displays of power. This includes parades commemorating May Day and the Bolshevik revolution, celebrations in honor of leaders' birthdays, portraits of Bulgarian leaders, and placards with exhortatory slogans. The resolution passing these measures pointed out that "the previously existing practice . . . suffered from excessive pomp, gigantomania [literally, *gigantomaniya*, in Russian], unnecessary state management, and so forth. In this connection, it is proposed to prevent wasting the time of citizens, specialists, and leaders in participation in insignificant events."[26] The Soviet response to the resolution pointed out that while other countries could, and do, take a different view of such matters, the Bulgarian decision was a "purely individual matter" which was "in line with the spirit of restructuring." Moreover, far from being chastised for being the first to introduce such a measure, the Bulgarian leadership was hailed for undertaking this "pioneering mission."[27]

It was again in Bulgaria that further substantial political reforms were announced at the beginning of 1988. A plenum of the Central Committee of the BCP, meeting immediately prior to a Party Conference, endorsed the introduction of a "mandate system" into the party in which, henceforth, "the top elective offices in the Party—from the Secretary General of the CC of the BCP down to the secretaries of the primary party organizations—should be held for two consecutive terms at the most, or, as an exception, for three terms."[28] The precise details of the changes, to be formally included in the BCP statutes at the next, 14th, BCP Congress due to be held in 1991, were not announced; but irrespective of the details, the impact of such a reform was likely to go beyond Bulgarian borders.

The reform of multilateral bloc mechanisms

The three major bloc mechanisms regulating political, military, and economic cooperation between member states are inter-Party links, the Warsaw Pact, and the Council for Mutual Economic Assistance (CMEA). Inter-Party links, as discussed above, have been greatly invigorated as the result of Gorbachev's own personal commitment to improved Party contacts.

The Warsaw Pact has not, however, as yet come under the influence of reformist aspiration in Moscow. Nor have East European military establishments decided that glasnost has proceeded far enough to allow for the open discussion of Pact doctrine. If such a debate were to begin, it is likely that at its center would be a document whose existence was revealed by former Polish Colonel Kuklinski. According to Kuklinski, in 1979, the Soviets gained East European acceptance (except Romania) of a document entitled "Statute of the Joint Armed Forces and Their Organization in Wartime." The document in effect provides for the complete subordination of East European military to the Soviet High Command during wartime. In essence, according to Kuklinski, the Soviets now are able to bypass national commanders in times of crisis and exert direct control over East European forces. Moreover, the document is so secret, Kuklinski maintains, that "even the branch and military district commanders only know those provisions that affect them directly."[29] Given the resistance encountered by Moscow in negotiating these and similarly constraining agreements with Eastern Europe, it is unlikely that this particular system of control will quickly come under the influence of revisionist forces in Moscow. Indeed some Western analysts are convinced that if anything Soviet preeminence within the Warsaw Pact has increased and not decreased since Gorbachev came to power.[30]

If the Soviets have been reluctant to reform the military basis of intra-bloc relations, the same is certainly not true in the realm of economics. Here, Moscow has presided over the beginning of a long-term process of thorough-going reform designed to increase bilateral and multilateral economic relations between CMEA member-states; raise the productivity of CMEA economies; improve the total efficiency of CMEA effort through the division of labor between the economies and greater integration; bring the quality of economic output up to world standards; and derive greater benefit from trade with the West, particularly in technology.[31]

In order to achieve these objectives, the Soviets are hoping first and foremost that the period of slow or negative growth in CMEA economies will be brought to an end through greater internal political and economic dynamism within all CMEA countries. Indeed, the improved growth rates achieved by the Soviet economy (in the region of 4% per annum) do suggest that some greater dynamism in intra-bloc economic relations can be achieved through this factor alone. Beyond this, the Soviets have specific reforms in mind for CMEA. Speaking at the 43rd Session of CMEA which met in Moscow in October 1987, Soviet Prime Minister Ryzhkov emphasized the objective of increased reliance on direct links between enterprises in the various CMEA countries. This implies that all CMEA countries will put into effect reforms which would give enterprises the rights to conclude contracts, exchange goods, transfer money abroad, and make and expend profits in different currencies. In accord with these plans, Ryzhkov also announced that agreement had been reached on "working out a collective concept of international socialist division of labor for the 1991–2005 period." The notion that "economic levers" would be used to solve the problem of integration suggested a realistic appraisal of the limits of political levers in achieving this goal in the past.

Closer cooperation within CMEA and increased trade with the rest of the world would not be obtainable, however, without changes in CMEA pricing and currency policies. Subsidies would have to be lifted gradually, prices would have to reflect world market prices, and currencies would gradually have to become convertible. Ryzhkov revealed the Soviet view on this latter particularly sensitive matter when he stated:

> We support the accord of the majority of countries on the introduction of the mutual convertibility of national currencies and the transferable ruble for servicing direct production links, joint economic activity, and scientific and technical cooperation.

As a goal for the future we should keep in mind the gradual transfer
. . . from the mutual convertibility of national currencies to the creation of
a collective monetary unit, which would be convertible in the future into
freely convertible currencies as well.[32]

He also revealed that not all CMEA countries were eager to implement reforms of any kind, emphasizing that "the Soviet delegation considers it important that countries not prepared to take part at the present moment in any sort of measures should not impede the settlements of others."[33] In this respect, the speeches delivered by the Romanian, East German, and Czechoslovak delegates in particular made little reference to interenterprise exchanges. The speech by Hungarian Prime Minister Grosz, on the other hand, indicated that they were impatient with the slow pace of CMEA reform, criticizing in particular the draft resolution of the session for containing so few concrete proposals for the reform of currency and monetary mechanisms.[34]

By any stretch of the imagination, it will be some time before CMEA begins to function as a true multilateral organization. Until then, economic relations will continue to be based primarily on bilateral links—links which themselves will be subject to qualitative transformation if even a portion of Soviet reform efforts make significant headway.

The elimination of "blank spots"

This phrase was first referred to by Gorbachev and Poland's General Jaruzelski when they signed an accord in May 1987 calling, amongst other things, for the elimination of "blank spots" in the official histories of the two countries. Meetings held since then between historians, in addition to statements by leading academics and intellectuals on both sides, indicate that all the most sensitive issues in the relations between the two countries and parties are being reassessed. These include: the prerevolutionary activity of the Polish workers' movement, particularly the Social Democratic party of the Kingdom of Poland and Lithuania, the Communist Party of Poland, and the Polish Workers' Party (with over 100,000 pages of previously classified documents given to the Polish Commission by the Soviets); the 1920 Polish-Soviet war; the circumstances surrounding the disbandonment and subsequent reinstatement of the Communist Party of Poland by the Comintern; the fate of Polish Communists who disappeared in Stalin's labor camps; and responsibility for the massacre of Polish officers in Katyn during the war.[35]

This call by Gorbachev himself for the open appraisal of all periods in Soviet foreign policy has led to a virtual avalanche of articles and speeches in Eastern Europe about subjects that had previously been sore points in bilateral relations with Moscow. The Hungarian leadership has brought up the fate of Hungarian communist leaders who emigrated to the USSR and disappeared in the 1930s[36]; Erich Honecker has paid tribute to the contributions of Karl Liebknecht and Rosa Luxemburg, with whom Lenin clashed, as co-founders, along with Ernst Thaelmann and others, of the German revolutionary movement[37]; and in Czechoslovakia, with the change of leadership from Gustav Husak to Milos Jakes, many attempts—still at the fringes of society—are being made to address the lessons of the Prague Spring.

Where Will It Lead?

It is difficult to judge the extent of commitment among the entire Soviet and East European elite to this process of profound reformulation which has taken place under Gorbachev's guidance. Most of the Soviet leadership appears to support it. East European populations and most of their leaders also have derived great hopes and inspiration from the changes taking place in Moscow.

On the negative side, however, it is certainly difficult to overlook the possibility that resistance—both political and bureaucratic—to these reforms could effectively blunt them or imperil them altogether. In Eastern Europe, Romania remains effectively beyond Soviet control; and Ceausescu is as impervious to influence from Moscow under Gorbachev as he was under Brezhnev. The leadership change in Czechoslovakia, which brought to power a leader—Milos Jakes—whose reformist credentials are scanty, if nonexistent, suggests the limits of Soviet capability, or conceivably even willingness, to influence succession outcomes in that country. And in East Germany, despite a softening in Honecker's view of domestic reforms inside the USSR, few examples can be found to indicate that these reforms are having a profound effect on East German policy.

Nonetheless, the unwillingness of individual East European leaders to implement Soviet reforms is not in itself an indication that Soviet-East European relations have failed to be transformed. Indeed, acceptance of diversity in political and economic policies is in some ways a benchmark of the Gorbachev era. What is of concern is that because glasnost and perestroika have not touched the issue of the reform of the Warsaw Pact, it is still very unclear what the reaction of the Soviet leadership would be to any fundamental and independent reformulation of Pact doctrine in Eastern Europe. This concern arises especially because the Soviet military and security elite have already shown themselves rather uncomfortable with certain aspects of glasnost in the Soviet Union. KGB chief Chebrikov, for example, delivered a speech in September 1987 in which he made the following charges reminiscent of the Brezhnev era:

> Imperialism's special services are trying to find new loopholes through which to penetrate our society, and are exerting targeted, differentiated influence on various population groups in the USSR with the aim of instilling in Soviet people the bourgeois understanding of democracy, removing the process of increasing the working people's sociopolitical activeness from the party's influence, splitting the monolithic unity of party and people, and installing political and ideological pluralism.[38]

The Soviet Minister of Defense, General Yazov, also expressed some misgivings about glasnost when in criticizing Soviet articles on Army life, he compared such work with that prepared by "imperialist propaganda."[39] Clearly, a major crisis in Eastern Europe would strain the loyalty of such men to the principles enunciated by Gorbachev since 1985.

Nevertheless, by way of conclusion it is important to underline that those East Europeans who think critically and carefully about such issues, and there are a large number of them, are convinced that the reform process begun by Gorbachev is wide-ranging, deep, and in certain key respects irreversible. Among this group is Alexander Dubcek who has perhaps had more cause and more time to think about such matters than anyone else in Eastern Europe. He, for one, has already reached his own firm conclusion about the depth and significance of the Gorbachev reforms. Commenting on all the ideological reformulations carried out in domestic and foreign policy since Gorbachev came to power—including those analyzed above—Dubcek offered the categorial opinion: "I can say that if the CPSU had then had the leadership it now has, the armed intervention in Czechoslovakia by the five armies would have been unthinkable."[40]

Notes

1. *Pravda*, March 12, 1985.
2. *Pravda*, October 15, 1987.
3. Karen Dawisha, *Eastern Europe, Gorbachev, and Reform: The Great Challenge* (Cambridge University Press, 1988), p. 9 fn2.
4. *Pravda*, June 29, 1988.
5. Mikhail Gorbachev, *Perestroika: New Thinking for Our Country and the World*, New York: Harper & Row, 1987, pp. 161-162.
6. Ye. Primakov, "Kapitalizm vo vzaimosvyazannom mire," *Kommunist*, No. 13, September 1987, p. 102.
7. V.I. Lenin, *Sochineniya*, Vol. 22, 2nd ed., Moscow, 1929, p. 265.
8. Primakov, *op. cit.*, p. 109.
9. *Ibid.*, p. 110 (my italics).
10. *Pravda*, February 26, 1986.
11. Gorbachev, *op. cit.*, pp. 162-164.
12. *Ibid.*, p. 165.
13. Budapest Television Service in Hungarian, April 26, 1987, in Foreign Broadcast Information Service, *Daily Report: Eastern Europe*, Washington, D.C. (hereafter *FBIS-EEU*), April 27, 1987, p. F6.
14. *Pravda*, September 26, 1968.
15. O. Vladimirov, *Pravda*, June 21, 1985. Vladimirov is generally accepted as the pseudonym of Oleg Rakhmanin.
16. Yu. S. Novopashin, "Political Relations of Socialist Countries," *Rabochiy Klass i Sovremennyy Mir*, Moscow, September-October 1985, pp. 55-65.
17. *Ibid.* For a more detailed discussion of this and other debates, see Karen Dawisha, "Gorbachev and Eastern Europe: A New Challenge for the West," *World Policy Journal*, Spring 1986; Karen Dawisha and Jonathan Valdez, "Socialist Inter-

nationalism in Eastern Europe," *Problems of Communism*, Vol. 36, March–April 1987; and Dawisha, *Eastern Europe, Gorbachev and Reform*.

18. Nikolay Shishlin, Moscow Domestic Service in Russian, May 15, 1987, Foreign Broadcast Information Service, *Daily Report: Soviet Union*, Washington, D.C. (hereafter FBIS-SOV), May 18, 1987, p. F1.

19. Gorbachev, *op. cit.*, p. 165.

20. Gorbachev, *op. cit.*, pp. 191–197, *passim*.

21. Gorbachev's speech to the 27th Party Congress, *Pravda*, February 1986.

22. Budapest Television Service in Hungarian, January 25, 1987, FBIS-SOV, January 30, 1987, pp. CC 3–4.

23. George Konrad, interviewed by Richard Falk and Mary Kaldor, "The Post-Yalta Debate," *World Policy Journal*, Vol. 2, No. 3, Summer 1985, p. 461.

24. *L'Unita*, January 10, 1988, FBIS-EEU, January 19, 1988, p. 18.

25. Gorbachev, *op. cit.*, p. 167.

26. *Pravda*, August 12, 1987.

27. Commentator Viktor Levin, Moscow Domestic Service in Russian, August 13, 1987, FBIS-SOV, August 14, 1987, p. G1.

28. "Todor Zhivkov's Report to the BCP National Conference," *Embassy of the People's Republic of Bulgaria, Press Release: BTA Report No. 103*, January 28, 1988, Washington, D.C., p. 5.

29. Interview with former Colonel Ryszard Jerzy Kuklinski, "Wojna z Narodem widziana od srodka," *Kultura*, No. 4/475, April 1987, Paris, pp. 54–55.

30. See Dale Herspring, "The Soviets, the Warsaw Pact, and the East European Militaries," in William E. Griffith, ed., *Central and Eastern Europe: The Opening Curtain?* Boulder, CO.: Westview Press, 1989.

31. All of these objectives are dealt with in greater detail in O. Bogomolov, "Sotsialisticheskiye strany na perelomnom etape mirovogo ekonomicheskogo razvitiya," *Kommunist*, No. 8, May 1987, pp. 102–111.

32. TASS, October 13, 1987, FBIS-SOV, October 14, 1987, p. 9.

33. *Ibid.*, p. 13.

34. Magyar Tavirati Iroda (MTI) in English, October 13, 1987, FBIS-SOV, October 14, 1987, p. 16. Speeches by the other delegates are also contained in this issue of FBIS-SOV.

35. Mention of the work of the joint commission of Polish and Soviet scholars is provided in the "Declaration on Soviet-Polish Cooperation in Ideology, Science and Culture," *Pravda*, April 22, 1987; an interview with Jaruzelski on Moscow Television Service in Russian, May 15, 1987, FBIS-SOV, May 19, 1987, p. F3; *Pravda*, May 22, 1987; and an interview with the head of the USSR State Historical Institute, Ye. Afanasyev, in the Polish weekly *Polityka*, calling for an investigation of Katyn, Hamburg DPA in German, October 4, 1987, FBIS-SOV, October 5, 1987, p. 34.

36. Interview with Janos Berecz, *Moscow News*, September 27, 1987.

37. Honecker speech in Moscow commemorating the Great October Socialist Revolution, East Berlin ADN International Service in German, November 2, 1987, FBIS-SOV, November 3, 1987, p. 26.

38. Speech by V. M. Chebrikov on the occasion of the 110th Anniversary of F. E. Dzerzhinskiy's Birth, *Pravda*, September 11, 1987.

39. Meeting between Yazov and writers, Moscow Television Service in Russian, January 16, 1988, FBIS-SOV, January 22, 1988, p. 69.

40. *L'Unita*, January 10, 1988, FBIS-EEU, January 19, 1988, p. 21.

2

Soviet Efforts to Restructure the CMEA: The Case of Regional Energy Relations

Carl H. McMillan

Relations with Eastern Europe must inevitably be a key consideration in any redirection of Soviet economic policy and reform of Soviet economic institutions. After all, the countries of Eastern Europe continue to be the Soviet Union's major economic partners, despite the high priority Moscow attaches to the development of economic ties with the industrialized West. Exchanges with the six East European members of the Council for Mutual Economic Assistance (CMEA) accounted for roughly half of total Soviet foreign trade at mid-decade, the share having risen significantly over the first half of the 1980s.[1] The comprehensive approach to the resolution of Soviet economic problems which the new leadership in Moscow has adopted therefore includes a reappraisal of both the CMEA and the Soviet Union's role in it.[2]

This chapter explores the conditions in which that reassessment is taking place and the lines which Soviet policy towards the CMEA has begun to take as a result. The full nature of Mr. Gorbachev's grand design for the Soviet economy, in terms of internal and external relations, is only gradually becoming known. We shall argue that there is nevertheless evidence of an important, new Soviet effort to revitalize the CMEA and to reshape it into a mechanism through which more effective, collective responses to the economic challenges of the 1980s can emerge. Developments in the energy sector will be used to illustrate the nature and process of adaptation.

From the Moscow perspective, the CMEA is a set of institutions through which the Soviet Union can seek to influence regional economic developments and a multilateral umbrella for Soviet economic relations with member countries. It is important to emphasize, however, that the "CMEA system" to which we shall refer is more multilateral in aspiration than in reality. Even when policies are coordinated in the framework of CMEA programs, the details are negotiated and the relations conducted through bilateral channels imposed by the centralized nature of the economic systems of the member countries. An aim of the reforms that are our subject is to loosen these bilateral binds, which have proved an impediment to achieving an integrated regional economy.

Ongoing Objectives

Soviet economic imperatives in Eastern Europe are not simply policy choices, but evolve under the force of circumstance which Moscow can only partially control. They may therefore be regarded as a fundamental part of the current leadership's legacy in the area of relations with the fraternal economies. As discernable from both statements and actions, Soviet regional objectives may be summarized as follows:

1. To develop an interdependent and prosperous group of socialist states headed by the Soviet Union. Interdependence, through processes of "socialist integration," has a dual aim: to foster cohesion—political as well as economic—among the member-states of the CMEA and to promote economic efficiency through regional specialization in production and trade. For the giant, relatively self-sufficient Soviet economy, interdependence implies less vulnerability to external (regional) developments than it does for the smaller, inherently more open, East European economies. Prosperity, in the dynamic context, means growing material wellbeing to provide a solid economic base for the maintenance of power by communist parties in the member countries, for the exercise of a desired degree of international influence by the Soviet-led alliance, and for the attraction of "socialist-oriented" states outside the CMEA to membership or association with it.
2. To limit the burden on the Soviet economy of relations with the other members of the CMEA. Here the role of the USSR as the principal supplier of fuels, energy, and raw materials to the regional economy has been at the heart of the issue. This imperative can be broken down into three, interrelated objectives:

a) To restrain and even reduce East European demand for Soviet fuels and raw materials, and thereby Soviet deliveries of these products to the CMEA. The need to curtail deliveries has been dictated by the increasing scarcity of supply within the CMEA region and the growing dependence of the Soviet Union on energy exports outside the region for its hard currency earnings. Pressure from the Soviet hard currency balance of payments has been reinforced by the decline in the world market prices of oil and related products. The corollary to this objective has been to encourage East European substitution of less scarce primary energy sources (such as natural gas) for increasingly scarce petroleum.[3]

b) To improve the terms of Soviet trade with Eastern Europe by raising the technical standards and other qualitative attributes of East European exports to the USSR. The East European economies are important sources to the Soviet Union not only of capital goods and technology but also of consumer goods, which more indirectly but still significantly contribute to the fulfilment of Soviet production plans. Raising the quality as well as the quantity of East European deliveries to the Soviet Union would also serve the interests of a more balanced trade and thereby reduce the growth of East European debt to the USSR.[4]

c) To share the cost of development of the Soviet resources required to meet regional demand. To this end, the USSR has put pressure on its allies to participate in joint projects which make future Soviet supplies of fuels, energy, and raw materials conditional on East European investment contributions. These investments, or advance payments, are typically in the form of goods and services, delivered on credit, for the project in question or for other, not directly related use.

3. To pursue these goals without undermining the political and economic stability of the East European countries. Stability considerations have restricted the scope of socialist integration to that consonant with East European national sensibilities. They have also limited the Soviet Union's ability to shift more of the burden of regional economic development to its East European allies. The constraint is heightened by awareness that instability requiring Soviet intervention in Eastern Europe would jeopardize efforts to achieve a rapprochement with the West.[5]

New Conditions

These objectives have been the economic foundations of Soviet policy toward Eastern Europe for more than a decade, with some modifications and shifts in emphasis. The impetus for a new approach to regional relations has come rather from changes in the conditions in which these ongoing objectives can be pursued. The economic difficulties which have beset Eastern Europe in the 1980s have been extensively analyzed, and have been regarded in many quarters as of "crisis" proportions.[6] Economic instability has not been accompanied by equally serious political instability outside Poland (which itself has been relatively quiet since the accession of Jaruzelski and the imposition of martial law in 1981).

The elements of the East European economic crisis can be briefly recalled. The difficulties faced were reflected most generally in planned rates of growth of aggregate output which were on the whole set well below those of the preceding decade. Cuts in investment were especially severe, and there was little net investment in most countries. Growth in fact fell even more sharply than planned, and most of the East European economies decelerated to their slowest pace of the postwar period. Difficulties were particularly pronounced in some of the more traditional sectors, and agriculture suffered not only from energy shortages but, in some countries, from unusually poor weather conditions. Several countries experienced zero and even negative rates of growth and others sustained decreases in per capita income levels. Real per capita consumption stagnated or declined in consequence, despite reduced investment targets.[7] Domestic imbalances were accompanied by dislocations in external relations: trade deficits, payments problems, enforced cuts in imports, etc. The Soviet economy also experienced some of the same internal problems, reflected in historically low overall growth, but did not face comparable difficulties in its external accounts.

The situation was rooted significantly in structural weaknesses in the East European economies and economic systems, which had developed over the long term.[8] Some problems were the legacies of poor planning and mistaken policies of the previous decade. Others were the cumulative outcome of long-standing deficiencies of an institutional nature and the failure to come to grips with them. In general, the CMEA countries had failed to give up the policies and institutions favoring the traditional pattern of "extensive" growth and to institute measures to foster a new "intensive" stage of development, based on more efficient use of resources and accelerated technical progress.

These structural weaknesses left the member economies more exposed to adverse external trends. The East European countries suffered a worsening in their terms of trade, including those with their major trading partner—the Soviet Union; all encountered declining demand, sharper competition, and mounting trade barriers in Western markets as the result of the economic recession of 1981–1983; all were affected, some critically, by the international payments crisis. To varying degrees all the East European countries faced tightened constraints on terms and supplies of raw materials and fuels, including the Soviet oil which most had grown heavily to depend upon.[9] For its part, the Soviet Union enjoyed a comparatively strong balance of payments position in the first years of the decade, but this situation changed as Soviet terms of trade began to reflect the weakening (after 1981) and then dramatic fall (after 1985) in the prices of oil and related energy products.[10]

The economic costs of its relationship with Eastern Europe is a matter of long-standing concern to the Soviet Union. It saw these costs escalate in the 1970s, principally as a result of the gap between the value of its oil on world markets and the preferential terms at which it supplied oil to its allies under CMEA arrangements.[11] The problems which beset the region in the 1980s had made it more difficult—but no less imperative—for Moscow to curtail these costs.

Adaptation at the CMEA Level

When in 1979 the CMEA entered its thirtieth anniversary year, the organization was in the doldrums. The 1971 Comprehensive Program had run out of steam, with its schedule for the gradual strengthening of multilateral approaches to socialist economic integration through a combination of plan and market, modest though it was, left largely unimplemented.[12] The creative spurt of new institutions and projects which the 1971 Program stimulated had quickly faded. No joint industrial enterprise had been established since 1975, and no major regional investment project had been initiated since the Soyuz (Orenburg) pipeline, agreed upon in 1974, and now nearing completion. The introduction of long-term "target" programs for integration in selected sectors had failed generally to breathe new life into the organization. Only in the area of nuclear power development was there a renewed attempt at multilateral coordination of any note, providing some vitality to the target program in the energy sphere.[13]

Surprisingly, this dormant state continued into the 1980s. Although mounting economic difficulties forced the East European member countries to adopt strenuous national adjustment measures, directed especially to their energy balances and their external accounts, the crisis did not evoke significant new initiatives at the regional level. The CMEA mechanism continued to operate largely as before.[14]

New regional initiatives had in the past generally come from Moscow, but circumstances in the Soviet Union now inhibited vigorous Soviet leadership. No doubt the initial windfall gains to the Soviet balance of payments from the 1979–1980 jump in the world price of oil encouraged Soviet complacency and reinforced in this area the policy inertia of the aging Brezhnev regime. Then the succession crisis preoccupied Soviet leaders from 1982 to 1985. When, at East European insistence, a CMEA summit (the first full-scale meeting of party leaders on economic matters since 1969) was finally held in Moscow in June 1984, it fell during the Chernenko interregnum and was anticlimatic. No new initiatives were revealed, and the Summit communique was if anything regressive in thrust, reinforcing the traditional bilateralism of intra-CMEA relations.[15]

It was only with the resolution of the Soviet leadership crisis the following March and the emergence of Gorbachev at the head of the Soviet party, that the CMEA system began to show signs of new forward momentum and the process of adaptation of the system to the conditions that were the economic legacy of the first half of the 1980s was initiated. A new "comprehensive program" now occupies the center of the CMEA stage. The "Comprehensive Program to Promote the Scientific and Technical Progress of the Member-Countries of the Council for Mutual Economic Assistance up to the Year 2000" was adopted at an extraordinary Council session held in Moscow in December 1985.[16] The new Soviet head of the CMEA Secretariat has referred to it as "priority number one."[17]

The Program in effect substitutes technical progress for resource development as the focus of CMEA activities. The acceleration of technical progress in the region as a whole is now to be the primary goal of the coordination of national policies at the CMEA level. A network of cooperation agreements and programs will be directed to all phases of research and development, from pure scientific research to the development and marketing of new products and processes. Policies coordinated bilaterally and multilaterally will be reflected in annual and medium term national plans.

The 1985 Program cites five broad areas in which cooperative efforts will be concentrated: electronics, automation, nuclear energy, new materials and related technologies, and biotechnology. Within these, 93 sub-projects or programs have been identified, with national participation in them to be on the basis of the "interestedness" principle. Each of these projects is to be directed by a Soviet "head" organization.

The designation of scientific and technical cooperation as the centerpiece of CMEA activity is a long overdue reflection at the regional level of the importance attached in the socialist countries since the 1960s to the "scientific-technical revolution" and its role in moving the socialist countries into a new intensive stage in their development.[18] It would also appear to represent a victory for the Soviet Union in its efforts to transform the CMEA system from the mechanism to channel Soviet fuels and raw materials to Eastern Europe, which it had increasingly become over the 1970s, to one through which the USSR can more effectively draw on the industrial and technical capacities of its allies to meet its own new development goals.[19]

Of scarcely less significance, however, is the way this reorientation is to be reflected in the institutional character of the CMEA. The 1985 Program emphasizes that direct relations among economic organizations in different member-countries must be the means of carrying out its objectives. This is made explicit in the text itself (Section III, "Implementation," paragraph 5):

> Member-states of the CMEA will foster direct relations among their enterprises, associations, and scientific-technical organizations, on the basis of the provisions of concrete bilateral and multilateral agreements and treaties. This is the effective method of achieving the cooperation necessary to implement the Program.

The priority now attached to inter-enterprise linkages has important implications.[20] It suggests a major departure from two of the institutional measures favored in practice since 1971.[21] Direct relations among national enterprises are not a return to joint planning on a sectoral basis through inter-state coordinating bodies. Nor are they to entail large international flows of capital, as in the case of joint investment projects. Rather, enterprises in the member countries will be encouraged to engage in a variety of direct contacts on a more decentralized basis, implying the strengthening of market instruments in intra-CMEA relations.

It is envisaged that inter-enterprise links should extend to the formation of "joint enterprises," for which the traditional CMEA environment proved to be unfavorable. A 1983 Soviet decree clarified the legal conditions for the operation of joint enterprises with CMEA partners on USSR territory.[22] There has since been a modest resurgence of joint enterprises between Soviet and East European partners, all bilateral in nature. Two Soviet-

Bulgarian machine tool enterprises have been established since 1974, both with a strong technological component and linking multi-plant production associations on the two sides. Several Soviet-Hungarian industrial ventures have been launched that appear rather different in character from the joint enterprises of the 1970s. Two have been established in Hungary: Mikromed Ltd., for the manufacture of electronic medical apparatus; and Intermos Microelectronics Ltd., for the production of integrated circuits. A third Soviet-Hungarian company (Littara-Volanpack) has been established in Soviet Lithuania to produce packaging equipment. An agreement signed during Soviet Prime Minister Ryzhkov's visit to Poland in October 1986 envisaged seven new joint enterprises, several of which have been created.[23]

For these enterprise-level ties to be meaningful, however, appropriate economic as well as legal conditions have to be created. The absence of these has in the past limited efforts to develop direct contacts and foster joint enterprises.[24] They require greater enterprise autonomy in the member countries and the means, as well as the authority, to engage directly in international operations. The prospects are improved by the fact that the Soviet Union is now a stimulus to (rather than a brake on) reform. The 1986-1987 Soviet foreign trade reforms, for example, are explicitly designed to provide the organizational basis for direct contacts between Soviet production enterprises and associations and their CMEA counterparts, as well as other foreign partners.[25] Officially, the Soviet Union proposes to allow each of the East European countries to proceed on its own reform path. There must, however, be sufficient homogeneity in the processes of reform in the member countries to provide a common basis for more decentralized interaction as envisaged by the Comprehensive Program. International cooperation at the enterprise level requires significant changes, nationally and regionally, in the role of money and prices so that they can be used more effectively in inter-enterprise accounting and perform new allocative and incentive functions. In terms of the CMEA, this entails further movement toward a more flexible system of pricing in regional trade and the establishment of a meaningful system of foreign exchange rates.

These conditions for effective inter-enterprise links, and through them for the success of the new Comprehensive Program, will not be easy to create, and at best can only be established in the long term. The obstacles—which are more political, sociological and psychological than economic—are great enough seriously to cloud the outlook. Meanwhile, although there has been some effort to "streamline" CMEA institutions, most of the regional organs established to facilitate state-to-state relations remain in place.

A key element in socialist economic integration in the past that is retained in the new initiatives and is to continue to play an important role is the East-West relationship. A Hungarian economist has recently concluded that "closer cooperation in the CMEA not only allows for, but positively requires, extensive ties with the West."[26] The new Soviet external economic policies and the measures adopted to implement them certainly signal this. Joint ventures with both CMEA and Western partners are being pursued, and these are clearly regarded as not only compatible but reinforcing.

Here again, however, desired effects are not likely to be easily attained. Long-standing structural weaknesses in East-West trade, foremost among them the limited export potential of the CMEA countries, continue to be a major constraint on its growth. Although the political climate for East-West trade has improved, two of the most dynamic economic ingredients in its expansion during the 1970s are no longer present in the same degree: Soviet oil and gas exports and Western (official and commercial) bank lending. These are unlikely to be able to give the boost to East-West exchanges that they did in the past. The recent rise in the share of CMEA trade in the total trade of the member countries (recall the Soviet shares cited in Note 1) is more the effect of these constraints on East-West trade than of any significant expansion in intra-CMEA trade.

The disillusioning experience of the 1980s has sobered Soviet and East European assessments of the economic benefits that can be realistically derived from relations with the West. Greater awareness of the limits to the expansion of East-West economic relations has increased interest in revitalizing the regional economy.[27]

The Energy Relationship in the 1980s

Energy is an area which illustrates sharply the increased interdependence between the CMEA countries and the rest of the world. It demonstrates the degree to which they have become vulnerable to extra-regional developments and to the policies that determine these developments. Thus OPEC pricing strategies, the US embargo on energy equipment and technology and the rise in real interest rates on international money markets all had important effects on energy relations within the CMEA in the first half of the 1980s. Current CMEA awareness of this reality is in marked contrast to the region's earlier sense of energy invulnerability and the complacency to which it gave rise.

Energy became the dominant factor in Soviet-East European economic relations in the 1970s, and continued to play a central role in the first half of the 1980s. The USSR employed the multilateral framework of CMEA institutions as well as direct bilateral relations to advance its objectives in this area.[28] Its approach was three-pronged: (1) It sought to improve the terms on which it supplied fuels and energy to Eastern Europe, initially by raising the relative prices of these products and more recently by pressures to increase the volume and to "harden" the structure of return flows of East European goods to the USSR. (2) It attempted to curb the volume of its energy supplies to Eastern Europe, through direct limits and by encouraging East European measures directed at domestic energy substitution and conservation. (3) It enlisted East European participation in the development of new Soviet sources of energy supply and the infrastructure required for the export of their output.

All of these policies have encountered serious obstacles. Because of the energy intensiveness of their industrial structures, which the earlier growth of Soviet energy supplies on easy terms had fostered, increases in Soviet energy prices resulted mainly in the growing ruble indebtedness of the East European countries. New East European energy management policies, while addressed more realistically to the problem, ran into serious institutional and structural obstacles. Efforts to harden East European counter-deliveries have been impeded by the technical and managerial limitations of East European production systems and by balance-of-payments pressure on the East European countries to raise the quantity and quality of their exports to hard-currency markets. Meanwhile, East European participation in Soviet resource development has encountered not only serious administrative problems but increasingly severe East European shortages of investment resources, both physical and financial.

The development and distribution of Soviet oil resources has not been the subject of major cooperative activities at the regional level since the 1960s, when the Druzhba pipeline was built. (The Adria pipeline of the 1970s was essentially extra-regional in orientation, although it involved two member countries: Czechoslovakia and Hungary.) One could say that national measures in the last five-year-plan period to limit consumption (and hence imports) of oil were region-wide, but they were essentially carried out unilaterally, albeit under Soviet pressure. As a result of these measures, the volume of Soviet oil exports to Eastern Europe declined by 15% between 1981 and the end of 1985.[29]

It is in the area of oil pricing, rather than oil development and distribution, that the CMEA framework has played a more influential part. In 1975, following the first jump in world prices, the USSR forced the CMEA member countries to modify the traditional method (the so-called Bucharest formula) for pricing goods traded within the regional system. Since that time, the negotiated price of Soviet oil deliveries to Eastern Europe has been fixed for the period of only a year and based on a five-year moving average of world prices. Because of the sharp upward trend in the world market price of oil, renewed in 1979–1980, the terms of trade of the East European countries with the Soviet Union deteriorated over the next decade. The price effect acted as an additional stimulus to adjustment in the oil-importing CMEA countries but, as noted, served primarily to force them into significant ruble indebtedness to the USSR.

It was widely rumoured that, at the June 1984 CMEA summit, the Soviet Union would seek to narrow further the gap between price developments inside and outside the CMEA by imposing a new pricing formula which would establish a closer link between the CMEA price and the world price. This did not happen. With the benefit of hindsight, this was unfortunate for CMEA importers of Soviet oil. With the precipitate fall in the world price in late 1985/early 1986 and the depreciation of the dollar that had begun some months earlier, the CMEA countries paid in 1986 an average ruble price for Soviet oil that has been estimated as roughly twice the world price at the official exchange rate. Some Western analysts question the relevance of this calculation and estimate that at a more realistic exchange rate the CMEA price was still below the world price.[30] Moreover, they estimate the advantage to Eastern Europe as still greater if one takes broader account of the terms at which Eastern Europe barters its goods for Soviet oil under bilateral agreements. Certainly, the fall in the world price has not seen any sudden shift on the part of the East European countries to world market sourcing. In any case, Eastern Europe would have benefitted earlier from world market trends if the 1984 summit had agreed on the abandonment of the existing ("modified Bucharest") formula for pricing Soviet oil deliveries within the CMEA.

Another facet of the Soviet regional energy strategy has been to encourage the substitution of natural gas for oil. The major CMEA cooperative project of the 1970s (the Soyuz pipeline to bring natural gas from the Orenburg fields in the southern Urals to Eastern Europe) proved to be well timed in this respect. It permitted a quantum jump in the volume of Soviet gas deliveries to Eastern Europe in 1980 (to nearly three times the 1975 level). Thereafter, however, exports of Soviet natural gas to Eastern Europe increased very slowly (and to some major East European countries—the GDR and Hungary—scarcely at all). Although the pipeline capacity was not available to permit a major rise in Soviet deliveries to a new plateau, their growth has been constrained primarily by demand factors. The increase in East European gas imports which the Soyuz pipeline permitted at the beginning of the decade was sufficient to meet the slack industrial feedstock requirements of the early 1980s. The emphasis in East European national energy policies has been on the substitution of domestic coal (rather than imported gas) for Soviet oil in electric power generation and on the development of nuclear capacity to attempt to meet growth of demand for electricity (which has slowed in the 1980s).

In these circumstances, plans for a major new CMEA gas project appear somewhat oddly timed. The Progress pipeline, one of half a dozen trunklines being constructed to provide an outlet for new output as the Yamburg gas fields in northwestern Siberia are developed, is to bring some of the Yamburg gas to the East European economies. It would seem to be pressure more from the Soviet supply side than the East European demand side that provides the rationale for the pipeline project.

The project has certainly received extraordinarily little publicity since it was first made public in 1984. It was not announced with great fanfare at the CMEA summit that year (nor even mentioned in the communique). Not one article devoted to it has appeared since 1984 in the official monthly magazine of the CMEA.[31] This treatment is in striking contrast to the play given to the Soyuz pipeline during its construction in the 1970s.

As a result, comparatively little is known about the nature and cost of the Progress pipeline project, especially the amounts and terms of the gas to be supplied to the participating East European countries or the form and extent of their contributions. The pipeline has variously been reported to have a projected cost in dollars (at the official exchange rate, which overvalues the ruble) ranging from $3 billion—about the cost of the Soyuz pipeline ten years earlier, although Progress is much longer (4,650 versus 2,677 kilometers)—to a more plausible $30 billion. The East European contributions to these costs will be repaid in deliveries of gas over a twenty-year period, in amounts apparently similar in magnitude to those of the earlier (Soyuz) agreement (a total of 15 billion cubic meters annually to the six East European participating states); but how the price of the gas will be calculated remains as much of a mystery as it did for the earlier project.[32]

All of the East European countries, including Romania (which chose to play a more restricted role than the other countries in the Soyuz project), are contributing to the financing of the Progress pipeline. No systematic picture of the nature of the East European contributions has emerged, however. Some countries are participating in aspects of the pipeline construction, but most contributions would seem to be in the form of advance deliveries of generally unrelated goods and services. Scattered bits of information about the East European contributions can be found. The Hungarian contribution was to be not to Yamburg, but to the development of a new Soviet gas field far to the south, at Tenghiz, in the area to the northeast of the Caspian Sea. Poland is to supply machinery for a Soviet steel mill at Magnitogorsk, as well as some equipment and labor for the construction of the pipeline itself. In the circumstances, it seems that the Progress pipeline is being built largely by the Soviet Union as a component of the major gas-pipeline construction program of the Soviet Twelfth Five-Year Plan.

This lack of information no doubt reflects ongoing uncertainties about the nature and extent of East European participation; uncertainties which arise in turn from the burden which the projected contributions place on already overstrained economies. If, for example, the cost of the Progress pipeline project is $30 billion, and half is financed by the six East European countries, their average share of the cost would exceed $2 billion. In September 1987, the Hungarian Prime Minister announced Hungary's reluctant withdrawal from the project.[33]

CMEA energy cooperation in the 1980s has emphasized the expansion of the unified power grid ("Mir") through the development of nuclear power capacity. Cooperation in this area has had two facets: East European participation in the development of Soviet nuclear power and of associated transmission lines to link the Soviet stations to the grid, and Soviet participation in the development of East European nuclear power.

The first major achievement in this area was the completion in 1979 of a 750-kv transmission line from Vinnitsa (USSR) to Albertirsa (Hungary) which—fatefully—linked the Soviet nuclear power station at Chernobyl to the East European system and permitted the expansion of East European (especially Hungarian) imports of Soviet electricity. In the same year, the

USSR, Czechoslovakia, Hungary, and Poland agreed to cooperate in the construction of the khmelnitsky station in the Ukraine and an associated high-voltage (750 kv) transmission line to the Polish city of Rzeszow (with a connection to the Vinnitsa sub-station). A later (1982) cooperation agreement between the USSR and the Balkan countries of Romania and Bulgaria provided for the "joint construction" of additional units of the South-Ukraine power station at Konstantinovka and an associated transmission line to Romania. Except in the case of Czechoslovakia, whose contribution is in related equipment, the East European contributions to these projects are in the form of credits (or goods and services supplied on credit) with repayment in exports of electricity over a twenty-year period in proportion to their contributions.

These projects to expand the CMEA electric power grid have experienced considerable delays. The giant Soviet nuclear reactor plant, Atommash (near Volgadonsk), designed to mass produce 1000-MW reactors of the Soviet VVER (pressurized water) type, has been plagued with problems. The reports on the source of these have ranged from severe construction faults— the plant was sinking into its swampy site—to more typical Soviet gestation problems. As a result, it failed to achieve its full scale of operations in 1985, as planned. The first Khmelnitsky unit was originally to have come on stream in 1984, but has yet to do so. Two units at Konstantinovka are reportedly in operation, but since at least the first of these predated the cooperation agreement with Bulgaria and Romania, the status of that arrangement is not very clear. The Bulgarian press has reported, however, that the 750 kv transmission line from the South Ukraine plant to Isaccea, in Romania, and on to Tolbukhin in Bulgaria, has been commissioned, with the larger share of power deliveries going to Romania.[34]

The Chernobyl disaster has been a further setback, causing additional delays in the program and raising its cost. It had the immediate effect of disrupting supplies through the Vinnitsa-Albertirsa line, and Hungarian reports of this disruption were among the first indications of trouble. Neither the Khmelnitsky nor the Konstantinovka stations are based on the RBMK graphite-moderated technology which was at issue in the Chernobyl accident. Nevertheless, the (at least temporary) closure of RBMK units in the USSR, at Chernobyl and elsewhere, put more domestic demand pressure on other Soviet nuclear and thermal power stations. Soviet exports of electricity to Eastern Europe in fact fell in 1986 (but not by a drastic 50% which the more pessimistic Western projections at the time of Chernobyl suggested). Moreover, Soviet assessments of the Chernobyl explosion indicate operating error rather than design weakness as the cause. This adds to the pressure to improve the safeguards (physical and procedural) at all of the plants, VVER as well as RBMK in design.

The repercussions of Chernobyl have also been felt in the East European nuclear development program. Under the 1978 Long-Term Target Program for Cooperation in Energy Fuels and Raw Materials, the 1980s were to be a period of major expansion in East European nuclear capacity, based on the 1000-mw units to be produced at Atommash. By the mid-1980s, the program had witnessed important increases in nuclear power generation in Bulgaria, Czechoslovakia, and the GDR (by 1985 nuclear power accounted for 16% of their combined electricity output) and the inauguration of the first Hungarian reactor unit (since followed into operation by two additional units). All of the East European reactors are based on the Soviet VVER technology, and hence not directly called into question by Chernobyl. In mid-1987—little more than one year after Chernobyl—in Eastern Europe, as in the USSR, the official commitment to nuclear power development remained, but the development program, already much delayed relative to ambitious plans, seemed likely to be further slowed and rendered more costly by the implications of the disaster.[35] For example, Bulgaria announced that steel reinforced containment buildings are to be erected around the reactors in its Soviet-designed nuclear power plants to prevent radioactive leakage into the atmosphere. Romania declared a general review of its nuclear program which although based initially on Canadian Candu technology, was in its later stages to employ Soviet-built reactors as well. Poland (whose first nuclear station is being constructed at Zernowiec on the Baltic) announced a similar review, following demands from the inhabitants of the city of Bialystok, which lay in the path of the radioactive cloud from Chernobyl.

Cooperation in nuclear engineering is one of the five basic themes of the 1985 Comprehensive CMEA Program for Scientific and Technological Progress. Of course cooperation in nuclear technology has been stressed for some time; witness the creation in 1956 of the Dubna Joint Nuclear Research Institute and in the early 1970s of the two international economic associations, Interatominstrument and Interatomenergo. More recently, one may cite the production of 440-mw nuclear reactors of the Soviet VVER design at the Skoda plant in Czechoslovakia to complement the production profile of the Atommash plant in the USSR. The Comprehensive Program is intended further to encourage cooperation along these lines and to cover the entire cycle from R&D to after-sale servicing.

Production specialization has in general, however, been an elusive goal of the CMEA for over three decades. The Paks nuclear power plant in Hungary (built on a cooperative basis with important Soviet, Czechoslovak, and other CMEA inputs) illustrates some of the problems. When the Hungarians failed to obtain the CMEA designation to supply the computer software for the facility, they simply went ahead and designed and employed their own software packages, which they regarded as superior.[36] These are the realities that often lie behind the official CMEA statistics of hundreds of "specialization agreements" concluded.

Cooperation in the development of new sources of electricity within the region is not limited to nuclear power. The hydroelectric project on the Danube border between Czechoslovakia and Hungary is interesting for several reasons. It is crucially based on inputs of capital and technology from Austria, in return for a share of the output. It is therefore a further example of the important link between East-West and East-East cooperation. Even more interesting is the extent to which environmental opposition in Hungary delayed the project, and for a time appeared likely to block it entirely. Austrian participation finally tipped the balance in favour of proceeding, and construction began in 1987.

Offshore oil and gas exploration and drilling is another area where Western inputs have been critically important to cooperative energy programs among CMEA member-states. It also illustrates the role of direct enterprise links, in the form of joint ventures, in an area of energy development which is of considerable potential importance to regional supplies of hydrocarbons in the 1990s and into the next century. Petrobaltic is a joint venture established in 1975 by the USSR, Poland and the GDR (50-25-25) respectively to explore and develop finds on their Baltic continental shelf and in adjacent territorial waters. The venture has met with moderate success: small commercial discoveries have been made off the Soviet coast near Kaliningrad and follow-up development of the most promising field has begun. Finds off the Polish coast have also been reported. On the other hand, exploration was recently reported to have been halted off the Lithuanian coast because of threatened environmental damage. The Soviet Union is cooperating with another CMEA partner, Vietnam, in the latter's China Sea explorations. Their joint venture, Vietsovpetro, has found oil and gas deposits on the Vietnamese shelf and has begun off-shore oil drilling operations. Western equipment and technology has been fundamental to these offshore projects, contributing either directly to them or to the development of Soviet-built ships and rigs.

We may conclude from our analysis of CMEA energy relations that large-scale, multilateral development projects are no longer the CMEA fashion. They savour too much of the "extensive" style of development, which present investment constraints will no longer allow. Joint energy development projects are no longer at the centre stage of CMEA cooperation as they were in the 1960s and 1970s. No new multilateral investment projects were agreed to in the period 1979-84.[37] Even then, the de-facto "freeze" was broken by a pipeline project (Progress) about which curiously little is said, and whose cooperative dimensions (in terms of the nature of East European inputs) are apparently quite limited. In the next decade, Eastern Europe will need more gas, so one of the trunklines being constructed under the 12th Five-Year Plan has been designated for the purpose, and the East Europeans appear to have contracted for it much as the West Europeans did in respect to their export pipeline in the last five-year plan period.[38]

Intensive development—*intensifikatsiia*—is the current emphasis, as reflected at the regional level in the new CMEA centerpiece, the Comprehensive Program for Scientific and Technological Progress. For the energy sector, this has implications that extend significantly beyond the supply side, where priority under the 1985 Comprehensive Program focuses on the coordination of research and development in the area of nuclear engineering. On the demand side, measures under the Program to raise the level of automation (robotization) and to introduce other new technologies in industry are intended to reduce the materials—(and especially the fuels)—intensity of the member economies. This is where the new CMEA energy priorities lie.[39]

High-level, state-to-state approaches are ill suited to these purposes. That is why direct forms of international cooperation among national production units are seen as essential to the introduction and diffusion of the new technologies which are now the principal hope of achieving a viable regional energy economy. "Policy coordination" is to substitute for "plan coordination" as a framework for relations at the enterprise level.

New technologies must necessarily take environmental effects into account and attempt to control them. We have seen that, at the present stage of development of the East European economies, policies to substitute domestic sources of energy (coal, nuclear, hydropower) for imported fuels have faced rapidly rising environmental costs. These have already delayed or otherwise shaped CMEA programs and activities, and will unavoidably be a growing factor in future regional energy policies.

Today, the East European countries are looking less to Soviet supplies, and more to joint investment programs in the USSR, to solve their energy problems. Attention (and debate) focuses on the potential for substitution of domestic energy sources for energy imports from the USSR: coal, nuclear power and, in Hungary and Czechoslovakia, hydroelectric power. Policy trade-offs are seen in terms of development of these domestic supply alternatives versus domestic investment in programs to reduce national energy consumption. The major area of increasing reliance on the USSR is gas, for which there is no practical alternative but the Soviet Union and on which, moreover, Eastern Europe sees its neighbours in Western and Southern Europe (and Turkey) increasingly dependent as well.

Only Romania, always the exception in East European energy matters, has turned more to the Soviet Union, at last concluding an agreement by which it is guaranteed additional supplies of Soviet oil at the CMEA rather than the world price (although apparently in return for the export of a specified quantity of "hard goods" to the USSR). In 1986, Romanian imports of Soviet oil were more than three times their 1985 volume, attaining a significant 6.3 mln. metric tons.[40]

The Shaping of a New Regional Relationship

Developments in the energy sector reflect the new Soviet thinking about the CMEA and the policy initiatives that have resulted. The energy sector also illustrates the mixed character of the CMEA system today and the nature of the related Soviet dilemma, and it seeks to adapt the regional system to the new conditions that have emerged in the first half of the 1980s, subject to the stability constraint described earlier.

The USSR wants to move the system in the direction of an "intensive type of integration," in which regional scientific-technical as well as production cooperation among national production units, interacting directly, will play a central role.[41] The traditional CMEA system is viewed as having evolved in the conditions of extensive growth. It must now be replaced by a system conducive to the intensive development of the member countries. The link between this conception of the regional system and economic reform in the member countries is clearly drawn. Gorbachev is quoted as affirming to the Eleventh Congress of the East German party that at issue is a "new economic mechanism for our cooperation."[42]

This theme was echoed by the official communique issued at the conclusion of the 43rd Session of the CMEA, held in Moscow in October 1987, which emphasized "the necessity of a *perestroika* of the mechanism of collaboration and socialist economic integration."[43] A contemporary *Izvestiia* article referred to a number of elements as essential to such a restructuring:

- creation in all the CMEA countries of the economic, legal, organizational, financial, and other preconditions;
- establishment of a system of interrelated exchange rates, convertible currencies, and a single common measure of value;
- freer movement of goods, services, and factors of production within the CMEA;
- improvement of information flows.[44]

Reform at the national level is therefore clearly regarded as a prerequisite to reform at the regional level. The vision of Gorbachev, his associates, and advisors is of a new CMEA system founded on direct enterprise-level collaboration and on the operation of jointly owned, multinational enterprises. These are the forms in which future investment cooperation among member countries is to be carried out.[45] To be effective, these organizational innovations require the restriction of centralized planning and management and the granting of increased enterprise autonomy in the framework of strengthened "commodity-money" (market) relations. Efficient international relations at the enterprise level demand not only the elimination of traditional legal and organizational impediments, but the creation of a system of prices and exchange rates which will provide appropriate incentives, permit meaningful accounting, and lay the foundations for currency convertibility.[46] These aims strongly imply comprehensive, market-oriented economic reform in all the member states.

Although Moscow signals this with increasing clarity in its statements, the USSR apparently does not feel that it can impose these requirements on its East European allies. Soviet policy thus urges CMEA countries to proceed with domestic reforms, while making respectful references to the concept of "different paths to socialism." The more conservative East European regimes (especially the German Democratic Republic and Romania) show little inclination, however, to follow the Soviet reform prescriptions.

At the same time, the fuels and other resource requirements of the East European countries cannot be ignored, given their present, materials-intensive industrial structures. Soviet Prime Minister Ryzhkov went out of his way at the November 1986 Session of the CMEA to reassure the East European countries that Soviet energy shipments would grow in the 1986-1990 plan period, despite the increased pressure on the Soviet balance of payments from the dramatic fall earlier that year in the world price of oil.[47] These commitments and programs imply joint planning at high official levels. The Progress (Yamburg) pipeline is being constructed, the regional nuclear power program is proceeding, and other large resource development projects are being pushed through (such as the Krivoi Rog iron ore combine).

In these circumstances, implementation of the 1985 Comprehensive Program will involve continued reliance on planned approaches at the state-to-state level. The traditional CMEA methods of plan coordination, followed up by bilateral, inter-governmental agreements, will therefore be the principal mechanism through which even the new programs of scientific and technical cooperation must be pursued. At the enterprise level, relations will have to continue to rely on old methods of accounting and settlement: barter, counterpurchase, and product-payback under (essentially bilateral) clearing arrangements. The transition to a decentralized mechanism of CMEA cooperation will inevitably consist of a contradictory mix of the old and the new.

It is the ambitious character of the Soviet initiatives, relative to regional realities, that raises this prospect of a long and difficult transition period. For the first time since Khrushchev, Soviet policy proposes a radical change in the nature of the CMEA system. Then the drive was to impose an integrated regional economy by means of centralized, supranational planning. The failure of that initiative resulted in two decades of virtual stagnation in the integration process. Now integration is to be determined through the decentralized action of market forces, subject to coordinated national policies. This strategy places reliance on institutions which are not well grounded in the still essentially administered economies of the member states. Whether the Gorbachev restructuring can be carried through successfully on the CMEA plane is as uncertain as it is at the national level. Meanwhile it represents a major redirection of Soviet policy for the regional system.

Notes

1. According to Soviet official statistics, the share of Soviet trade with the East European members of the CMEA (Bulgaria, Czechoslovakia, GDR, Hungary, Poland, and Romania) rose from 42.5% in 1980 to 47.2% in 1985 and 53.9% in 1986.

2. See, for example, L. Csaba, "The Council for Mutual Economic Assistance and the Challenge of the Eighties," *Külpolitika*, Vol. 13, No. 5, 1986, and Vol. 14, No. 1, 1987, summarized in *Abstracts of Hungarian Economic Literature*, Vol. 16, No. 6, 1986, pp. 263-265, and Vol. 17, No. 1, 1987, pp. 266-268.

3. See J. Hannigan and C. McMillan, "The Energy Factor in Soviet-East European Energy Relations," Research Report No. 18, *East-West Commercial Relations Series*, Institute of Soviet and East European Studies, Carleton University, Ottawa, 1981.

4. The East European debt to the USSR is denominated in an inconvertible unit of account, the "transferable ruble." Cumulative surpluses in Soviet trade with Eastern Europe over the period 1975-1986 amounted to 18.1 billion rubles, according to calculations based on official Soviet sources. Harriet Matejka notes a considerable discrepancy between Soviet and East European official statistics in this regard, with the latter indicating a cumulative imbalance of only 12.1 bln. rubles in the Soviet favor. See her "Déséquilibres, endettement et ajustement au sein du CAEM," *Etudes Internationales*, Vol. 19, No. 2, June 1988, pp. 293-300.

5. Moreover, as Karen Dawisha points out, instability in Eastern Europe has more than once in the past undermined efforts at reform in the USSR. See Chapter 2.

6. Cf. J. Drewnowski (ed.), *Crisis in the East European Economy: The Spread of the Polish Disease*, London: Croom Helm, 1982. For detailed analysis of the economic situation in Eastern Europe in the first half of the 1980s, see *East European Economies: Slow Growth in the 1980s* (three volumes), A compendium of papers submitted to the Joint Economic Committee, Congress of the United States, 99th Congress, 1st Session, Washington, D.C.: U.S. Government Printing Office, 1985-1986.

7. For example, according to Western estimates, per capita living standards declined in Poland and Romania and stagnated in Hungary over the first half of the 1980s. See T. Alton et al., Research Project on National Income in Eastern Europe, Occasional Paper No. 98, "Money Income of the Population and the Standard of Living in Eastern Europe," New York: L. W. International Financial Research, Inc., 1987.

8. Jan Vanous has provided a clear analysis of the factors involved. See his "East European Economic Slowdown," *Problems of Communism*, July-August, 1982, pp. 1-20.

9. See Hannigan and McMillan, *op. cit.*

10. The effect of the fall in the price of oil was reinforced by the depreciation of the U.S. dollar, in which Soviet oil exports are settled.

11. These arrangements are described later, in the section on energy relations. The most comprehensive, if controversial, analysis of the costs of the relationship is M. Marrese and J. Vanous, *Soviet Subsidization of Trade with Eastern Europe*, Berkeley: Institute of International Studies, University of California, 1983.

12. See the author's "The Council for Mutual Economic Assistance: A Historical Perspective," published as an annex to *Czechoslovakia, A Country Study*, Foreign Area Studies Series, Washington, D.C.: American University, 1982 (and other East European volumes in the series).

13. East European participation in the financing of the Khmelnitsky nuclear power station, to be constructed in the Western Ukraine, was announced later in 1979 (see following).

14. Cf. J. van Brabant, "Recent Growth Performance, Economic Reform, and the Future of Integration in Eastern Europe," Working Paper No. 5, Department of International Economic and Social Affairs, United Nations, July 1987.

15. On the context of the summit meeting, see M. Lavigne, "The Evolution of CMEA Institutions and Policies and the Need for Structural Adjustment," paper presented at the conference on the Soviet Union and Eastern Europe in the World Economy, held at the Kennan Institute, Washington, D.C., October 1984; for a resumé of the meeting itself, see A. Tiraspolsky, "Le Sommet du CAEM: Vers un Politique Economique Commune," *Le Courrier des Pays de l'Est*, No. 289, November

1984, pp. 48-65; for an interpretation of its significance, see J. van Brabant, "The CMEA Summit and Socialist Economic Integration: A Perspective," in *Jahrbuch der Wirtschaft Osteuropas*, Vol. 12, Part 1, 1987, pp. 129-160.

Some have argued that the summit communique (which was short, vague, and very traditionalist in character) was backed up by more substantive unpublished agreements. (Cf. "A Blueprint for Gorbachev's Integration Strategy?" *PlanEcon Report*, Vol. 11, No. 36, September 4, 1986). It seems odd, however, that if it had been possible to agree on important new initiatives, these would not have been made public at the time. The fact that a program on scientific and technical cooperation (already raised at the 1982 CMEA session) was briefly alluded to but not elaborated upon in the summit announcements, suggests that full agreement had not been reached. A Hungarian economist has referred to the summit as taking place in a "Brezhnevian" atmosphere (L. Csaba, "Le CAEM sous le signe de la restructuration," *Le Courrier des Pays de l'Est*, No. 313, Décembre 1986, p. 7.).

16. For the Russian text of the agreement, see *Ekonomicheskoe Sotrudnichestvo Stran-Chlenov SEV*, Moscow, 1/1986, pp. 1-13.

17. TASS, June 17, 1987. The appointment in 1983 of Viacheslav Sychev to succeed Nikolai Fadeev, who had been Comecon Secretary since 1958, helped to pave the way for a new period in the history of the organization.

18. We may also note that the CMEA program was launched at the same time as the counterpart West European "Eureka" program. It is perhaps the latter that finally stimulated the socialist countries to action. The CMEA has a history of initiatives taken in apparent reaction to developments on the Western side. The organization itself is generally regarded as having been created in response to the American Marshall Plan for the postwar economic recovery of Western Europe.

19. Philip Hanson has calculated that by 1985 imports from Eastern Europe accounted for about 30% of Soviet equipment investment, and that this investment is planned to increase by nearly 40% over the 1986-1990 plan period. See his "The Soviet Twelfth Five Year Plan" in R. Weichhardt, ed., *The Soviet Economy: A New Course?* Brussels: NATO, 1987, pp. 10-28.

20. The promotion of inter-enterprise linkages is also not a new idea. It was one of many concepts incorporated in the catch-all 1971 Program, and has since received growing attention in the authoritative CMEA literature. Cf. Iu. Shiriaev, "Problems in the Development of Direct Relationships among Economic Organizations of CMEA Member Countries," published in *Zahranicni obchod*, No. 1, 1982; English version published in *Soviet and East European Foreign Trade*, Vol. 18, Fall 1982, pp. 1-14. The author is the director of the CMEA's International Institute for Economic Problems of the World Socialist System in Moscow.

21. L. Csaba, "Le CAEM sous le signe . . ." *op. cit.*, who cites other CMEA authors in this regard.

22. Decree of the Presidium of the USSR Supreme Soviet of May 26, 1983, "On the Procedure Governing the Activity of Joint Economic Organizations of the USSR and other CMEA Countries on USSR Territory." It has been supplemented by the Presidium decree of January 13, 1987, "On Matters Concerning the Establishment on USSR Territory and the Activity of Joint Enterprises and International Associations and Organizations with the Participation of Soviet and Foreign Organizations, Firms and Management Organs" and a resolution of the USSR Council of Ministers of the same date, "On the Procedure for the Creation on USSR Territory and the Activity of Joint Enterprises and International Associations and

Organizations of the USSR and Other CMEA Countries." The last provides the most detail on the conditions for the establishment in the USSR of joint ventures with CMEA partners. These can take three organizational forms: joint ventures proper (with shared equity), international business associations (contractual rather than equity ventures) and joint organizations (joint equity ventures for R&D purposes).

23. *Bulgarian Foreign Trade*, No. 4, 1986, pp. 4-7, *Hungaropress*, various issues, and *Foreign Trade* (Moscow), 3/1987, p. 60.

24. See, for example, M. Lavigne, "Problématique de l'entreprise multinationale socialiste," *Economies et Sociétés*, Vol. XI, Nos. 1-2, 1977, pp. 35-78. The point was stressed again, in the context of current moves to strengthen direct contacts, by the Hungarian economist I. Wiesel in "K.G.S.T.," an article on the CMEA published in *Figyelö*, Vol. 31, No. 7, 1987, p. 3 (summarized in *Abstracts of Hungarian Economic Literature*, Vol. 17, No. 1, 1987, pp. 264-265).

25. The 1986 reforms of the Soviet foreign trade system were designed to create the conditions for the "direct participation" of domestic enterprises in the implementation of the CMEA Comprehensive Program in cooperation with partner enterprises in the other CMEA countries (*Pravda*, September 24, 1986, p. 1).

26. L. Csaba, "CMEA and East-West Trade," *Comparative Economic Studies*, Vol. XXVIII, No. 3, Fall 1986, p. 57. The Hungarian economist A. Köves has questioned whether turning inward is a feasible choice in his *The CMEA Countries in the World Economy: Turning Inwards or Turning Outwards*, Budapest: Akad. Kiado, 1985.

27. In reviewing the background to the CMEA's "strategic response to the challenge of the 1980s," Bogomolov has asserted that "the CMEA countries have had to draw far-reaching conclusions from the worsening international situation and the continuing crisis in the world socialist economy. Cold war winds blowing from across the Atlantic have damaged trade conditions between East and West. This is all the more alarming because it has given rise to problems of a purely economic nature." O. T. Bogomolov, "CMEA Economic Strategy in the 1980s" in *The World Socialist Economy*, Moscow: Nauka, 1986, p. 20. In the same volume, an article by H. Vlasin and N. Alekhin on CMEA scientific and technical cooperation ("Scientific and Technological Cooperation") calls attention (pp. 186-187) to the constraints on scientific cooperation with the West.

28. The Soviet imperatives defined at the beginning of this paper should be recalled here.

29. Statistics on oil trade published by the International Energy Agency, Paris.

30. *PlanEcon Report*, Vol. 111, No. 1, January 7, 1987.

31. *Ekonomicheskoe Sotrudnichestvo Stran-Chlenov SEV*, Moscow. In a monograph published on the Soviet role in socialist economic integration published by the CMEA Secretariat in 1986, the pipeline is the subject of the briefest possible reference in a short paragraph listing joint development projects in the period of the Twelfth Five-Year Plan. (O. Bogomolov, *SSSR v Sisteme Sotsialisticheskoi Ekonomicheskoi Integratsii*, Moscow: CMEA Secretariat, 1986).

32. On the financing of the earlier project, see J. Hannigan and C. McMillan, "Joint Investment in Resource Development: Sectoral Approaches to Socialist Integration," in *East European Economic Assessment, Part 2—Regional Assessments*, A Compendium of Papers submitted to the Joint Economic Committee, Congress

of the United States, 99th Congress, 1st Session, Washington, D.C.: U.S. Government Printing Office, 1981, pp. 259-295.

33. Reuters dispatch from Budapest, September 24, 1987.

34. *Sofia News*, August 26, 1987, p. 4.

35. John M. Kramer has reviewed the East European nuclear power program in the light of Chernobyl, in his "Chernobyl and Eastern Europe," *Problems of Communism*, Nov.-Dec. 1986, pp. 40-58.

36. J. Warnock, "The Soviet Union's Role as an International Supplier of Nuclear Technology, Equipment and Materials," unpublished M.A. thesis, Institute of Soviet and East European Studies, Carleton University, Ottawa, 1986.

37. The period spanned by the announcements of the Khmelnitsky nuclear power and the Progress pipeline projects. Bulgarian and Romanian participation in Konstantinovka, formally agreed in 1982, was decided earlier, as a Balkan counterpart to Khmelnitsky.

38. That is, providing some needed equipment and technology and contracting for long-term counter-deliveries. The Soyuz (Orenburg) concept of cooperation, involved complete East European construction responsibility for designated sectors of the line, with coordination performed by a Soviet agency.

39. In illustration, a chapter (by A. Zubkov) on "CMEA Energy Supply" in a recent, authoritative Soviet source (*The World Socialist Economy*, op. cit.) devotes primary attention, despite its title, to energy-saving policies and programs in the region and only secondarily to measures to boost regional energy supply.

40. *Financial Times*, April 28, 1987. This compares with Romanian crude oil production of 10.1 mmt and estimated total (crude and products) oil imports of 16.6 mmt in 1986.

41. Bogomolov, *SSSR v sisteme* . . . ; Academician Bogomolov is director of the Institute of the Economics of the World Socialist System, USSR Academy of Sciences, and is regarded as a close advisor to Gorbachev on external economic relations.

42. Quoted in *ibid.*, p. 25.

43. TASS International Service, October 13, 1987.

44. *Izvestiia*, October 10, 1987, report (p. 6) of a roundtable of international economists at the Academy of Sciences, Moscow.

45. Cf. L. G. Abramov, *SEV: Kapital'nye vlozheniia—perspektivnaia sfera strodnichestva*, Moscow: Nauka, 1987.

46. Soviet Prime Minister Ryzhkov's speech to the 43rd Session referred to the need to expand the use of national currencies in intra-CMEA settlements as a first step towards eventual convertibility and the institution of a collective monetary unit. TASS International Service, October 13, 1987.

47. Statement to the 42nd regular session of the Council held in Bucharest, November 3, 1986 (TASS International Service). Ryzhkov did not explicitly state that oil deliveries would increase; and added the typical provision that East European participation in joint projects would continue and that East European counter-deliveries would have to grow and improve in structure.

3

Soviet Military Concerns and Prospects in Eastern Europe

Edward N. Luttwak

Introduction: Scope and Limits

Soviet "concerns" are of course subjective and very much culturally determined, not a fit subject for a non-Sovietologist who must limit himself to the interpretation of military externalities. But to speculate on "prospects" is now almost compulsory: with the disposition of the peoples of Eastern Europe still fundamentally resting in the Kremlin, the advent of a new ruler—especially one who proclaims devotion to structural reform—naturally evokes welcome possibilities of positive change in Eastern Europe as well. Certainly there is much room for that: notwithstanding the profoundly different circumstances of each country, in all of them the political landscape is a petrified forest of suppressed change.

The world has turned many times since that most murderous winter of 1944–1945 when Germany's final retreat left Eastern Europe in Stalin's power. The colonial empires that once engulfed Africa and much of Asia have disappeared, an unprecedented prosperity has arisen in diverse parts of East Asia, both North America and the Soviet Union itself have been transformed in their own ways, and in non-Communist Europe the advance of affluence has left only pockets and extremities unconquered. Only in Eastern Europe is the status quo of 1944–1945 fundamentally perpetuated: what Stalin's troops conquered the Soviet Union still keeps, and that basic political fact ultimately governs all else, no matter what deviations from the ideal model of totalitarian and subservient satellites may exist in each country. That to note as much is mere banality, merely shows that one may become habituated even to tragedy on the largest scale, manifest in Czechoslovakia's degradation, the arrested development of Hungary and Poland as well as Bulgaria, the continued division of Germany and Romania's reversal to oriental despotism.

But now Gorbachev's regime has evidently decided that varied forms of liberalization are required to achieve the actual aim of a more efficient

Soviet Union. Subject to the stated refusal to allow any diminution in the CPSU's monopoly of power, the scope of what is to be allowed in the various categories (expression, economic activity, movement) is the key contention of Soviet politics at present, in lieu of the prior focus on central-planning priorities. Therefore, no well-defined Soviet "liberalization model" has yet been offered to the ruling elites of Eastern Europe. But the liberalization-for-efficiency formula has certainly been advertised, and the great question is just how far the process might go.

What follows is an attempt to define the presumptive outer limits of liberalization set for the role of East European *territory* in Soviet grand strategy, which of course does not tell us what will actually happen in each country within those limits. No attempt is made to address other limits to liberalization which might be imposed by Moscow to preserve its considerable non-military interests in the region, both economic and political. And what Moscow may choose to allow might be disallowed by the ruling group in each country. Ever since the dissolution of the standardized Stalinist model during the 1950s, the governance of the various countries has evolved on divergent paths with localized adaptations, the residue of past policy reversals and the dynamics of inner-party politics combining to create vastly different regimes not only among countries but also among the different sectors of national life. An East European composite of the most liberalized sectors today would define a state substantially authoritarian, with wide freedoms of expression except in regard to politics narrowly defined, a mixed economy with as much scope for free enterprise as in some countries of Western Europe, and almost unimpeded freedom of movement. Equally, one could construct another composite of the most rigidly controlled sectors that would substantially replicate the pure Stalinist model circa 1952, minus the executions.

Specifically, in Hungary and Poland, *de facto* liberalization of cultural and religious expression as well as of the agricultural and service sectors already goes beyond whatever has been proposed in the Soviet Union by even the most reformist of official voices. In East Germany, the leadership still resists in principle Moscow's liberalization-for-efficiency formula as an unnecessary devolution of power. In Bulgaria, attempts at conformity with the new Soviet "line" have a farcical air given the stolid continuity of the leadership, and its evident difficulties in following a "line" so poorly defined. As for Romania, the Gorbachev formula offers a purely abstract hope for a population that would see improvement even in a return to an orderly Stalinism. It seems irrelevant for the ruling family, devoted as it is to the perfection of despotism. It is against the background of these diverse realities that the present analysis of the role of East European territory in Soviet grand strategy unfolds, beginning with a retrospective overview.

The Pre-Nuclear Period

It might seem that there was hardly a pre-nuclear period at all, inasmuch as the Soviet Union had only been in control of Eastern Europe for a few months when the first fission bomb was detonated. Actually, Stalin knew of the bomb's existence well before that, thanks to the skillful espionage that kept him, unlike Vice-President Truman, informed of the Manhattan project. But those facts must not be interpreted anachronistically: fission devices were seen merely as more powerful bombs. The true significance of the novelty (i.e., that with its help "strategic air bombardment" could finally achieve the war-winning role that its historic advocates had so prematurely claimed) did not sink in even long after Hiroshima, as the evidence of Soviet decisions at the time clearly shows.[1]

Despite the change in mentality that nuclear weapons eventually induced, Soviet military policy remained essentially pre-nuclear not only after Hiroshima but even as the Soviet Union itself acquired its first nuclear weapons. Inevitably that meant that the entire strategic landscape and the role of Eastern Europe within it were also seen in pre-nuclear terms, with Germany as the problem and Soviet military control of Eastern Europe as a partial solution.

Germany was utterly defeated after World War II, but the danger of a renewed German invasion remained Moscow's salient preoccupation, more so than the urgencies of reconstruction when choices had to be made between the two.[2] The victory had been a damnably close-run thing, as the Iron Duke said of Waterloo, its catastrophic ravages still very much in evidence long after V-E day. As Stalin saw it, either later at the hands of a reconstructed, once again aggressive Germany, or much earlier if American production combined with the devilish war skills of Germans, the Soviet Union would be re-invaded. The Volga might once again form the last line of resistance. Stalin used this scenario to justify the acquisition of big-gun warships under the first post-war naval construction program; arguing that by steaming upriver they could add their firepower to the land defenses.

Such fearful expectations did not exclusively reflect the continuing psychological impact of that most catastrophic of wars. In addition to whatever ideological predispositions (and projections) may have been at work that transcend the scope of this analysis, fears of renewed invasion could also be sustained by hard-headed military calculations. This was so, notwithstanding the seemingly overwhelming capabilities of the Soviet armed forces at the time vis-à-vis the extinct German military power and the feeble strength of Anglo-American ground forces after the 1945/1946 demobilization. There was a very specific notion of the operational form of an invasion: converging deep-penetration offensive thrusts by echeloned armor-spearheaded mobile forces, advancing by successive bounds through fronts breached by massed artillery fires, with tactical-air support being of crucial importance throughout.

It was that last component of the overall operation that had very adverse strategic implications for Stalin and his men as they contemplated the post VE-Day military balance. For, by the end of the war Soviet military planners had learned that tactical air support when it was applied in both heavy and sustainable doses, could nullify even sharp disadvantages in quantity and quality between the spearheading armored units of an offensive and the armor contingents reacting defensively (or vice-versa), in spite of the substantial immunity of the battle tanks themselves to most air to ground weapons then available. The battlefield interdiction of their constantly-needed resupply could wholly neutralize armor units even without their direct destruction; the operational impotence under sustained air attack of German *Tiger* and *Panther* units of formidable quality, whose vehicles had exceptional armor protection which totally outclassed Anglo-American armor forces, had been dramatically illustrated again and again after D-Day.

Secondly, tactical air support could efficiently replace laboriously assembled concentrations of field artillery even in its initial front-breaching role at each remove. The vastly greater potential for locational surprise inherent in airpower outweighs its daylight/fair weather limitations. Consequently, for the continuing fire support of on-going offensive thrusts, tactical air strength was absolutely superior to artillery, only a fraction of which could be carried forward with the advancing forces to be deployed within range of its targets.

More generally, tactical air power could nullify the impact of numerical disadvantages on the ground *in toto* within the terrain conditions of central and eastern Europe (no jungle-cover, etc.). Thirty or even fewer divisions could prevail against one hundred if the latter could only move to engage the former at night or in foul weather, then to fight under one-sided air attack.

That being the 1945 state of the military art, Stalin's planners could obtain little comfort from the vast superiority of Soviet armor, artillery and numbers in general—even if the potential of *strategic* air bombardment with fission bombs was wholly discounted (because of the extreme scarcity of fission bombs or because of presumed inhibitions to their use). Given the new operational reality revealed by 1945 (to paraphrase: ground forces occupy the territory that tactical air power conquers) the superior Anglo-American capacity to *produce* military aviation (airframes, engines, crews, ordnance) had to mean that the military balance was decisively skewed, as production/mass oriented Soviet evaluators would see it; the production ratio was of the order of 4:1 in favour of the West at least, if not more.[3] Actually from the Soviet point of view the situation was even more unfavorable. The *qualitative* superiority of Anglo-American fighters was such that it would serve little purpose to divert resources from ground weapons (already in surplus) in order to increase aircraft production. In any realistic appraisal, P-51s could be expected to obtain 10:1 or more likely 20:1 success ratios in air combat, establishing a decisive air superiority that would nullify the potential of Soviet attack and bomber types, almost regardless of their numbers.

Once airpower was placed in the equation not only was the balance decisively altered but the time-horizon of the threat was greatly foreshortened. True, for the West to recruit German ex-servicemen and form them into

U.S.-equipped units, to remobilize Anglo-American forces, prepare their equipment and stock supplies would take a long time if the aim was to achieve superior strength on the ground. Even Soviet planners, insensitive to the insurmountable political obstacles to remobilization, must have known that by the end of 1946 the once-mighty U.S. ground forces had been largely disbanded rather than demobilized in orderly fashion; and that in any case in the crucial armor sector equipment could only come from new production. But air power could be reconstituted much more quickly because the huge left-over inventories were far from obsolete, production capacity was still in place, and war-trained aircrew and ancillary manpower was still very much current, needing no retraining to speak of (as opposed to the unit training of ground formations). Hence the more airpower figured in the mix, the quicker could an invasion be conspired.

What to us now seems nightmarish fantasy was the essence of realism in Moscow, as the urgency given to the air-defense build-up irrefutably shows.[4] Amidst the ruins and hunger of a devastated Soviet Union, it was the production of anti-aircraft guns, the mass-production of copied lend-lease radars, the frantic development of German *Wasserfal* surface-to-air missiles (eventually deployed as the NATO-designated SAM-1), and the first MiG-15 jet interceptors that had the highest priority.

Given this world-view, in which Soviet strength on the ground was so much less formidable than it seemed to most Western observers, the territory of Eastern Europe was perceived in classic terms as a protective glacis. To the extent that the depth of the Soviet zones in Germany and Austria as well as of Czechoslovakia, Hungary and Poland could absorb the momentum of an invasion out of the Western parts of Germany, to the degree that Yugoslav, Bulgarian and Romanian territory could do the same for an Anglo-American invasion out of Italy, Greece or Turkey, the maximum enemy penetration would be foreshortened, and perhaps this time their armies might not even reach the Volga. Last time round the Soviet Union had only had Lithuania, Latvia and Estonia to shield Leningrad and only Bukovina and Bessarabia to add depth before Kiev. For the next time, which thanks to airpower, could come very soon, Moscow was determined to have much more.

There were to be sure other motives for the imposition of Soviet control in country after country. The expansion of Soviet-style governance was ideologically satisfactory, it widened the circle of obedience to Moscow's orders, and also ensured that loot could continue to be extracted in systematic fashion through the notorious joint companies. But even if none of these other reasons had obtained, the military value of each hectare of Eastern European territory meant that Moscow would try to secure as much of it as possible, even if it had to tolerate the ambiguities and delays of subversion, in fear that a straightforward imposition of control might precipitate the invasion so actively expected.

During this nuclear phase therefore, which certainly lasted into the 1950s, even as the Soviet Union was acquiring thermonuclear weapons, only a successful invasion could have loosened the Soviet hold on Eastern Europe.

The Nuclear Period

Because it only began when the mentality of the Soviet leaders absorbed the implications of the cataclysmic nuclear innovation—by then magnified a thousand-fold in destructive power—no precise date can be given for the inception of this second period. But we know that we are dealing with a new world-view when we take note of the belated demobilization carried out by 1960, in which the substantial disbandment of the field artillery formations was especially significant.[5] In spite of the prominence of Soviet armor, it was the field artillery that was the largest and most expensive component of the Soviet ground forces by the end of the war—much of it in the independent artillery brigades and divisions under direct Army and front command—and it was regarded as the key tool of ground warfare.

When this huge mass of howitzer and gun batteries was disbanded, to be replaced by the handful of nuclear rockets (F.R.O.Gs in NATO-speak) assigned to each maneuver division and later the few battalions of SCUD nuclear missiles assigned to Army echelons, the meaning of the matter was clear: any serious war would be nuclear from the start (a war both serious and non-nuclear would have required the mass of field artillery then disbanded), even if it could be hoped that the (nuclear) fighting might be confined to the theater in dispute (the Soviet "Local War" concept) without extending it to the American and Soviet homelands. But even if "Local War" was fervently advocated, it was actually "strategic" nuclear war that was in prospect, because that, of course, was what the United States threatened if there was any serious war at all.

In those years—as we would later see it—perceptions of the utility of nuclear weapons were grossly inflated.[6] The widespread expectation that nuclear weapons would be used from the very beginning of a serious war gave the doctrine of "Massive Retaliation" (a strictly unofficial label) enunciated in January 1954 sufficient plausibility to allow significant military economies with undiminished security. To be sure, that brilliant diplomatic construct which exploited the advantage of the defensive, and the moral intensity of contemporary American public attitudes, was not literally meant—if three drunk Russian soldiers stumbled across the inter-German border, the immediate nuclear bombardment of Moscow would not automatically follow. And it is also true that the logical consequences of the doctrine were not in fact accepted; if they had been, the U.S. Army, Navy, Marine Corps and Air Force should have been substantially disbanded. Nevertheless, the American intent to use nuclear weapons was sufficiently plausible to make large-scale continental warfare by non-nuclear forces an unlikely possibility as far as the Soviet leadership was concerned. Only that explains the post-1955 unilateral reductions in the Soviet ground forces.

The new strategic conditions sharply reduced the *military* value of Eastern European territory. Defensively, it would no longer provide significant protection—if the U.S. sent its bombers to drop nuclear weapons on Soviet cities it would hardly matter which side occupied the intervening terrain.[7] Offensively, forward jump-off bases in Saxony and Bohemia would count for little given that in any case a successful Soviet offensive on the ground would merely trigger "strategic" nuclear retaliation by the United States.

Soviet acceptance of the Austrian State Treaty of 1955 was certainly congruent with the new strategic circumstances whatever its motives may have been. The former Soviet zone in eastern Austria had lost value as a protective glacis for a Soviet-dominated Hungary, just as the latter had lost much of its value as a forward shield for Soviet territory. Given the successful negotiation of the Austrian arrangement in the newly favorable strategic setting, it is possible to speculate that further reciprocal withdrawals under the premise of neutralization might also have been negotiable for other territories under Soviet occupation.

No doubt Soviet leaders had fully sufficient non-military reasons for retaining control of East Germany and the rest of the bloc, but from a strictly military point of view what had been essential before had become merely desirable, at most.[8] When the importance of nuclear weapons within the overall military balance was at its peak, the defensive/offensive value of East European territory was at its nadir, and other things being equal that was the period when the chances of emancipation should have been at their highest. It is suggestive that in 1956 the Soviet leadership could accept the 1956 Gomulka coup in Poland, as it might have accepted a Nagy coup in Hungary, had the principle of the Party's monopoly of power and Hungary's affiliation to the bloc been preserved. Now that the military prerequisites were relaxed to a level at which the mere exclusion of hostile forces was deemed sufficient (viz. the need to use the territory for defensive preparations and offensive deployments), Soviet political and economic interests became the salient factors, and they could be satisfied just as well with looser forms of control.

In theory, "Massive Retaliation" could have kept the Soviet Union and the United States in a state of extreme tension; in practice, it de-fused the military competition between them, by discounting the value of (the much more costly) non-nuclear forces while justifying only modest "counter-city" nuclear forces on each side. Under its aegis, Eisenhower could resist (up to a point) pressures for military preparedness in general (the "New Look" defense-budget cuts) and later for the building of a large force of ballistic missiles; equally Khrushchev was able to carry out his vast demobilization while proclaiming the power of an intercontinental ballistic missile force that consisted of a handful of SS-6 missiles produced by artisanal methods. As war-experienced leaders on each side confronted one another with forces so largely symbolic in nature, it was certainly not their mechanical interaction that precluded a relaxation of tensions that might have had profound consequences for Eastern Europe. In fact the emphasis of both sides on the political/economic competition in the Middle East, and the exposure of both sides to other political pressures (Mao's China in the Soviet case, domestic activism in the American case) shows in oblique fashion to what extent the military competition in Europe had waned in importance.

The Decline of Nuclear Weapons

Once again it was the United States that took the initiative to change the strategic rules, not necessarily to its own advantage. By 1961, with the advent of a new Administration in the United States, the longstanding critiques of "Massive Retaliation" acquired official endorsement. Academic and professional military officers (General Maxwell Taylor most notably) especially had made much of the theoretical defects of Massive Retaliation from its inception, while obscuring its substantive merits. Both emphasized the twin dangers that if challenged, the Massive Retaliation stance would dissolve into mere bluff, leaving the United States in a position of great weakness—or else that it might not be a bluff after all, leading to a nuclear catastrophe.

Both pointed out that the logical Soviet course was to carry out an aggression by small slices, each one too insignificant in scope to warrant a "massive" retaliatory attack on the Soviet Union. The professional military critique naturally emphasized the virtual impossibility of coherent preparations in the Army, Navy, Air Force (minus the Strategic Air Command) and Marine Corps under the official assumption that any serious war would be nuclear from the start: there were no force-structures, operational methods, tactics or equipment choices that could make sense amidst multi-megaton explosions on the respective cities.

While the logic of the critique seemed compelling at the time, we can now recognize that it—and reciprocally the rationale of the "Flexible Response"—had a very transient basis. Their tacit premise was that nuclear weapons *were* usable for the deliberate, purposeful, conduct of war—so long as they would not be used from the start for indiscriminate attacks on cities. In other words, the credibility of nuclear warfare itself was then in a middle stage, its continuing erosion as yet unnoticed.

The new strategic stance called for much more elaborate (and costly) nuclear forces with many more "tactical" and "counterforce" weapons of greater accuracy and with smaller warheads, in lieu of the cheaper nuclear forces that had sufficed for Massive Retaliation (which required only the ability to attack a modest number of the largest, most easily hit targets (i.e. cities) with multi-megaton explosions). If a war escalated, only "tactical" nuclear weapons would be employed at first, starting with the "battlefield" sub-category of artillery shells, short-range missiles and smaller bombs; further flexibility was retained after that by a capacity for selective though "strategic" nuclear attacks, and only if all else failed and the aggressor persisted would counter-city attacks follow.

But the flexibility to be obtained for varied nuclear attack "options" was only supplementary to a restored capacity for sustained non-nuclear warfare. That was the sovereign if costly remedy for the much-emphasized threat of a slice-by-slice Soviet invasion: each slice would be met, flexibly, by an appropriate non-nuclear response.

The detailed elaborations of American nuclear strategy did not affect the predicament of Eastern Europe but the substantial rehabilitation of non-nuclear warfare under Flexible Response almost certainly did. The refusal to engage in it proclaimed by the United States under the policy of Massive Retaliation had undermined the purpose of Soviet preparations for large-scale continental warfare, to the extent that the threat of a prompt escalation was believed. As noted, the Kremlin leadership under Khrushchev had chosen to believe in the threat so as to carry out the largest unilateral military reductions in Soviet history, while promoting its own (also very economical) "Local War" concept of prompt nuclear use.

When the United States repudiated Massive Retaliation and launched a significant effort to restore realistic combat capabilities in the armed forces, it would have been difficult for any Soviet leadership to persevere in Khrushchev's path. No doubt the increasingly broad and eventually monumental Soviet armament effort that began in 1963 (not coincidentally as Khrushchev's power waned) derived from purely internal impulses as well (Maxwell Taylor's Soviet colleagues, and the heavy-industry "Metal eaters") but even if it was not a response to "Flexible Response," the latter certainly provided a rationale for professional-military and political proclivities that Khrushchev could no longer resist, and which his successors clearly had no intention of resisting.

The ensuing Soviet build-up covered the full spectrum of military forces; both nuclear and naval developments acquired great prominence within it, but the priority of ground and air forces for large-scale continental warfare was in evidence from the start. At the beginning of the build-up, Soviet tactical air forces were equipped largely with lightweight fighters, very efficient for the air defense role along with missiles and guns, less useful for the offense/defense "air superiority" role over the battlefield, and of very little value for ground attack and still less for interdiction. During the next two decades, Soviet tactical air power was transformed by the introduction of strike/interdiction and ground attack aircraft in large numbers, while the standard fighters in production were increasingly heavy, multi-purpose machines—far better suited to support the ground operations of continental warfare on a large scale.

The changes manifest in the Soviet army were even more suggestive and much more costly. The Soviet divisional count did not increase dramatically immediately or even later (140 in 1968; 168 in 1978; 200+ in 1988[9]) but the vast effort devoted to the upgrading of the ground forces became evident in the growth of the "Armya" and "Front" echelons above division. The bulk of Khrushchev's reductions had been achieved by the substantial disestablishment of the two echelons above the division level, and the post-1963 build-up emphasized their reconstitution. The effort was prolonged as well as very extensive. It took years for the effects to mature but eventually the reconstituted echelons emerged with (a) vast artillery forces now self-propelled, a full division at Front level, and a large brigade's worth at Armya level; (b) contingents of air assault and armed helicopter forces, in brigade strength at Front level and in battalion strength at Armya level; (c) large anti-aircraft forces with both missile and gun units at each echelons; and (d) a full panoply of engineer, signals, electronic warfare, chemical warfare, nuclear/biological/chemical defense, tank-transport, supply and maintenance units at each echelon.

Standing back from the details of the force-structure, the wider implications can be readily recognized. First, the specialized manpower they required as well as their especially costly equipment made the 16 Front and 40 Armya echelons along with the line divisions they supported the single most costly element of the entire Soviet build-up; their reconstitution and continued development over the span of two decades therefore expressed Soviet strategic priorities in unambiguous fashion.

Second, and conclusively, whereas the line divisions themselves were needed for internal (and imperial) security in any case, and were also essential as territorial markers even under a Massive Retaliation/Local War all-nuclear strategy, the Armya/Front echelons have little or no value for either function. They only become important in the context of *non-nuclear* operations on a large scale, when their support can be applied selectively to chosen groupings of line divisions, in order to endow them with offensive or defensive strength in concentrated form.

In the circumstances, the role of Eastern Europe in Soviet strategy naturally underwent a very unfavorable change. To the extent that non-nuclear operations became more important, the control of territory became more important also, whether to provide depth on the defensive or jump-off positions on the offensive. If an Austrian arrangement could be acceptable for Germany as well under the earlier dispensation, (at least from a purely military point of view) it became less and less acceptable as the plausibility of non-nuclear war increased. And if the Soviet Union could view the absence of forward deployments in Czechoslovakia or elsewhere with relative equanimity under the earlier strategy, they became essential under the new strategy which was designed to utilize the costly non-nuclear strength that was being acquired.

As it happens, Soviet ground forces arrived in Czechoslovakia in 1968 in the context of an invasion meant to reverse political changes that the Kremlin had strong reasons to resist—quite aside from any strategic considerations. A subservient government fully capable of enforcing its control was duly stabilized within a year or two. But Soviet ground forces have remained in place just the same till this day: while their forward deployment had not been needed during the Massive Retaliation/Local War period, in the new strategic conditions it was becoming steadily more useful for both offensive and defensive purposes.

For the change was not a one-time shift. The non-nuclear content of NATO's Flexible Response as well as that of Soviet military preparations continued to increase from the later 1960s, in a process that continues still. Hence the utility of Eastern European territory in Soviet strategy continued to increase also. Had those years been marked by political liberalisation in the Soviet Union and Eastern Europe, a harsh contrast would have been seen in the growth in Soviet divisional garrisons, the expansion of air bases and supply depots, and the construction of new headquarters and ancillary facilities for Armya, Front and Group echelons (notably in East Germany). As it was, because the post-1964 period was also characterized by a reversion to rigidity in Soviet domestic controls ("neo-Stalinism"), which was reflected in Eastern Europe too in some degree, the unfavorable evolution of the strategic situation was congruent with the deteriorating political climate in a most unhappy harmony.

The Emerging Post-Nuclear Era

The observed change is the steadily increased reliance of both East and West on (costly) non-nuclear forces and on the outcome of many small decisions to acquire this or that non-nuclear capability, in order to delay the moment when nuclear weapons would first have to be used in war. The synthetic depiction of that change is the diminishing role of nuclear weapons in the overall military balance. The proximate cause of the change is the diminished acceptability of nuclear use in both declaratory policies and operational war-planning. Finally, the ultimate cause that seems most plausible is the redefinition of the threat: for the United States, the perception of the Stalin-era threat as a global conspiracy with absolute aims had been displaced by a classical, *territorial*, threat perception, in which the Soviet Union is seen as threatening this or that zone which its forces can reach. For the Soviet Union, on the other hand, we may infer that perceptions of the threat of a renewed (and now American-backed) German invasion must have waned with the passing of each day from the climax of 1942, as the dissipation of the terrors of invasion allowed more sober appraisal. And, the observed evidence of an offensive re-orientation in the detailed composition of Soviet military power from the mid-1960s onwards [10] indicates that hopes of military gain took the place of fear in the Kremlin's "who-whom" worldview, instead of the tranquillity that another political culture might have allowed. Still, as each side perceived a less monstrous threat the use of monstrous nuclear weapons became less acceptable; limited threats call for a limited response. Moreover, on the Soviet side, the realism of offensive ambitions was dependent on the hypothesis of nuclear *non-use*.[11]

When will quantitative change—the declining role of nuclear weapons within the overall military balance—become qualitative? That "post-nuclear" state is reached when the threat to use nuclear weapons in response to an attack that is (a) non-nuclear and (b) aimed at a protected third party, is repudiated, (i.e. when the attempt to compensate for non-nuclear weakness by means of nuclear threats is finally given up). In the obfuscating shorthand of strategical discourse that application of nuclear strength is labelled "extended deterrence"; actually it should be thought of as "twice-extended deterrence," because nuclear strength is invoked against a non-nuclear threat, and one moreover aimed at a third party. As such it is the most ambitious application of nuclear strength, at the opposite extreme from "strike-back" deterrence, (i.e. the threat to use nuclear weapons against direct nuclear attack). The latter is as credible now as it ever was: the aggressor who would attack with nuclear weapons cannot reasonably assume that his victim will not respond in kind, if he still can. Nuclear deterrence "extended" just once, i.e. the threat of a nuclear response to nuclear attack against a protected third party, implies a degree of solidarity that may or may not obtain, but it does not violate proportionality: the aggressor who uses nuclear weapons is sufficiently monstrous to be attacked with monstrous weapons.

The attitudinal shift that has been registered, and which still continues, therefore specifically erodes "twice-extended deterrence" as it has been labelled here. Explicit calls for its repudiation ("No First Use") have already been voiced by noted figures of no current official standing. But with NATO's entire strategy still squarely based upon it, no early change in official policy is to be expected. Yet declarations do not determine strategic phenomena; they sometimes reflect them and more often they seek to modify them by exhortation, reassurance or threat. In the meantime, actual decisions do reflect the evolving trend: the emphasis on the conventional part of "Flexible Response" continues to grow, nuclear use against non-nuclear attack continues to lose plausibility, and Soviet investment in capabilities that are only useful if there is *no* nuclear use, continues to increase.[12]

We are therefore witnessing a slide towards post-nuclear conditions, caused by an attitudinal shift but materially promoted by the changing composition of military power. Moreover, this is strongly encouraged by Soviet declaratory policy (and all other means of influencing Western public opinion) in a process that is certainly not restrained by internally-contradictory U.S. and NATO policies. For, both of the latter combine vehement reiterations of "twice-extended deterrence" with active participation in the delegitimization of nuclear weapons *in toto* (e.g. by the presentation of the 1987 INF Treaty as merely a first step towards the complete abolition of all nuclear weapons). And the U.S. continues to urge the need for more non-nuclear strength, even though the more NATO non-nuclear defenses are resilient, the greater the scope thereby allowed for the continuation of politics after the outbreak of war, and therefore the more likely that the nuclear option would be renounced.

What full-scale "post-nuclear" conditions would mean for Soviet military attitudes towards Eastern Europe is evident: if nuclear weapons are wholly eliminated from the theater-level military balance, the ground forces must recover their ancestral role as *the* strategic instrumentality of continental warfare. With that the possession of territory must also recover its full significance. There is therefore a bitter irony in the present conjunction between a reformist and partially liberalizing regime in Moscow, and the accelerated drift towards post-nuclear conditions which that same regime is so actively promoting.

Residual hopes must therefore focus on the potential for "conventional" arms control, and specifically for disengagement measures that would remove Soviet forces to the East. To be sure, from a strictly strategic point of view which disregards notably the *possible* Soviet intention of reducing substantially current military expenditures, the emergence of post-nuclear conditions should dissuade any reductions in the Soviet Union's non-nuclear forces aimed at the European theater. For of course the prospective elimination of nuclear weapons from the European balance, should finally make it possible for the Soviet Union to secure the full benefit of its non-nuclear strength, which nuclear weapons have denied it ever since 1945. If therefore no other considerations applied, the Soviet Union should now take good care to preserve if not enhance its non-nuclear strength, in anticipation of the arrival of full post-nuclear conditions when nuclear strength would no longer be fully validated for either coercive diplomacy or actual war.

The prospects of a Soviet military disengagement from Eastern Europe therefore depend on the willingness of the Kremlin leadership to sacrifice short/medium-term strategic gains for long-term economic gains. It is impossible to assess what those strategic gains might be worth to the Kremlin, or what uses present leaders might see in a post-nuclear situation for the kind of non-nuclear advantage that Soviet planners might have dreamt of at various times during almost half a century of nuclear frustration. By contrast, it *is* possible to determine the scope of the possible savings (though not their subjective value of course). Two rough approximations suffice for that: the ground and tactical-air forces as a whole account for not less than 70% of Soviet military expenditures excluding central overheads; and not less than 60% of those forces are assigned to the European theater.[13] Hence the theoretical maximum of possible savings is of the order of 42% of total Soviet military expenditures, as opposed to the maximum of 20% (also excluding central overheads) that a total elimination of Soviet strategic-nuclear forces would yield.[14] To be sure, the idea that the Soviet Union could get along with a mere 80 divisions, 14 "armies" and 9 "fronts" is chimerical, but the comparison does show that the potential for savings is twice as great in the Europe-assigned theater forces as in the strategic-nuclear forces, whose total elimination is also chimerical.

It is perhaps more realistic to envisage a partial Soviet disengagement. Some of the forces in Eastern Europe would be withdrawn to the USSR, some of them in turn to be placed in Cat II, or even Cat III reserve status,[15] in order to reduce operating and maintenance expenditures and to allow the release of technical cadres for other employment (as noted, the "armya" and "front" combat-support and service-support echelons now absorb especially large numbers of career technicians, many of them highly skilled, and presumably much-needed in industry).

What a reduction in the Soviet garrisons would mean for the political evolution of each one of the Eastern European regimes is far from clear;

even a retreat from such liberalization as has taken place might be the result in some cases, with tighter controls being imposed to compensate for the loss of latent Soviet military support. In that regard, one may recall that in Romania the absence of Soviet troops coincides with the most repressive of all Eastern European regimes. On the other hand it is easy to foresee what the results of a *complete* Soviet troop withdrawal would be. For in yet one more conjunction that need not have been (on top of the sheer coincidence of Gorbachev's ascent with the post-nuclear drift), "inherent" political stability (what stability would be minus repression) is perhaps at an all time low throughout Eastern Europe. Both the party loyalty, even fervor, that energetic indoctrination secured among younger segments of the population during the 1950s, and the hopes of rapid economic growth that variously prevailed during the 1960s and into the 1970s have been dissipated. An irremediable aversion for the several regimes is now the norm in the public opinion of each country, while the internal cohesion of the several CPs now rests entirely on the sum total of individual calculations of material self-interest, with the last remnants of ideological commitment long gone. This last conjunction means that political conditions are less favorable than ever before for total Soviet troop withdrawals—if, that is, the Soviet leadership is both politically well-informed and prudent. But of course the evidence of four years is that the present Kremlin leadership is neither of these things, at least judging by what happened in Alma Ata, and between Armenians and Azeris in the Caucasus.

Notes

1. See, e.g., R. L. Garthoff, *Soviet Military Policy: A Historical Analysis*, London: 1966, and Stalin's call for rearmament in *Pravda*, February 10, 1946, p. 20.

2. Soviet force levels show how limited was the immediate post VJ-day demobilization, notwithstanding the acute shortage of able-bodied manpower for reconstruction and production; T. W. Wolfe, *Soviet Power and Europe 1945–1970*, Baltimore: Johns Hopkins Press, 1970, pp. 8–15.

3. In the peak production year, the U.S. produced 96,318 airframes, the U.K. 40,300, Canada/Australia 26,263, and the U.S.S.R. 40,300; that understates the gap because of the many Anglo-American four-engine types versus the predominance of single-engine airframes in Soviet production. The 1944 aero-engine totals were 256,912 for the U.S., 56,931 for the U.K. and 52,000 for the U.S.S.R. R. J. Overy, *The Air War 1939–1945*, London: Europa Publ., 1980, Table 12, p. 150.

4. The emphasis on air defense is illustrated by the 1948 elevation of the relevant forces into a separate service, "Troops of national air defense," PVO *Strany*. Harriet Fast Scott and William F. Scott, *Armed Forces of the U.S.S.R.*, 2nd Edition, Boulder Colo.: Westview Press, 1981, p. 147.

5. Wolfe, *Soviet Power and Europe 1945–1970*, pp. 301–310.

6. An incidental consequence was the imminent expectation of widespread nuclear proliferation: how could the appeal of weapons so useful be resisted by those who could have them?

7. Preferred bomber flightpaths would avoid Eastern Europe; the shortest routes from CONUS would be over the Pole, and the least-defended approaches would be from the south.

8. Because they are inherently more exposed and also more costly (higher transport costs), forward-deployed garrisons are not desirable, unless there is use in their forward deployment.

9. See successive editions of the IISS *Military Balance* for 1968/1969, 1978/1979, and 1987/1988.

10. E.g., the changed composition of Soviet tactical aviation as lightweight interceptors/air superiority aircraft of the MiG-21 family gave way to a mix of multi-purpose MiG-23/-27 types and Su-19s, outright interdiction aircraft; in the ground forces the greater stress on offensive capabilities is exemplified by the introduction of otherwise counter-doctrinal elite forces (notably the air assault troops) as well as the new "Operational Manoeuvre Group" format, which required, inter alia, the acquisition of costly helicopters in large numbers.

11. In theory, there was a simple technical remedy for the diminished appropriateness of nuclear use against a diminished threat: nuclear weapons themselves diminished—"mini-nukes" in the jargon. Their advocacy has been recurrent and uniformly unsuccessful on the reasoning that attempts to secure advantages by the use of, say, 0.01 kiloton weapons would evoke 0.02 kiloton attacks, and so on.

12. Of which the prime exhibit is the conversion of the field artillery to much more costly self-propelled configurations and its concurrent expansion.

13. These calculations are the author's estimates derived by inspection of the detailed force structures, rather than of financial data such as it is; for a summary of the gross uncertainty that persists in regard to the latter see, inter alia, the IISS *Military Balance 1987/1988*, pp. 29–31.

14. Idem.

15. The O & M costs (and technical-manpower requirements) of Soviet ground forces vary according to their mobilization status. All 30 of the Tank and "Motor-Rifle" divisions in Eastern Europe (and their respective Army and Front echelons) are Category 1 formations, fully manned and with complete sets of late-model equipment; Category 2 formations have complete equipment sets but are only manned at 50–75% of authorized strength; Category 3 forces (the largest part) have older equipment sets and not much more than 20% of total authorized manpower, i.e., a mobilization cadre. See IISS *Military Balance 1987/1988*, pp. 34 and 39.

PART TWO

East European Concerns

4

East European Political and Ideological Perceptions and Concerns

Andrzej Korbonski

Introduction

This chapter focuses on the Soviet-East European relationship in the second half of the 1980s and on the prospects for the adaptation of that relationship to changing conditions in today's world. Obviously, these changes have been occurring at different levels: global; East-West; European; and regional. For reasons of space it was not possible to cover all these levels and the analysis will be confined to the regional perspective only. Under this particular rubric I have concentrated on the East European perceptions of the recent changes and current developments in the Soviet Union and the resulting concerns experienced by the East Europeans regarding the impact on its junior allies of the changes in the USSR.

The topic of perceptions and misperceptions has not been neglected by political scientists and there is no need to delve deeply into the meaning and theoretical implications of the concepts of image and image formation, perception and misperception, deception, rationality and irrationality. The pioneering work in this field was done by Robert Jervis and we are all in his debt. However, as suggested by Trond Gilberg,[1] it is imperative for us to distinguish between elite and mass perceptions in both the Soviet Union and Eastern Europe and also to differentiate among different elites and oligarchies—political, economic, and military. As will be shown, at times there have been striking differences between the elites and the masses, and sharp contrasts and conflicts among various elite groups. Similarly, we ought to be as precise as possible about the object of the perceptions. The meaning or substance of a belief, or an issue, or a policy lies in the eye of a beholder—who can perceive and interpret the real meaning of a behavior or a policy by having advance information. The problem, as pointed out by Tadeusz Kowalik[2], is that the absence of basic information is endemic in Eastern Europe, representing a major bottleneck which tends to slow down the progress in Soviet-East European relations that may take several years to eliminate.

It was Jervis who hypothesized some time ago that "scholars and decision-makers are apt to err by being too webbed to the established view and too closed to new information, as opposed to being too willing to alter their theories."[3] He also suggested that this was at least partly related to a tendency to fit incoming information into existing theories and images and that it gave rise to still another tendency whereby "actors see the behavior of others as more centralized, disciplined, and coordinated than it is."[4] This is an important warning, particularly for those discussing East European perceptions of Soviet behavior not only under Gorbachev but also under his predecessors.

East European Perceptions of the Soviet Union: The First Forty Years

In examining East European perceptions of Soviet behavior in the second half of the 1980s, we cannot entirely ignore the history of Soviet–East European relations as they evolved in more than four decades since the Soviet-sponsored Communist takeover of the so-called "East European Six"—Bulgaria, Czechoslovakia, East Germany, Hungary, Poland, and Romania. In looking at the past, it is easy to discover elements of both continuity and change.[5] On the one hand, many aspects of the Moscow-led alliance in Eastern Europe remained until today essentially unchanged after more than forty years of Communist rule; on the other hand, behind an impressive and seemingly impregnable facade of the alliance, some major changes have taken place over time. It is clear that the mix of continuity and change has greatly influenced the perceptions of the Soviet Union held by successive East European leaders, including the latters' reactions to Soviet policies. The reverse was also true, and it may be taken for granted that different Kremlin leaders have held different views of their East European counterparts.

It is clear that Soviet perceptions of Eastern Europe could not be easily separated from East European perceptions of the USSR. In contrast to an almost uniformly highly favorable image of the West, the East Europeans' perceptions of the Soviet Union on the eve of the Communist takeover varied sharply from country to country. Historical circumstances accounted for most of the variations, although some images were strongly conditioned by geography and such factors as political culture and religion. To put it simply, Poland, Hungary, and Romania were most hostile to Moscow whereas Bulgaria, Czechoslovakia, and Yugoslavia appeared most friendly. The future East Germany did not offer a clear-cut picture.

The seizure of power and the subsequent imposition of the Stalinist model did not essentially change their existing reciprocal national images and stereotypes, at least not right away. However, soon after the takeover, the traditional perceptions began to change, often quite drastically. Thus, for example, the Soviet-Yugoslav rift of 1948 was actually an interesting case of misperception on both sides: Stalin believed that Yugoslavia would not resist and would eventually collapse and surrender to Soviet demands; and for several years after the break Tito was still firmly convinced that it was all a misunderstanding that would soon be cleared up and Yugoslavia once again would be welcomed to the camp.

Stalin's death and the gradual dismantling of the Moscow-led monolith, resulted in an internal relaxation throughout the bloc and this, in turn, had considerable impact on the East European perceptions of ensuing changes, especially those affecting the relations between the center and the periphery. Probably the most telling aspect of the break-up of the Soviet colonial empire was the emergence of striking differences in the reactions on the part of the individual East European countries to changes occurring in the bloc. The East European reactions to the 20th CPSU Congress and to Khrushchev's secret speech provided probably the most interesting example of the varying images and perceptions arrived at by the different countries and their respective leaders. It soon became obvious that in delivering his speech Khrushchev himself was guilty of a serious misperception of the deep crisis in the region which affected some of the countries.

Since the late 1950s, with two significant exceptions, the relations between the USSR and Western Europe have tended to be reasonably stable. The two exceptions were the 1968 crisis in Czechoslovakia and the "Solidarity" upheaval in Poland in 1980-1981.

It may be argued that the events of "Prague Spring" and the Soviet intervention in August 1968 were perfect examples of false images, misperceptions, and wrong inferences drawn by all sides to the dispute. The Soviet leaders were largely misled about the changes in Czechoslovakia which they perceived as a threat to the survival of the Communist system in that country. At least two of the leaders of the neighboring states—East Germany and Poland—formed an exaggerated image of the Czechoslovak liberalization process spilling over to their own countries. And, finally, the leaders of the Czechoslovak Communist Party, badly misjudging Soviet attitude and behavior, were totally unprepared for the intervention. The great majority of the Czechoslovak people who have traditionally held warm feelings towards Russia, were taken aback by the Soviet action and the popular friendship turned to hostility.

The events of 1980-1981 in Poland were also affected by mutual misperceptions. The "Solidarity" leaders, very much aware of the potential impact of the labor movement on Soviet-Polish relations and reaffirming the Soviet intervention in Czechoslovakia, tried to assuage Moscow's fears by reaffirming the leading role of the Polish Communist Party and Poland's alliance with, and loyalty to, the USSR. As it became apparent only too soon, these assurances created little impression on the Kremlin. At the same time, the Soviet leaders were guilty of misperceiving the ability of the Polish regime to keep "Solidarity" under control.

More recently, the leaders of Bulgaria and East Germany misperceived the true nature of the personal changes in the Kremlin during the Andropov-Chernenko period and they endeavored to build bridges to West Germany only to be rudely brought down to earth by Moscow.

To summarize, insofar as Eastern Europe as a whole was concerned, the key problem was to determine the threshold of autonomy vis-à-vis the Kremlin for both the individual countries and the region as a whole. This was no mean feat when the Soviet Union has been both player and umpire in a rigged game whose rules are constantly changing and frequently fuzzy, if they exist at all. It was up to the leaders of the individual countries to estimate the margin of freedom at their disposal which would allow them to conduct foreign and/or domestic policy that might depart to a greater or lesser degree from the norms specified by Moscow. There were some striking differences in this respect among the various countries in the region, once again testifying to the presence of disparate perceptions of the Soviet Union within the European Communist camp.

In answering an obvious question regarding the reasons for the above disparity as well as for the continuity versus change in the East European images and understanding of Moscow's motives, policies and behavior, I would analyze these perceptions as being a function of three variables: the Soviet perceptions of the individual East European countries; the domestic situation in the region; and the state of East-West relations.

There is little doubt that the Soviet leaders' perception of Eastern Europe has been (and continues to be) a major factor in determining Moscow's policy toward the region and, in conformity with the principle of action-reaction, undoubtedly has influenced the perception of the individual East European countries vis-à-vis the USSR. In looking at Eastern Europe ever since the end of World War II, the successive Soviet leaders were from the very beginning faced with a built-in conflict between the region's cohesion and stability and its viability,[6] or, to put it somewhat differently, between the region being an asset or a burden or liability to the Kremlin.[7] Cohesion in this context was derived from general conformity of East European domestic and foreign policies to Soviet prescriptions and a rough congruence of institutional arrangements between the USSR and its allies. Viability suggested the presence of confident, efficient, credible and at least partly legitimate regimes in Eastern Europe that would obviate the need of continuous Soviet preoccupation with, and intervention in, the region. The concepts of asset and burden can be defined as sources of a stream of recurrent gains or losses, tangible and/or psychic, accruing to the owner, which is likely to continue for more than just a brief period of time.

Thus, the early postwar period might be seen as reflecting Stalin's preference for viability of the newly formed Communist states in Eastern Europe which still faced many problems connected with the process of state building. In the late 1940s, this rather benign attitude was drastically transformed into Moscow's policy of strict cohesion and Eastern Europe became a major economic, military and political asset of the Soviet Union. Throughout most of his rule, Khrushchev adhered to the principle of viability as did Brezhnev, at least until the "Prague Spring" of 1968, whereupon his perception of Eastern Europe changed dramatically in favor of greater cohesion. The results of a cost-benefit analysis were less clear:

Eastern Europe continued as a military asset but it was gradually becoming an economic and even a political-ideological burden. It was only toward the end of Brezhnev's rule that the Soviet grip over the region began to show signs of relaxation, which was again interrupted by the "Solidarity" crisis in Poland.

The four year period, 1981–1985, which saw four successive leaders in the Kremlin, is hard to categorize: Andropov was viewed, at least by the Hungarians, as essentially sympathetic to Eastern Europe, and the opposite appeared to be true for Chernenko who was generally seen as Brezhnev's *alter ego*. The early signals out of Moscow suggested that Gorbachev might assume a tough stance vis-à-vis Eastern Europe but, as will be discussed, the predictions proved false.[8]

All this suggests that the Kremlin has not succeeded in achieving a balance between cohesion and viability which has been its major objective in Eastern Europe. This is not surprising. Moscow has been saddled with an impossible task as the proper mix of cohesion and viability requires the presence of preconditions, some of which do not exist in the region. There is not doubt, for example, that after being in power for about 40 years, the East European regimes are still perceived as illegitimate by their populations which means that all countries in the region have been experiencing a crisis of legitimacy that varies in intensity from country to country. Faced with an area-wide legitimacy crisis, the Soviet Union has little choice, especially in the early 1980s, but to emphasize cohesion at the expense of viability.[9]

Insofar as the individual countries are concerned, the main focus of Soviet attention in the first half of the 1980s was East Germany, for some time the linchpin of the Soviet control system in Eastern Europe. The German Democratic Republic remains a key Soviet asset, making an important contribution to the military and economic power of the alliance, despite being strategically the most exposed of all Warsaw Pact members. Poland, which unwillingly relinquished its number one standing in the alliance to GDR, has long been viewed by the Kremlin as a complicated and frustrating case. It may be argued that even in the mid-1980s, despite many problems, Moscow still considered Poland as a military-strategic asset; in every other aspect, however, Poland appeared mostly as a liability.

Soviet perception of Hungary has been positive. In the ideological realm Hungary has undergone a striking metamorphosis from being a liability in the 1950s to becoming an asset twenty years later, and the same was true for its economy in the first half of the 1980s. On the other hand, if Hungary was perceived by the USSR as a major asset or at least a useful ally, Romania has been most likely regarded as a liability in just about every respect except possibly for the ideological context in which the country's performance must have given the Soviet leaders little cause for complaint.

The Kremlin most likely viewed Czechoslovakia as an important ally from both the strategic-military and economic points of view, despite the debacle of 1968 and its replacement by East Germany as the chief supplier of technologically advanced goods to the USSR and the rest of CMEA. Bulgaria has traditionally been Moscow's most faithful ally in Eastern Europe in the four decades since the Communist seizure of power, and there was little evidence of any serious diminution of Sofia's devotion to the cause.[10]

Turning to the internal situation within the region, limitation of space precludes a detailed discussion of the state of affairs in each of the individual countries and only some generalizations can be made, which tend to be risky. In the mid-1980s it was clear that in the domestic political arena the East European countries were showing less similarity to each other than to some of their neighbors in Western Europe. A neo-Stalinist Romania had little in common with a relatively liberal Hungary which, in turn, appeared closer to Austria. The conservative regime in Czechoslovakia was quite different from the reasonably relaxed government in Poland and it was also true that the relatively efficient and well-managed East Germany was rather distant from stagnating Bulgaria.

An interesting question concerned the ability of the various East European regimes to adapt to changing circumstances, to overcome the growing differences, and to remain in control of their respective societies (to the considerable relief of Moscow). One of the reasons has undoubtedly been the considerable leadership skills exhibited by the then powerholders in the area, such as Kadar of Hungary, Zhivkov of Bulgaria, Ceausescu of Romania, Husak of Czechoslovakia, and Honecker of East Germany. Kadar and Zhivkov had been in power for about thirty years and the remaining leaders for close to two decades which reflected their ability to survive a series of crises, both foreign and domestic. Poland was the sole example of its leaders' ineptitude—with the exception of its current leader, General Jaruzelski, who took over at the height of the "Solidarity" crisis in 1981. The differential rate of survival obviously contributed to differential perception of the Soviet hegemon on the part of the individual East European leaders and their oligarchies.

A good test of the ability of the individual leaders to remain in power and in control of their countries was provided by the "Solidarity" crisis in Poland. The record shows that the impact of that crisis on the rest of Eastern Europe was insignificant. To some extent, this was not surprising or unexpected. The various regimes had more than three decades to develop institutions and mechanisms that could absorb a variety of shocks and deter internal and external challenges to their rule.

To repeat, much of the credit for this achievement should go to the individual Communist parties and their leaders. Political stability in the respective countries has been, as a rule, a function of the character and cohesion of the ruling party, especially the strength of its leadership and bureaucracy, and their control over the instruments of coercion—the security police and the military. In the mid-fifties only one East European party, that of Poland, faced major difficulties in this respect; everywhere else, the ruling parties were clearly in control and the only potential fly in the ointment was the inescapable ageing of the top leaders which was bound to affect the East European political landscape sooner rather than later.

From a purely ideological viewpoint, the Kremlin's stake in Eastern Europe has rested on the success or failure of a Communist polity to become firmly embedded in a given East European society, thus validating if not legitimizing the Soviet brand of Marxism-Leninism as a universal model. Although the USSR must have derived considerable satisfaction from the fact that the Communist rule in Eastern Europe remained relatively unimpaired since the end of the war, it was equally clear that the past leadership in the Kremlin has been greatly concerned with the viability of that rule. Events in Hungary in 1956, in Czechoslovakia in 1968, and in Poland in 1956, 1970, 1976 and 1980–1981, provided clear signals that Communist rule in those countries was fragile and that the political systems have been unsuccessful in generating popular support.

Despite its obvious concern for ideological conformity, Moscow has seldom spelled out its parameters exactly. Even the "Brezhnev Doctrine," proclaimed after the Soviet intervention in Czechoslovakia, reserved for the USSR the right to determine what was or was not ideologically correct and acceptable, without establishing the threshold which the East European countries could not cross. The record shows that in recent years, Moscow's ideological stance with regard to Eastern Europe has been full of contradictions and inconsistencies, illustrating once again the perennial Soviet dilemma with regard to its policy toward the region, that of viability versus cohesion. The Kremlin must have realized that conditions for political stability and economic efficiency did not necessarily coincide with requirements for ideological conformity and cohesion. As a result, Soviet policy toward Eastern Europe has vacillated over the years and Moscow's attitude toward developments in the region has been characterized, at least until the recent period, by a mixture of relative relaxation and recompression.

Finally, in the realm of economics, it was the 1960s which first witnessed a significant downturn in the East European economic performance which had two important consequences. On the one hand, several countries initiated reforms of their economic systems, and on the other, the USSR decided to continue supplying its clients with increasing quantities of raw materials at favorable prices. Nonetheless, despite the reforms, the Soviet economic help, and large Western credits, the East European economies continued to falter during the 1970s and the first half of the 1980s.

There is no doubt that the deteriorating economic situation in nearly all East European countries has exerted considerable impact on Soviet domestic and foreign policy. As mentioned earlier, the Soviets have long been concerned with the viability and legitimacy of Communist regimes in the region and they have been aware of the close correlation between economic wellbeing and regime legitimacy, and of the latter's crucial role in the attainment of Moscow's security, and political, and ideological objectives—not only in Eastern Europe but also in the world at large.

This brings me to the third variable in the Soviet-East European matrix— the state of East-West relations. It is generally agreed that Eastern Europe has been a major beneficiary of East-West detente from its earliest beginning in the late 1960s. Its highlights are well known: the normalization of relations with West Germany, including the agreement on the status of Berlin; the start of the troop reduction talks in Vienna; the Conference on Security and Cooperation in Europe in Helsinki and its follow-ups in Belgrade and Madrid; expansion in East-West trade stimulated by generous Western credits; the signing of the SALT I and SALT II treaties and, finally, the arms control negotiations in Geneva. Moscow's junior allies clearly welcomed all signs of rapprochement between East and West and for that reason they were clearly chagrined with the Soviet intervention in Afghanistan and even more unhappy with the Kremlin's decision to withdraw from the START and INF negotiations, followed by the deployment of additional Soviet missiles in Eastern Europe which spelled the demise of detente. The damage caused by these events was made worse by Western reaction to the imposition of martial law in Poland in December 1981, which took the form of harsh sanctions against the region that further aggravated its already difficult economic situation.

Here also the Soviet Union was facing a dilemma. On the one hand, one of the long-standing cherished goals of the Kremlin has been to weaken NATO by decoupling Western Europe from the United States, using Eastern Europe as a sort of a Trojan horse. On the other hand, Eastern Europe could only prove useful in this respect if it was perceived by Western Europe, as a relatively free region which meant, in practice, Soviet willingness to emphasize its viability at the expense of its cohesion. The individual East European leaders were well aware of Soviet designs in this respect and, as will be shown, adjusted their policies accordingly.

What conclusions can be drawn from the Soviet-East European interaction on the eve of Gorbachev's assumption of power in early 1985? One possible way of answering this question is to contrast the initial Soviet and East European objectives in the region with the degree to which these original goals have been fulfilled forty years later. Twenty years ago, a distinguished British authority in the field of international relations made the following observation:

> Alliances are a means to an end, whether it is primarily to increase the security of a group of sovereign states in the face of a common adversary, or to increase the diplomatic pressure which they can bring upon him, or to share the economic cost and the political risk with either objective.[11]

Yet multilateral regional linkages also did not prove to be entirely satisfactory. I am prepared to argue that after more than thirty years of their existence, both the Warsaw Pact and CMEA did not greatly strengthen the security of either the Soviet Union or its East European members. I would also submit that from the economic standpoint, the value of CMEA was limited, if not deleterious to East European interests.[12] Did it all mean that the Kremlin-led alliance in Eastern Europe was dead? The simple answer was no: to borrow a phrase from Charles Gati, the alliance was "alive but not well."[13]

The view that the Soviet imperium in Eastern Europe has been ailing has been shared by many experts who concluded that the crisis in Eastern Europe would force the Kremlin either to provide more room for manoeuvre for the individual countries or to impose tighter controls over the region. Only very few observers of the scene claimed that the crisis in Eastern Europe was not unprecedented and that the Soviet policy toward the regime under the new leadership in the Kremlin would essentially continue on its present course of "muddling through" and "more of the same."[14]

The East European leaders themselves were most likely highly confused by the signals emanating from the Kremlin. At least two of them—Zhivkov and Kadar—were put in charge of their respective countries with the blessing of Khrushchev and the rest owed their position to Brezhnev (Husak and Honecker) or were chosen by their ruling oligarchies without Moscow's objections (Ceausescu and Jaruzelski). Khrushchev appeared strongly interested in Eastern Europe and was presumably willing to listen to his opposite numbers in the region. The same was true for Brezhnev, at least until the Czechoslovak crisis of 1968. During the 1970s, Brezhnev's interests shifted and became primarily focused on East-West relations, including arms control, and on Soviet expansion in the Third World. It may be argued that Brezhnev took Eastern Europe for granted and in the waning years of his life, when he may not have been in full control of Soviet policy, no one else in the Kremlin appeared to be particularly concerned with Eastern Europe.

Because of that, the East Europeans generally seemed to welcome Andropov's succession to power in the belief that he would listen with sympathy to their problems. Chernenko was generally perceived in the East European capitals as Brezhnev's clone and hence, at best indifferent and at worst hostile to Eastern Europe.

The disarray in the Kremlin coincided with the rapid deterioration in East-West relations which compounded East Europe's problems, confused its leaders, and negatively affected Soviet-East European relations. The obvious unhappiness expressed by Czechoslovakia, East Germany and Hungary on the occasion of the Soviet withdrawal from the INF talks in Geneva, followed almost immediately by Moscow's announcement about the deployment of additional SS-21 missiles on the territory of Czechoslovakia and East Germany, was a case in point. The clear disagreement between the Soviet Union on the one hand, and the strange alliance of East Germany, Hungary and Romania on the other, regarding the role of small states in the process of East-West rapprochement, provided another illustration of a more independent stance adopted by Moscow's East European allies, apparently no longer afraid to make their views known and presumably hoping to have an impact on Soviet behavior.[15] Chernenko's veto of the proposed visits to West Germany of Honecker and Zhivkov was another example of a growing strain between the USSR and the rest of the alliance.

While the remaining countries in the area stayed out of the fray, the fact that with the exception of Czechoslovakia they refused to take the Soviet side, was a telling testimony to the breakdown of the traditional consensus imposed from above by the Kremlin.[16]

East European Perceptions of the Soviet Union Under Gorbachev

It may be taken for granted that the ruling oligarchies in Eastern Europe did not know what to expect of Gorbachev when he assumed power in the USSR in March 1985. This was not surprising, considering the fact that the new Soviet leader was essentially a darkhorse in the Soviet Union itself and his prior experience in the government and the party did not include dealing with Eastern Europe. It may also be assumed that the individual East European leaders were hoping that the new occupant of the Kremlin would be more understanding of their needs and difficulties than his immediate predecessors. Many of the leaders remembered Brezhnev's rude treatment of Poland during the 1980-1981 crisis, which included the threat of reviving his own "Doctrine," as well as Chernenko's arrogant veto of Bulgaria's and East Germany's rapprochement with Bonn in 1984. The initial signals out of Moscow, were not encouraging: following his ascent to power Gorbachev staged several multilateral and bilateral meetings with his East European counterparts and the overall impression was that he was ready to adopt a tougher stance toward the East Europeans than his predecessors.

I propose to discuss the reciprocal, Soviet-East European perceptions and concerns under Gorbachev again in terms of three issue-areas: the Soviet goals in Eastern Europe; the internal situation in the individual countries in the region, and the state of East-West relations.[17]

It was generally assumed that Gorbachev would pay more attention to Eastern Europe than his predecessors and that he would give top priority to the replacement of most of the East European leaders who were in their seventies and who could easily be blamed for the difficulties faced by the respective states. Even though several East European Communist parties held their congresses in 1985 and 1986 (which would have provided a tailor-made opportunity for a wholesale ouster of the aging leaders), to everyone's surprise no one was actually retired and replaced by a younger member of the ruling elite. The common explanation offered by the East European observers of the Moscow scene was that Gorbachev had his mind set on other things—rapprochement with the United States and China, and domestic reforms in the Soviet Union—and that Eastern Europe was to be relegated to the back burner, at least for the time being. Gorbachev's seeming indifference toward the region was also interpreted by some of the East European leaders as giving them a free hand to pursue their policies at will, without Moscow's interference. With the exception of Hungary and Poland this meant in essence maintaining a conservative course emphasizing the *status quo*, which the various leaders had pursued in the previous two decades with Soviet *imprimatur*.

In time, the early hopes of Soviet policy of benign neglect toward Eastern Europe turned to near certainty. After initially proclaiming his determination to re-assert Eastern Europe's important role in Soviet policy, Gorbachev had very little to say about the region in his major address at the 27th CPSU Congress in February 1986, except for emphasizing the need for closer economic integration under the aegis of CMEA.[18] This seemed further to reaffirm the view that contrary to initial expectations, Eastern Europe did not, after all, appear very high on Gorbachev's policy agenda, with a possible exception of economics.

The record of the last few years has shown rather conclusively that there has been an unmistakable change in the Kremlin's *modus operandi* vis-à-vis Eastern Europe, in the style and manner of making policy by the Soviet leadership, especially on the bilateral level, and in the general atmosphere of conducting business in the Warsaw alliance and CMEA.[19] Gone are the arrogance of Brezhnev allowing his military overlord, Marshal Kulikov to treat Poland as Moscow's fiefdom, in a manner strongly reminiscent of Stalin's days.[20] Chernenko's disapproval of East European bridge-building to West Germany was replaced by a much more permissive Soviet attitude reflected, for example, in apparent indifference of Moscow with respect to Honecker's visit to the Federal Republic in September 1987 and to France in January 1988.

Moreover, serious questions have been raised in both East and West challenging the continuing validity of the "Brezhnev Doctrine" which was perceived as governing Soviet-East European relations ever since 1968. Although Gorbachev himself has rather carefully avoided making unequivocal statements about the "Doctrine," his close advisers and spokesmen tried to create an impression that the "Brezhnev Doctrine" was essentially dead[21], and Gorbachev himself, by formally denying the Soviet primacy in the Warsaw alliance, at least implicitly confirmed that view.[22]

The "new thinking" in the general area of Soviet-East European relations affected also the relationship between the USSR and the individual countries. A truly striking change, for example, could be observed in the relationship between Moscow and Warsaw. General Jaruzelski, who only three years earlier was viewed by the Kremlin as a black sheep in the East European flock, has now become Gorbachev's strongest supporter and closest friend. Kadar also continued as Gorbachev's close ally (until his replacement by Karoly Grosz) while Honecker, who under Brezhnev assumed a leading role in the alliance replacing Poland's Gierek, seemed to have lost that position in the mid- 1980s, for reasons that are not entirely clear. There has been no change in Gorbachev's attitude toward Ceausescu and Husak which continued to be cool on both sides. It may be assumed that it was that coolness that contributed to Husak's ouster from party leadership and his replacement by Miloš Jakeš in December 1987.[23] Zhivkov, the perennial survivor, who lagged behind the Poles and Hungarians in embracing *perestroika* as the new dogma, ultimately saw the light and accepted Soviet reformism as the new creed.

In contrast to Moscow's seeming indifference in the military, political and ideological spheres, Gorbachev right from the start indicated his strong interest in tightening economic cooperation within the alliance, using a three-way approach. On the one hand, the Kremlin appeared determined once again to use CMEA as the chief instrument of closer economic integration. On the other hand, Moscow, at least implicitly, urged its junior allies to follow its lead in introducing radical economic reforms. And finally, without publicizing it too widely, the Soviet Union undertook what might be easily interpreted as a new economic penetration of Eastern Europe, which took the form of joint Soviet-East European ventures. The USSR usually supplies the raw materials and its smaller partners the rest, repaying Moscow with a rather high share of the final output, to be marketed in the Soviet Union.

Relatively few details of these bilateral arrangements are known and fully understood in the West and as a result, opinions differ as to the real significance of this new policy. Nonetheless, it is clear that Soviet interest in the East European economies in the late 1980s appears much stronger than in the past. It is not inconceivable that the main reason for it has been Gorbachev's belief that an economically viable Eastern Europe would also be a politically stable and viable region and that, in turn, economic efficiency, well being and interdependence would most likely strengthen the cohesion of the bloc.[24] While this formula resembled somewhat Khrushchev's emphasis on legitimacy based on consumerism, it went beyond it by stressing economic interdependence as providing an important linkage and enhancing cohesion without necessitating coercive or oppressive measures.

Turning to the internal situation within the individual East European countries, it is clear that in the past three years it was been strongly influenced by the winds blowing *ex oriente*. Obviously it was not the first time in the more than four decades since the Communist takeover that the Kremlin was determined to impose its will on the region. What was unique about this particular situation was that it was only the second time in the history of Soviet-East European relation that the winds from the East were pushing in the direction of political and economic reforms, echoing similar appeals from Moscow in the mid-1950s.

One can easily imagine the genuine astonishment of the East European leaders with Gorbachev's policy of *glasnost* and with his announcement of far-reaching reforms in the USSR.[25] While the new Soviet leader at no time insisted that the policy he intended to introduce at home was to be immediately followed and emulated in Eastern Europe, those in the region who remembered Khrushchev and Brezhnev understood only too well that sooner or later they would have to adopt the Soviet example in the name of proletarian internationalism and initiate similar reforms in their own countries. Not that all of them were inherently opposed to political and economic liberalization. Poland's Jaruzelski, who for his own reasons embarked on a similar policy earlier on, enthusiastically endorsed Gorbachev's new course and welcomed it as indicating Moscow's approval of his own reforms in Poland (which were viewed with suspicion by some of Poland's neighbors as well as by both the liberal and conservative elements in the Polish party and society at large).[26] Similarly Hungary, long in the forefront of economic and societal reforms in the region, seemed to approve of Gorbachev's reform blueprints.

The reaction of the remaining East European leaders has been and continues to be strikingly different.[27] They indicated their displeasure with the Soviet reform plans using a variety of means: emphasizing the superiority of their own systems and policies (East Germany)[28], ignoring wholly or in part Gorbachev's key ideas and pronouncements (Czechoslovakia)[29], openly criticizing some of Gorbachev's plans (Romania)[30], and so on. Western visitors to the above countries would be told in no uncertain terms that the new Soviet leader would not last very long or that he would share the fate of Khrushchev who also tried to introduce far-reaching reforms in the Soviet Union and who ultimately fell victim to bureaucratic resistance. What has been and is striking about all this is that the criticism is voiced quite openly and often quite sharply, thus providing an ironic testimony to the spread of the policy of glasnost started by the Kremlin.

The negative reaction to Gorbachev's ideas in most of the East European countries was not really surprising. After all, the current leaders in Bucharest, East Berlin, Prague and Sofia managed to stay in power for a long time by adhering to cautious and conservative policies, by toeing Moscow's line which until recently excluded the possibility of meaningful reforms, and by developing a certain *Fingerspitzengefühl* which allowed them to divine and predict changes in Moscow. Were they to embrace the new faith unquestioningly, this would put their leadership at risk, and since few if any of them would be likely to agree to relinquish their leadership voluntarily, this would carry a threat of a power struggle and political instability the cost of which would be hard to calculate. Moreover, many of the East European leaders managed to survive at least three successive occupants of the Kremlin and presumably hoped to survive the fourth; hence their belief in Gorbachev's ultimately succumbing to conservative pressure in the Soviet Union and their reluctance to jump on his bandwagon.

Not unexpectedly, the surprising improvement in East-West relations, symbolized in the Geneva, Reykjavik and Washington summit meetings, predictably was welcomed by Eastern Europe. As suggested earlier, Eastern Europe saw itself as a major victim of the demise of East-West detente and could not but be pleased with renewed rapprochement between the Kremlin and the White House. Apart from the general improvement in East-West climate, which in the past has nearly always benefited Eastern Europe, the INF agreement called for the removal of Soviet missiles from Czechoslovakia and East Germany, which were first deployed there in 1983 to the open chagrin of both the local oligarchies and populations at large.

While the removal of the medium range missiles represented an important concrete benefit for Eastern Europe, the simultaneous elimination of American and West German missiles was received with considerable satisfaction in the East European capitals as still another sign of better relations between East and West. For the East Europeans this could also mean further economic benefits, resulting, for example, from closer collaboration between CMEA and the European Economic Community.[31]

Altogether, one may generalize that unless something unexpected were to happen, such as Gorbachev's sudden removal from leadership or a major deterioration in Soviet-American relations, the incremental improvement in, and expansion of, East-West detente could only bring further advantages to Eastern Europe, especially in the economic sphere.

Conclusion

Our analysis throughout this chapter focused on the interaction between the East European political and ideological perceptions and concerns, and the prospects for adaptation in Eastern Europe to changes taking place in the Soviet Union. One of the possible results of the interaction and adaptation to the new circumstances influencing Soviet-East European relations might be a creation of a more "viable," "cohesive" or "organic" Soviet-East European relationship. The question remains, however, whether such a relationship is likely to emerge in the foreseeable future.

The foregoing discussion suggested that prospects for the creation of a qualitatively different alliance in Eastern Europe are remote. There are several reasons for this rather pessimistic forecast. Probably the fundamental obstacle is historical. More than forty years of Soviet-East European interaction have shown rather clearly that despite periodic attempts by Soviet leaders, such as Khrushchev and Gorbachev, to change the nature of the alliance by reducing Soviet hegemony and allowing more elbow room for the East Europeans, the latter have continued to be rather distrustful of Moscow's good will, and as a result, many of Gorbachev's ideas simply have lacked credibility. The Soviet willingness to loosen controls over Eastern Europe produced one unexpected result: instead of generating uniformly enthusiastic support for the "winds of change," it provided an opportunity for some of the East European leaders openly to criticize Gorbachev, apparently without a fear of retribution.

The continuing rift between the Soviet and some of the East European leaders raises at least three interesting questions. The first one concerns Moscow's ability and willingness to tolerate the criticism emanating from the various East European capitals. So far there has been no sign of Gorbachev's trying to stem the tide of discontent or to impose his reforms on the region. In the past the Kremlin was the sole judge of what constituted the threshold of permissible action by the East Europeans and it is not inconceivable that at some point the Kremlin would be forced to abandon its policy of benign neglect and to adopt tougher measures against the recalcitrant leaders, especially if and when the East European resistance would strengthen the hand of those members of the Soviet ruling oligarchy who have been and continue to be less than enthusiastic about Gorbachev's reform in the USSR.

The second question concerns the future shape of domestic politics and economics in Eastern Europe. Thus far, only Hungary and Poland appear to be reasonably firmly in Gorbachev's camp. However, if for one reason or another, the conservative leaders in Eastern Europe were to be replaced by younger, reform-oriented individuals, the whole character of East European politics could be radically changed. Ultimately, this transformation might give rise to a serious challenge to Moscow's supremacy in Eastern Europe, with all its consequences. Although Gorbachev does not appear as of yet to be ready and willing to preside over the dissolution of the Soviet empire in the region, chances are that he realizes that the logic of his reform movement might ultimately lead in that direction.[32]

Insofar as the economic situation is concerned, much will depend on the success or failure of the economic reforms in the region. It now appears that with the exception of East Germany and Romania, the other countries are now more or less committed to a fairly drastic *perestroika* of their economic systems. As yet, however, there is no evidence of the reforms being adopted and supported by the populations of the respective countries: on the contrary, even countries such as Hungary, are experiencing economic difficulties which are being linked to reforms which have celebrated their 20th anniversary.[33] If Hungary, whose reforms were praised by one of the more conservative members of the Soviet ruling elite, Igor Ligachev[34], could not fully satisfy the Hungarian masses, the probability of a major economic upturn in the rest of Eastern Europe is slim, creating as a matter of course serious political difficulties not only for the local leaders but also for Gorbachev himself.

Finally, what should be the Western reaction to recent developments in Eastern Europe? Much the same question has been raised more than once regarding the American and West European attitudes to Gorbachev's reforms in the Soviet Union and the most sensible answer seems to be that while the West should in principle welcome any policy that benefits the Soviet people, the West should not necessarily, tailor its own policy toward the USSR in order to ensure Gorbachev's success but to satisfy its own national interest.

In dealing with Eastern Europe today, both the United States and Western Europe are once again faced with a dilemma. Insofar as Washington is concerned, the basic premise of American policy vis-à-vis Eastern Europe in the past thirty years or so has been to encourage the loosening of bonds between the Soviet Union and its allies in the region, and to encourage the latter's independence of Moscow's commands. On the other hand, the United States has always been sympathetic to those countries in Eastern Europe which pursued a liberal course and showed concern for the welfare of their citizens. Ironically, today those countries which seem to oppose

Moscow are also those which are politically most oppressive whereas those states such as Hungary and Poland which have adopted a more relaxed stance, are those that support Gorbachev and thus, willy nilly, favor closer relations with the USSR.

While the dilemma is less acute for Western Europe, there is no easy way out of it. The best that can be done in the circumstances is for the West to keep an eye on the evolving situation in Eastern Europe which is changing rapidly. Any precipitous action on our part, trying to take advantage of Soviet troubles in the region, is bound to backfire and hence the best part of wisdom is to adopt a wait-and-see attitude while showing interest in both the present and the future of the region.[35]

To sum up, the conclusion that the prospects of a radically different Soviet alliance system in Eastern Europe appeared poor in the foreseeable future, must be qualified in the short run. To begin with, it may be argued that the experience of three years of Gorbachev's rule was not long enough to offer a conclusive evidence one way or another. The record shows that since March 1985 Gorbachev accomplished more than some of his predecessors in the course of many more years. Moreover, as suggested earlier, the process of economic reforms in Eastern Europe has began about quarter-of-a-century ago and it is still continuing today which means that we should not expect concrete results for many years to come.

Secondly, the belief that "nothing succeeds like success" is as valid in Eastern Europe as anywhere else in the world. This means that the success of perestroika in the USSR is bound to persuade those East European countries still lagging behind, to jump on Gorbachev's band wagon. The reverse, of course, is equally true: a failure in the Soviet Union is bound to generate a negative demonstration effect with all its consequences.

Thirdly, the problem of leadership succession has not been resolved in Eastern Europe as of the time of this writing. The changeover in Prague offered no clues in this respect as Jakeš was clearly Husak's clone and was expected not to deviate from the conservative course adopted nearly twenty years ago. The changeover in Hungary continues the policies of reform. Elsewhere, the incumbent leaders have appeared firmly in the saddle and so far there has been no evidence of Gorbachev being actively engaged in preparing an ouster of his adversaries.

Finally, is Eastern Europe at the end of the 1980s still a key asset for the Kremlin whose control over the region is not likely to be diminished? Intuitively, one is inclined to respond in the affirmative. On the other hand, ever since his ascent to power, Gorbachev has been trying his best to create a different impression. The record shows that Eastern Europe is less and less being mentioned in formal and informal declarations issued by Moscow and that Gorbachev has clearly decentralized his rule and granted considerable autonomy to the East European leaders, even in such highly sensitive issue areas such as amnesty, popular participation or expansion of the private sector.

Whether all this means that another fresh policy threshold has been established by Gorbachev is anybody's guess. Time will only tell whether the new Soviet-East European relationship is likely to remain unchanged in the foreseeable future or whether it will change once again sooner rather than later.

Notes

I want to express my appreciation to Walter Connor, Mary Ellen Fischer, and Trond Gilberg for their perceptive and helpful comments on the first draft of this chapter.

1. In his comments on the first draft of this chapter.
2. In his comments on the first draft of this chapter. My own lengthy experience in Eastern Europe strongly supports this view.
3. Robert Jervis, "Hypotheses on Misperception," *World Politics*, Vol. XX, No. 3, April 1968, p. 459.
4. *Ibid.*, pp. 455 and 475.
5. Andrzej Korbonski, "Soviet Policies in Communist Alliance," paper delivered at conference, "The Roots of Soviet Power: Domestic Sources of Foreign and Defense Policies," Los Angeles, U.C.L.A., October 10-11, 1985.
6. James F. Brown was the first to draw attention to the inherent incompatibility of Soviet goals of cohesion and viability in Eastern Europe. For details, see his "Relations Between the Soviet Union and Its East European Allies: A Survey," *RAND Report R-1742-PR*, 1975, passim.
7. Andrzej Korbonski, "Eastern Europe: Soviet Asset or Burden? The Political Dimension," in Ronald H. Linden, ed., *Studies in East European Foreign Policy*, New York: Praeger, 1980, pp. 289-297.
8. Vladimir V. Kusin, "Gorbachev and Eastern Europe," *Problems of Communism*, Vol. XXXV, No. 1, January-February 1986, pp. 39-53.
9. Andrzej Korbonski, "Eastern Europe," in Robert F. Byrnes:, ed., *After Brezhnev: Sources of Soviet Conduct in the 1980s*, Bloomington, Indiana: Indiana University Press, 1983, pp. 303ff.
10. On the other hand, after decades of strong support, Moscow began to have second thoughts about Bulgaria's economic performance. Jackson Diehl, "Bulgaria, Once a Soviet Favorite, Faces a Squeeze," *New York Herald Tribune*, May 9-10, 1985.
11. Alistair Buchan, "The Future of NATO," *International Conciliation*, No. 565, November 1967, p. 5.
12. Valerie Bunce, "The Empire Strikes Back: The Evolution of the Eastern Bloc from a Soviet Asset to a Soviet Liability," *International Organization*, Vol. 39, No. 1, Winter 1985, pp. 1-46.
13. Charles Gati, "The Soviet Empire: Alive But Not Well," *Problems of Communism*, Vol. XXXIV, No. 2, March-April 1985, pp. 73-86.
14. Korbonski, "Soviet Policies in the Communist Alliance," *passim*.
15. Mátyás Szűrös, "Wir sind inzwischen erwachsen geworden," *Der Spiegel*, No. 37, September 8, 1986, pp. 173-184.
16. James M. Markham, "Sovereignty Made Soviet Bloc Issue," *New York Times*, March 7, 1985. See also, Vasil Bilak, "Unser Löwe is noch immer ein Löwe," *Der Spiegel*, No. 44, October 28, 1985, and Ronald D. Asmus, "The National and the

International: Harmony or Discord," *Radio Free Europe Research, RAD Background Report/144 (Eastern Europe),* December 10, 1985.

17. By now, there is already a substantial volume of literature dealing with Gorbachev and Eastern Europe. Among the most recent items, see Magarditsch A. Hatschikjan, "Der Ostblock und Gorbačov 1986," Konrad-Adenauer-Stiftung Forschungsinstitut, *Interne Studien,* No. 7, 1987; Karen Dawisha and Jonathan Valdez, "Socialist Internationalism in Eastern Europe," *Problems of Communism,* Vol. XXXVI, No. 2, March–April 1987, pp. 1–14; Charles Gati, "Gorbachev and Eastern Europe," *Foreign Affairs,* Vol. 65, No. 5, Summer 1987, pp. 958–975; and Fred Oldenburg, "Osteuropa-Basis or Bürde für die Weltmacht UdSSR," *Berichte des Bundesinstituts für die ostwissenschaftliche und internationale Studien,* No. 29, 1987.

18. Mikhail Gorbachev, *Political Report of the CPSU Central Committee to the 27th Party Congress,* February 25, 1986. (Moscow: Novosti Press Agency Publishing House, 1986), pp. 88–89.

19. For a recent reaffirmation of the "new thinking" in the context of Soviet-East European relations, see Philip Taubman, "Soviets Won't Push Policy on Allies, Gorbachev Says," *New York Times,* 5 November 1987. See also, Henry Kamm, "Russians Extend Call for Candor to Relations with East Bloc," *ibid.,* April 23, 1987.

20. Ryszard J. Kuklinski, "Wojna z narodem widziana od srodka," *Kultura* (Paris), No. 4/475, April 1987, pp. 21ff.

21. Vladimir Kusin, "Brezhnev Doctrine Rejected in Stockholm Agreement?" *Radio Free Europe Research, RAD Background Report/138 (East-West Relations)* September 29, 1986. For a recent statement to that effect, see Robert C. Toth, "Soviets Appear to Soften Policy on Intervention," *Los Angeles Times,* December 28, 1987.

22. Jackson Diehl, "Gorbachev Calls on Eastern Europe to Change but Not to Mimic," *Washington Post,* April 13, 1987, and Elizabeth Teague, "Gorbachev Addresses Prague Rally," Radio Liberty, *Research Bulletin,* No. 16, April 22, 1987.

23. John Tagliabue, "Husak Steps Down as Prague Leader," *New York Times,* December 18, 1987.

24. Mary Ellen Fischer in her comments on the first draft of this chapter.

25. Michael T. Kaufman, "Glasnost Upsetting to Soviet Allies," *New York Times,* April 5, 1987.

26. Kaufman, "Poles Show Weariness on Gorbachev's Policies," *ibid.,* March 27, 1987.

27. See, for example, Michael T. Kaufman, "Gorbachev Draws a Mixed Reaction from Soviet Bloc," *New York Times,* February 12, 1987; Mathis Chazanov, "Gorbachev's Reforms Draw Mixed East Bloc Reaction," *Los Angeles Times,* April 9, 1987; Tad Szulc, "Perestroika Gets Mixed Reviews in East Europe," *ibid.,* July 19, 1987; and John Tagliabue, "East Bloc Seems Divided on Speech," *New York Times,* November 4, 1987.

28. William Tuohy, "East German Official Says No to Soviet Style Reforms," *Los Angeles Times,* April 9, 1987.

29. "Czechoslovakia's Husak Backs Soviet Reforms and Hints He May Follow Suit," *Los Angeles Times,* March 21, 1987.

30. John Tagliabue, "Rumania, Ever the Maverick, Resists Soviet Spirit of Change," *New York Times,* December 2, 1987.

31. John Zoubek, "EEC-CMEA Relations," Radio Free Europe Research, *RAD Background Report/98 (Economics)*, June 16, 1987, and "Recent Moves in EEC-CMEA Relations," Radio Free Europe Research, *RAD Background Report/191 (Economics)*, October 21, 1987. See also, John M. Markham, "East Trade Bloc Seeks Tie to West," *New York Times*, December 2, 1987.

32. Bill Keller, "Soviet Bloc Feels the Reins Loosening," *ibid.*, January 3, 1988.

33. John Tagliabue, "Austerity and Unrest on Rise in Eastern Bloc," *ibid.*, December 6, 1987, and "Soviet Letting Trade Partners Shop Around in Hard Times," *ibid.*, January 4, 1988.

34. Elizabeth Teague, "Ligachev Endorses Hungarian Reforms," Radio Liberty, *Research Bulletin*, No. 18, May 6, 1987.

35. Flora Lewis, "Gorbachev's Messages," *New York Times*, October 14, 1987, and David K. Shipler, "U.S. Applauds (Softly) at Changes in Eastern Europe," *ibid.*, January 3, 1988.

5

Reforms in the USSR and Eastern Europe: Is There a Link?

Paul Marer

Introduction

This chapter will try to assess economic reforms in the USSR and their impacts from the perspective of East European countries.

Assessing Soviet economic reforms is a very difficult task. There are vast differences among the East European countries in how they view the reforms. Furthermore, in some countries the top leader or the leadership may have one view, economists (most of whom are reform supporters) another, and the average person a different perception still. Moreover, we in the West have no comprehensive information on the views of these groups, only small bits of evidence that are difficult to interpret authoritatively. Therefore, instead of just trying to state the "East European view" on Soviet reforms, I will first attempt to seek answers to the following questions:

1. What motivates Gorbachev to try to introduce "radical" reforms in the USSR?
2. What is the essence of the Soviet reform blueprint?
3. Assuming that Gorbachev's economic-reform blueprint is implemented, what kind of economic system will the Soviets have?

I will then discuss a further set of questions that examine possible links between Gorbachev's new course and developments in Eastern Europe:

4. How does the Soviet reform blueprint compare with reform experiences in Eastern Europe and what explains the large differences among the individual East European countries in their attitudes toward economic reform? What do we know about the views of different countries and groups in Eastern Europe on Gorbachev's new course?

5. What did reforms in Hungary—the CMEA country with the longest experience with comprehensive reforms—achieve, and what could reforms in Hungary not accomplish?
6. What lessons can be drawn from the Hungarian experience for economic reforms in the USSR and elsewhere in Eastern Europe?
7. What is the impact of Gorbachev's new course on Eastern Europe?

What Motivates Gorbachev's "Radical" Reforms?

Before answering this question, we should try to pick out the voices that, at this juncture, are the most influential in shaping policy and public opinion in the USSR.

Traditionally, there are four principal sources of influential economic advice in the Soviet Union: the Central Committee apparatus and its institutes, the various organs of the Council of Ministers, Gosplan and its institutes, and the economic institutes of the Academy of Sciences.[1] Ordinarily, a major new proposal is prepared by a commission or working group whose members are drawn from the organizations listed.

The key commission given the task to elaborate an economic reform program for Gorbachev is that established by the Council of Ministers in 1985, the "Commission for the Perfection of Management, Planning, and the Economic Mechanism," headed by the Chairman of Gosplan, Nikolai Talyzin. The Commission has set up a "Scientific Section," comprised of about 15 prominent academic economists, reportedly in charge of drafting the technical details of the reform blueprint; it coordinates the work of a large number of subcommittees and working groups. A key position thus is held by the person who heads the Commission's "Scientific Section" and simultaneously serves as deputy chairman of the Commission. This post was originally held by Dzhermen Gvishiani, son-in-law of former Premier Alexei Kosygin, who when appointed was also the director of the Institute for Systems Analysis and the Deputy Chairman of Gosplan.

In the fall of 1986 Gvishiani was dismissed from all three of his posts, allegedly for his failure to produce a concrete reform blueprint.[2] Abel Aganbegyan (who since 1966 had served, in Novosibirsk, as director of the Academy of Sciences' Institute of Economics and Organization of Industrial Production, where he directed the work of a reform-oriented group of economists) took over as Chairman of the "Scientific Section" of the Talyzin commission. At about the same time, Aganbegyan also became permanent secretary of the Economic Department of the Academy of Sciences. Thus, at present, Aganbegyan holds the two most influential economic posts in the USSR. His prominence is further shown by the fact that an important speech of Gorbachev on the economy, given on June 11, 1985, was based on Aganbegyan's ideas, as reflected in his August 1985 article in his Institute's journal, *EKO*.[3] Thus, we can turn to Aganbegyan's writings to obtain a reflection of the thinking of Gorbachev and his reformers on what is ailing the Soviet economy and what they think needs to be done to cure it.

Aganbegyan poses the question: "Why is a radical reform of [Soviet economic] management needed?" and stresses two points in answering it.[4] First, since 1975 there has been a dramatic slowdown in the rate of growth of the labor force and in the capital stock. The old economic mechanism was geared to "extensive growth," that is, to deploy additional inputs to obtain additional output, but it is not at all suited to improving the combined productivity of capital and labor. Since in the future much of the growth must come from improved productivity, a radically new economic system is needed.

Second, a scientific and technological revolution is sweeping the world and without fundamental reforms, the Soviet Union will be unable to participate in it. Aganbegyan implies that without reforms, the Soviet Union would become a second- or third-rate economic power.

Aganbegyan and his colleagues recognize that official economic growth rates—which have shown substantial declines since the mid-1970s—are becoming less and less meaningful as economic performance indicators. One reason is that in all centrally planned economies the methodology of constructing them has a built-in upward bias.[5] This is now admitted also by Gorbachev and his advisors. A further important reason is that growth rates do not reveal that a growing share of production is not saleable on the world market and would be purchased neither by domestic producers as inputs nor by domestic consumers as final products if they could obtain the better-quality goods and services that are readily available in much of the rest of the world, or if the economic system would motivate enterprises to be cost-conscious. Aganbegyan noted:

> A significant share of produced goods does not satisfy social requirements and is, consequently, superfluous. . . . While we produce twice as much metal as the USA, we buy rolled metal in other countries. The USSR produces 4.5 times more tractors than the USA, though we have a smaller grain-growing area. . . . Eliminating this wasteful production is the key task in restructuring the economic mechanism.[6]

A further reason for the reform is the large and growing technology and consumer "gaps" between the West and the USSR. To illustrate the latter some examples may be useful. A North American, for instance, is 12 times more likely to own an automobile than a Russian. An American with an average salary needs to work for five months and a West European for about eight months to afford a small car—a Russian must labor for four years. But even if he has the money, the Russian will have to wait in a queue for eight years. And the car he eventually buys will break down more often and finding spare parts and service will be headache.

On why and how the existing economic mechanism and policies are responsible for all these shortfalls, there is substantial agreement between Soviet and East European reformers and standard Western assessments of the problems of a Soviet-type economic system.

What Is the Essence of the Soviet Reform Blueprint?

There is a tug of war between those who desire simply to "perfect" the existing mechanism and those who wish to radically reform it. At the moment, the "radical" reformers have the upper hand. However, even among them, there is agreement only on the broad objectives and not on the details of the reform blueprint.

The basic approach, spelled out in Gorbachev's speech at the June 1987 party plenum and in the accompanying economic reform document (reported, respectively, in *Pravda's* June 26 and June 27, 1987 issues and summarized by Edward Hewett),[7] is that producing units are to gain much greater economic independence, together with the right to fail. The ultimate consequence may be closing down the business and letting go of the workers. In the new system, to be introduced gradually by 1991, producing units will have to cover their operating costs out of current proceeds and much of their investment costs from repayable bank loans.

Enterprises will no longer receive compulsory annual plan targets, only "control figures," at the beginning of each five year period, "orienting" them in constructing their own plans. Enterprises, instead of "doing what they are being told," should "do what they think best, while making sure they follow the guidelines."

Enterprises will be told to maximize profits, subject to a set of constraints:

1. Many will have to fulfil state orders at fixed (supposedly incentive) prices for specified goods and services (there may be competition between enterprises for state orders).
2. Certain categories of inputs, investments, and construction will remain centrally allocated.
3. The prices of all other goods are to be agreed upon between buyers and sellers, but they must follow rules of price-formation that will be established and enforced by the authorities.
4. Each enterprise (or sector) will receive a set of coefficients (norms) that ties its taxes, wage bill, bonus fund, investment fund, and welfare fund to some measure of its economic performance (yet to be determined). These economic "regulators" supposedly will remain fixed for five years.

The size of the central bureaucracy will be reduced substantially, eliminating all departments currently involved in operational decisions. The role of the central organs will be limited to ensuring macroeconomic balance, the desired structural change, and setting and enforcing a set of internally consistent financial and price "regulators" which, in their aggregate, should guide and motivate enterprises to fulfil the central plan.

Strategic supervision over enterprises and the selection of top management will be delegated to some type of workers' self-management; details are yet to be worked out. A much greater differentiation in wages and salaries between and within enterprises is to be allowed, based on enterprise profitability and individual employee contributions. And certain ministries as well as large enterprises will receive foreign trading rights and could retain a share of hard-currency export revenues, which (theoretically) they can spend freely on imports. Finally, greater scope is to be allowed to small-scale private and truly cooperative activities, especially in agriculture and in consumer services.

Under the new system, prices will become much more flexible. A significant amount of open inflation is almost certain to result, at least initially, as costs are defined more comprehensively and as the huge subsidies currently granted to many enterprises and on many consumer goods will be reduced. All of this will increase prices immediately, whereas the improvements in production efficiency and in supplies, which are expected to put a downward pressure on prices, will take time to be realized.

The associated political reforms include allowing greater "openness" ("publicity") in the media to discuss society's ills and alternative solutions to them, lowering the intensity of the campaigns against dissidents, easing the "nomenklatura" system (the practice of restricting all important positions to persons approved by the party), and a promise of competitive and secret elections for state (and perhaps even party) positions. In June 1987, for instance, the Supreme Soviet voted to permit popular referendums on regional political and social issues and to let citizens appeal to the courts decisions made by Communist Party officials.[8]

What Kind of Economic System Does the Blueprint Envision?

If and when this blueprint is implemented, it will be a drastic departure from the traditional, Soviet-type system operating in the USSR for sixty years (since the late 1920s). At the same time, the reform blueprint should not be considered a huge step toward the type of capitalist or mixed market economies that are in place in the industrial and newly-industrializing countries around the world. The similarities between the Soviet blueprint and the market economies are more apparent than real. What appears to make them similar is that private-sector activities will be given a somewhat greater scope and that the authorities intend to use financial instruments— prices, interest rates, exchange rates, credits, taxes, and profits—to implement the central plan. The crucial differences are the following.

First, the "capitalist" private segments of the economy—which may include newly-established cooperatives that are in essence private ventures— are not intended to develop into more than marginal significance for the economy as a whole, however important such activities may become for producing a given commodity or service. In 1986 an influential Soviet economist, L. Abalkin, stated that in ten years, the private sector might account for 4% of national income and cooperatives 10–12%.[9] And in 1988 cooperatives were supplying less than 0.04% of all Soviet consumer goods and services.[10] Moreover, the operating conditions of the private and cooperative sectors are likely to remain severely constrained—in terms of access to inputs, imports, finance, labor, and markets—as compared with the operating conditions faced by apparently similar private firms in market economies.

The second and much more crucial difference is that prices, interest rates, exchange rates, credits—and thus profits—will not be determined fundamentally by market forces. Rather they will emerge from bargaining between producers and the authorities about how these regulators should be set and applied in specific cases. Says Agenbagyan:

> In contrast to capitalism, commodities and money relations [the term used in Centrally Planned Economies to describe genuine markets] are not universal categories. Land and natural resources cannot be bought and sold. Since there is no unemployment and the economic base of society accords with socialist ownership, there is no labor market. A market for capital is not envisaged as part of perestroika. There are no plans for a Soviet stock exchange, shares, bills of exchange, or profit from commercial credit. . . . Prices for most essential products are also to be set by state bodies. Major capital investment and other economic levers and stimuli are in the hands of the state and can be directed at greater or lesser production of certain goods and thus have a major influence on the market.[11]

In sum, the Soviet reform blueprint is to create a system in which "horizontal" links between enterprises are at least as important as the "vertical" chain of command from the authorities that has dominated up to now. Thus, perestroika is not a blueprint for restoring capitalism—not even about introducing a market economy, although it moves in that direction. The economy is to remain centrally planned and, with minor exceptions, publicly owned. The large apparatus of central command is being trimmed, not abolished. The intention is to create a system that combines central control with local initiative. "Impossible," say the cynics. "Imperative," says Gorbachev.[12] Both logic and the experience in Eastern Europe, though, suggest that it is exceedingly difficult, perhaps even impossible, for such a mechanism to achieve anywhere close the efficiencies of a genuine market system.

The Soviet Reform Blueprint and Experiences in Eastern Europe

Most of the six East European members of the CMEA are out of step with developments in the Soviet Union: Hungary is way out ahead. Poland is perhaps a little ahead. Bulgaria's reforms appear to move approximately on a parallel track with those of the USSR. Although there are certain similarities between the economic reforms of the USSR and the GDR, the differences are much more substantial, as is the case also for Czechoslovakia. Romania has unconditionally rejected Gorbachev's new course.

Hungary is ahead of the Soviet Union, since it had implemented practically all of the Soviet reforms now being proposed. Poland is also ahead because of the political tolerance for public criticism of the regime. Regarding economic reforms, in 1982 Poland adopted a reform program that has many parallels with the Soviet blueprint. To be sure, since the implementation of Poland's economic reform program has lagged up to now,[13] in the economic arena the country is not out of step with the USSR. Still as early as in October 1987, a radical new reform program was proposed that is more far-reaching than that in the USSR. Of all the East European countries, Jaruzelski's regime has given the most enthusiastic public endorsement to Gorbachev's reform initiatives. One reason is that Jaruzelski, like Gorbachev, is a relative newcomer to his leadership post. Therefore, he, too, can claim to have "inherited" his country's problems, and is thus free to strike out in new directions in attempting to solve them.

Bulgaria's case is very interesting, and more complex than would appear at first glance. Ever since Todor Zhivkov assumed power in the mid-1950s, Bulgaria seems have been continuously on a "reform treadmill."[14] Since as yet the economy does not appear to operate very differently from that of a traditional CPE, it makes Western observers understandably sceptical that radical changes are indeed afoot. A further reason for scepticism is the timing and content of the country's recently announced radical reforms (a series of decrees between December 1986 and early 1988). They share many similarities with the Gorbachev blueprint. Are the changes real or are they put on the books for "show" only? Still another reason for scepticism is that accurate information and statistical data are much more difficult to obtain from Bulgaria than from Hungary and Poland, or even from the USSR.

A closer examination of Bulgaria's reforms, however, suggest that there are persons in important political positions, supported by a group of economic advisors, who not only have a good understanding of the need for fundamental reforms but also have a strong commitment to them, independently of developments in the USSR.[15] But they face the very same problems that reformers in the other East European countries run up against: inertia; the power of the bureaucracy and vested interests; ideological opposition; and the political forces that support them. Be that as it may, Bulgaria has a reform program that is quite radical in its conception and blueprint—in fact, it is quite similar to Hungary's New Economic Mechanism (NEM). The extent to which it will be implemented remains to be seen.

All the East European leaders except Jaruzelski (and now Karoly Grosz) have been in power for a long time and this makes it difficult for them to criticize their country's past policies and performance. Furthermore, all of them are old and at or near the end of their political careers. This makes them cautious, avoiding political risks whose possible economic payoffs would be realized years in the future. One risk they appear to be concerned about is the uncertainty about whether Gorbachev, or his new course, can survive politically.[16]

There are further, country-specific reasons for the differences among the reform policies of the countries of East Europe. A major difference between the GDR and the USSR for instance, is that the leadership of the GDR does not admit that the economy is at or near a crisis or that fundamental reforms are needed. The leadership of the GDR has several reasons for being especially cautious about embracing Gorbachev's program. One is that East Germany's economy, although facing many of the ills of a traditional CPE, has been performing a shade better than most of the others in Eastern Europe, thanks to the ability of the East Germans to make the best of a bureaucratic economic system, the modest "kombinat" reforms introduced years earlier, and the subsidies they obtain through the "special relationship" with West Germany. The other reason for caution is that the division of the two Germanies, symbolized by the Berlin Wall and all it stands for, makes the GDR's leadership especially weary of embarking on a course of domestic liberalization which might unleash forces that it may be unable to control.

A major similarity between the two countries is that the USSR reforms incorporate certain aspects of the earlier "kombinat" reforms of the GDR. Kombinats are large associations of enterprises in related areas of production. A great deal of the planning and resource allocation tasks previously carried out at ministry levels have been delegated to kombinat directors. The Soviet reforms, too, envision the formation of several thousand large associations modeled on East Germany's kombinat system (which Gorbachev reportedly admires), grouping together enterprises and research institutes in related fields, to link technical research more closely with development and production.

The current leaders of Czechoslovakia have less confidence in the good performance of their economy than their East German colleagues, and yet are reluctant to follow Gorbachev. The most basic reason, of course, is that they came to power twenty years ago to reverse the reforms of the Prague Spring—very similar to Gorbachev's reform program—a task in which they succeeded. At the same time, the leadership does not ascribe the economy's obvious problems just to the shortcomings of the system.[17] They can point to mitigating circumstances in foreign trade: the 25% deterioration during 1970-82 in the country's terms of trade (while the Soviet Union had enjoyed a large gain); the financial difficulties of their Third World trading partners (during much of the postwar period Czechoslovakia specialized in developing ties with Third World countries); and their economy's increasingly heavy dependence on trade with the USSR, which is an obstacle to economic decentralization (while for the USSR, trade with other CPEs is relatively much less important).

To be sure, the leadership does not speak with one voice. The top party leaders, Gustav Husak and his December 1987 replacement, Milos Jakes, are against fundamental economic reforms even though they are giving lip-service to it. Reluctance to follow the Soviet line is, therefore, giving rise to the paradox that the very same leaders who for decades have made it their career to be loyal to the Soviet leaders now talk about national sovereignty and the right of every socialist country to choose its own path.[18] By contrast, more pragmatic leaders, such as Prime Minister Lubomir Strougal, believed that significant economic reforms should be introduced.

Pressures from the Soviet Union (whether explicit or implicit is not clear); from the pragmatists in the leadership; from some economists, other intellectuals, and the youth (i.e., from "below"); and from deteriorating economic performance have forced the Czechoslovak authorities, though, to take some cautious reform steps since 1987. Several reform commissions were organized, discussion about reforms became somewhat more open in the press, and several reform measures were or are expected to be introduced. These include abolishing(!) the association of enterprises, reducing the number of compulsory plan targets, splitting the monobank into a central bank and a limited number of commercial banks, loosening the foreign trade monopoly, allowing modest increases in private and cooperative activities, and some "hardening" of the budget constraints of enterprises.[19] But these "reforms" are clearly more in the spirit of perfecting than transforming the traditional CPE system.

Romania, under the autocratic leadership of Nicolae Ceausescu, follows its own course. My visit to Romania during June 1987 convinced me that Romania's policies are based on its leadership's misguided pursuit of economic and political independence—first and foremost from the USSR. Romania's history is fraught with foreign conquests and domination. Ceausescu has a siege mentality, coupled with simplistic and outmoded views on what it takes for a country to maintain its economic and political independence. Ceausescu's "vision" is that the country must pursue broad-based industrialization and self-sufficiency at all costs, that strict central planning should be maintained, that the forces of market and "greed" must be suppressed, that he alone knows what is the best for Romania, and that a leader should not be deterred from his "correct" course by obstacles and hardships. To be sure, Ceausescu is probably unaware of much of the costly consequences of his policies and the suffering of the Romanian people, because he appears to surround himself with officials who tell him only what he wants to hear. Ceausescu is thus not at all receptive to adopting Gorbachev's initiatives, and has been publicly criticizing the course followed by the Soviet leader. Concludes Gati:

> By so dissociating Romania from Gorbachev's path, Ceausescu has thus signalled both his contempt for what the Soviet Union is doing and his unequivocal opposition to emulating the new Soviet model. Accordingly, chances for Ceausescu's maverick Romania to return to the Soviet fold have further decreased since Gorbachev's ascension to power. This is so despite the dramatic expansion of trade between the two countries since 1984, which reflects Ceausescu's determination to eliminate Romania's hard-currency debt.[20]

There is much that is similar, however, between Hungary's comprehensive economic reform blueprint, the NEM, developed during the mid-1960s and introduced in 1968, and Gorbachev's reform blueprint. To be sure, there are notable differences also. Still, Hungary's reform experience is the most directly relevant for understanding the possibilities and problems the Soviet Union is likely to face.

The main similarity is the strategic concept of the reform, which has the following essential components in both cases:

First, the goal is to make the reform comprehensive and thereby affect many aspects of the economic mechanism. This is to be done more or less simultaneously rather than piecemeal, (or only experimentally), in selected enterprises or sectors. When Agenbagyan for instance was asked:—"Considering that you have lived through two previous reform attempts, why are you optimistic that Gorbachev's reforms will be successful?"—he replied: "The previous reforms were not successful because they were only partial reforms. Because the administrative system remained dominant, it was not possible for the economic regulators to function. For example, in 1985, only industry and agriculture was reformed, construction and transportation were not. Planning methods, the regulatory mechanism, and the banking system had remained unchanged. Thus, the new economic methods became alien bodies within the organism. Because the alien parts could not function, they simply disappeared."[21]

Second, they both maintain central planning, but reduce greatly its scope and change its instruments of implementation. The blueprint envisions the elimination of compulsory plan directives: the granting to enterprises of a great deal of autonomy over the composition of current production and inputs, the distribution of output, and replacement investment; and the assumption that enterprise decisions would be guided by "market" forces, as reflected in profits. Enterprises that are unprofitable would be reorganized and, if they remained loss-makers, they might go bankrupt. Enterprises making good profits would expand. The authorities would "guide" market forces by establishing and manipulating a series of financial "regulators:" rules of price formation, rules for managers for granting personal compensation to employees, rules of access to bank credits, rules of taxation and subsidization, rules for allocating after-tax profits among "reserves," "expansion," and "profit sharing," and so on. Direct controls would be maintained over the output of some key products, a significant part of new investments, and over much of trade with CMEA partners.

Third, they allow a significant, but on balance still modest expansion of the private (and genuinely) cooperative sectors, especially in agriculture and in the services. This means legalizing more private economic activities and allowing the small-scale private and cooperative ownership of some means of production (or providing close substitutes for it, such as the long-term leasing of land and other fixed assets).

What Did Reforms in Hungary Achieve and What Could They Not Accomplish?

Before attempting to answer the question posed, though, we must establish whether the reform blueprint sketched above was actually introduced.

The short answer is that the reform blueprint was not introduced exactly as envisioned. The reality is that enterprises and cooperatives have remained, in many respects, much more under direct central control than was envisioned, even though the instruments of control have changed. The most important reason why the NEM blueprint did not operate as envisioned was that a sufficiently strong market mechanism was not created, either in the factor or product markets. While product markets were developed quite extensively in agriculture and in the consumer sector, in industry and in other sectors their emergence was hindered by the highly concentrated structure of industry and construction, by the absence of import competition, and by the unwillingness of the authorities to allow prices to reach market-clearing levels (fearing too rapid inflation). The development of a labor market, where wage rates would approximately equate the supply and demand for labor, was hindered by the absence of a countervailing power by the "owners of capital" (who are they?) to resist the always strong pressures for wage increases. The development of a market for real and financial assets, whose prices should be based not on costs but on expected rates of return, was prevented by the absence of financial intermediaries or some institution to fulfil the functions of a stock market, namely to revalue assets continuously. A further constraint on introducing a real market mechanism was the decision of the authorities not to allow large enterprises to go bankrupt (the "soft-budget constraint").

In brief, owing to: (1) an absence of the institutional prerequisites of genuine marketization; (2) the ideologically- or politically-based mistrust of genuine market forces; and (3) an unwillingness to countenance the initially traumatic consequences for certain vested interests of redeploying human and material resources from less to more productive uses and allowing prices to move to market-clearing levels, much of the economy did not become market-oriented but remained authority-oriented. Those segments of the economy that were allowed to be guided (to a greater or lesser extent) by market forces—namely, much of agriculture, many small state enterprises and cooperatives, the marginal activities of a certain number of large firms, and the private sector—did contribute to a significant improvement in Hungary's economic performance. But the predominant state industrial sector did not improve its performance significantly because it was provided neither sufficient pressures nor adequate opportunities to do so.

Hungary's improved economic performance as compared with the pre-1968 period or relative to those of the other CMEA countries is difficult to detect from statistics. One reason is that Hungary's official statistics are subject to much less of a statistical bias. Also, much of the improvement has taken the form of the better availability, quality and assortment of food and other consumer items. Official growth rates in CPEs do not distinguish between producing goods that end up as unsalable inventories or reluctant purchases by unhappy users who have no choice, versus products that meet the buyers' specifications. Thus, the Hungarian reforms, limited as they were, did bring significant though limited economic improvements, more apparent to those who travel throughout Eastern Europe than to those who make their assessments by pouring over economic statistics.

Still, a further aspect of Hungary's economic performance is that the authorities have been making a series of costly mistakes in economic policy. The most important of these is the soft-budget constraint on large enterprises. That is, the state has been willing to cover losses in order to maintain full employment, because the output of each large producer appears to be essential to supply the domestic, the CMEA, or the Western market. Moreover, as many factor and product prices have remained arbitrary accounting profits or losses may not reflect true economic performance.

A further mistake was initiating during 1968-1973 a series of mammoth "central development programs" to increase exports to the CMEA or to substitute for convertible-currency imports. Implementing these projects and obtaining the inputs needed to operate the (outdated) industrial capacity these projects created preempted, under the direction of the state and not that of the market, a large share of Hungary's investment resources, leaving insufficient resources—and freedom—for enterprises to expand modern manufacturing and exports to the West.

Reinforcing these errors was the decision during the 1970s to borrow large amounts from the West and the failure to invest the credits wisely. The mistakes, together with the many remaining shortcomings in the economic system and unfavorable developments in the external economic environment, resulted in a level of foreign indebtedness that has forced the authorities to institute and maintain economic austerity since 1979. The austerity, and its adverse impact on the standard of living, tend to veil the modest but not insignificant improvements in economic performance that should be attributed to the reforms.

The Lessons of Past Reforms for the USSR and Eastern Europe

What lessons can we learn from the experiences of Hungary and the other "reforming" countries in the region?

First, with the possible exception of the GDR and Romania, most economists in the CMEA (as well as in Yugoslavia and China) seem to agree that the CPE system has fundamental shortcomings. There is growing realization by influential persons in Hungary, Poland, Bulgaria, and the USSR that a modern economy has become too complex to be planned by directives from a center and that "marketization" is the only feasible direction of change. This is the common denominator in these countries' reform blueprints. But there is no clear notion of how markets should operate and how the markets for factors of production, intermediates, and final goods and services are interrelated. As a consequence, the ongoing experimentation with change can be described as "reforms without theory." We do not find a clear vision of a desirable future economic system. Consequently, there is no uniform reform blueprint nor agreed reform strategies or principles of implementation.[22] This imperfect understanding is an obstacle to meaningful change. Further important constraints to marketization are that they represent a threat to the political power structure and that they disturb vested interests.

Second, Hungary's experience helps us evaluate the logic of its reform blueprint that has many common features with those that several other CMEA countries may soon be introducing. In my view, the real issue is not central planning *versus* the market. In any country, the government is responsible for important economic tasks, whose implementation may be called "central planning." The real issue, it seems to me, is that central planning should remain limited, should not involve detailed instructions to most enterprises, and that real market forces be given sufficient scope. That is, most factor and product prices should be determined largely by market forces, under competitive conditions. Without competition, factor and product prices will remain arbitrary and profits will not be reliable performance indicators. Furthermore, competition means that there will be winners and losers among producers, investors, and workers who should enjoy or suffer the consequences of their performance. To be sure, open markets cannot be introduced or sustained politically without institutions designed to soften the social impact of swift changes triggered by market forces. But that is not the same as the practice of CPEs of attempting to insulate large enterprises—as well as every producer, manager, and worker—from market forces or the consequences of their own inadequate performance.

It seems to me that neither Hungary's NEM, nor the GDR's kombinat reforms, nor Gorbachev's reform blueprint reveals a sufficient appreciation of the role of competition. For example, neither blueprint mentions exposing domestic producers to import competition, much less sets a timetable for its gradual implementation. To be sure, the thinking on this has begun to change in Hungary, so far more among economists than policy makers.

Third, a further lesson we can learn from Hungary's experience is that before market forces can be unleashed with good results, the institutional preconditions of a market mechanism must be created. That is:

- Industrial organization cannot remain as highly concentrated as it was when the NEM was introduced. While Hungary has made some progress in breaking up enterprises, and the rules of entry and exit have been eased, much still remains to be done. Although the large size of the Soviet economy makes industrial concentration less of a problem, without sufficient domestic and international competition, even if

enterprises will be allowed to contract with each other directly, many fundamental problems will not be solved.
- The monopoly banking system must be replaced with a network of profit-oriented and competing financial institutions. Hungary has made an important step in this direction in 1987 when it created a commercial banking system.
- The large central planning apparatus, including the branch ministries, must be disbanded. Hungary's example shows that this is an exceedingly difficult task because it touches essential political nerves and large vested interests.
- One of the thorniest issues—one that has not yet been solved adequately even in the Hungarian blueprint—is that if the means of production will continue to remain predominantly non-private, who can—and how should they—exercise various essential ownership functions. That is, who will resist the strong pressures from workers for higher compensation? Who will appoint, evaluate, promote and sack managers, and on what basis? Who will decide where after-tax profits should be invested? Who is to risk large sums to back ventures that are risky but have potentially large payoffs for society and the investor? In a market economy, ownership functions are exercised mostly by private capitalists, either directly or through profit-oriented financial intermediaries. In a traditional CPE, they are exercised by the authorities. But who will do so in a radically-reformed socialist economy? In enterprises or cooperatives where the workers do not own (or members did not contribute) the assets, workers' self management is not likely to be a viable ownership mechanism.
- Regardless of who will exercise the ownership functions, enterprises will need good managers. Under the old system, managers were more like bureaucrats than business executives. As radical reforms are introduced, managers must learn to operate under new rules, and eventually these have be set predominantly by market forces.

Fourth, market-oriented systemic reforms must be complemented by proper macroeconomic policies: full employment should not be pursued by subsidizing too many loss-making ventures. Economic equilibrium must be maintained by not pushing growth rates, investment rates, and domestic and foreign borrowing beyond prudent limits. Price and incomes policies must ensure that markets will be cleared: exchange rates should be realistic; and the tax system should not impinge too much on individual incentives to work, or on enterprise incentives to produce and to take risks. Yet, at the same time, disparities in personal incomes and wealth must be kept within reasonable limits.

Finally, Hungary's experience tells us that implementing radical economic reforms will take a long time, even under favorable political circumstances, something that of course cannot be taken for granted. Hence, our assessments and expectations must be realistic.

The Impact of Gorbachev's New Course on Eastern Europe

The most important impact of Gorbachev's new course is that it gives a much freer hand to the leadership in Eastern Europe to shape the content of their individual reform blueprints and pace of implementation. Why the dynamics of economic reforms differ so much among the East European countries has already been touched upon. Much more work remains to be done to understand the historical, social, political, and economic forces that shape an individual country's reform dynamics.

Paradoxically, however, the foreign economic aspects of Gorbachev's reform program do not fully support the introduction of market-oriented reforms in Eastern Europe. The Soviet Union is pushing for both increased and improved economic integration with the countries of Eastern Europe. The following are the key building blocks of how the Soviets desire to implement this.

First, the Soviet Union wishes to alter the structure of its exports to East Europe. In place of providing growing quantities of energy, raw materials and intermediate goods—products that have become increasingly scarce and expensive to mine, process, and transport to their destination—the Soviets wish to sell increased quantities of manufactures. Although the growing difficulty of acquiring more of these "hard goods" from the USSR are considered a serious economic constraint by the planners in Eastern Europe, I believe that in the long run this is really a blessing in disguise for them. The easier it is to acquire these hard goods from the USSR and to pay for them with "soft" manufactures, the longer Eastern Europe will maintain its increasingly outdated structure of production and the less pressures they will face to restructure their production and to give high priority to erecting capacity whose output can be competitive on any market, not just in the CMEA. Such restructuring, in turn, requires market-oriented economic reforms and economic policies that support them. The Soviet intent to export more manufactures will help the reform process only if the quality, modernity, and customer-orientation of these goods also improves considerably. Since this is a possibility only if the Soviet's own reform program succeeds, say, by the mid-1990s at the earliest, if the East Europeans decide or are pressured to take more Soviet goods sooner, that would be counterproductive to their own reform efforts.

Second, the Soviets would like the East Europeans to make a greater contribution to the Soviet economy by:

1. Participating in joint research and development and providing high-quality exports to assist the expansion of such priority sectors in the Soviet economy as machine tools, robotics, electronics, chemicals, and energy and raw material production as well as conservation. By itself, Soviet pressure on the East European countries to modernize and improve the quality of what they export can be evaluated as positive, provided that Soviet orders can be manufactured economically and

that the same or similar products can be exported to non-CMEA destinations also. But, I am afraid, Soviet jawboning on this is not backed by a trade, pricing, and financial mechanism in the CMEA that would actually motivate producers to improve quality and to become customer-oriented. And such reforms are not now on the CMEA's agenda.

2. The Soviets would also like to receive from the East Europeans much greater quantities of agricultural and industrial consumer products. Although these are not high priority in Soviet production plans, they are high priority for improving the lot of the consumers, and East European suppliers are supposed to play an important role in this endeavor. But planners in Eastern Europe are resisting this Soviet demand because its implementation would have an adverse impact on their convertible-currency balance of payments. Agricultural goods can always be sold, at however low a price, on the world market, whereas expanding the production of consumer manufactures would require a great deal of new investments as well as relatively large convertible-currency inputs. On the one hand, the Soviets apparently are not willing to pay good prices for such "soft" products or to compensate the East European by paying with additional supplies of hard goods or convertible currency. So far, there has been something of a standoff on this issue.

3. As a result of their reforms, the Soviets now not only permit but would even like to encourage the development of interenterprise relations between in the CMEA. This is an idea that sounds good because it appears to be supportive of the reforms, except that with the existing domestic and CMEA pricing and trading mechanisms, interenterprise relations cannot be implemented effectively on a substantial scale.

4. The Soviets would like the East Europeans to contribute much more to so-called CMEA joint investment projects located in the USSR, in exchange for a greater assured future supply of project-related "hard goods." This is being resisted, to some extent successfully, by the East Europeans since short of investment funds.

5. The Soviets would like the East Europeans to start repaying the modestly large terms of trade credits they received during the second half of the 1970s and early 1980s. This, as any new investment contribution, would increase the shortage of resources available in Eastern Europe, increasing the economic pressure on their planners, which in turn may or may not be conducive to further economic reforms.

In sum, since Soviets reforms are not likely to improve, substantially and within a relatively few years, the quality, modernity, and service features of the country's manufactures, nor is it likely that the CMEA's trade and financial mechanisms will be fundamentally altered, growing Soviet economic pressure on the East Europeans to contribute more to the Soviet's modernization effort is not likely to bear rich fruit to the Soviets nor is it likely to be a major factor in East European's own improved economic performance. Paradoxically, tightening the supply and conditions of Soviet energy and raw material exports may be the only thing that, in the long run, will yield substantial benefits for the countries of East Europe.

Notes

1. Anders Aslund, "Who Are Gorbachev's Economic Advisers?" Unpublished paper of September 16, 1987, the Kennan Institute, the Wilson Center, Washington D.C., p. 2.
2. Ibid.
3. Ibid.
4. A.G. Aganbegyan, "Problems in the Radical Restructuring of Economic Management in the USSR" (in English translation), August 1987 (unpublished).
5. Paul Marer, *Dollar GNPs of the USSR and Eastern Europe* Baltimore: The Johns Hopkins University Press for the World Bank, 1985.6. A.G. Aganbegyan, "Problems in the Radical Restructuring of Economic Management in the USSR" (in English translation), August 1987 (unpublished), pp. 4-5.
7. Edward A. Hewett, "The June 1987 Plenum and Economic Reform." *PlanEcon Report*, Volume III, No. 30, July 23, 1987.
8. David S. Mason, "Soviet Reforms and Eastern Europe: Implications for Poland." Paper prepared for delivery at a conference on "New Dimensions of the Polish Economy," Wichita State University, Wichita, Kansas, October 6, 1987.
9. *Economist*, (London), April 9, 1988.
10. *Pravda* report, quoted in the *Economist*, April 9, 1988.
11. Abel Aganbegyan, *The Economic Challenge of Perestroika* Bloomington, IN: Indiana University Press, 1988, p. 127.
12. *Economist*, April 9, 1988.
13. Paul Marer and Wlodzimierz Siwinski, (eds.), *Creditworthiness and Reform in Poland: Western and Polish Perspectives* Bloomington: Indiana University Press, 1987.
14. Marvin Jackson, "Bulgaria's Economic Reforms—How Long is the Road Ahead?" *PlanEcon Report*, Volume III, Nos. 34-35, August 27, 1987.
15. Ivan Angelov, "Driving Forces and Resistance," *Sofia News*, July 29, 1987.
16. Charles Gati, "Gorbachev and Eastern Europe," *Foreign Affairs*, July 1987.
17. Josef C. Brada, "Sartor Resartus? Gorbachev and Prospects for Economic Reform in Czechoslovakia." *Harvard International Review* November 1987.
18. Igor Lukes, "The Reform or Not to Reform: Gorbachev's Initiatives and Their Impact on Czechoslovakia," *Harvard International Review*, November 1987.
19. Vaclav Klaus, "Socialist Economies, Economic Reforms and Economist: Reflections of a Czechoslovak Economist." Paper presented at the Conference on Alternative Models of Socialist Economic Systems, Gyor, Hungary, March 18-22, 1988.
20. Gati, *loc. cit.*, p. 962.
21. *Die Zeit*, "Interview with Agenbagyan," as reported in *Heti Vilaggazdasag* Budapest, October 10, 1987.
22. Klaus, *loc. cit.*

6

The Lesser Allies' View: Eastern Europe and the Military Relationship with the Soviet Union

Ivan Volgyes

This chapter examines the behavior of states in the Warsaw Pact by evaluating the interrelation between Soviet goals, purposes, and behavior on the one hand, and alliance aspirations regarding the military relationship with the Pact in general, and the USSR in particular, on the other. In Part I we will examine the emerging new foreign policies of the Gorbachev era and the potential impact of the "new" policies on Soviet-East European external relations. In Part II we will analyze the concept of "lesser" allies, while Part III will be devoted to the dominant views within the Pact regarding their military relations with the hegemony—and with each other. Finally, Part IV will address the thorny subject of "adaptation" in military relations with the USSR. This essay, however, is largely predicated on the hitherto unproven assumption that in the Gorbachev era there is a fundamentally different set of external circumstances that warrant a serious re-examination of previous tenets. If this is not the case, *caveat lector*, my motto still remains: "I have not *always* been wrong."

The Gorbachev Era in Foreign Policy: Implications for Change

There can be no doubt that Gorbachev's efforts in domestic policies, his continued emphases on *perestroika cum glasnost* at home, have altered the political landscape of the USSR to an extent unprecedented since Khrushchev's reform years. Although we do not know the future changes that may result from such efforts—as the Russians would say—*poka* (for the time being, or meanwhile), the changes appear to be significant and affect the very bases of the operation of the USSR. While real reforms in the economy and society, not to mention in political life, lag behind the dominant verbiage, there cannot be any doubt that the USSR is undergoing "interesting times."

In foreign policy as well, since mid-summer 1987, new approaches seem to be noticeable. In a groundbreaking article, Evgenii Primakov, the present Director of the Soviet Academy of Sciences' prestigious Institute of World Economic and International Relations, advocated the adoption of a new approach to foreign policy.[1] Primakov discussed a "new philosophy of foreign policy," implying that the USSR must turn inward in order to succeed in its domestic modernization efforts. Consequently, Primakov implies that the Soviet Union must seek a less confrontationalist approach vis-à-vis the West, and must decrease those expenses—aid to the Third World, "excessive" military costs, even increasing assistance to Eastern Europe—that would hinder these efforts. While this may be a "new philosophy" regarding foreign affairs, it hardly amounts to new "foreign policy;" the publication of the article, nonetheless, indicates a re-prioritization of long-utilized instruments of foreign affairs.

Primakov's study was followed up the very next day by a second "theme" article written by Aleksandr Bovin in *Izvestiia*.[2] Noting that Soviet and Communist advances are not viewed by most people in the world as very bright accomplishments that would merit emulation, Bovin chastises foreign policymakers and challenges them to come up with new approaches and alternatives that would reflect existing realities. And as if that were not enough, the party's theoretical journal chimed in by explaining how the new approach—philosophy or theory?—can be viewed in the broader context of Marxism-Leninism.[3]

Two things appear remarkable about these articles. The first is that they all seem to hark back to an earlier formulation of Marxist-Leninist theory, Stalin's concept of socialism in one country: that concept in its practical applications, in fact, subordinated external considerations regarding the course of advances in world communism to domestic Soviet developmental desiderata. Just as in 1936, the implication of advocating the "new approach," once more is simply to suggest that under the current conditions, in order to ensure the survival of communism as a whole in the future, the Soviet state—through its *perestroika*—must become strong and viable. As Bovin notes, the successes of a *"perestroika-*d" society will result in not merely talking about creating a new society "but by demonstrating its successes as well."[4] In other words, the necessary retrenchment and changes in Soviet domestic and foreign policy, will result in a sort of demonstration effect for the rest of the world.

The second remarkable element delineated in these articles lies in the candid admission that the changes are necessary both because the Soviet Union is no longer an emulatable model, and because Marxist-Leninist precepts were simply wrong. On the first point, the sharp phrasing by Bovin bears repeating: "the reversals, contradictions, crises and the stagnation in the development of the Soviet Union, of the other socialist countries, and of world socialism . . ." have not resulted in the USSR "becoming a model to be imitated" abroad.[5] On the second point, repeating several themes that have been bandied around both by Gorbachev and others pertaining to the evaluation that Marxism-Leninism has not been infallible as a guide to action, contemporary Soviet critiques call for a re-examination of foreign policies that were based on "erroneous assumptions." All of the articles on the topic fault ideology for providing a false sense of security; e.g. the conviction, on the one hand, that capitalism is bound to fail, and that—consequently—the victory of communism is predetermined, and, thus, it is inevitable. Again, as Bovin notes: "It should be accepted that the ability of capitalism to adapt to new historical circumstances surpassed our expectations. The prospect of transformation to socialism in the developed capitalist states receded indefinitely." And the successes of capitalism— contrary to the very bases of Marxism-Leninism—are taking place at a time when in many socialist states "the situation is unstable (and) fraught with the possibility of regression."[6]

The new foreign policy orientation—or philosophical restructuring— suggests both a retrenchment of Soviet policies, probably, toward a mild case of isolationism, and the external utilization of less expensive, less confrontational instrumentalities. The evidence for that retrenchment appears to be sketchy at best, but some foreign policy initiatives undertaken by the Gorbachev leadership appear to indicate its existence. Hence, the 1987 signing of the INF treaty, the acceptance of some American demands as valid conditions for the desirable reduction of long-range strategic weaponry, the withdrawal from Afghanistan, all are signs that such retrenchment is actually taking place. Even if these activities may not be evidence of a *general* retrenchment, at least the philosophical-theoretical bases for such an activity already seem to be in place. Such a potential retrenchment obviously also has been on the mind of the East European elites, whose major question remains the implications of the new directions for Eastern European-Soviet external relations, a topic to which we will now turn.

At this juncture, time and space constraint force us to delimit our evaluation of that relationship to a few generalities.[7] It should be noted, first, that Soviet-East European relations, generally, are carried on "formalistic" bases; once Stalin decided not to incorporate the East European states into the USSR, Soviet leaders were compelled, at least ritualistically, to treat the leaders of the Warsaw Pact states as "sovereigns." Only in atmospheres of crisis—e.g. Czechoslovakia in 1968—do the brutality of reality invade the "ritualized consultative" respect.[8] Therefore, in obtaining the optimally desirable outcomes in Eastern European foreign policies, especially since 1968, Gorbachev as well as other recent Soviet rulers, have been compelled to use such instrumentalities available that fall considerably short of instruments of open violence.

Second, on the one hand, it should also be noted that the present Eastern European rulers are not Gorbachev's own choices for the job, and they all seem to feel that they owe very little to the Soviet leader. On the other hand, however, while Moscow, undoubtedly, does reserve the right to veto any successor, in its present domestic preoccupation, the men in the Kremlin are not likely to rock the boat of stability present in Eastern Europe by forcibly replacing the gerontocrats of the region. As a Soviet diplomat recently remarked in a private conversation: "They will drop dead by themselves, without any help from us." Given the accumulation of interests that favor the limitation on Gorbachev's "reformist" policies within the USSR, the latter evaluation may be all too optimistic.

Third, it may be observed that three distinct (but occasionally overlapping) approaches seem to have been developed by the Eastern Europe power holders regarding existing or potential "innovations" in Soviet policy taking place both at home and abroad. The first approach is to follow the old, "time-tested" policies: Ceausescu, Honecker, Husak (and recently Jakes), and Zhivkov in domestic affairs, and Husak, and Zhivkov in foreign affairs apparently follow this "line." Their motto is: stability *ueber alles*. The second technique is to follow the new Soviet line without any question. In domestic affairs, Jaruzelski and Grosz, in foreign affairs, Honecker, Grosz and Jaruzelski seem to be taking this stance. And the third approach is to go beyond what Moscow is doing. In domestic affairs, Grosz and Jaruzelski, in foreign affairs Ceausescu—and perhaps Honecker?—are tending in this direction. While we note the existence of these varied approaches, or techniques in dealing with changes in Soviet policies we must reiterate that, to date, there is no "unified" policy adopted by the East European elites either in accepting or rejecting the "new philosophy of foreign relations" mentioned above.

When we come to the military-political relationships within the existing alliance systems, we have to look long and hard for any real or apparent changes that are the results of adopting "new philosophies." It is not that there have not been innovations: the debate over Ogarkov's suggestion for a prospective change in Soviet military affairs, the adoption of a "more defensive" Soviet strategy by the Soviet army, the consequent agreements on offensive limiting nuclear missile deployments, and unilateral Soviet military reductions etc., all have had their obvious and well-documented reverberations in Eastern Europe as well. There have also been dissenting voices heard regarding the costs borne by the various Eastern European states for force modernization, and the costs of the new military equipment acquired by the East European states for updating their arsenal.

Yet, these debates within Eastern Europe—with the exception of vociferous Romania—have all been muted, because *the domain of the Warsaw Pact, military affairs, and defense policies remains beyond the pale of openly discussable topics.* While there are many small complaints regarding costs, integration, limits of autonomy, etc., expressed openly in East European military journals, the bigger implications of foreign policy changes and their impact on military integration—or disintegration?—within the Warsaw Pact, remain largely taboo subjects. Eastern Europe's military relations with the USSR, therefore, can only be seen in the light of the present wait-and-see attitude, marked by caution even in raising this topic in any but the most oblique manner.

The Lesser Allies' View:
Thoughts on a Definitional Challenge

At the outset of this section it is very important to emphasize that, at least in the WTO parlance, the term "lesser" ally, or "little brother" is never utilized; conversely, however, the Soviet Red Army frequently has been referred to as "our elder brother." This duality is not totally unintentional; while the Red Army elite tries to lessen the tension that exists between their "naturally senior" role and those played by "co-subordinated" armies, sycophantic, overly pro-Muscovite local elites have found it hard not to pay homage to the men and institutions "from whom all blessings flow." Thus, the usage of the term "lesser ally," at once identifies the user as: (a) an objective, Western observer; (b) a sycophantic Muscovite; or (c) a sarcastic East European.

In real life, however, the Warsaw Pact's role as *the* lesser ally is totally justified by any objective measurement. Thus, the Pact comprising around 100 million people fields a combined army of less than a million men, while the USSR with some 280 million people fields an army of around five million men. The ratio in equipment, or military expenditure even more dramatically indicates the superiority of the hegemon, and, conversely, the inferiority of the "lesser" allies. If we were to analyse still other elements of the alliance system, the not-so-surprising conclusion of total Soviet superiority would clearly emerge; this is true in command, control, and decision-making as well. On every level, including the staffing of combined *shtabs*, commanding exercises, or deciding on the location of deployment, the Red Army acts like the hegemon over the "Lesser Allies": the non-Soviet Warsaw Pact partners.

The weakness of the NSWP members and their inferior position is further emphasized by the fact that the Warsaw Pact is not now, nor has it ever been, united *vis-à-vis* the hegemon. This lack of unity, to date, has been especially notable in intra-Pact practice, because the Pact so far has been deployed only in combat against various members of the WTO itself—even though the theoretical justification for the very existence of the alliance is to "combat NATO aggression." To wit: the Pact was split on the Soviet decision of invading Hungary in 1956, split on the decision to invade Czechoslovakia in 1968, split on the best available solution for Poland in 1981, and split on myriads of smaller decisions ranging from the "proper" size of defense expenditure to the placement of the INF missiles.

It is worthwhile to ask whether such splits are beneficial or harmful to Soviet decision-making. To the extent that such splits exist in regards to the formulation of a common front *vis-à-vis* Moscow—e.g. a potentially unified opposition to the Soviet decision of increasing the costs of defense—they are clearly welcomed by Moscow; a joint declaration of *not increasing* defense expenditures when the Red Army calls for them would be quite embarrassing, even for a not easily embarrassable Kremlin. Consequently, Ceausescu's decision, *not to* officially increase defense expenditures, while regrettable from Moscow's point of view, is not as negative in its consequences as a joint, and unified East European call to limit such spending contrary to what Moscow's wishes would be. Moreover, such splits in intra-Pact affairs is also desirable on the basis of the ancient principle of *divide et impera*. Hence, while Hungary had opposed the use of force against Poland, the latter opposed the use of force against Hungary, and Czechoslovakia opposed the use of Pact forces against Czechoslovakia, such individual deviation in behavior is far more easily tolerated than a *potential coherence* of anti-Soviet activities. The overt and covert use of nationalism by the USSR, in preventing such a coherence is a fact of daily political life in Eastern Europe.

The Lesser Allies, of course, are lesser not just in macro, but in microterms as well; because of deep divisions within the NSWP partners, they do not ever achieve a coherence as a Bloc. There are, for instance, well marked divisions within the alliance that delineate "more" or "less" senior allies. The Northern Tier, for example, is more important, better supplied, possesses more important missions, and is considered by the Soviets to be more reliable than the Southern Tier. Poland is more important in political deliberations than Bulgaria, East Germany is more important in planning military exercises than Hungary, and Czechoslovak military leaders are far more trustworthy than their Romanian counterparts. Moreover, from an offensive perspective, East Germany is more valuable—and vulnerable—than Romania, while from the defensive perspective, Czechoslovakia and Hungary are more valuable—and vulnerable—than Bulgaria or its northern neighbor. In fact, the stationing of Soviet troops on the territory of the WTO states does serve as a rough indicator of the extent of value and vulnerability differences within the alliance.

Soviet, and official East European, sources are equally careful to indicate that the alliance is based on equality, and is supposed to be a "comradeship in arms" between sovereign equals and not between "greater" or "lesser" partners. In spite of the care taken by these sources to assuage easily hurt sensitivities, the very fact that the NSWP allies *respond* or *fail to respond* to new Soviet initiatives is an indicator of the real weight of Moscow within the alliance. It is a role, of course, to which the Soviets have been accustomed throughout the last four decades. And even the tiniest alteration of this causes them discomfort. Thus, for instance, Bucharest's call for the removal of *all INF* missiles from Europe—a call made *before* Moscow made its double zero concessions—caused the Soviet elite to climb down the throats of the East German leaders who were toying coyly also with advocating such an option, and sent the German "emissaries of peace" hastily back into the fold of obedience. The limits of freedom *to act only in concurrence with those desiderata Moscow deems to be of primary importance* was carefully and clearly explained to them, once and for all. In this sense, they have been compelled to remain "lesser allies," whether they wished to be in that position or not.

The Divergence of Views and Attitudes Among the Lesser Allies: Some Thoughts on Soviet–East European Military Relationships

In evaluating the actual extent of divergence, it is necessary for us to discern those categories where differences are most clearly manifest. Accordingly, there seem to exist basically two types of divergence. The first concerns issues that involve the domestic and the second the external aspects of the military relationship between Eastern Europe and the USSR. Within the domestic category differences of views and attitudes can be identified in regards to the objects of: (a) the system; (b) the types of policies to be followed; and (c) the elites in power. Let us now try to identify and briefly analyze these domestic divergences.

While among the East European and Soviet members of the alliance some obvious cleavages can be noted in regards to the systemic elements of the military relationship, it should also be observed that there is no divergence whatsoever in regards to the declaration that the primary purpose of the WTO is the defense of the socialist system. But this is not to be understood exclusively in terms of an external threat. In this respect, the primary goal of the alliance is also to serve as an internal police mechanism within the Pact. As the armed invasion of Czechoslovakia in 1968 indicated, the internal guarantor function of the WTO was clearly invoked.

The Red Army's or the WTO's guarantor function, however, has not been uniformly accepted with great joy—even publicly—by all of the members of the alliance for various reasons. First, there seem to be great divergences in regards to the location of the right to interpret and evaluate the existence and extent of the "threat" to the socialist order; on this issue the alliance has repeatedly been rent asunder. Thus, according to the Hungarian government of Imre Nagy, there was no threat to the social order on November 1, 1956 with which the internal forces at Nagy's disposal could not deal. Consequently, on November 4, 1956 there was no need to bring in the Red Army to guarantee the survival of the socialist system, and hence the decision to evaluate the threat should have rested with the territorial authority (i.e. Imre Nagy) and not with the men in Moscow. Similarly, in 1968, according to the Czechoslovak, Hungarian and Romanian leadership—and contrary to the evaluation of Brezhnev, the Soviet, East German, Bulgarian and even the Polish ruling elites—there was no such threat posed to the social order that had called for armed "guarantors" in the form of WTO forces to be sent into Czechoslovakia by the military leadership of the Pact as directed from Moscow. Or again, alternately, in 1981, neither the Hungarian, nor the Romanian leaders felt that the threat to the socialist order in Poland called for WTO "guarantor activities"—although their counterparts in Prague, East Berlin or Sofia openly called for such eventualities.

These divergent interpretations have been discussed often in a theoretical manner. Thus, according to Ceausescu, it is the sovereign right of the sovereign head of the sovereign state to determine that an actual threat exists. While the Soviet and non-Romanian WTO elites never openly argued this proposition with Romania—in fact, both in Hungary and in Czechoslovakia the Soviets have insisted that they were "invited" by the relevant native party authorities "begging for fraternal assistance"—in recent years there has emerged a fuzzy theory of "collective responsibility" for the future evaluation of potential threats. In fact, an oft-stated purpose of many of the joint exercises of recent years had been to assure the close working relationships between units and staffs in fulfilling the duties derived from that collective responsibility.

The impact of such divergences upon evolving military relationships among the members of the Pact is hard to fathom. Clearly, the ruling, native political elites are interested in assuring their final say regarding the existence or severity of threats to the social order taking place on their own territory. Just as importantly, they also wish to have a say in formulating the "correct" perceptions of such threats, as well as having the *right* to make any decision about what to do in regards to such threats on the territory of *any* other alliance member. Yet, these elites are ultimately dependent upon both the support of their own army, and—lacking that—upon the support of the fraternal armies. Put differently, while Grosz may not trust his own armed services to come to his aid, he must trust the Red Army. Or alternately, while Ceausescu must trust his own army to come to his assistance come what may, he certainly does not trust the armies of the WTO to regard potential revolts against his rule as "threats to the social order."

Closely related to the systemic *cleavages*, but analytically clearly apart from them, are the cleavages that exist in regards to the distinctive *policies* pursued by the various East European regimes. In this respect, *inter alia*, the following divergences may be analytically identified: 1. cleavages between Soviet and NSWP desiderata; 2. between intra-NSWP desiderata; and 3. within single NSWP country desiderata. Thus, in the first instance, Moscow may develop priorities for the Pact that are opposed by the NSWP members to varying extents. The 1978 demands for sharp increases in military spending caused such a cleavage in military relationships. The Kremlin, originally, stood alone on the issue—even if later all but Romania fell in line. Second, there can also be significant cleavages regarding intra-NSWP desiderata; the intervention to remove a domestic threat in a single country, the presumed threat posed by the adoption of a "liberal" economic or social system, or, for example, the demands for "normalization" in Poland, split the Lesser Allies within the alliance just as much as the "offending" country or countries seemed to have been split from Moscow. And, finally, a split within a single country can also be cause for cleavages between the various members of the alliance itself. Thus, for example, the varied interpretation regarding the domestic situation in Poland in 1980–1981, the extent to which the party was or was not in control enough for the maintenance of the desired social order, has also caused documentable cleavages and differences of opinion among the Pact members. The types of policies, in other words, that are implemented in a single country or in a set of countries, can easily cause stresses within the military and political establishments, and these stresses that can contribute either to the integration or disintegration processes within the alliance as a whole.

Finally, in the domestic sphere the position of the rulers can also impact upon alliance relationships in the military realm. Thus, for example, the Soviet military was more in favor of Ferenc Munnich than Janos Kadar in 1956, and the nearly unified military support that General Jaruzelski enjoyed among the various military allies, certainly tilted the powers that be in favor of his selection as Moscow's *Gauleiter* over that of a better-known "party-hack." In regards to Romania, however, the problem could be reversed; it is doubtful whether the Warsaw Pact military elite would come to the assistance of Ceausescu over a challenge from a potentially pro-WTO military leader, even if Ceausescu continued to insist that his personalized dictatorship represented the "true socialist order."

While these cleavages in regards to domestic political considerations continue to be nagging problems, they are usually posed more abstractly than the external political considerations that tend to be more concrete. The external considerations involve: (a) the goals of the alliance as a whole; (b) the question of alliance leadership; (c) the policy choices facing the alliance; (d) the costs of the alliance; (e) the role of the member-states of the alliance and (f) the tasks that are set for the "Lesser Allies" within the alliance as a whole. While these considerations are often country and/ or issue-specific, and while they differ both in weight (according to the individual member's perception) and time (according to the politico-historical chronology of the region), generally they are the more thorny issues between the Lesser Allies and the Kremlin.

The most significant conflicts occur between the USSR and some of the members of the alliance—notably, Romania, Hungary, and sometimes Poland—in regards to the further integration of the Pact as a whole. The conflicts take place in spite of the fact that the officer corps of all WTO states, with the exception of that of Romania, especially above field grade levels, appear to be well-integrated in the WTO. The upper-level service academies that provide further training to senior officers, joint exercises, and other well-established mechanisms, have, indeed, created solid bases for *personal* integration. Even the institutionalized penetrative activities—liaison officers, mechanisms within, for example, the SGSF, or the GSFG, etc.—all provide additional bases for continued integration.

In spite of the success of personal integrative processes, major differences regarding goal orientation continue to plague the alliance. For example, Romania's defensive doctrine of the "War of the Entire People," provides a clear challenge for the offensive activities of the Pact, including the joint preparation for such an eventuality. Or, once again, in the case of Romania, further integration within the Pact is clearly hindered by the lack of joint, massive exercises, or exercises that cannot be held on the territory of the Romanian state. While one could argue that Romania's case is an extreme example, other instances seem to indicate severe problems as well. Thus, on a more subtle level, while the top-level integrative mechanisms seem to work in Hungary, on the lower level, there remains severe doubt about the ability and capacity of the Hungarians to perform well-integrated alliance function with proper enthusiasm—and there is very little that the current elite does or cares to do about this dysfunction. The tendency of "resurgent nationalism," especially with its negative potentialities in the GDR, must also be a cause for worry for those concerned with the total integration of the WTO.

As far as the question of alliance leadership is concerned, problems arise on two different levels. On the first level, while there is little or no doubt about the *theoretical* hierarchical order within the Pact, the confusion not long ago regarding Ogarkov's and Kulikov's position, for instance, muddied the waters in the Pact. This is especially important in light of the fact that these powerful individuals each had coteries of followers who had banked their careers on the future success their patrons can achieve. With uncertainty in the ranks of the top levels, some personal integrative mechanisms have been placed on hold.

A far greater problem is observable regarding the issue of "wounded pride" among some of the native commanders, who feel that they are, indeed, "second class" citizens. These native commanders argue that the number of Soviet commanders heading joint exercises is nearly three times greater than those commanded by the "lesser brethren." Joint exercises, moreover, are rarely truly joint exercises involving pass-through activities. Rather, they are side-by-side, or boundary operations that frequently subordinate NSWP participation to the desiderata imposed upon the exercises by the needs of the Red Army. While some of the specific issues can easily be resolved, the continuous lack of general resolution is precisely what bothers (especially) some Polish and East German officers of field grade ranks.

A lack of interest in further integration on the part of the Lesser Allies, and an expectation of greater cooperation on the part of the USSR, also can be observed regarding the formulation and operationalization of alliance policies. Even among the East European political leadership the "three percent solution" caused considerable anxiety, some debate, and occasional public dissension. Although, ultimately, only Romania chose—at least publicly—not to raise its defense expenditures (since 1979) in accordance with the "Pact decision," political elites in Hungary and Poland, and also even to a minor extent in Czechoslovakia, grumbled about the lack of consultation, about the fact that the "Soviets just sprang this on us," as an Hungarian official related to this author. Force modernization timetables, costs of equipment, delivery priorities, etc. all tend to make the Lesser Allies resentful, for no central plans relating to these matters are detailed and discussed in advance with them. And the Lesser Allies also grumble about the unilateralism of the Soviet decision-making process in regards to the stand-down on the INF; it is not, necessarily, the outcome they debate, or they complain about, but the fact that these policies—and the attendant, apparent concessions—have not been discussed in detail, and in advance with them. As a Czech officer maintained during the summer of 1987 in a private interview:

> I am glad they will get rid of the INF missiles, but this means that all the rockets below 500 kilometers range will be exploded on Czech, German, and Hungarian soil. The least they (the Red Army decision-makers) could have done is to discuss this potentiality with me and the political leadership in some detail. The fact that we were just 'informed' of this decision really shows what they (the Russians) think of us.[9]

Nowhere is this resentment greater than in regards to the utilization of native forces as part of the Soviet armed forces. Colonel Kuklinski's study detailed the use of Pact armies *as direct parts of Soviet army operations.* While we have always known that in time of war, Pact units would be directly subordinated to operational control of the Soviet Army, Kuklinski revealed that the Pact members—with the exception of Romania—had all signed a new protocol with the USSR in 1979.[10] The protocol entitled "Statute on the Commanding Organs of the Combined Armed Forces during Wartime," in fact establishes the right of the Soviet High Command to take control of the member-states' armed forces in time of such crises that the Soviet High Command *perceives to be a threat.* Coupled with the establishment of "parallel operational units" of Category I forces, such control activities that result in the effective subordination of the Pact armies even during peacetime activities, add up to a stress between at least *some* native commanders and the Soviet High Command.

Added to these problems is the issue of the increasingly high costs of the "alliance." At present—with the possible exception of the GDR—all of the economies of the alliance are strapped, and are truly scraping the bottom of the barrel, as far as growth is concerned. The economic crisis severely delimits the amount that the Pact countries can conceivably spend on defense; this crunch also takes place at a time when the USSR—in accordance with its "new philosophy of foreign relations"—is demanding that the East Europeans pull their own weight. With the normal fifteen year cycles of generational replenishment, the NSWP members are unable to meet the mandated levels of new equipment purchases. They are also unable to spend on defense expenditures amounts that are mandated by Pact considerations, just as they are unable—where applicable—to assume ever greater burdens for the stationing of Soviet troops on their soil. From the Soviet perspective the inability of the NSWP member states to carry great burdens, ultimately, is viewed as a proof of their unwillingness to share equally in meeting their common defense obligations, while from the NSWP perspective, Soviet demands for increased performance are viewed as unreasonable—given the existing economic constraints. These specific problems in the selection of equitable policies, clearly diminish further Soviet desired integration activities within the Pact, and fuel specific, national developmental goals in the NSWP states.

The twin issues of projected roles and specific missions, established by the Pact High Command and set out for the Lesser Allies in a potential war, are intertwined in causing additional conflict between the NSWP and the hegemonic actor. They both contain perceptual as well as real elements. Perceptually, many NSWP decision-makers and commanders feel that the Soviets really do not trust them; this is especially noticeable among Hungarian, Czech and Polish officers. While Romanian military officers loyal to Ceausescu, who do not trust their Russian comrades the least bit, openly express concern over Soviet tasks set for them, and do not trust the Red Army, and while these very officers do recognize the validity of Soviet concerns *vis-à-vis* Romanian performance, other NSWP officers feel that they deserve greater trust than that accorded to the "dissident" Romanians, and certainly greater trust than that which is implied in the 1979 Statutes. In short, they all would prefer to have their "own front," to have "special missions." They do not wish to fight in positions that are subordinate to Red Army desiderata, sandwiched—as it were—between Red Army units. The same resentment caused by the lack of trust is also evident in regard to the air-defenses of the region that are controlled solely by the Soviet *PVO Strani* and not by native commanders, let us say, in Czechoslovakia or East Germany. To put it simply, the NSWP allies feel that equality within the alliance cannot be achieved through a continuation of the present unequal allocation of tasks and responsibilities. The NSWP member-states fear that, in a generalized conflict with the West, they will be relegated to play supporting, cannon-fodder roles. As long as the Red Army and its high command perceives these states to be simply Lesser Allies, their reliability is bound to be perceived as questionable and a cause for worry, both for the Soviet and the native politico-military elites.

The Prospects For Adaptation in Military Relationship: Concluding Thoughts

Given that Gorbachev is still in power as of this writing, given his "genuine interest" in restructuring Soviet foreign policy priorities, given that a "new philosophy" guiding foreign relations may yet emerge, the question of the impact of these changes upon Soviet-NSWP relationship still cannot be easily answered. For any such changes as those indicated above will have long-term implications in regards to: 1. alliance goal restructuring; 2. force modernization; and 3. the continuing reliability of the alliance members. In each of these areas, of course, the limits of future changes will be determined by the extent of decisive alterations in the Soviets' perception of their own national interests; while the NSWP members would be *forced* to go along with these changes, they may or may not be happy with the end results.

Clearly, the restructuring of alliance goals toward a less confrontationalist approach *vis-à-vis* NATO would be a welcome objective for the NSWP states. It would mean lower levels of readiness for at least part of their troop structure, and less extensive participation in costly joint exercises, to cite but the most obvious short-term benefits. But a "diminution" of the perceived threat from NATO, on the one hand, would also make these armies less potent weapons in the hand of a narrow elite for the defense of their own, personal rule; a heightened Cold War hysteria, on the other hand, would help to preserve the East European armies as sharp instruments which guarantee regime stability at home. Thus, while in their external relations with the USSR, the East European regimes would welcome goal restructuring and a somewhat less aggressive WTO stance, (especially regarding regional policing) not all of the present rulers would be wildly enthusiastic about the "new philosophy in foreign relations."

Similarly, in regard to force modernization, there remain some problem areas for the NSWP members. The potential conclusion of INF and START treaties between the USSR and the US, would force both alliances to pay more attention to conventional arms modernization. Conventional weapons and instruments are, however, expensive to develop, deploy, and maintain, and the increased number of men who must be removed from badly needed economic activities for the maintenance of perceived conventional "parity," would also hurt their strapped economies. Simply put, nukes are cheap, men and machines fulfilling non-nuclear functions are expensive. Therefore, the "joy" over the conclusion of a INF and the potential conclusion of a START treaty series, will be mitigated by nagging questions as to *how much more* these NSWP states will *have to pay* for force and weapons modernization, who will pay for equipment development and maintenance, or for the even more expensive troop deployment, and especially, the alternative, eventual allocation of roles for the production and sale of the new Pact arsenals. It is little wonder then, that the East European states so eagerly supported the Soviet decision in December 1988 to start to unilaterally cut some of their conventional forces and promptly followed Moscow's example. They concluded that these limited reductions should give them at least some respite, however temporary.

All the remaining problems signify further headaches for the Soviet leadership in assuaging their NSWP partners. They must convince the latter that all of the new Soviet foreign policy initiatives are in the best interests of the East European brethren, while continuing to extend "perpetual" guarantees for the survival of these elites. They must convince the present NSWP rulers that the ultimate guarantors—the armies of both the Lesser Allies and the USSR—will remain there to back them up whatever crisis may take place. Hence, all of these developments *directly compel the USSR to reiterate its "permanent" interests in Eastern Europe and continue to maintain the region as its sphere of sole influence.* Conversely, however, this becomes a "Catch-22" situation; such a declaration is likely to meet with ever greater resentment on the part of an already resentful population, and the increased resentments, in turn, will heighten the Soviet doubts in the reliability of—at least some of—their Lesser Allies. Unfortunately for the Soviets, in international politics one cannot always have one's cake and eat it too, but such is the nature of the burden of the hegemonic power. They chose to maintain the Empire in Eastern Europe, and we should not feel sorry for them for having to pay the ever-spiralling costs of their unsavory enterprise.

Notes

1. E. Primakov, "Novaia filosopfii vneshnei politiki," *Pravda*, July 10, 1987.
2. A. Bovin, "Perestroika i sud'by sotsializma," *Izvestiia*, July 11, 1987.
3. "Novaia myshlenie i perspektivy sotsial'nogo obnovleniia mira," *Voprosy Filosofii*, No. 6, 1987.
4. Bovin, "Perestroika. . . ."
5. *Ibid*.
6. *Ibid*.
7. For a broader treatment see I. Volgyes, "Between the Devil and the Deep Blue Sea: Gorbachev and Eastern Europe," *International Journal*, Winter, 1987-8, Volume XLIII, No. 1, pp. 127-41.
8. Zdenek Mlynar, *Nightfrost in Prague*, New York: Karz, 1980, p. 24.
9. Interview No. 27, June 7, 1987.
10. Ryszard J. Kuklinski, "Wojna z narodem wydzania od srodka," *Kultura*, Paris, 4/475, April 1987, pp. 3-57

7

Lands In-Between:
The Politics of Cultural Identity
in Contemporary Eastern Europe

Melvin Croan

We . . . huddle here on the western margin of the [Soviet] empire and on the eastern side of the Iron Curtain, with a cautious strategy of limited self-preservation and a troubled mind, because we don't want to identify with the East and we can't identify with the West.

—Gyorgy Konrad, Antipolitics

With no precise borders with no center or rather with several centers, "Central Europe" looks today more and more like the dragon of Alca in the second book of Anatole France's Penguin Island *to which the Symbolist movement was compared: nobody who claimed to have seen it could say what it looked like.*

—Danilo Kis, "Variations on the Theme of Central Europe"

Today's Eastern Europe came into existence as a distinct geopolitical entity only after World War II. Many observers—critical East European commentators foremost among them—chalk it all up to Yalta. However one may feel about code words, the 1945 Yalta agreements surely did foster the establishment of a novel "supranational space," comprising a conglomeration of peoples and cultures knowing little and caring less about one other. The ensuing disarray, in turn, greatly facilitated the region's Sovietization which the West, for its part, effectively failed to counter.[1]

Now, more than four decades after Yalta, Eastern Europe can look back to a bewildering sequence of crises and adjustments. From Stalinization with all its horrendous consequences, through the fitful bouts of de-Stalinization of the Khrushchev era, to the elaborate efforts of the Brezhnev period and beyond to consolidate Communist rule domestically and push regional integration with the Soviet Union, the area's fate has appeared at once sealed and yet also open to the possibility of renewed challenge.[2] What Gorbachev's innovative dispensations may augur for Soviet-East European relations and for individual regimes remains to be seen.[3] It is quite certain, however, that more than perhaps ever before, crucial facets of cultural identity will help shape political issues and outcomes. The discussion that follows will, therefore, analyze the politics of cultural identity in present-day Eastern Europe, with special emphasis on the idea of Central Europe which has recently come to be much touted in the West as a "new political identity."[4]

Cultural Identity

Although it constitutes a crucial strand of that knotty complex of considerations denominated as "political culture," there need be nothing particularly elusive about the concept of cultural identity. One's identity is typically defined by the group or groups to which one belongs or aspires to belong.[5] In highly politicized systems, like those of Communist-ruled Eastern Europe, cultural identity and political identity are closely linked: indeed, the two terms often seem to be virtually synonymous. In each of these systems, however, there may be more than one politically relevant cultural identity. This is true of the ruling elite as well as for society as a whole. Basic identities at the societal and the elite levels are, of course, rarely coterminous and frequently appear to be mutually exclusive. Yet, the two sets of very different identities can and do interact with one another.[6] Finally, if identity determines policy at least to the extent of delimiting the range of available alternatives, changes of policy direction, sustained over time, may well contribute to the formation of novel identities. One salient example may serve to illustrate the point: As the result of its web of vested interests in East-West detente in general and in relations with West Germany in particular, East Germany's Communist ruling elite has added a distinctive German as well as a regional mid-European identity to augment and in some ways modify its ingrained orthodox Marxist-Leninist regime community identity.[7]

As concerns cultural identity throughout Eastern Europe as a whole, it seems reasonable to conclude that, *pace* various Czechoslovak emigre intellectuals who despair about the ultimate fate of their homeland, Sovietization has failed just about everywhere.[8] Genuinely felt cultural self-expression *a la sovietique* was always restricted to a small, albeit once seemingly almighty, elite group. Authentic cultural Sovietization was thus destined to decline and doomed to virtual extinction with the demise of that earlier generation of Stalinist functionaries whose very identity had indeed been predicated upon willing obeisance to the Kremlin. "One of the great achievements of Soviet rule in Eastern Europe," a knowledgeable western analyst aptly notes, "has been to make citizens of the region feel more *Western* than they ever did."[9] The forced draft Russification of culture that accompanied the Soviet-style revolution from above imposed upon the satellites in Stalin's time remains little more than a distant bitter memory. Manifestations of Russian culture do exist, of course, but they are scarcely determinative anywhere, including in Bulgaria where the persistence of traditional orientations toward Moscow tends to set that country apart from most of its neighbors in Southeast Europe, not to mention countries further afield. For all the rest, even during the heyday of Brezhnev's comprehensive program for the integration of the "socialist community in Europe" with the USSR, the development of ideological and cultural ties lagged markedly behind the fabrication of other integrative mechanisms.[10]

How, then, do things stand today with respect to cultural identity in Eastern Europe at the elite level? While the situation varies from country to country, several general characteristics are worthy of note. In the first instance, Communist political elites—much like rulers everywhere, only more so—are nothing if not power-conscious. This much they owe to their Leninist upbringing which also predisposes them to cling to the remnants of the ideological justification for their exercise of power. This, in turn, inclines Communist rulers to continue to identify themselves in terms that remain largely at odds with the aspirations and values associated with traditional nationalism. At the same time, the evisceration of "proletarian" (more recently, "socialist") "internationalism," impels those who are constrained to continue to espouse the old formulas to seek recompense elsewhere for the emotional aridity and practical inadequacy of their erstwhile credo. Recourse to renewed expressions of national identity has come increasingly to fill the bill. In addition to its value as a compensatory mechanism, elite identity in terms of the nation that it governs is a distinct asset as a device with which to endeavor both to enlarge leeway abroad and enhance legitimacy at home. But such national identification also poses a basic question, viz., is the political elite willing or able to countenance a diminution of its heretofore sacrosanct "leading role" to the extent of accepting society's views of *its* politico-cultural identity?

As is the case with the various ruling elites, so too do East European societies differ among themselves in terms of the identities they have spawned. To a greater or lesser degree, however, all countries' societies harbor both sub- and countercultures. The latter, a transnational phenomenon originating in the West, has taken root among disillusioned and disoriented youth. Utterly anathema to the ruling elite, this amorphous and essentially antisocial counterculture finds no favor beyond its own generational borders which nowhere encompass anything like youth as a whole.[11] Many young people seek their cultural identity in nationalism or in religion or else in both. In this they are similar to their elders, differing perhaps only in the intensity of their commitment. Concurrently, the younger generation has proved far more receptive to cultural influences emanating from the United States, thereby contributing to the entrenchment of an Americanized popular subculture throughout the entire region. All this must be borne in mind in assessing the major alternative cultural identity unfolded by the most articulate segment of society, the critical intelligentsia.[12] Its most articulate spokesmen now contemplate a regional identity that transcends national limitations, rejects transnational nihilism, and eschews the dominance of peripheral superpowers. Their ideal is

Eurocentric with its epicenter at the heart of the old continent in precincts newly redesignated "Central Europe."

The New *Mitteleuropa*

The old-new concept of Central Europe abounds in ambiguities and is beset by contradictions. On the one hand, it conjures up shades of German imperialism; on the other, it prompts remembrance of the repudiation of all reactionary imperial systems. The German expression, *Mitteleuropa*, gained currency during the First World War, thanks to the exertions of various patriotic publicists, Friedrich Naumann the best remembered of them. The notion of *Mitteleuropa*, as expounded by Naumann and others, provided a rationale for Imperial Germany's expansionist schemes: subsequently it also served Nazi Germany's aggressive designs.[13] As against this unwholesome pedigree, a quite different vision of a "New Europe" (focused on Central Europe or, rather, as he preferred to call it, East-Central Europe) was advanced by Thomas G. Masaryk. The concerns of the scholarly President-Liberator of Czechoslovakia centered on the lands between the Germans and the Russians, an area whose peoples had been subjected to alien rule and deprived of any opportunity for their own free development. This sorry state of affairs owed less, Masaryk felt, to ethnic conflict than it did the political and cultural oppressiveness that he believed to be built into the very structure of outmoded monarchical despotism. His prescription for a new Central Europe called for political democracy and national independence.[14]

It is tempting to see in Masaryk's reflections something of a prefiguration of the views of Central Europe developed many decades later by some of the leading dissidents of Communist Eastern Europe. In fact, their preoccupation with the internal foundations of international independence may owe something, if only indirectly, to Masaryk's linkage between the domestic and external realms of political expression and action. Much more tenuous is the relationship between German speaking exponents of the notion of *Mitteleuropa* today and their forebears before 1945.[15] The really important point, however, is not to confuse the ideal of Central Europe championed by East European dissidents with any version of *Mitteleuropa*, past or present. The two expressions reflect two very different sets of special interests. In its latter day usage, *Mitteleuropa* can stand for anything from the nationalist-neutralism of the Left in West Germany to the politico-strategic concerns of the Honecker regime in East Germany; it also includes long dominant Austrian aspirations to regain that country's previous regional influence.[16] East Europe's critical intellectuals, by contrast, are not particularly interested in Austro-German perspectives; they display little real understanding of the practical politics of the "German problem," are roundly critical of the peace movement in the west,[17] and can scarcely be expected to invest all that much emotional capital in the prospect of basking in the renewed radiance of Vienna's cultural splendor. Rather, their passion for

Central Europe is animated by the desire to break loose of the fetters which have bound *Eastern Europe* ever since Yalta (as most of them would date things).

Beyond this powerful common motivation, those critical spirits who espouse a Central European identity differ among themselves on a whole range of quite basic issues, including such crucial matters as the precise delineation (territorial or other) of their novel allegiance, the definition of its essential contents, its origins, and strategies best tailored to guarantee that it has a future. Merely to offer a random (and necessarily incomplete) listing of those who in one way or another have embraced the idea of Central Europe, or at least flirted with it, is already to suggest how diverse are the many approaches to this elusive paramour. Consider only the following names, here presented in no particular order: Milan Kundera, Gyorgy Konrad, Vaclav Havel, Adam Michnik (whose Central European agenda is kept well hidden), Czeslaw Milosz, Miklos Haraszti, Danilo Kis, Gyorgy Oalos, Jiri Oienstbier, the editors and writers for the underground Prague journal, *Stredni Evropa* (i.e., *Central Europe*). . . . Czechs, Hungarians, and Poles (if only the tiniest handful), to which there might be added a sprinkling of East Germans, some Yugoslavs (especially Slovenes and Croats), and possibly even one or two Romanians (one thinks willy-nilly of Paul Goma, for example). All of them, whether living abroad or still in residence in their native countries, are exiles, in the most profound sense.[18] Some of them are of mixed ethnicity, many of Jewish background but they are all Jews functionally, i.e.. "aliens everywhere and everywhere at home, lifted above national quarrels" and therefore "the principal cosmopolitan, integrating element in Central Europe."[19] By much the same token, however, none of them is anything like fully representative of his own nation. Small wonder that there is no general agreement about Central European identity even among its most avid protagonists.

Cultural-Political Perspectives

In the absence of a single, coherent, integrated body of thought about Central Europe, one can only hope to identify recurrent themes and analyze salient characteristics. As concerns the politics of cultural identity, now and for the future, three facets are particularly pertinent. They are: the implicit elitism that attends most thinking about Central Europe, its cultural pessimism, and the emphasis it accords to what might be termed metapolitics.

Elitism

The *elitism* of all major protagonists of the ideal of Central Europe becomes immediately apparent as soon as one subjects their fundamental premises to critical scrutiny.[20] In the first instance, most consider regional identity to be morally superior to national parochialism, not to mention, to any supranational allegiance based on the big power blocs bequeathed by Yalta and cemented in the course of the ensuing Cold War. Since, however, the horizons of popular identity throughout Eastern Europe tend to be restricted to those of one's own nation, and no vision of Central Europe can claim to have enlisted anything even vaguely approximating mass support, it follows that those few critical spirits who have been able to perceive the promise in all its majesty must be singularly endowed. But since Central Europe disposes of an ambivalent historical legacy of questionable overall moral value, it falls to those who champion it today to sift and winnow so as to recover and cultivate all that is positive in Central Europe's many different traditions. This mandate presupposes talent and finesse, such that those who are able to discharge it successfully constitute unto themselves, if not necessarily for others, veritable paragons of the region's virtues, intellectual and spiritual.[21]

In all of this, Eastern Europe's independent minds are recreating, albeit in a wider geographic context, the traditional role of the area's intelligentsia as the conscience of the nation, its moral preceptor, and its tutor in one absolutely crucial subject: preservation of the national culture. Traditionally, for the intelligentsia this also entailed an ascriptive claim to the august status of guardian of the nation's destiny. Small wonder that so potent an historical legacy should posit certain political presumptions. In the post-World War II period, this factor has come repeatedly into play, prompting the active involvement of intellectuals in all the major crisis of Communist rule in Eastern Europe from Hungary in 1956 through Czechoslovakia in 1968 to Poland from the 1970s to the present. To acknowledge this is not, of course, to agree with the grotesque charges levelled by various Communist ruling elites to the effect that, for example, during the Prague Spring the intelligentsia organized itself into a "vanguard of counterrevolution," sought to defy Marxist dialectics by substituting itself as a class for the proletariat, and aimed at arrogating unto itself the Party's "leading role" over society.[22] Neither ought we subscribe to the interpretation, advanced by at least one well known Western political scientist, holding that Communist regimes are well advised to neutralize their intellectual critics by mobilizing against them all the anti-intellectual reflexes they may conjure up throughout society as a whole.[23] At issue, however, is a somewhat different and rather more important point: Almost all the rumination, emanating from Eastern Europe about Central Europe is tinged with elitism—mostly only implicit, but occasionally rendered quite explicit as, to cite one striking example, in Gyorgy Konrad's notion of an "international intellectual aristocracy." As Konrad depicts it, this formation, the natural outgrowth of the intelligentsia's "rich historical tradition," is novel in its "really catholic universalism—one that holds all particularism in check"—and can lay claim to a powerful "cultural and moral stature" which alone and entirely without "any electoral legitimacy" provides it with an overriding "right" to keep watch on the political process and exert pressure to direct it into desirable channels.[24]

To be sure, far from all East European intellectuals would insist that their confreres' record has always been completely admirable. Some criticize their forebears for having fuelled ethnic animosities or at least fed nationalist egotism.[25] One, Vaclav Havel, faults his intellectual colleagues of the post-World War II period for their tendency too easily to "lapse into utopianism."[26] Nonetheless, the common refrain would seem to be "if not us intellectuals, then who?" And, they would continue, if there is blame to be assigned for the general state of affairs throughout Eastern Europe today, it surely is not deserved by the intellectuals but rather should be placed entirely on the Communist system itself. What the system has wrought, in turn, both necessitates and justifies a special mission for the critical intelligentsia, or so its members believe.

"A little open [intellectual] aristocratism is necessary," Konrad stipulates with accustomed irony, "lest the great democrats run off with democracy."[27] The reasons behind this aphorism have been aptly recorded by the much persecuted Czechoslovak dissident, Milan Simecka. As he bitterly notes, the order euphemistically known as "real existing socialism" is not only oppressive and corrupt but, worst of all, utterly mindless. Its "politics" are "tedious, boring, inaccessible, and [an] anonymous annoyance coming from somewhere on high."[28] It deliberately transforms otherwise decent people into venal consumers who gladly turn their backs on public affairs, regarding "no political ideal [as] . . . tempting enough . . . to jeopardize one's full enjoyment of the benefits of consumerism. . . ."[29] So, if the system, as Kundera has asserted, "deprives people of memory and thus retools them into a nation of children," doesn't the resultant "relentlessly juvenile society" cry out for instruction and guidance from mature, genuinely virtuous adults?[30] And what more appropriate grown-ups than the independently minded critical intellectuals?

Cultural pessimism

Such, then, is the compound of factors that goes into the intelligentsia's elitism. Many of the very same ingredients also make for its cultural *pessimism*. Much as they may prefer the myth of a Central Europe endowed with a whole range of quite special virtues, few of the region's intellectuals are oblivious to the darker aspects of its modern history. Perhaps that is precisely why they so readily warm to Central Europe as what Konrad terms "a cultural counter-hypothesis."[31] It may also, as Konrad further suggests, indeed convey "the allure of nostalgia and utopia."[32] If so, that scarcely suffices to generate optimism about the present and foreseeable future. On the contrary, it may rather nurture sentiments more nearly akin to morbidity.

The most ominous forebodings are a particularly striking characteristic of the Central Europe thinking of Milan Kundera. Even before the appearance of his widely known essay, "The Tragedy of Central Europe," Kundera had spoken of the mortality of nations as well as human beings and gone on to caution that "the end of Central Europe" heralded "the beginning of the end for Europe as a whole."[33] For him, Russia as a civilization "anchored in the Byzantine world" was even more to blame than the Communist system that Soviet power had imposed on vast tracts of what had long been western civilization.[34]

Although one may well be tempted to attribute such pessimism to the kind of fatalism that has become particularly prevalent among Czechs, it would be mistaken to do so. Consider Kundera's deeply anti-Russian sentiments, extending to his expressed distaste for such major figures of Russian (and indeed universal) culture as Dostoyevsky. It is a safe bet that Kundera's antipathy toward things Russian, though rarely expressed in terms as sweeping or outspoken as those he employs, is widely shared by most East European intellectuals. It certainly affects many Polish critical thinkers, among whom any inclination toward the notion of a Central European culture identity is conspicuous by its very absence. On the other hand, most Polish intellectuals are not nearly as pessimistic as their counterparts elsewhere in the Soviet orbit. In fact, the Pole most known for his endorsement of a Central European culture, Czeslaw Milosz (long resident in the West) waxes more optimistic than almost anyone else when he addresses such themes.[35] Could it be that the Polish intelligentsia has been the least ready to rally to the banner of Central Europe not simply because to many of its members that may smack of a *Mitteleuropa*, past or present, that they cannot stomach, but also because they fear far less for the survival of their national culture than others elsewhere is Eastern Europe? The reasons for the Poles' sense of confidence are many and fairly obvious: emphasis here need only be accorded to the apparent correlation between politico-cultural despair and the quest for a different, seemingly more promising cultural identity.

Metapolitics

This apparent correlation, in turn, points toward the third and most elusive facet of recent thinking about a Central European cultural identity, viz., its *metapolitical character*. The late Kwame Nkrumah's precept, "Seek ye first the political kingdom," would be totally out of place in these precincts. Rather, the message appears to be the very opposite, "To hell with all politics!" as in the "anti-politics" of Konrad's title. True to that summons, Konrad himself totally rejects what he calls the "Jacobin-Leninist tradition" which he regards as absolutely repugnant to all Central European cultural aspirations.[36] He also alleges that "the intellectual aristocracy has no desire to bring down governments, since its members don't want to be government leaders."[37] About all to which intellectuals should aspire is to influence policy so as to "push the state" in more rational (i.e., intelligent) and humane directions.[38] But even this may be less important than other objectives such as self-government within the intellectual community itself and, should this prove impossible, among loosely knit networks of like-minded friends.[39]

Beyond that, however, there remains for Konrad only the pursuit of "the article in shortest supply"[40]—Truth. A small matter or a tall order? There can be no doubt about which if one considers that, unlike any other commodity, truth alone can redeem individuals from the multitude of sins they have been compelled to commit by the political system and thereby restore some semblance of a moral life to society as a whole.

Judging by Konrad and his ilk, one may be forgiven for concluding that all the contemplation about a Central European cultural identity really amounts to a kind of transcendental *Heilslehre* (i.e, teaching designed to lead to salvation) of scant relevance to anything approximating real politics. Nonetheless, designations such as "anti-politics" are completely off the mark. A term like "metapolitics" is more nearly evocative of what is at stake. Every thinking East European is only too well aware that there is no real escape from politics even in the "autonomous sphere of culture" or in the "kingdom of the spirit."[41] Propagating "antipolitics" is itself a political tactic, contrived to disarm the wielders of power through the ever so slightly disingenuous assurance that their intellectual critics do not seek their jobs. Of course, thinkers may not desire to become ministers. After all, what is a share of power compared to possession of Truth? And yet, are the two dichotomous, especially in the East European context? One suspects that they are not or rather that the intellectuals would like nothing better than to forge a linkage between truth and power. Some, like Konrad, may choose to dissemble. Others, like Vaclav Havel, elect to speak out quite openly. Under what he chooses to label "the posttotalitarian system," Havel forcefully insists, "truth, in the widest sense of the word, has a very special import, one unknown in other contexts."[42] He is not in the slightest reluctant to emphasize the crucial point:

> . . . living within the truth is more than a mere existential dimension (returning man to his inherent nature), or a noetic dimension (revealing reality as it is), or a moral dimension (setting an example for others). It also has an unambiguous *political* dimension.[43]

Practical Applications and Europeanization

Here, then, is a modern secular expression under contemporary East European conditions of the scriptural injunction, "Ye shall know the truth and the truth shall make you free." Or, better yet, here is a restatement of the commandment of an earlier Central European martyr, Jan Hus, who ordained, "Seek the truth, listen to the truth, teach the truth, love the truth, abide by the truth, and defend the truth, unto death." Freedom and death—yet, apart from these polarities, worthy of the rhetorical reach of a Patrick Henry, are there no other outcomes that are likely or at least possible? How, in other words, to assess the practical import of the rediscovery of Central Europe, and what contributions to systemic change in Eastern Europe can be expected from the cultural identity?

Of the foregoing queries, the issue of the practical importance of all the recent contemplation about Central Europe is at once the easiest and the most difficult to address. In the first instance, one might take the pertinent thinkers at their own word and treat Central Europe as a "counter-hypothesis," a cultural aspiration rather than an historical reality or a political possibility. Maybe the whole thing is at bottom merely a figment of a fecund imagination, but otherwise next to worthless for any practical purpose. Yet even were the notion of Central Europe to be so dismissed, something more would still have to be added to take account of its quite considerable psychological appeal. In fact, confused though they may appear to those who do not share them, vistas of *Central* Europe have offered hope where otherwise there might have been only despair in *Eastern* Europe. As the Hungarian dissident, Miklos Haraszti, has been quoted as putting it, "the vision behind the notion of [Central Europe] is that Communist rule is temporary," and he further insisted that such aspirations constitute "a powerful force that should not be ignored."[44]

Visions of Central Europe are far from going totally ignored on the part of East Europe's ruling Communist establishments. Noteworthy have been such backhanded compliments as the denunciation of "the myth of *Mitteleuropa*" by the Polish party paper, *Tribuna Ludu*, comparable polemics by Czechoslovak authorities, and, interestingly enough, criticisms by various Yugoslav commentators, more particularly from Serbs.[45] Nor have regional aspirations gone unnoticed in western Communist circles. The Italian Communist Party (PCI), for one, has treated the dissidents' search for a Central European identity as a positive development. The PCI's leading specialist on Eastern Europe, Adriano Guerra, has written of these countries' "crisis of identity," catalyzed by intellectuals who through thick and thin had always continued to regard themselves as "Europeans of the East." He has urged Soviet policy makers to recognize and accommodate "the idea of Europe" that has taken root in the Soviet Union's erstwhile satellites.[46]

Beyond its demonstrated ability to elicit Communist commentary, favorable in the West, critical in the East, the proclivity to the idea of Central Europe (in this instance, *Mitteleuropa* would seem the more appropriate term) has sired a regional intergovernmental organization, founded in 1987 and known as Alpe-Adria. This novel configuration includes one West German *Land*, Bavaria, five Austrian provinces, the two most westerly districts of Hungary, the Yugoslav republics of Slovenia and Croatia, and four northerly and northeasterly Italian districts. (Shades of a rump Habsburg realm?) Any body consisting of such politically diverse parts might be expected to proceed slowly and with great caution and so indeed has this one, limiting its activities to such non-controversial matters as the coordination of measures against pollution, the promotion of culture, tourism, sports, and the like. Unspectacular though these doings may seem, Alpe-Adria is proving to be a significant symbol in its own right, exemplifying the practical power of the idea of a Central European identity.[47]

For East European champions of Central Europe, every practical step, however small, is a step in the right direction—away from the "provincialism of national culture" toward the goal of an eventual "global culture."[48] This cultural internationalism should not be discounted as merely so much empty rhetoric. On the contrary, over the last several years, the democratic opposition in Eastern Europe has joined forces across national lines to commemorate the thirtieth anniversary of the 1956 Hungarian uprising (1986), protest against violations of the Helsinki accords (1987), foster ties between Poland's Solidarity and Czechoslovakia's Charter 77 (1987), and most recently to demonstrate jointly against repression in Romania and petition on behalf of human rights in East Germany. All told, the extent of transnational coordination among the various opposition groups spawned by the critical intelligentsia has been little short of remarkable. The success of this effort constitutes a quite practical manifestation of the sentiments of regional identity expressed so poignantly by Konrad:

> . . . we have said before that "we Czechs are not Hungarians," "we Poles are not Czechs," . . . "we Hungarians are not Poles." There wasn't much point in that. We are Hungarians and Poles and Czechs and—the list could go on. The strivings of every people of our area for freedom are ours.[49]

These are without any doubt entirely noble sentiments and ones that are now being acted upon. Still, when one asks: toward what larger end and with what prospects of success, one has immediately to acknowledge a number of omissions that render the vision something less than a full fledged action program. Foremost among these shortcomings is an apparent inability or unwillingness to recognize and come to grips with the rampant materialism that has come to shape popular attitudes and mass culture throughout Eastern Europe. They also include failure to undertake a serious analysis of international politics, whether at the level of the strategic relationship between the superpowers or with a regional focus on the seemingly intractable German problem or in the all-important area of international political economy with its many crucial implications for "Central Europe," as well as for individual East European debtor-states.[50]

For seers to become doers requires a willingness to tackle economics and international politics, each of which may well seem to be a dismal science. For seer-doers to entertain any expectation of practical progress toward their ideal would seem also to call for much closer and much more serious consideration than heretofore of the colossus to the East—Russia. Critical intellectuals may get some gratification from intertwining their specific cultural disdain for Russia with the general popular animus against the Soviet Union as a political system. But as the regional hegemonial power whose massive influence may have to be reckoned with for a long time to come, Soviet Russia merits an approach that combines searching analysis with a generosity of spirit, a combination that would do credit to the much vaunted agility of the Central European mind.

Actually, not all champions of the ideal of Central Europe go to the extreme anti-Russian lengths of say, a Milan Kundera. For Kundera, Russian cultural influence together with Soviet political control have proved so deadening that he is not willing to countenance anything less than their complete elimination from Europe. As he sees it, the further westward the Russians advance, the more they retreat "culturally toward their own

Byzantine past."[51] Since he is not particularly optimistic about a political withdrawal by the Russians, he is forced to fall back to a strategy of cultural self-defense. In the end, Kundera's "supranational Europe" can only be conceived spiritually rather than spatially, "not as a territory but as a culture."[52]

The eastern horizons of others are much more open. This is true even of Polish writers and thinkers. Milosz would willingly make room in his Central Europe for Russian culture—just as soon as "Russian art and literature again recover their spontaneity."[53] Adam Michnik, for his part, believes that the idea of Central Europe ought to be anti- anti-Russian, i.e., in every respect "an anti-xenophobic idea."[54] Still, the general attitude toward Russia that prevails among the intellectual partisans of Central Europe is condescending at best. In this respect, Konrad may be most representative. His Central European perspectives are geographically broad and sufficiently flexible to accommodate the Soviet Union as far as Vladivostok; in fact, he relishes the thought of a Eurasian construct, with its foundations in Central Europe, of course.[55] He treats Soviet-East European relations in zero-sum terms, leaving no doubt about who would win out over whom, given the right kind of contest. "I know of no way for Eastern Europe to free itself from Russian military occupation," Konrad writes, "except for us to occupy them with our ideas. Think about it: in a free exchange of ideas, who would colonize whom?"[56]

While the Europeanization of Russia is surely an eminently desirable goal, it is one of truly historical proportions and an altogether complex task calling for patience, tact, and finesse rather than presumption and cultural arrogance. The latter risks provoking a powerful backlash in the form of Great Russian chauvinism and/or neo-Panslavism, both of which would augur ill for the future of Soviet–East European relations, to leave aside entirely the realization of any idea of Central Europe. Culturally based superciliousness seems particularly inappropriate at a time when, thanks to his advocacy of *glasnost* and *perestroika*, Gorbachev has gained unexpected popularity in Eastern Europe, ranging from sober-minded proponents of domestic reforms all the way to devotees of the rock counter-culture. In a sense. the Gorbachev leadership may have stolen the march on all the many East European intellectuals who have been ready to turn their backs on the East in order to face squarely West. For the moment, it seems to be an astonishing case of *ex oriente lux*. Whereas only a short while ago it was the idea of central Europe that seemed to offer the West hope of eventually throwing off the yoke of Communist rule, today it is the prospect of restructuring affairs on the spot at home that generates a guarded optimism. In the words of one Czechoslovak oppositional activist, "if real reforms are implemented, it won't be communism any more."[57]

Is systemic change in Eastern Europe really in the cards? And by systemic change does one mean change of the system or rather in-system changes? And, if the latter, what is to keep such changes from culminating in a fundamental transformation of the entire system itself? These are, of course, the crucial issues and they beg, in turn, the question of the role of the politics of cultural identity in a number of different possible scenarios.

To begin with, it is the safest of bets to assume that, all of his novel dispensations notwithstanding, Gorbachev did not become CPSU General Secretary in order to preside over the liquidation of the Soviet empire. It is highly improbable that the Kremlin under his leadership would countenance, much less push perestroika in Eastern Europe to the point where Moscow's clients restructured themselves right out of the Soviet orbit and rejoined Europe. A host of traditional Russian geopolitical reflexes militate against this, as do vital Soviet strategic considerations that continue to put great store in holding onto Eastern Europe physically. By much the same token, it seems highly unlikely that the Soviet Union would wish to cut a superpower deal by, for example, renegotiating Yalta so as to Finlandize Eastern Europe. Were something like this ever to occur, it might well give major impetus to the realization of a host of Central European projects; on the other hand, by simply occurring, it might serve to render the ideal of Central Europe superfluous; wholly new identities might easily come into play.

Apart from one or another form of superpower diplomatic settlement for Eastern Europe, it is always possible (some might say likely) that indigenous developments within the region could get out of hand resulting in even greater turmoil and even more serious upheavals than this crisis-ridden area has experienced before. In that eventuality, any concomitant paralysis and/or breakdown in Moscow could lead to something like the vision (or was it a nightmare?) presented by Andrei Amalrik with "the de-Sovietized countries of Eastern Europe . . . dash around like horses without their bridles."[58] Under these conditions, nostalgia for Central Europe might rapidly give way to a pan-European identity, even though the banner to which the Soviet Union's ex-client states would now rally would doubtless be that of a Europe *des patries* (or perhaps more trenchantly formulated as: *des chevaux nationalistes*). In the more probable event that unrest in Eastern Europe brought about a Soviet crackdown, identification with Central Europe, with Europe as a whole, or with "the West" more generally would become more widespread and grow in intensity—only this time as a *cri de coeur*, only too expressive of what would amount to the renewed subjection of the East European peoples and the utter impotence of their self-appointed intellectual mentors.

Conclusion

While dramatic changes ought never to be ruled out entirely, the prudent forecaster is well advised to focus on the likelihood of a protracted but inconclusive period of alternating cycles of reform and retrenchment, relaxation and reimposition of controls, with the basic pattern varying only in details in accordance with specific circumstances from one country to the next. This is what one astute Western journalist has described as "the regress of a would-be totalitarianism" and labelled "the Ottomanization rather than the Finlandization of the Soviet empire."[59]

Reasoning by historical analogy is always treacherous. In this instance, one must beware of the enticement of treating Eastern Europe as if it were or else could become a kind of socialist millet system: one is also well advised against succumbing to the temptation of dismissing the Soviet Union as "the sick man" of Europe, if not of the planet. On the other hand, East Central Europe together with Southeast Europe (however we may wish to define each in terms of territory and/or culture) does constitute something of a contemporaneous "sick heart of Europe."[60] Much of the sickness grows out of the continued political dependency of proud peoples who have long been deprived of the opportunity for free national expression. It is precisely "this lack of independent national development," a Hungarian scholar reminds us, that has "created a special role for cultural identity because the national culture, the native language, and the native histories of this region became the integrating force."[61] That being the case, the politics of cultural identity bids fair to constitute the epicenter of political life throughout Eastern Europe. And whether or not the idea of Central Europe has any real future, its contemporary exponents have already bequeathed it a rich legacy, destined to provoke renewed intellectual controversy and certain to be subject to repeated partisan challenge but, for all of that, a bequest of no small moral worth.

Notes

1. For a poignant discussion, see Ferenc Feher, "Eastern Europe's Long Revolution Against Yalta," *Eastern European Politics and Societies*, Vol. 2. No. 1, Winter 1988, pp. 1-34. The felicitous phrase, "supranational space," is Feher's, see p. 21. On the background and role of Eastern Europe as a regional "actor," see Vernon V. Aspaturian, "Eastern Europe in World Perspective," in Teresa Rakowska-Harmstone, ed., *Communism in Eastern Europe*, Bloomington: Indiana University Press, 1984. Cf. also Janos Kis, "Das Jalta-Dilemma in der achtziger Jahren," *Kursbuch*, 81, September 1985, pp. 153-164.

2. For one view of a strategy by the domestic democratic opposition that might overturn the Yalta "settlement" and result in a kind of "self-Finlandization," see Feher, *loc. cit.*, pp. 30-34.

3. Apart from the implications of Gorbachev's advocacy of *glasnost* and *perestroika* for various East European countries, there is also the greatly reduced claim on behalf of the Soviet Union as a normative "model" of development and an international "center" of command, including an apparent deemphasis if not quite renunciation of the Brezhnev Doctrine. For a recent analysis of these developments, see Vladimir V. Kusin, "The 'Yugoslavization' of Soviet-East European Relations?" Radio Free Europe, RAD Background Report, No. 57, March 29, 1988. Cf. Eric Bourne, "May East-bloc States Now Chart Their Own Socialist Paths?" *Christian Science Monitor*, April 18, 1988.

4. See, for example, George Schopflin's "Central Europe: A New Political Identity," a presentation to the East European Program of the Wilson Center, Washington.

D.C., May 1987, The Wilson Center, East European Program, *Meeting Report*, No. 21. Cf. Andrew Nagorski, "The Rebirth of an Idea." *Newsweek*, March 30, 1987, and Elizabeth Pond, "Pursuing the Ideal of a Central Europe," *Christian Science Monitor*, March 6, 1987. For a brilliant analysis, full of insights, see Timothy Garton Ash, "Does Central Europe Exist?" *New York Review of Books*, Vol. XXXIII, No. 15, October 9, 1986, pp. 45-52.

5. Cf. Kenneth Jowitt's observations in Sylvia Sinanian, Istvan Deak, and Peter C. Ludz, eds., *Eastern Europe in the 1970s* New York: Praeger, 1972, pp. 180-184.

6. In discussing the distinction between the "second" or "underground" culture and the "first" or "official" culture in Eastern Europe, Gordon Skilling notes that "the line between the two cultures and the two forms of communication is not always sharp and distinct." Skilling cites a leading exponent of the "parallel culture" in Czechoslovakia, Vaclav Havel, to the effect that "the once well defined and impenetrable dividing line between the two cultures appears to be growing fuzzy. . . ." H. Gordon Skilling, "Independent Communications in Communist East Europe." *Cross Currents*, 5, 1986, pp. 53-75, esp. pp. 69-70.

7. The single best general treatment of this development may be found in A. James McAdams, *East Germany and Detente* Cambridge: Cambridge University Press, 1985. For a discussion of the relationship between East Germany's ideological orthodoxy and inter-German detente, see Melvin Croan, "The Politics of Division and Detente in East Germany," *Current History*, Vol. 84, No. 505, November 1985, pp. 369-390.

8. For the contrary view that, as a result of the destruction of indigenous culture and intellectual life, "the Sovietization of contemporary Central and South East Europe has put down deeper roots than commonly supposed," see Michal Reiman, "Die 'Sowjetisierung' Mittel- und Sudosteuropa," *Kursbuch*, 81, September 1985, pp. 137-151, p. 149. Cf. the lugubrious, deeply anti-Russian ruminations of Milan Kundera to which reference will be made in our subsequent discussion.

9. J. F. Brown, *Eastern Europe and Communist Rule*, Durham and London: Duke University Press, 1988, p. 400. Italics added.

10. James F. Brown, "Relations Between the Soviet Union and Its East European Allies: A Survey," *RAND Report R-1742-PR*, 1975, passim.

11. For a discussion of "the situation among youth," see Brown, *Eastern Europe*, pp. 399-403.

12. The term "critical intelligentsia," as used here, is synonymous with "dissidents" and "independent thinkers." Some of the people in question (and some of their sympathizers in the West) prefer the designation "independent" (thinkers, actors, etc.) and object to the notion of "dissidence" as already tainted by that from which it dissents. For an example of these sensibilities, see H. Gordon Skilling, *loc. cit.*, (note 6) and his "Independent Currents in Czechoslovakia," *Problems of Communism*, Vol. XXXIV, No. 1, January-February 1985, pp. 32-49. Cf. Milan Kundera's avowal of his "allergic" reaction to "today's political terminology" (i.e., the term "dissident") and his refusal to "make use of it." "Milan Kundera's Interview," *Cross Currents*, 1, 1982, p. 15.

13. A detailed treatment of these issues may be found in Henry Cord Meyer, *Mitteleuropa in German Thought and Action*, The Hague: Martinus Nijhoff, 1955.

14. For a good discussion of Masaryk's conceptions with bibliographical references to the pertinent primary sources, see Roman Szporluk, "Defining 'Central Europe': Power, Politics, and Culture," *Cross Currents*, 1, 1982, pp. 30-37.

15. Cf. Garton Ash, loc. cit., p. 51.

16. Of course, the influence of Austria on Communist Eastern Europe is already a factor and has been for at least two decades. For a brief discussion, see Brown, *Eastern Europe and Communist Rule*, pp. 69-72 ("The Attraction of Austria").

17. On both points, see the apt observations of Garton Ash, loc. cit., p. 52. For a vivid sense of the distaste, not to say disgust, of East European dissidents for western "peaceniks" together with a trenchant critique of the Western peace movement's egocentrism, see Vaclav Havel, "Anatomy of Reticence," *Cross Currents*, 6, 1986, pp. 1-23.

18. For his part, Milan Kundera would deny this. In answer to the question of whether he felt "like an emigre, a Frenchman, a Czech, or just a European without specific nationality," he replied, "my stay in France is final, and, therefore, I am not an emigre. (!) France is my only real homeland now. Nor do I feel uprooted. For a thousand years, Czechoslovakia was part of the West. Today, it is part of the empire to the east. I would feel a great deal more uprooted in Prague than in Paris." Olga Carlisle, "A Talk with Milan Kundera," *New York Times Magazine*, May 19, 1987, p. 74. But what does Kundera's answer manifest if not that sense of irony so often deemed to be a major element in the Central European character!

19. The quote is Milan Kundera's and refers to the Jews themselves whom Kundera describes as Central Europe's "intellectual cement, a condensed version of its spirit, creators of its spiritual unity." He adds, "that's why I love the Jewish heritage and cling to it with as much passion and nostalgia as if it were my own." Milan Kundera, "The Tragedy of Central Europe," *New York Review of Books*, Vol. XXXI, No. 7, April 26, 1984, p. 36.

20. This is not the place to enter into a lengthy discussion of elitism in either theory or practice. Suffice it only to note that the concept itself connotes both the infusion of value and the elevation of the specially selected. Webster's Unabridged Dictionary (2nd ed., 1979) defines elite as "the choice or most carefully selected part of a group, as of a society or profession." A British political philosopher, Geraint Parry, has noted that for many observers, "elites are the sole source of values in the society or constitute the integrating force in the community without which it may fall apart." Geraint Parry, *Political Elites*, London: George Allen and Unwin, 1969, p. 13.

21. For a brief but pointed commentary, see Garton Ash, loc. cit., p. 46, which, *inter alia*, quotes Francois Bondy's cutting quip that "if Kafka was a child of Central Europe, so too was Adolf Hitler." With respect to Havel's description of the "Central European mind," Garton Ash asks, "*since when* has [it] been 'skeptical, sober, anti-utopian, understated'?" ibid., italics as given.

22. See, for example, *On the Situation in the Czechoslovak Socialist Republic*, II, Berlin 1969 *passim* but especially "Intellectual Vanguard of the Counter-Revolution," pp. 76-93. Cf. the Husak regime's notorious "Lessons," widely circulated during the 1970s as a rationalization for the Soviet-led invasion and subsequent "normalization" of Czechoslovakia.

23. Samuel P. Huntington, "Social and Institutional Dynamics of One Party Systems," in Samuel P. Huntington and Clement H. Moore, *Authoritarian Politics in Modern Society*, New York: Basic Books, 1970, pp. 3-47, esp. pp. 36-38.

24. Gyorgy Konrad, *Antipolitics*, New York and London: Harcourt Brace Jovanovich, 1984. The quotes are all taken from the section entitled, "The Power of the State and the Power of the Spirit," pp. 216-243.

25. Garton Ash refers to moving remarks to this effect at an unofficial culture symposium held at Budapest in 1984. See Garton Ash, *loc. cit.*, p. 46
26. *Ibid.*
27. Konrad, *op. cit.*, p. 225.
28. Milan Simecka, *The Restoration of Order*, London: Verso Press, 1984, p. 17.
29. *Ibid.*, p. 71.
30. Kundera's interview with Philip Roth, *New York Times Book Review Section*, November 30, 1980, p. 80.
31. Konrad, "Is the Dream of Central Europe Still Alive?" *Cross Currents*, 5, 1986, p. 115.
32. *Ibid.*, p. 118.
33. Interview with Philip Roth, *loc. cit.*, p. 80.
34. *Ibid*, p. 7. Cf. Kundera's "Tragedy of Central Europe," *loc. cit.*
35. It is not surprising that Milosz, as a Pole who hails from Wilno (the ancient Lithuanian capital of Vilnius), should celebrate the memory of the Polish-Lithuanian Union of yore. With respect to the issue of pessimism, Milosz observes that "dark visions of the future . . . seem to be a specialty of Central European writers." Czeslaw Milosz, "Central European Attitudes," *Cross Currents*, 5, 1986, p. 105.
36. Konrad, *Antipolitics*, p. 114ff.
37. *Ibid.*, p. 224
38. *Ibid.*, p. 225.
39. See Konrad, "The Democracy We Have—Among Ourselves," *Antipolitics*, pp. 195-207.
40. *Ibid.*, p. 196.
41. The phrases are Garton Ash's. See Garton Ash, *loc. cit.*, p. 48.
42. Vaclav Havel, "The Power of the Powerless," *Cross Currents*, 2, 1983, p. 17.
43. *Ibid.*
44. Miklos Haraszti as quoted by Andrew Nagorski, *Newsweek*, March 30, 1987, p. 40.
45. See *The Economist*, December 26, 1987, p. 52.
46. Adriano Guerra in *Rinascita*, April 11, 18, and 25, 1987, as quoted, summarized, and analyzed by Kevin Devlin, "PCI Scholar Assesses Impact of Soviet Changes on East European Regimes." *Radio Free Europe Research*, RAD Background Report, No. 83, May 21, 1987, and *idem*, "Italian Communist on Contradictions and Crisis in Eastern Europe," *Radio Free Europe Research*, RAD, No. 91, June 5, 1987.
47. *The Economist*, December 26, 1987, pp. 51-52.
48. Konrad, *op. cit.*, p. 210.
49. *Ibid.*, p. 117.
50. On the first two matters, see Garton Ash, *loc cit.*, p. 51.
51. Milan Kundera, "Prague: A Disappearing Poem," *Granta*, 17, 1985, p. 102.
52. Kundera's address on receiving the Jerusalem Prize, "Man Thinks, God Laughs," *New York Review of Books*, June 13, 1985, p. 11.
53. Milosz, *loc. cit.*, p. 108.
54. Michnik as quoted by Nagorski, *Newsweek*, March 30, 1987, p. 40.
55. He writes, "I would like to think of myself as some utopian son of Europe able to touch the Pacific at San Francisco with one outstretched arm and Vladivostok with the other; and keeping the peace everywhere within my embrace." Konrad, *op. cit.* p. 129.
56. *Ibid.*

57. Jana Chrzova of Democratic Initiative (Prague), as quoted in *Newsweek*, April 25, 1988, p. 38.

58. Andrei Amalrik, *Will the Soviet Union Survive Until 1984?* New York and Evanston: Harper and Row, 1970, p. 61. Amalrik also prophesied that the countries of Eastern Europe "finding the Soviet Union powerless in Europe, will present territorial claims that have long been hushed up but not forgotten: Poland to Lvov and Vilna, Germany to Kaliningrad (Konigsberg), Hungary to Transcarpathia, Rumania to Bessarabia." *Ibid.* He omitted mention of the even more likely possibility of a rekindling of ethnonationalist passions within Eastern Europe—already apparent— and the fresh pursuit of territorial claims as the result of the eruption of various disputes that simmer just below the surface within the region.

59. Garton Ash, *loc. cit.*, p. 52.

60. For the origins of this phrase and a highly pertinent discussion of its applicability in the Communist period, see Hugh Seton-Watson, *The "Sick Heart" of Modern Europe*, Seattle and London: University of Washington Press, 1975, *passim.*

61. Ivan Berend, "The Role of Cultural Identity in Eastern Europe," in Ivan Berend, Josef Brada, Charles Gati, and Peter Sugar, eds., *Eastern Europe: A Question of Identity*, Washington, D.C.: East European Program, The Wilson Center, Occasional Paper No. 2, 1985, p. 12.

PART THREE

Dilemmas and Prospects

8

On Reform, Perceptions, Misperceptions, Trends, and Tendencies

Aurel Braun

There is, as we have seen, a sense of movement in the Soviet Union and in parts of Eastern Europe. Certainly under Gorbachev a good deal of energy has been devoted to change. In view of such fluidity it is healthy to provide a historical perspective for change, particularly when it affects Soviet and East European relations (as Andrzej Korbonski, for instance, has shown in Chapter 4). Without historical perspective one may magnify certain aspects of what may be merely an evolutionary process and thereby distort the analysis. There are, moreover, great expectations as well as some fears both in the Soviet Union and in Eastern Europe. And expectations can generate a momentum for further change, often unpredictable, or they may set the stage for disillusionment.

The Soviet-East European relationship is also deeply affected by the environment within which foreign policy is formulated. For instance, Harold and Margaret Sprout have noted that foreign policy is subject both to the operational environment and the psychological one.[1] The former refers to the circumstances of world politics as they exist at any moment in time whereas the latter involves the perception of the policymaker of the existing circumstances. In other words, there is a distinction between objective conditions and subjective perceptions of them. This somewhat oversimplifies the position of the Sprouts, but it is clear that their conceptual distinction is meant to apply to all states. The two environments can mesh, in a sense, but they do not always do so. In terms of analysis of policies and processes it is also very difficult to distinguish between the two environments, yet the perception of the analyst may differ from the operational environment. Therefore, it may be a worthwhile exercise to divide, at least broadly, the evaluation of the Soviet-East European relationship between the nature of the change—both domestic and regional—that may be taking place and the perception that the parties have of the process and of the actors involved.

The Nature of Change

For our purposes we are not merely concerned with the magnitude of the change in the Soviet Union, the East European states, and in the Soviet-East European relationship. Rather, we are primarily interested in assessing whether the change is meaningful in terms of adapting the relationship to a more organic form. But because external relations especially in this region are so profoundly influenced by domestic change, several of the contributors have found it essential to examine the nature of domestic change, particularly in the Soviet Union. The asymmetry in size alone makes it natural that developments in the Soviet Union should be the focus of a good deal of analysis. Domestic developments in all states, though, have an impact on the external relationship because of the particular political and economic circumstances of Eastern Europe. Several years ago, Rezso Nyers, who with some justice is referred to as the father of Hungarian economic reform, stressed the linkages between domestic change and intrastate relations among Socialist states.[2] For instance, he argued that for integration to proceed successfully in the Socialist bloc there would have to be a reform both of the Council for Mutual Economic Assistance (CMEA) and of the domestic economic mechanism of its member-states. The domestic changes that he suggested were along the lines of the Hungarian New Economic Mechanism (NEM). Without such changes, he suggested, the success of domestic Hungarian reform, would be endangered. Thus linkages between domestic and external factors are particularly strong in the socialist community. Ideally, then, domestic changes in the socialist community should be synchronized or at the least be compatible.

Strong economic ties between the Soviet Union and Eastern Europe are also reflected in the trade figures. Even though the combined economic output of the East European states is far smaller than the Soviet gross national product, as Carl McMillan shows (in Chapter 2), the countries of Eastern Europe continue to be the Soviet Union's major economic partners. This is so despite the high priority that Moscow has attached to the development of economic relations with the industrialized West. Moreover, as McMillan points out, in the 1980s the share of the six East European members of the CMEA in Soviet trade grew and accounted for slightly over half the total.

External economic linkages, though, operate within a larger political context and although there are significant economic, military, cultural, and psychological dimensions to the Soviet-East European relationship, the paramount factor remains political. Even though the Soviet Union under Gorbachev may be willing to allow the East European states a significantly greater degree of leeway both in domestic and foreign policies, Moscow continues to retain political primacy in the region. Changes in Soviet policies may be under way that could conceivably affect this in the future (as we shall discuss later) but in certain respects, from the beginning of his rule Gorbachev has presented himself as the leader of Eastern Europe as well as of the Soviet Union.[3] The broad outlines of his future policies focus on the Soviet Union, of course, but they also include Eastern Europe.

Soviet leadership, in terms of its impact on Eastern Europe, may be employed flexibly but by his insistence on retaining a central position Gorbachev has ensured that his program should have a major effect on Eastern Europe. Karen Dawisha, as we have seen, argues forcefully (Chapter 1), that Gorbachev has already had a significant impact on Soviet–East European relations. Consequently, it should be worthwhile to assess further the "operational environment" of Gorbachev's reform program both by comparing the evaluations of the contributors in this volume and by delving more deeply into certain aspects of *perestroika* in order to ascertain the nature of the change that the Soviet leader is trying to effect in the Soviet Union. Furthermore, it should be helpful, to do a comparative analysis (as Marer has in economic terms in Chapter 5) of Soviet and East European reforms in order to gain a better perspective of the objective environment before one examines Soviet and East European perceptions of reform and change in the region.

Reform Plans

Societies in general tend to view reform with some trepidation. In the Soviet Union and in Eastern Europe where change has often had a very negative impact, it is especially difficult to generate not only party but at times popular enthusiasm for reform. Lenin himself had remarked that "the habits of hundreds of million of people are a tremendous force"—a statement that, as Karl W. Deutsch has pointed out, shows an appreciation of the difficulty of bringing about major changes and the extremely lengthy period that it takes to alter habits in this region.[4]

The antecedents of reform

Nevertheless a number of Soviet leaders, including Lenin, have sought to bring reform to the Soviet system. In the post-war period, Nikita Khrushchev set seminal precedents that may be worth examining in brief. This is not meant to downplay the significance of what Gorbachev is trying to accomplish, but some historical perspective as noted, is useful to better understand the current environment in which changes are being introduced. For, history shows that effective reforms produce a synergy that leads to a widespread positive transformation while poorly conceptualized and implemented reforms ultimately lead to dysfunction.

Khrushchev, like Gorbachev, had a bold vision of change. But the former, especially in economic matters, was driven far more by a sense of dynamism than of desperation. Still, although Khrushchev concentrated more on personalities, he also subjected the Soviet system to severe criticism. In the domestic realm he sought changes in industry, agriculture, the military, law, and cultural policy. While some of his proposals were borrowed or poorly conceived, in his broad approach Khrushchev was quite innovative.

In external matters, Khrushchev chipped away at the rigid barriers to intercourse between the Soviet population and the outside world that Stalin had created and maintained. Furthermore, in 1956 he and the Kremlin endorsed the principle of "many roads to socialism." This at least appeared to give the individual East European countries license to behave in a somewhat more autonomous manner but allowed the Soviet Union to retain its status of *primus inter pares* in the socialist community.[5]

Soviet interest in Eastern Europe, though, is not merely based on *realpolitik*, and changes in the Soviet–East European relationship have been due to more than the factors of personalities and leadership. Systemic factors have also played a pivotal role. It may be something of an exaggeration to state, as Nish Jamgotch had, that the Soviet Union as an "ideologically oriented great power . . . must ultimately depend on its political transplants abroad."[6] But ideological considerations have played an important part in the Soviet–East European relationship in legitimating and in systemic terms, in large part due to the nature of Marxism-Leninism. Ralf Dahrendorf, for instance, has noted that there is a closer link in communist states than in Western ones between economic growth and political organization.[7] Citizens in such societies have grown accustomed to their political leaders taking a large share of the credit for economic successes and thus conclude that the leaders must also bear responsibility for economic failures. Therefore, not only does the Soviet Union have ideological concerns that are community-wide (within the socialist system), but socialist states share key, if somewhat worrisome, systemic characteristics. Consequently, transmission of ideas, innovations, and processes is made both more necessary and easier between the Soviet Union and the East European states.

As the hegemon, the Soviet Union has certain intrinsic advantages in transmission, but the East European states, at least in the past, have often shown themselves to be more innovative in the ideological and the economic realms. Thus, there has been a diffusion of innovation from Eastern Europe to the Soviet Union as part of a process of mutual influencing. For example, it was a study by the Czechoslovak Academy of Sciences in 1966, using Marxist doctrine, that came to the conclusion that the urgency to embark and succeed in the scientific-technological revolution was impeded by a "directive system of management" which, as part of the superstructure, was incapable of nourishing the free spirit of enquiry and competition of views that was essential to the optimal development of science.[8] In Eastern Europe, even before 1968, there were suggestions of electoral reforms, revitalizing of representative institutions, broadening trade union rights, and easing censorship.[9] Following 1968 and the invasion of Czechoslovakia, the Soviet Union took a less flexible view of East European developments and showed greater concern over the possibility of undesirable "spillovers" from technological or economic developments into political and social areas. But Soviet literature did not ignore East European innovations completely even after the tightening up that occurred in the wake of the 24th CPSU Congress in 1971. Moreover, following the ascension to power of Yuri

Andropov there was more innovation in Soviet ideological writings, some of which could clearly be traced back to East European thinking of the 1960s.[10]

In some ways it is rather curious that Andropov would have been a Soviet leader who allowed greater innovation or facilitated the transmission of innovations from Eastern Europe. As ambassador to Hungary in 1956, Andropov loyally carried out Soviet foreign policy, which included armed invasion. He consulted with Imre Nagy, the new Hungarian Prime Minister, at every step,[11] leaving the impression that Moscow concurred with Nagy's measures. And he tried to mislead Nagy about Soviet invasion plans. On November 1, 1956, for instance, Andropov went to Nagy's office to assure the Hungarian Prime Minister that Soviet troops had *entered* Hungary only in order to safeguard the security of Soviet forces *leaving* the state.[12] In effect, though, the Soviet invasion had already begun.

Yet, Andropov's tenure in Hungary also provides clues to his subsequent behaviour. He tried to understand the causes for discontent in Hungary and built a wide network of contacts. As a new ambassador in the summer of 1956, he kept inviting Imre Nagy, who then was just a pensioner, for long and apparently pleasant discussions.[13] He was thus pursuing a KGB-influenced pattern of behaviour which took a more sophisticated approach to controlling the bloc states and the three Baltic republics which had been annexed only in 1940. It appears that Andropov appreciated the need for reform in Hungary as part of a process of legitimation, as long as the central role of the Party and core Soviet interests were not threatened. Moreover, such an approach seems to have influenced Khrushchev and Andropov's protégé, Mikhail Gorbachev. The latter has not only taken a more flexible approach toward Eastern Europe than his immediate predecessor, but also to the three Baltic republics, where he has been willing to make more concessions to nationalistic concerns than elsewhere in the Soviet Union. It is, therefore, not unreasonable to assume that although all Soviet leaders have sought to retain control over Eastern Europe, those who had better information about local conditions and needs (as a result of their connections with the secret police) seem to have felt that they could afford to become more flexible and more confident in their dealings with the states in the region. It was perhaps not just a coincidence then, that Leonid Brezhnev and Konstantin Chernenko, who did not have the kinds of contacts and interests in Eastern Europe that Andropov had, were more rigid in their policies toward Eastern Europe, particularly regarding the question of reform.

Still, Gorbachev has sought to ensure that the KGB is restricted to a subordinate role during his tenure. In a reshuffle of the Politburo on September 30, 1988, he had the Central Committee move Viktor M. Chebrikov from the directorship of the KGB (a post he had held for 6 years) to the job of party secretary in charge of a new Central Committee commission on legal policy.[14] He named 64-year-old Vladimir A. Kryuchkov, a colonel-general in the KGB, as head of the organization. The latter is not a member of the Politburo, and thus the KGB lost its direct representation in the most powerful political body in the Soviet Union. Nevertheless Gorbachev, in appointing Chebrikov to head a commission overseeing all legal affairs, allowed a former KGB man to have a potentially very powerful position in the formulation and implementation of domestic reform. And, in appointing a professional security man as the head of the KGB, Gorbachev may have also improved the reliability of the information coming to him from this security agency.

Gorbachev's reform plans appear to be quite ambitious and, as Dawisha and McMillan show, urgent. Some of the East European reform plans (especially in Hungary and Poland) seem to be even more far-ranging. Still, the Soviet leader has also shown that he is cognizant of the problems and risks of trying to reform a stagnant political system that is imbued with a profound sense of pessimism.

Perhaps it was such intrinsic problems that led Gorbachev to be more cautious in the beginning. During the 27th Party Congress he spoke of the steady decline of economic growth during the 1970s but referred to radical reform only once.[15] By the Central Committee Plenum on January 27 and 28, 1987 he talked of a "new stage" and referred frequently to the need for "radical reform."[16] Thus there has been an acceleration in the Soviet reform program combined with a seeming broadening of its scope. In fact, among the terms most frequently employed by Gorbachev is that of *uskorenie* (acceleration). Some Western scholars, particularly Gail Lapidus, have argued that the regime now has a broad strategy for reform and that there has been a radical evolution in Gorbachev's thinking since the summer or fall of 1986.[17] Carl McMillan (Chapter 2), has suggested that the "grand design" for the Soviet economy is now beginning to be apparent and Paul Marer (Chapter 5) has referred to Gorbachev's "blueprint" for reform. Gorbachev himself, responding to domestic criticism that his reform program was ill thought-out, contended in January 1989 that the directions for perestroika were mapped out in more than 100 studies by various specialists, even before he came to power.[18]

If indeed there is *now* an operational blueprint or a grand design for reform, in the Western sense, then the delay in bringing this forth may provide some clues to future developments. If the delay has been caused primarily by Gorbachev's desire to first entrench himself more firmly in power, then he is indeed a good Fabian he may be contemplating a systemic change and, as such, may still have a good many more surprises in store depending on his future political circumstances. The broad outlines of the current plan, though, should still make the identification of some trends, or at least tendencies, easier. If, on the other hand, Gorbachev's intent is to preserve the Marxist-Leninist system but his own thinking on reform was not well-formed at the time of his rise to power or as many believe he still does not have a comprehensive plan or detailed blueprint and what we are perusing is a four-year learning period, then the uncertainty of future policy outcomes grows but there will be no deliberate moves to

On Reform

effect a systemic change. He may gain a greater appreciation of the need and potential for reform, particularly in the economic realm, but he may also become more reluctant to push for change as the risks and constraints become more daunting. The central dilemma that he faces is enormous— how to unleash initiative without endangering the political power of the Communist party. And, as he encourages reform throughout Eastern Europe these states are or will be confronting a similar dilemma.

Motives

Gorbachev's motives for seeking reform, as far as we may be able to ascertain them, could provide some indications as to whether he is a Fabian who may be moving deliberately toward systemic change in the Soviet Union. Paul Marer (in Chapter 5) argues very persuasively that Gorbachev's reason for introducing reform were twofold. First, since 1975 there has been a dramatic slowdown in the rate of growth and in the capital stock buildup in the Soviet Union. Second, it has become clear that without deep reforms the Soviet Union will be unable to participate in the worldwide scientific and technological revolution and that consequently the "gap" with the West will continue to grow. In another work[19] Marer points out that in the Soviet Union and in most of the East European states, official statistics on economic growth rates are becoming less and less meaningful as economic indicators since the statistical methodology employed has a built-in upward bias. Yet, despite this statistical bias, official figures have shown a very substantial decline in growth rates. It is reasonable to assume that the true decline in performance growth rate has been dramatic and has created a need for urgent solutions. As Gorbachev's principal economic adviser, Abel Aganbegyan put it rather delicately, "for the last fifteen to twenty years the Soviet Union's development has not been satisfactory."[20] And he added that the deeper reason for reform though is that the system of management which had been created under different circumstances in another age has been kept in operation to the present when in essence it ceased to be relevant to the real growing needs of progress in the Soviet Union.[21] Therefore, although power considerations may have played a role in Gorbachev's initially cautious behaviour, the urgency of the problems has been such that he could have ill afforded to play the role of a Fabian.

It is more likely that Gorbachev, though aware of many of the Soviet problems, has had to go through a learning process before formulating more clearly defined policies of reform of the Marxist-Leninist system. And among the things that he seems to have learned is that political changes are needed in order to bring about effective economic reform. As Georg Brunner has suggested, part of the political reform includes a form of liberalization, to be understood in the sense of combating dysfunctional administrative and judicial arbitrariness and creating the basis for a rule of law as well as extending personal freedoms in those spheres of social life where it can be done without endangering the fundamentals of Communist one-party rule.[22] It also involves enhancing popular participation in public affairs. *Glasnost* has been part of the political reform in the Soviet Union, both as a symbol of change and as part of change itself.

By comparison, two of the East European states, Hungary and Poland, are more advanced in political (and in economic) reform than the Soviet Union. In Hungary, in particular, the realization of the need for political reform in order to facilitate and stimulate economic change came well before Gorbachev's rise to power. For the Hungarians it has not been a matter of learning from the Soviet example but rather a case where Gorbachev's policies have acted as a catalyst for speeding up reform processes already under way. The question now is whether Hungary's new reforms might move it beyond the stage of political development that the Soviet leadership envisages or finds acceptable.

Political restructuring

Often, it is difficult to separate political and economic reform but it is useful to do so here for analytic purposes. Political reform in the Soviet Union is similar in certain crucial respects to those that have preceded them in Eastern Europe, particularly in Hungary. As noted, there is increasing recognition in the region that growing economic problems can be solved only when accompanying political reforms are pursued. There is a need to restrain the exercise of uncontested party power, to introduce some limited pluralism at least in terms of personnel choices that can be achieved through certain electoral reforms, to develop further the rule of law, and to extend some personal freedoms. In all of these areas Hungary and Poland are significantly ahead of the Soviet Union.[23]

There are also important distinctions that are derived from differences of political culture. In the Soviet Union glasnost is part of a reform from above. In the case of Hungary, reforms have produced a multiplicity of debates on the direction that change is to take. In a sense, they are part of a movement that had developed much more from below.[24] In the Soviet Union the style of reform from above is part not only of the socialist political culture but also of the Russian one and, as such, glasnost may play a significantly different role than in Hungary.

The absence of civil society in the Soviet Union, or in Russia before it, makes the introduction of glasnost potentially more volatile since it appears as a sharper threat to those who wish to preserve traditional processes and privileges. It is true that in the Soviet Union the relationship between state and society is changing. And as Gail Lapidus has suggested there is a possibility that civil society will emerge in the Soviet Union.[25] The road though is fraught with dangerous obstacles and it is too premature to talk of a civil society in that state. Perhaps one of the most difficult impediments is the lack of understanding or at least adequate appreciation on the part of the current Soviet leadership of what constitutes civil society and what are the pivotal ingredients of political culture. Gorbachev in a discourse on politics and reform stated that the Soviet Union lacked political culture but then confidently predicted in true Leninist fashion that "we will master that *science* too."[26] (emphasis added). Given differences in political culture, at least for the time being, openness of communication is more organically linked in Hungary and in Poland to ongoing reforms than in the Soviet Union.[27]

However, it would be a mistake to minimize the importance of political change in the Soviet Union. It is not just a matter of glasnost and perestroika but also of *pereotsenka* (or reappraisal) and *perevyazka* (bandaging or healing of old wounds) as Karen Dawisha points out in Chapter 1. Even though the two latter terms apply more to external relations with the Socialist states in Eastern Europe, they also have a domestic dimension. Even limited constraints on the role of the Party and the development of greater legality enhance political freedoms in socialist states and can facilitate economic reform.

It is not inconceivable that at a certain stage there may be a movement, for instance, toward what may be called "Communist constitutionalism"[28] as contradictory as that term may be. Such a development would involve a modernization of the leading role of the party, the reduction of the role of the state and the creation of a more autonomous civil society. We see elements of this, both in the Soviet Union and in some of the East European states.

Yet, even though such changes are significant and they have far-reaching implications, it is important to place them within the context of the goals and capabilities of the regimes, particularly that in the Soviet Union. What these changes quite clearly are not is a movement to a full-blown Western style constitutionalism. Though Gorbachev has expressed considerable impatience with the pace of political as well as economic reform in the Soviet Union, he has also made it clear that there are definite limits to political reform. He wishes to restore the vitality of a Leninist party—he is not about to allow the monopoly of the power of the Communist party to slip away. Political participation is to be increased but it is to be guided by the Communist party within the socialist system.

Gorbachev, as noted, clearly understands the seminal linkage between political change and economic reform. The success of perestroika depends on political change that "shakes" up all of society. Nikita Khrushchev had also recognized the need for political change though ultimately his reforms failed. His basic approach though may have been sound. And in a fashion similar to Khrushchev who cultivated support "from below" for the purpose of shaking up the bureaucracy "from above," Gorbachev has referred to the need for a simultaneous revolution "from above" and "from below."[29] (Though the initiative is clearly coming from above). This is not to suggest that Gorbachev is merely reintroducing ideas or policies first formulated by Khrushchev. There are, however, similarities in their approach to political issues that are salient and that indicate some of the parameters inherent in current political reform. In politics Gorbachev may be substituting a cybernetic approach for the more mechanistic one employed by Khrushchev but this still represents a "technological" solution.

Still, the Soviet leader has been willing to experiment. Gorbachev has proposed fixed terms of office which could limit his own tenure as General-Secretary of the Communist party, and electoral competition for party and state officials (from approved lists).[30] In the March 26, 1989 elections to the 2250 seat Congress of People's Deputies two thirds of the seats were subject to multi-candidate elections. Though the remaining one third of the seats were allocated to the Communist party and affiliated organizations and despite the fact that many of the contested seats had only one candidate, the elections were a radical departure from the past and produced a number of surprises. Not only did the hundreds of candidates find themselves facing run-off elections because no one had garnered a majority of the votes in their constituency but scores of individuals who had run unopposed failed to get the necessary 50% approval to gain a seat. Among the more prominent losers in the latter group were the Leningrad regional party boss, Yuri F. Solovyev and the Mayor of Moscow, Valery T. Saikin. At a Central Committee Meeting in April 1989 both openly criticised Gorbachev for what they claimed was the creation of ideological disorder[31] but the Soviet leader pushed ahead with his reforms. He forced the resignation of 110 members of the Central Committee who were holdovers from the Brezhnev era and promoted 24 candidate members to voting rank, including such well-known supporters of perestroika as the vice-president of the Academy of Sciences, Evgeny Velikhov and think-tank chief Evgeny Primakov.[32]

Several of the keenest reformers were also elected to the new Congress of People's Deputies. Boris Yeltsin who had been removed from the Politburo for his criticism of the slow pace of reform made a triumphant political comeback (at least in terms of public visibility) when he gained the largest number of votes for any candidate in the Soviet elections. In the Moscow city-wide district election Yeltsin captured 89% of the vote.[33] Two state prosecutors, Telman Gdlyan and Nikolai Ivanov who had made a reputation for their inquiry into state corruption, were overwhelmingly elected in run-off elections to the Congress.[34] The latter had even alleged that Yegor Ligachev's (the party secretary in charge of agriculture) name had "appeared" in the corruption inquiry. This in turn prompted not only an indirect denial by Ligachev but also an angry denunciation of the prosecutors by a Government commission.[35] Moscow citizens, however, supported the prosecutors and rallied by the thousands to protest corruption.[36] Lastly, the Soviet Academy of Sciences reversed its earlier stand and sent Andrei Sakharov to the Congress as part of its allocated slate of representatives.

Furthermore these reformers have continued to voice their concerns openly. In May 1989 at the openly televised session of the Congress of People's Deputies, Andrei Sakharov called on Gorbachev to speak not only of his successes but also about the failures of perestroika and then tried (unsuccessfully) to amend the agenda so that voting for the president would not take place until the end of the congressional session.[37] Boris Yeltsin, in an interview with *The Washington Post* just days before the opening of the Congress (which was supposed to choose a new administrative president, vice-president and Supreme Soviet), asserted that the Gorbachev leadership suffered from "inconsistency, indecisiveness, half-measures and susceptibility to pressure from the right wing" and questioned the high-profile role of Raisa Gorbachev.[38] Furthermore at a political rally before the Congress, Yeltsin told the 20,000 people in attendance that during a long private meeting he had with Gorbachev on May 12, 1989 he turned down an offer by the Soviet leader which would have guaranteed him a seat in the new Supreme Soviet in exchange for toning down his criticism.[39]

The open criticism of reformers or dissidents is significant but what is even more remarkable is the entire change in the political atmosphere in the Soviet Union. The tremendous popular interest in politics that was manifested not only during the March elections but also in the eagerness with which the population followed the televised proceedings of the May-June 1989 Congress meeting indicates the potential for dramatic change. The open criticism of Gorbachev and his admission that there had been mistakes during his first four years as party leader all represent major departures from the past.

Yet a change in the political atmosphere as significant as that may be, especially for longer term prospects, should not be mistaken for a fundamental alteration of the political system itself. Though we should not underestimate the importance of current developments in the Soviet Union and we should certainly not exclude the possibility that systemic change will take place in the future, these changes should be viewed with some caution. Even if we are witnessing the inchoate stages of a systemic change similarities in form with Western developments may be deceptive. There are several factors which suggest that it would also be unwise to overestimate the depth of political change in the Soviet Union which in turn impacts on Soviet-East European relations.

First, the Soviet elections and the changes in the structure of the government are at best selective applications of democracy. One third of the seats in the Congress of People's Deputies were allocated *ab initio* to the Communist party and affiliated organizations. Neither Gorbachev nor any other full member of the Politburo for instance, had to seek a popular mandate at the ballot box on March 26, 1989. The new Congress then approved Gorbachev (who ran unopposed) for the newly-created powerful post of (administrative) president by an overwhelming 95% of the votes cast (87 opposed him and 11 deputies abstained).[40]

Furthermore, though the Soviet Union allowed multi-candidate elections this is quite different from the creation of a multi-party system. Gorbachev has not proposed that other political parties arise to compete with the Communist party. Although *samizdat* publications have talked of political pluralism, the official press is yet to broach the subject. Valentin B. Yumoshev, the letters' editor of the free-wheeling official weekly *Ogonyok* said in May 1988 that although they had received letters suggesting a multiparty system, they had been unable to publish them.[41] And several of the group of about 100 dissidents who formed the Democratic Union (a party which intends to pursue parliamentary democracy) have been harassed or arrested by Soviet authorities.[42]

Gorbachev's "pluralism" does not go so far as to allow a substantive challenge to the party's monopoly of power. At a Central Committee meeting in March 1989 Boris Yeltsin was called to account for daring to suggest that the idea of having alternative political parties was a fit subject for public discussion in the Soviet Union.[43] It is also worth noting that even though a number of party officials were defeated in the March 1989 elections, more than 90% of the deputies in the new Congress of People's Deputies are members of the party or the Young Communist League. Thus, despite far greater public involvement in the elections and the "scare" it gave to some hard-liners, this was to a considerable degree a controlled experiment which allowed Gorbachev to better gauge the problems and prospects for political reform.

It is true that the spectrum of opinion among the Communist deputies is quite broad. Yet it is allowed to operate within certain parameters for the party is still governed by the principle of democratic centralism. The effect of this approach has been manifested not only in angry statements by Gorbachev at the May 1989 meeting of the Congress, accusing the Lithuanian delegation of trying to foment a crisis[44] or the conservative majority interrupting and reviling the reformers who failed to gain election to the Supreme Soviet[45] at that same meeting. Rather, it is reflected in the new procedures and rules of public debate evident at the May 1989 Congress which allowed the party apparatus to enforce its will almost as easily as it did before. The dissenters could speak but the party apparatus got its way.

Reformers who disagreed with the scope or pace of Gorbachev's glasnost or perestroika were rejected by the apparatus in their quest for election to the Supreme Soviet. Whereas the full Congress is to set major directions of national policy it is to meet very infrequently for short periods only. The substance of legislation is to be formulated and passed by the bicameral Supreme Soviet which is to sit in extended sessions in the manner of Western parliaments. Loyal lieutenants of glasnost and perestroika, such as Evgeny Primakov, the scientist Evgeny P. Velikhov and newspaper columnist and chairman of an official commission on human rights, Fyodor M. Burlatsky did make it to the Supreme Soviet,[46] clearly with Gorbachev's blessing.

Boris Yeltsin who had criticized Gorbachev but had gathered the largest number of votes of any candidate in the March election was rejected for membership in the Supreme Soviet.[47] But following the demonstration by about 70,000 supporters of reform in Moscow in May 28, 1989 a newly-selected deputy to the Supreme Soviet resigned in order to allow Yeltsin to take a seat in that body.[48] There were no reversals in the case of the other prominent reformers who were rejected: the eminent sociologist Tatyana I. Zaslavskaya, who had called for deep reforms and had asked the Congress to suspend a law which banned public demonstrations; Gavril K.

Popov, an economist who had criticized attempts to limit the power of Congress and who also called for the replacement of central economic planning with a free market; Aleksei V. Yablokov a prominent ecologist and many other reformers.[49] Andrei Sakharov and a number of other well-known proponents of change were not nominated by the Congress for the Supreme Soviet.

The party apparatus thus signalled the limits to pluralism and Soviet-style democracy. The danger is that if the perception grows that glasnost and pluralism is not more than a "wink and a nod" the kind of cynicism that would ensue would make it difficult to implement reform. The bitterness and disillusionment of those who did not make it to the Supreme Soviet gives an indication of the danger. The historian Yuri Afanaseyev deplored the "aggressively obedient majority" at the Congress.[50] Gavril Popov contended that:

> Yesterday the machine of majority rule was started in full swing. Delegates whose opinions differed from those of the majority of their respective delegations were pushed aside and lists for the Supreme Soviet were made up on this basis . . . to form a Supreme Soviet obedient to the will of the apparatus and to keep up the pressure on the progressive wing in the leadership of the country.[51]

And Andrei Sakharov contended that there were hardly any deputies sent to the Supreme Soviet who could even talk about the real problems of the country.[52]

Secondly, the March 1989 elections and the decisions of the Congress in May-June 1989 reflect the deeper problems posed by Soviet political culture. During a break at the Congress Gorbachev told reporters that, "we have yet to master the art of democracy, political culture and the ability to listen to each other."[53] His own domineering, intrusive style during the sessions, though, showed not only an ignorance of or disregard for parliamentary procedure but was emblematic of Soviet political culture and the problem that it poses to democratization.

Still, glasnost, even if commenced from the top, is an encouraging sign that Soviet political culture does contain a spirit of liberty. But socialism and particularly Stalinism has interrupted what may have been an evolution in Russia toward a more Western political culture. Instead authoritarian traditions were reinforced. There is therefore a high degree of mistrust, fear and envy. A 1989 study published in *Interlocutor* by Mark Urnov, a sociologist with the Soviet Academy of Sciences, found an extremely high degree of popular cynicism about recent political reforms and Soviet society in general.[54] Only 7% believed that public figures were honest and 93% feared the authorities.[55] A 1989 poll by a Moscow sociologist, Leonti G. Byzov also showed that there are sharp differences between most workers and the intelligentsia.[56] Most Soviet workers incline, it seems, toward a notion of "social justice" that wishes to ensure that no one gets too far ahead. Intellectuals, in contrast were much more receptive to the Western ideals of individual advancement and initiative.

Workers though vastly outnumber all other strata in society and given these indicators of political culture they are very likely highly susceptible to the politics of envy and to populist demagoguery. Yeltsin's appeal to the population, for instance, is not really based on demands for more freedom or democracy but rather on a populist platform which promises to provide more food, consumer goods, and better services and to eliminate corruption and privilege.[57] Worthwhile goals, but they do not address the vital political issues. Perhaps Yeltsin has sensed that the population is not ready for a profound political transformation but then this only demonstrates further the brake that Soviet political culture is to change. As Walter Laqueur argues, the uprooting of the authoritarian tradition in the Soviet Union will require a cultural revolution and a real change in the attitude and nature of the people.[58] And Laqueur is quite right that there is no sign that this is yet happening.

Thirdly, political reform may have been limited by Gorbachev's concentration on consolidating his own power base. On the one hand Gorbachev's actions are quite understandable, for without solidifying his own position he could have been removed by hard-liners who resisted any change. The purging of the old guard from the Politburo and the Central Committee is logical and understandable. On the other hand, his constant preoccupation with enhancing his own power, including the restructuring of the role of the presidency (while he accepted a whole series of compromises on political and economic issues) breeds apprehension if not cynicism. Gorbachev's dual position of president and party head combine the elements of power in the presidential and the prime ministerial systems in the West without the democratic checks on power in either form of government. There has to be a fine balance between political survival and the implementation of a program of reform and Gorbachev's focus on the former raised the suspicion of the more radical reformers at the meeting of the Congress. Much of the credibility of reform in the Soviet Union rests on the personal credibility of Gorbachev. Loss of faith in Gorbachev's motives if he does not emphasize further political change and economic improvement over political consolidation could stifle support for reforms.

Fourthly, political change is further inhibited by the continued presence of most of the instruments of repression. This was starkly illustrated in April 1989 when special internal security troops used sharpened shovels and toxic gases to put down a large demonstration in Tbilisi, Georgia and killed twenty-one people in the process.[59] On April 8, 1989 a decree was passed by the Presidium which broadly interpreted could be used to jail citizens for "discrediting" the state.[60] The Congress session in May 1989, for instance, overwhelmingly rejected a call by Tatyana Zaslavskaya to at least suspend for the duration of the meetings a law banning public demonstrations in Moscow.[61]

Despite four years of glasnost the Soviet Union has continued the practice of confining some political dissenters to psychiatric institutions. In 1989

Amnesty International confirmed that several dissidents had been sent to such institutions and that many others had been imprisoned.[62] And despite an easing of censorship there are tight limits on what can be published. For instance, Soviet medical researchers cannot publish details of studies linking air pollution to the high numbers of birth defects in certain parts of Moscow.[63]

Pressures from the Periphery. Thus in the political realm systemic change is yet to take place though there has been significant improvement. Given the difficulties confronting a systemic transformation, the overall political prospects in the Soviet Union do not appear to be particularly encouraging. Pressure for change though, appears to be greater in the peripheral areas of the Soviet Union, such as the Baltic states or Georgia or Armenia. If systemic change does take place the catalysts may come in these areas first.

These republics have a different political culture from that of Russia, though socialism has had an important impact. In the case of the Baltic states socialism was imposed only in 1940. They are also closer culturally to Europe than the rest of the Soviet Union and so the Baltic people are more receptive to Western ideas. In Georgia there are strong memories of the three years of independence and here as in Armenia, nationalism is a powerful force. Throughout these republics there is also a greater sense of entrepreneurship than elsewhere in the Soviet Union. Thus there is greater pressure for both political and economic reform.

Despite the riots and demonstrations in Georgia which focused largely on issues of nationality, language and territory, the political challenge to glasnost and perestroika coming from the Baltic states is even more immediate. In Estonia, Latvia and Lithuania independent popular fronts, largely with the support of local Communist party officials are asking for nearly total political and economic autonomy from Moscow and, in some cases, for independence.[64] The people of these three republics thus have availed themselves more quickly of the opportunities presented by glasnost and perestroika than elsewhere in the Soviet Union. In Lithuania, for instance, a popular front movement "Sajudis" which captured a large number of seats in the March 1989 elections has advocated independence and neutrality.[65]

Furthermore, there are no clear divisions between Communist party members and dissidents in the Baltic republics. In Estonia for example, many communists joined the Popular Front, a pro-reform alliance and ran successfully as radical candidates on the Front's platform.[66] In May 1989 a leading member of the Front was named Deputy Prime Minister of Estonia and head of a commission to oversee Estonia's transition to economic independence.[67] The radicalized Estonian parliament set itself on a collision course with Moscow when in its mid-May 1989 session it adopted a plan for economic sovereignty which once in force in 1990 would introduce not only deep market reforms, far beyond what is envisioned by Gorbachev's perestroika, but would give Estonia its own currency—the *korus*.[68] The Estonian parliament also demonstrated its political differences with Moscow when it unanimously condemned the use by troops of shovels and toxic gas to break up a demonstration in Tbilisi, Georgia that left a score of people dead.[69]

In the Baltic states there appears to be a widespread popular belief that the protection of national rights and the revitalization of the economy requires profound political reform. There is, therefore, in these states an interlocking of issues and concerns that involve not only the centrifugal forces of nationalism but a quest for a kind of political pluralism that seems to challenge the core concepts of socialism.

It remains to be seen whether political changes in the Baltic republic (or the other republic on the Soviet periphery) may act as a catalyst for greater political changes throughout the Soviet Union or whether Moscow will view them as unacceptable challenges. There are some disquieting signs. At the May meeting of the Congress Gorbachev declared that all people should put the Soviet Union ahead of their own feelings about their ethnic nationalities.[70] Then, as noted, he angrily accused the Lithuanian delegation of trying to forment a crisis.[71] Thus the Soviet leadership also finds it difficult to separate the issues of nationalism and political reform in the Baltic republics and this does not bode well for reform. Evgeny Primakov and Georgy Shakhnazarov, an assistant to Gorbachev (and former first deputy chief Liaison with Socialist Countries Department of the Central Committee) both have suggested that the situation in the Baltic states is one of the graver problems facing the Soviet Union.[72]

The East European Impact. Stimulae or challenges to reform in the Soviet Union also emanate in Eastern Europe for a process of mutual influencing is at work. Shakhnazarov spoke of the possibility of synergy when he asserted that successful reform in Eastern Europe can reinforce Soviet reforms.[73] But he also warned that if the East Europeans were to cross the line to "extremism" and "chaos," Soviet perestroika could be dealt a "death blow."[74]

But in addition to the direct impact the East European experience can provide some useful clues to the changes and prospects in the Soviet Union. True, Romania, the GDR and Czechoslovakia have rejected reform. And developments in Poland and Hungary are not completely analogous to those in the Soviet Union. The differences in size, historical evolution, political culture and strategic interests should make one cautious about drawing too close comparisons. Nevertheless, there are crucial similarities in the domestic systems of the East European states and that of the Soviet Union and the interrelationship in the bloc further emphasizes the relevance of East European developments for Moscow.

Two East European states, Poland and Hungary, as noted, have considerably more experience with reform than the other states in the region. For the Soviet Union, Poland is the strategically more significant country but Gorbachev has placed greater emphasis so far on economic and political matters. Consequently, Hungary which has the longest experience with economic and political reform is more relevant to an understanding of current developments in the Soviet Union and the bloc states. Hungary's experience may also provide clues to potential regional and sub-regional developments. Various sub-regional plans had been circulated in the late 1940s and greater flexibility in the future could conceivably allow the creation of sub-regional units which could include some East European states in an economic relationship with certain Soviet republics.

Still, the East European reform experience should be kept within the perspective of general political and economic developments. Even in Hungary and Poland political change is still radically different from Western constitutionalism. This is not meant to diminish the importance of what has occurred or may take place in a country such as Hungary. There is considerable potential for a rapid political change since the ouster of not only Janos Kadar as General Secretary of the Party but also of several Politburo hardliners.[75] Kadar was replaced by the Prime Minister Karoly Grosz who is viewed as a pragmatist. He has urged a "renewal" of Communist rule that would incorporate at least some of the features extant in Western political systems.[76] Just as importantly the new eleven-seat Politburo has as new members the reformist Imre Pozsgay who heads the Patriotic People's Front (PPF) which works under the umbrella of the Communist party, and Rezso Nyers, the father of economic reform in Hungary. Pozsgay is 55, Grosz is 58 and another new Politburo member Miklos Nemeth, who has become Prime Minister, is 41 years old. Therefore, there has been not only a leadership but also a generational change. The quick and warm congratulatory message from Gorbachev to Grosz conferred the Soviet stamp of approval on the change in the Hungarian leadership.

Reforms in Hungary can help the process of reform in the Soviet Union, at least in terms of that small state functioning as a relatively safe laboratory. The potential for external intervention from the Soviet Union can help ensure that political and economic reform in Hungary remains a controlled experiment though it would be erroneous to view this as an iron-clad guarantee. Public and repeated Soviet reassurances that each socialist state has a right to follow its own road to development has led to a popular perception in Hungary that there are few, if any, external constraints on domestic reform. There is considerable volatility in Hungary as popular dissatisfaction with economic deterioration (in a state that had been viewed as perhaps the most successful socialist model), continues. This dissatisfaction has reached into the Communist party itself. Between December 1987 and March 1988, for example, over 40,000 party members left and many senior members in the reformers' camp, especially academics, threatened to resign in protest.[77] Hungarian dissidents have long called for the creation of a multi-party system and true political pluralism. Even some members of the Communist party have called for profound reforms that would result in a change of the political system. These include proposals for the dismantlement of democratic centralism.

As late as 1988, though, non-party organizations such as the Hungarian Democratic Form (HDF) and the Federation of Young Democrats (FIDESZ), were branded as illegal organizations.[78] Furthermore, on April 9, 1988, a little over a month before the Party Conference, Kadar and party hardliners tried to reimpose party discipline by expelling four key communist reformers.[79] The attempt to discredit reformers and dissidents, however, backfired as we have seen when Kadar and several hardliners were removed from the Politburo at the May 1988 Party Conference.

It appeared at first highly unlikely that Grosz would adopt the position of those who called for fundamental, systemic change. He defended the right of the party to select its members and stood by the expulsions. And, in his speech to the Conference, Grosz turned aside calls for the recognition of social movements, unions and political parties outside Communist control.[80] He indicated that he intended to concentrate on economic measures though he recognized the need for greater political liberalization. As a pragmatist he advised the Hungarians to be patient.

Economic and political pressures, however, forced the Hungarian leadership to accept far greater political changes than it had at first contemplated. It is somewhat ironic that the Hungarian regime, which for decades under Kadar had sought legitimacy through economic means and which in exchange for a steadily improving standard of living asked for political acquiescence, now is driven to make political concessions in order to try to compensate for a massive economic failure.

Signs of major change came in the fall of 1989. There was increased talk of constitutional restraints and Western notions of liberalism not only in intellectual circles but also among government officials. For instance, Kalman Kulcsar, the Minister of Justice in a scholarly piece on human rights cited Edmund Burke.[81] It was Kulcsar who announced in November 1988 that the Government would be introducing a bill on the right to form association which could lead to a multi-party system.[82] In January 1989 the Hungarian Parliament passed two breakthrough laws which not only gave people the right to demonstrate but also to form associations, including independent political parties.[83] Another law was to be passed later regulating the operations of new political parties but the stage was set for multi-party elections in 1990.

The January laws have been followed by a veritable frenzy of political activity. First, the Hungarian Socialist Workers' Party (HSWP) jumped on the bandwagon of multi-party elections. Even Grosz reversed course and reluctantly endorsed the creation of a multi-party system as "another form of democracy."[84] The new Prime Minister, Miklos Nemeth declared that if the NSWP was defeated at the polls it would be the party's fault alone and it would have to accept it.[85] The leading reformer in the Politburo, Imre Pozsgay has also fully endorsed the proposition that the party will have to risk its position in multi-party elections.[86] New parties have been formed and old ones revived. The *Peter Veres* society became the *People's Party*, a *Christian Democratic Party* was formed, and the Hungarian Social Democrat Party was revived.[87]

Secondly, a re-examination has begun of the 1956 Revolution, the role of the then Prime Minister Imre Nagy and that of the show trials conducted between 1945 and 1962. The party reached a compromise solution on the 1956 Revolution, recognizing that it was a popular uprising but that there were counter-revolutionary elements present in the latter stages. The reformers have also pressed for the rehabilitation of Nagy and the party agreed at least to allow his body to be exhumed from an unmarked grave and to have it reburied on June 16, 1989 in a national day of mourning.[88] In May 1989 the Party admitted that Nagy was executed illegally after a show trial.[89] Thus Hungary seems to be moving resolutely to eliminate important "blank spots" in its history.

Thirdly, the party and the government has engaged in major personnel changes. For example, in April 1989 the Party removed four members from the Politburo.[90] Shortly afterwards, Miklos Nemeth dropped several members of his cabinet and promoted a number of reformers.[91]

The momentum of reform then, seems to be so great that it is not unreasonable to ask whether the process that seems to be underway will lead to a transformed system that could no longer be called socialist. There is a significant split in the HSWP already with the hardliners coalescing in the *Ferenc Muennich Society* and many of the reformers grouping around Pozsgay and Rezso Nyers.[92] Regarding a possible split, Pozsgay declared in May 1989 that:

> it would be my desire that the fundamentalist and Stalinist wings bolt. Without them the HSWP can become a genuinely democratic and European party in which socialism would become synonymous with its original definition: Economic prosperity and social justice based on democracy and individual freedom.[93]

It is little wonder that many in Hungary wonder if Pozsgay is still a communist.

Rising popular expectations have also contributed to the momentum for change. And as Zbigniew Brzezinski has pointed out, if the viewpoint that a Soviet military intervention is in fact unlikely becomes more widespread, this perception might make a revolutionary upheaval more probable.[94] Moreover, recent opinion polls show that only 24% of Hungarians trust the party and that as matters stand now they would get fewer votes than an alliance of non-Communist parties in the 1990 elections.[95] Political reform in Hungary has thus moved considerably ahead of that in the Soviet Union. It is possible then that transcendence or even systemic change may take place in the future. Yet a number of factors in Hungary also suggest caution and consequently it should be premature to assume that Hungary is on an irreversible course to social or liberal democracy.

First Hungarian political and legal culture has strong authoritarian roots which were greatly reinforced under communist rule. The traditional vesting of rights in the state rather than the individual helped to stifle democratic instincts. The Kadarist formula that distinguished among those views that the party would *support*, those that it would *tolerate* and those that it would *prohibit*,[96] represented a significant improvement over Stalinist precepts but still reinforced the paramountcy of the party over the individual. Though the rediscovery of the liberal notions of constitutionalism by a number of reformers is most encouraging, a shift in political culture requires a radical change in the mentality of the entire nation. It is a fairly lengthy process and political maturity is essential in the period of transition. The latter requires a fine balance between the push for change and self-restraint in order to avoid provoking those forces that can block transformation. It also includes the art of political compromise and the ability to turn from slogans to realistic policies. The task before radical Hungarian reformers is not an impossible one but changing the political culture is going to be difficult. Hungarians in March 1989 celebrated openly for the first time in 41 years the unsuccessful revolt against Austria in 1848. As 60,000 people gathered in front of the parliament a number of banners reading, "Ivan, Don't You Feel Homesick?" in English, were held aloft.[97] Given Hungary's international circumstances and historical experiences, such acts are hardly encouraging signs of political maturity.

Secondly, it would be a mistake to underestimate the ability of the HSWP or any communist party to adapt to changing conditions or by the same token to overestimate the ability of a fragmented and inexperienced opposition to present itself as a viable, political alternative. The HSWP may be wrecked by factionalism but under Grosz it has nevertheless moved vigorously to assume the mantle of populism and nationalism. Widespread poverty, especially among the aged, a widening income differential as a small but successful entrepreneurial class emerges, the threat of unemployment and inflation combined with authoritarian traditions make the country ripe for a Peronist-style populism which could retain at least some of the core of Marxist-Leninist doctrine. This party, albeit at great economic cost, could offer to protect the jobs of the several hundred thousand who are manning inefficient state industries and to continue to provide a social welfare net to millions of poor perhaps by redistributing more of the income from the economically successful segment. Thereby it could also play on the politics of envy which holds such appeal in states where civil society is ill formed. Such a platform would contribute to further economic stagnation but it is probably the best recipe for political survival for the HSWP. The fragmented opposition in offering to introduce a market system and pluralistic democracy would be asking a risk-averse society to make large sacrifices and accept significant social dislocations in exchange for future pay-offs in terms of political freedom and economic improvement. Most in the opposition, moreover, cannot offer to the electorate proof of political experience or administrative skill. Furthermore, in a multi-party election campaign, the HSWP would have the advantages of superior funding, a vast electoral organization and control over the most important elements of the media.

It is also conceivable that the HSWP could follow the model of the Italian Communist Party. The latter in fact has long supported the "liberal" sectors of Hungarian and Polish parties. The Italian party has formally abandoned the precept of democratic centralism, is emphasizing such fashionable causes as ecology and feminism and is promoting a broader concept of the Euroleft that also embraces social democrats.[98] The Italian party, though, presents only limited analogy for it operates in a radically different political and military environment—Italy is a wealthy, successful liberal democracy that is a member of NATO and the European Community. Furthermore, changes by the Italian party are yet to bear political fruit. In fact in municipal elections in 1988 its share of the vote fell to 21.9% from 34.4% in 1976. Consequently, for a ruling East European party, the Italian model may present few attractions.[99]

Nationalism, though, can be a useful platform if employed cautiously. In the 1960s and the early 1970s Nicolae Ceausescu for instance, managed to combine successfully communism and nationalism both to increase the legitimacy of the party and to enlarge Romania's area of autonomy in foreign policy.[100] In Hungary, nationalism has been a volatile factor especially when directed at Soviet domination. The Hungarian regime, however, now has a relatively safe target—the brutal and internationally discredited regime of Nicolae Ceausescu which rules over an ethnic minority of about two million Hungarians. Romania has been widely condemned for human rights violations in the West.[101]

The persecution of the Hungarian minority in Romania is real and tragic. Public attacks between the two states[102] have continued despite some efforts at resolution. In June 1988, in Budapest, with the government's permission, 100,000 people in the largest mass demonstration since 1956, protested the treatment of the Hungarian minority in Romania and specifically Ceausescu's plans to raze 7-8,000 villages which are inhabited predominantly by Hungarians and move the population to larger centers.[103] Grosz's decision to meet with Ceausescu at the end of August 1988 in the Romanian city of Arad, also failed to resolve any of the major outstanding disputes.[104]

Grosz was criticized in Hungary for failing to achieve positive results and polemics between the two states, in fact, have intensified. The intensity of the anti-Romanian campaign in Hungary though, raises the suspicion that the Hungarian party is doing more than just expressing a justifiable concern for the welfare of the Hungarian minority in Romania. The play on nationalist theme helps the party assume a mantle of legitimacy. It is, however, a dangerous game. Hungarian nationalism has a history of considerable volatility and by encouraging it the regime runs the risk not only of damaging relations with two other neighbours, Czechoslovakia and Yugoslavia, which also have substantial Hungarian minorities but also of arousing strong historic anti-Russian feelings. The latter in turn could cause the kind of complications in Soviet-Hungarian relations that Budapest can ill afford as it tries to implement its ambitious plans for reform. But in a desperate search for legitimacy the Hungarian party does not seem to be able to resist the temptation of using nationalism and that may thus diminish the possibilities for transcendence or systemic change.

As in the case of Hungary, the Polish regime has also found that it has had to agree to deeper political reforms than it envisioned even a few years ago. And as in Hungary it is quite uncertain how far these reforms will go in transforming the political system. The Polish party has been in desperate straits. Unable to stop the country's downward economic spiral, resolve labour strife or crush Solidarity the Polish party has had to make dramatic concessions to political pluralism.

In April 1989 the Jaruzelski regime not only agreed to relegalize Solidarity but also to hold partially competitive elections in June 1989.[105] It seemed to be a brilliant victory for Lech Walesa and Solidarity and a major step towards pluralistic democracy as the country moved toward the first truly multi-party elections in four decades.

True, the rules assured the Communists and their allies 65% of the seats in 460-member lower house, the Sejm. And in stipulating that the President was to be chosen by a joint session of the Sejm and the 100-seat Senate the rules assured that a Communist candidate (Wojciech Jaruzelski) would win. But the restoration of the Senate where all the seats were to be freely contested was a major concession by the party. Moreover, the regime's negotiators pledged to Solidarity that in four years all seats in both houses of Parliament would be freely contested.[106] Though the Communists seemed to have assured themselves of at least four more years in power following the June 1989 elections both the partially competitive elections and the agreement in principle for completely free future elections appear to signal that the antiquated, highly monopolized, political structure in Poland is about to change.

Yet the population has shown little enthusiasm for the elections. Small numbers of dissenters have even protested against the pact between the party and Solidarity.[107] They contended that the elections were a trap by the regime for it would retain power but it would force Solidarity to share political responsibility for solving the country's dire economic problems. This may indeed prove to be correct but to an extent it is an unfair assessment. Clearly both the regime and Solidarity have a vested interest in discrediting each other and both are taking a gamble on building or solidifying their public support. The gamble is very likely greater for Solidarity for unlike the regime it does not carry the stigma and burden of a failed economy. Nevertheless, the regime has also come to realize that it cannot resolve the problems confronting it unless it can build some consensus in the country. And this is not possible without the creation of a degree of political pluralism. It is the level and the type of pluralism that will emerge that will determine the nature of the change taking place in Poland. Political culture, political vision and domestic and external realities in turn will set the parameters and determine whether political transcendence or systemic change will take place.

As in the case of Hungary, Polish political culture has been affected both by authoritarian traditions and its reinforcement by socialism. Perhaps even more than in Hungary, though, socialism and economic chaos have induced in the population a sense of tiredness that is evident even to casual foreign visitors. It is little wonder then that the elections have not excited a weary and demoralized population. The palpable apathy which is also reflected in the decision of many Poles not to bother to vote in the June elections,[108] bodes ill for Western-style political reform and makes future change more unpredictable. Moreover, the deep pessimism and cynicism of the population makes reform particularly difficult for it inhibits the willingness to take political risks. Successful reform requires at least some optimism regarding the outcome as well as credibility.

Furthermore, given the history of Polish politics, which were largely characterized with swings between dictatorship and anarchy (with some short democratic intervals) in a transition to pluralistic democracy, the West may not be the model envisioned by many of those who seek a systemic change. Lech Walesa has said that the problem was not reforming the system but "how to get out of this abnormal system that leads to absurdity and move toward normality."[109] Yet it is not entirely clear what even Walesa means by "normality." Clearly committed to political freedom, is he able to separate that from his quest to provide Polish workers with economic security? A devout Catholic, Walesa has often shown considerable scorn toward the West as a soulless society consumed by material acquisitiveness.[110] Is he envisioning some sort of "paternalistic" democracy for Poland? Thus, it is unclear even what the competing political visions in Poland are and as such the possibility for unexpected developments and consequences tend to magnify.

Nevertheless, there is also the possibility that at least in the short term political uncertainty may work to the advantage of Jaruzelski and the party. Though Solidarity has not committed itself to a full free-market economy, it is the Communist party that is associated with the preservation of the social safety net (as inadequate as it may be) and the mass subsidies to the huge and inefficient state industries. Two groups in particular, the several million pensioners and the millions of workers in the steel, coal and shipyard industries are a highly susceptible constituency to party assurances against mass unemployment and drastic social welfare cutbacks. The vast bureaucracy also depends on the party to maintain their jobs. The Solidarity-supported candidates who have to balance the need to protect workers' jobs with the necessity of deep economic reform if the country is to avoid falling irretrievably behind Europe, will have considerable difficulty in reassuring the above group in the near future.

Moreover, in a legislature in which the electoral agreement ensures that the opposition has a minority of the seats and thereby is restricted to either blocking legislation or supporting the regimes' majority, it faces a considerable dilemma and the danger of losing political credibility. If the opposition tries to consistently block legislation it risks appearing as an irresponsible, obstructionist or inept group that is unfit to govern. This could destroy its chances in the 1993 elections. But if the opposition acquiesces to legislation put forth by the party it has to share the responsibility if the effects are negative. If the outcome is positive, the opposition, as the "juniorgarten" in the legislation, is likely to derive little credit.

But in the June 1989 elections the Polish party also undertook concrete steps to improve its chances in the election. It tried to take advantage of its vastly superior funding and access to the media. By timing the election for June 1989 it also caught the opposition by surprise, giving it little time to prepare. It put forth many candidates who had built independent reputations for themselves and played down their connections with the party. The party logo did not appear on their literature and posters.[111] For instance, Antoni Gucwinski, a television personality and the director of the Wroclaw zoo, was one of the party's candidates but nominally ran as the candidate of the Association for the Dissemination of Knowledge.[112] Jerzy Urban the notorious former government spokesman and vitriolic critic of Solidarity decided to run as an independent in Warsaw's Srodmiescie district.[113] Technically, he was never a member of the party but he had been one of the most outspoken defenders of the Jaruzelski regime and its policies. In some respects, though, the regime's tactics may be of greater significance as a dress rehearsal for the 1993 election. In 1989 the elections represented more of an opportunity to protest than a chance to select an alternative government. The regime, the population, and to a lesser degree, Solidarity, could better afford to experiment.

Lastly, Solidarity itself is more divided than in 1981 and its popular support has diminished. As noted, some Solidarity members and supporters in other opposition groups have denounced the pact. On the one hand this, of course, may also be interpreted as a sign of healthy political pluralism. On the other hand, it shows dangerous fragmentation at a time when the opposition needs to build cohesion if it is to challenge the party successfully and help guide the country towards becoming a pluralistic democratic, post-Communist state. Many factions in the union itself have become radicalized and do not take direction easily from the leadership. There has been a dramatic decline in membership as well from the heady days of 1981. Wladyslaw Frasyniuk, a top union leader expressed the hope in June 1989 that by the end of the year Solidarity membership would rise to between 5 and 6 million (compared to 10 million in 1981).[114] All these problems did not necessarily diminish the chances of Solidarity-supported candidates to do well in the June elections. The greater danger is in the longer term as Solidarity prepares to offer the Polish people a real alternative in completely free elections.

In fact, Solidarity-supported candidates appeared to do extremely well in the June 4, 1989 election (and the June 18, 1989 run-offs). They swept all of the 161 seats that were open to free competition in the Sejm, and all but one of the seats in the 100 seat Senate. Also, many of the 35 government candidates for the Sejm on a special list (including the Prime Minister, Mieczyslaw Radowski) who ran unopposed were defeated when more than 50% of the voters crossed out their name. The regime not only readily conceded that its candidates did badly but rather ingenuously declared that Solidarity "must now accept its responsibility and join a coalition government."[115]

Though this election is clearly a progressive step towards pluralistic democracy there is also cause for caution. First the voter turnout at 62% was unexpectedly low indicating that many Poles still did not accept the legitimacy of the political system. There is thus a strong signal of disapproval of Solidarity's election agreement with the regime which indicated the possibility of splits in the opposition in the future. Secondly, the eagerness with which the regime has sought to bring Solidarity into a coalition presents both a historical opportunity and the danger of cooptation. The regime still controls the majority of the seats and Solidarity must ensure that it does not become the scapegoat for the failures of the larger partner should it join in a coalition. And thirdly, the very poor showing of the party could induce hard-liners to try to block further movement to democratization. And if Gorbachev's reforms falter in the Soviet Union then the hard-liners would also get a sympathetic hearing in the socialist bloc.

Very likely then among the larger issues confronting Solidarity will be its ability to hold its membership together over divisive issues in the years to come, to play a constructive role in conditions of economic chaos and to maintain or enhance its credibility as the center of an opposition that would be a viable alternative to the communist regime in power. These is also a danger that the current situation will suddenly deteriorate. Beneath the surface, there may be more than apathy and disillusionment in Poland. Anger and frustration is widespread as well, and ironically, major political reforms can help set into motion truly cataclysmic forces. Sarah Terry, for instance, has argued that radical political changes coupled with a pauperized economy have turned Poland into a "pre-revolutionary society" that can erupt at any time.[116] If that is indeed the case then one of the most onerous tasks confronting the opposition is how to effect a peaceful political transcendence or systemic change.

In Poland and in Hungary then opposition forces have an exceedingly difficult task ahead of them if they are to bring about transcendence and especially systemic political change. Even in these two states where political reform is far more advanced than elsewhere in the socialist community, the communist parties are desperately trying to adapt to changing circumstances. They seem willing to tolerate more pluralism but even in Hungary they seem intent on surviving as the leading political force in the country. Even in these two states it is premature to speak of a "post-Communist" era though the possibility for systemic change is far greater than elsewhere and perhaps the people of these two states have the best chance to take what the Hungarians have called a "leap into the future."

But the significant domestic constraints, as we will discuss later, are reinforced by some external ones, though here too change is taking place. As Melvin Croan has put it (in Chapter 7), Gorbachev did not become CPSU General Secretary in order to preside over the liquidation of the

Soviet empire. Nor, for that matter, is there any reason to believe that Gorbachev would be willing to allow the disintegration of the Leninist system in the Soviet Union itself.

Thus there are limits to political reform in the Soviet Union and throughout Eastern Europe. What is envisioned by the various regimes (with the possible exception of Hungary's) is a reform of the current system rather than a systemic political change. What is also important, however, about the nature of the change that is occurring is that it is primarily motivated by economic factors. To that extent political reform, though part of a broader approach, plays a secondary role to economic change, particularly in the Soviet Union's perestroika.

Economic changes

Moscow is moving ahead vigorously with the introduction of a variety of economic reforms as part of perestroika. For instance on May 24, 1988 Nikolai Ryzhkov, the Chairman of the Council of Ministers, introduced a draft law on cooperatives in the Supreme Soviet which will allow Soviet citizens to join cooperatives with no limits on taxable earnings.[117] Ryzhkov was particularly enthusiastic about the new law and declared that "in a short period of time, cooperatives can solve the most acute problems of perestroika."[118] The law is part of the Soviet regime's attempt to give market forces a greater play—as Carl McMillan and Paul Marer show in their chapters. The strong, persistent, and often vociferous, opposition to these measures in the Soviet Union gives but some indication of the magnitude of the economic changes that are taking place. Far more freedom will be allocated to the enterprises, both domestically and in foreign trade, and more play will be given to wage differentials.

Gorbachev has not only emphasized that economic reform requires political change but also seems to have concluded that if he is to succeed in carrying out his policies he must consolidate his power. We witnessed this, as noted, at the meeting of the Congress of People's Deputies in May 1989 when Gorbachev was acclaimed for the powerful new post of executive and administrative president. In the election for the Congress in March 1989, by allowing people to choose among candidates or even by simply exposing them to the 50% vote requirement in constituencies, where they ran unopposed, he managed to dispose of or humiliate "conservative" opponents of perestroika. At the session of the Congress during May–June 1989, Gorbachev, working together with the party apparatus that controls that body, also winnowed out the most radical reformers by preventing their election to the Supreme Soviet. Though it will contain some dissenting voices such as Yeltsin's, the Supreme Soviet should be quite a malleable instrument in Gorbachev's hands.

But perhaps trends are as important as Gorbachev's current success in consolidating his political power. The Soviet leader from the beginning of his tenure has equated personal power and economic reform. Bringing in his own people into the Politburo and dismissing more than 100 Central

Committee hold-overs from the Brezhnev era have been part, it seems, of a kind of dual-track approach.

In the reshuffle of the Politburo of September 30, 1988 and the subsequent votes in the Supreme Soviet, for example, Gorbachev significantly enhanced his position and his ability to pursue economic and political reform. He not only became the titular President (Chairman of the Presidium of the Supreme Soviet) but appeared to succeed in weakening the power of those who seemed to be less enthusiastic than he, about reform. He had the number two man, Yegor Ligachev formally stripped of responsibility for ideology and personnel (key portfolios that some analysts contend had been taken away from him in previous months).[119] Ligachev moved to the agriculture portfolio and still retained his Politburo seat. Thus he could continue to wield considerable power but would not be able to play as central a role as before. On the other hand, Gorbachev's choice for his replacement as head of ideology significantly strengthened the Soviet leader's hands. Vadim A. Medvedev, Gorbachev's selection to head the ideology portfolio was also given full membership in the Politburo. He has a reputation as a strong proponent of economic reform and had been a part of Gorbachev's inner circle of advisors. In addition, he had the rather difficult job of explaining Gorbachev's reforms to the East European leaders. He had to encourage change, ensure Eastern Europe support and yet make certain that the states in the region did not go too far along the road to reform. Thus, Gorbachev promoted someone who not only shares his views on reform but is also knowledgeable about conditions prevailing in Eastern Europe.

Medvedev's support is important to Gorbachev. The Soviet leader has been emphatic that there must be visible improvements in the standard of living in the Soviet Union. In his acceptance speech following his election as state President, Gorbachev declared:

> It is extremely important for the Soviets to master more quickly the new methods of management, to take charge of supplying the population with foodstuffs and industrial goods, construction of housing and its equitable distribution, the development of services, the insurance of legality and maintaining of public order, and environmental protection . . . The principles of self-financing, self-support, self-management must be introduced everywhere.[120]

Medvedev fully supports Gorbachev's position on the nature of socialist state control of the domestic economy. In contrast to Ligachev who derided the Western idea of free markets and declared it anathema to communism, Medvedev is far more flexible on the questions of markets and ownership of productive property. In his first statement as chief ideologist, he contended that "the market is an indispensable means of gearing production to fast-changing demand and a major instrument of public control over quality and cost".[121] He also declared himself in favour of current experiments with cooperative ownership and the renting of property to farmers and small entrepreneurs. Moreover, he argued that this should be expanded to heavy industry. He added, "our previous concepts of public property and our attitudes to this problem have proven to be untenable."[122]

As major as these changes are, though, it is worth heeding Marer's *caveat* (Chapter 5) that the Soviet reform blueprint should not be considered a step toward the type of capitalist or mixed market economies that are in place in the industrial and newly-industrializing countries around the world (though there are clear similarities between Soviet reform plans and the nature of market economies). A number of measures are more form than substance. Profound differences persist which make analogies between the two systems misleading. But then it is not merely a matter of the Soviet Union replicating a Western economic system. Rather, it is a question regarding the very nature of the Soviet reforms and whether they do envisage fundamental change. Such a transformation, though, does not necessarily entail a wholesale switch from central planning to a market economy for in all states the government is responsible for some vital economic tasks and therefore what is involved is really a balance between "central planning" and the market.

There is, however, a radical difference between market-style reforms and a market. An acceptance of the market involves the adoption of the "market idea." The Soviet Union, as Herbert S. Levine has stated, has not yet developed the "ideological faith" that markets can benefit society generally.[123] That is, there has to be a shift in the ideological perception of the market as something fundamentally beneficial rather than as a remedy for certain problems that have arisen in the application of an ideology that is basically sound. Even those Western economists who contend that the Soviet bloc needs to combine both market and plan, call for major changes. Alec Nove, for example, has suggested as minimal measures the abandonment of quantitative output targets, the allocation of resources by non-administrative (cost) means, an end to state subsidies for inefficient industries and the acceptance of temporary unemployment.[124] This would necessitate, however, profound economic restructuring, including the freeing up of prices.

The pattern of development in all the socialist states has created fundamental problems, though the acuteness of the difficulties varies among them. "Extensive" development, where production is capital, material and fuel intensive, has brought about economic stagnation. More than that the administrative command planning employed by the socialist states has created a whole series of disequilibria. The Hungarian economist Janos Kornai has written perceptively both about the theory of soft budget constraints (i.e. weak punishment for poor financial performance, which is manifested in supply constraints) in socialist economies and the problems of controlled disequilibrium.[125] Some economists, including Igor Birman have suggested that the Soviet economy is in an acute state of cumulative disequilibrium that threatens to reduce productivity to the crisis point.[126] This may be an exaggeration but the Soviet Union and the East European states do face economic disequilibria and contradictions. These deep disequilibria become more evident as reforms proceed. In the case of the Soviet Union we have begun to see the hidden inflation, hidden unemployment and hidden balance of payment problem where the deficit was covered by the state monopoly of foreign trade and the use of arbitrary exchange rates. The issues of price, capital flow, wage differentials and competition all need to be addressed. Soviet success in addressing these issues have an impact not only on political reform and the survival of Gorbachev but also on Soviet-East European relations.

Moscow's Economic Dilemmas. The Soviet approach to the dilemmas confronting it has been perhaps best illustrated in the policies on cooperatives, on agriculture, on alcoholism, and on prices. Cooperatives in some respects have become emblematic of the hopes and contradictions of perestroika in the Soviet Union. A year after Ryzhkov introduced the law his assumptions about cooperatives appear to be vastly over optimistic. Certainly, they have mushroomed all over the country to more than 60,000 with 7,000 in Moscow alone.[127] In terms of the large Soviet economy, however, they occupy a very small portion of the country's economic activity. But perhaps more importantly the trends in the development of cooperatives is disquieting. In December 1988, for instance, the Council of Ministers announced a ban on certain types of services that had been provided by medical, printing and film cooperatives.[128] Medical cooperatives, for example, can no longer perform abortions (legal under Soviet law) or a whole range of minor surgery and treatment. As a result, over one-third of the medical cooperatives have already closed down.[129]

Further restrictive measures have been introduced. In February 1989 the Soviet government announced that cooperatives would be subjected to higher taxes. The rate of taxation is to be determined by the 15 local Soviet republic governments.[130] This means that in the Baltic states, where the economic and political soil is much more fertile for cooperatives, taxes will be relatively low but elsewhere in the country Soviet entrepreneurs will have to content with a heavy tax burden. Government officials have declared that they do not want cooperatives to turn people into instant millionaires with "unearned income."[131] As well, in March the government approved legislation which severely limited cooperatives in their dealings with foreign firms.[132] But this measure will have a negative impact not only on trade with the West but also on the enterprise-to-enterprise relations with East European states which Gorbachev has sought to encourage. Thus, what the Soviet government has given to the cooperatives with one hand it has often taken away with the other. Moreover, an atmosphere of uncertainty, and the unpredictability of government regulations all discourage the risk-taking that is so essential to the growth of private enterprise.

Cooperatives also suffer from an economic structure that has a centralizing bias and relegates private enterprise to the periphery of economic activity. The Soviet economist Gavril Popov charged that many cooperatives, particularly in construction cannot secure bank loans and have to pay high prices for supplies.[133] He pointed out that, for instance, cooperatives have to pay five times more for trucks than do state enterprises. Those cooperative enterprises that do get bank loans are subjected to harsh terms and then have to bid against powerful state enterprises for scarce supplies.[134] It is little wonder, then, that cooperatives need to charge higher prices.

Perhaps the greatest obstacle to the development of cooperatives, however, comes from the attitude of the Soviet people, which in turn involves Soviet political culture. At the meeting of the Congress of People's Deputies, Vitaly Kanishev received wild applause when he said that private cooperatives set up at Mr. Gorbachev's urging "not only get their hands into our pockets, they undress us and want to kill us, too."[135] It is a dissatisfaction that is deeper than just a complaint about prices. Cooperatives reflect the contradiction between the impulse of the Gorbachev government to liberalize the economy and the ingrained conservatism of the population. Gorbachev himself has expressed his own ambivalence about private enterprise. In February 1989 he told the citizens of Lvov that "Cooperatives are necessary, but they should help people, not empty their pockets." And, a few days later in Kiev he stated that it was true that cooperatives were driving up prices and were "intensifying shortages."[136] Among the population, after seventy years of socialism there is a feeling that profit is evil. There is also the Russian heritage of envy of those who move ahead in society. Andrei Konovalov, the chairman of the Moscow Union of Cooperatives perhaps best summed up the effect of these traditions on popular attitudes. He said, "there exists a stereo-type that makes it a virtue to do away with the rich. We still have the psychological tendencies of the poor."[137]

Contradictions also abound in Gorbachev's policies on agriculture. The virtually uniform complaint in the Soviet Union that the economic restructuring that Gorbachev is trying to implement has so far led only to shortages,[138] is based to a significant degree on the inability of agriculture and the distribution system to supply adequate quantities of food. Soviet economist Aleksandr S. Zaychenko recently debunked official claims about the high-protein Soviet diet. In fact he showed that Soviet citizens eat a third as much meat as Americans. Furthermore, he cited figures showing that in 1988 the Soviet population had a poorer diet than it did in 1913 under the Czars.[139] Soviet authorities also admit that at least 20% of the Soviet population lives below the poverty line.[140]

Gorbachev himself told newspaper editors in March 1989 that agricultural reform was imperative. He added that, "the food problem is the fundamental problem at present . . ." and that if food shortages persist, "frankly speaking, we can ruin the whole of perestroika and bring about serious destabilization of society."[141] Yet Gorbachev's own reforms have been responsible, at least in part, for some of the problems in agriculture. It was he who had created, *Gosagroprom*, the giant state agriculture superministry three years earlier. In March 1989 he proposed and the policy-making plenum accepted the dismantling of *Gosagroprom* and of some other parts of the cumbersome agro-industrial complex. He also gained the acceptance of a leasing system for family farms.[142]

At best, however, he achieved only a compromise solution. A variety of ministries continue to exist and their very presence creates or reinforces centralizing tendencies. Ligachev has remained in charge of agriculture and he has contended that state and collective farms will remain the main focus of agriculture.[143] It is true that an extensive leasing program of land by families and cooperative farms has been introduced but the state farms have been left with a whole series of blocking mechanisms. Nikolai Shmelev, head of the economics department of the Institute of the U.S.A. and Canada, in Moscow, has called the March 1989 changes "half-hearted."[144] For the near future agriculture as a whole, will not be subject to the market and the availability of land for leasing is yet to be determined.

Gorbachev's anti-alcoholism campaign also reveals some of the dilemmas of reform in the Soviet Union. Started by the Soviet leader as a means of increasing worker discipline and productivity it produced unexpected and unwelcome consequences. The population soon found means of producing alcohol at home and the heavy use of sugar in these private stills helped cause a shortage of sugar in the country. But more importantly the reduction in the sale of alcohol by the state resulted in a huge drop in revenues. Alcohol is very heavily taxed in the Soviet Union and has been a key source of state income.

To complicate matters, the Soviet Union, it seems, has been running a budget deficit for years.[145] In early 1989 Leonid Abalkin, then the director of the Economic Institute of the Soviet Academy of Sciences, revealed that the budget deficit for the year would come to the equivalent of $162 billion (three times the October 1988 government estimate) and asserted that it endangered the national economy.[146] Thus this attempt at reform which resulted in the loss of tens of billions of dollars of tax revenue has resulted in economic dysfunction rather than progress.

As the Soviet economy stagnates, as the Soviet Union tries to redirect more spending to consumer goods and attempts to reduce the deficit, the critical piece that is missing, as Murray Feshbach has suggested, is major price reform.[147] Without a change in the way prices are determined, decentralization, competitiveness and ultimately economic efficiency cannot be achieved. Abel Aganbegyan, Gorbachev's key economic advisor argued in 1988 that "there definitely would have to be reform of retail prices" and that moreover, this would have to be a priority.[148] But in February 1989 the Soviet Union published a decree to curb "growing prices" and in a *Pravda* article Aganbegyan suggested that the retail price reform issue should be shelved for three or four years[149] (so as to allow popular support for perestroika to solidify).

So there is an awareness among some Soviet economists that more fundamental solutions are needed but they find it difficult to overcome the contradictions inherent in the socialist system. For example Nikolai Shmelev, has argued for radical solutions, including moving to higher prices as determined by the market, and the elimination of poorly performing factories.[150] This would raise the possibility, he has acknowledged, that some workers in inefficient operations would find themselves unemployed. Moreover, he has contended that workers need to be given economic incentives and industry must become interested in innovation. But he has also been aware of the problems of introducing such reforms since higher prices for consumers, especially for food, are a "socially dangerous problem," in his words.

He has stated, in a 1989 interview, that in theory he is against any control over prices. But he added that because of the very high degree of monopolization of the Soviet economy, any real reform of prices first required a decentralization of the economy, recognition of enterprises and the creation of the new companies to demonopolize prices.[151] Only when the monopoly control of the economy is reduced could *wholesale* prices be set by the margin. He added that very optimistically this could be done by the mid-1990s. At the same time he contended that because of the possibility of "unbearable social tensions" *retail* prices should not be touched at least for the first half of the 1990s.[152]

He has also admitted that the full benefits of perestroika may not be seen for another decade. Consequently he has argued that the Soviet Union should be willing to increase its foreign debt to import cheap consumer goods for the next three to five years so that Soviet workers could see more quickly the benefits of perestroika.[153]

There are, however, significant difficulties with Shmelev's approach that illustrate the overall dilemmas of reform. First, his proposals for decentralization operate within strict parameters. He is also in favour of developing the high technology sector and his solution contradicts his general goal of decentralization. Growth in this sector he argues should come from state investments, state credit facilities and even price supports all to be "accomplished through central planning." Secondly, it is difficult to see how wholesale prices could be freed up but retail prices kept under control. If the tax portions of the retail price are reduced then that would increase the budget deficit so eventually the retail prices would also need to be adjusted. And thirdly, the advice to increase the foreign debt underestimates the burden and overstates the benefits. The Soviet Union already has a large hard-currency debt. In 1988 sharply higher imports from the West left the Soviet Union with a deficit of $2.6 billion.[154] And in the first quarter of 1989 the Soviet trade gap widened to 600 million rubles ($1.1 billion) from 40 million rubles in the same period the previous year.[155] Yet there has been no appreciable improvement in the lot of the Soviet consumer.

More radical measures, in Soviet terms, need to be followed through but as Marer shows, that requires a proper appreciation of competition and prices, a resolution of the ownership function, and the introduction of proper macro-economic policies. This is yet to happen in the Soviet Union. Even the more reformist economists have not resolved the contradictions of socialism. Some of the policies that have been implemented have managed to magnify them. At times these Soviet policies seem to resemble an individual who is driving with one foot on the brake and the other on the accelerator. There is not much movement but there is considerable damage to the vehicle. And thus, using the criteria for systemic change suggested by William Odom[156], the economic reforms in the Soviet Union do not constitute such an alteration.

The East European Experience. In the economic realm the relative newness of the Soviet reform program, though, necessitates an examination of other socialist economic reforms of longer duration. This should help not only in understanding the future course of Soviet reforms but also that of Soviet-East European economic relations. In this instance Hungary, as noted, with the longest reform record, is a logical choice. It is not a matter of simple analogies and the transfer of the Hungarian reforms and innovations to the Soviet Union. There are salient differences, including size, external control, the availability of natural resources, the depth of the crisis and differences in political culture as we have noted. Nevertheless, there are vital similarities as well between the Hungarian program introduced in 1968 and Soviet perestroika. A seemingly comprehensive approach, but the application only of halfway measures, is characteristic of both programs. And the Hungarian experiment is now particularly relevant, but not only because of its longevity or because it is further advanced than the current Soviet reforms. With the generational change that has occurred in the Party leadership, both the pace and the nature of Hungarian economic reform may be changing more radically.

As they stand, Hungarian reforms have enjoyed only limited success. Economic stagnation, massive inflationary pressures, rising unemployment and the largest per capita hard-currency debt in Eastern Europe provide little confidence in the Hungarian model. Yet the Hungarian experiment has been viewed as the most sophisticated one in Eastern Europe. On closer examination, though, the process of change has been far less well thought-out than it appears. Basically, it has been more a matter of responding to immediate, or short-term, needs rather than dealing with fundamental long-term issues. Again form has often prevailed over substance.

Certainly there has been economic progress in Hungary. Market forces have been given greater play. Industrial concentrations have been diminished somewhat and some limited progress has been achieved in the creation of a capital market. The role of fiscal policy has increased and the reorganization of the banking system has advanced and with it monetary policy has received a boost. There has even been legislation on the liquidation of inefficient and money-losing enterprises.

Bold measures (though on a limited scale) have been instituted. A small stock market with forty state-owned companies listing their shares was opened in July 1988. It only meets once a week but optimists at the Hungarian National Bank expressed the hope that within a few years up to one-third of the country's operations could become Western-style joint-stock companies.[157] In January 1989 many of the restrictions on foreign purchases of Hungarian companies, were lifted. And in May, thirteen western banks paid $110 million for 49.65 percent of Hungary's leading lighting company, Tungsram.[158]

The Hungarians have tried to encourage foreign investment. They have appealed to Western governments, corporations and even Hungarian expatriates. There has been an increase in foreign investment but hardly a rush. Until Hungary institutes deep reforms with a realistic market-determined pricing system foreign investors will find few attractions and will operate largely on the periphery. Economic reforms in Hungary, though, have been constrained in large part by the desire of the political leaders to sustain socialism even if in an altered form.

Insufficient incentives and inadequate competition plague Hungary despite twenty years of reform. Even those who have an optimistic outlook regarding the prospects for the Hungarian economy, such as Jan Adam, argue that successful reform cannot be achieved without a resolution of the problem of the lack of strong incentives in the economy.[159] Incentives, though, and the consequent wage differentials are not a remedy that can be easily implemented in Hungary. Income differentials which have grown wider are deeply resented.[160] As well, growing inflation has further impoverished the already large percentage of the population that was at the margin or below the poverty line.[161] Further wage differentialization, therefore, could become a politically explosive issue.

Perhaps such political constraints have inhibited reformers from delving more deeply into the basic issues and potential solutions. Regardless of the motives and difficulties, though, the end result has been that reform in Hungary as well as elsewhere in Eastern Europe has not been particularly well thought-out. Marer (Chapter 5) and others are then quite justified when they characterize the ongoing experimentation with change as "reforms without theory."

Despite considerable innovativeness the Hungarian reformers have not been able to resolve the contradictions of socialism. Attempts at increasing economic efficiency have instead further deepened Hungary's economic quagmire. Reforms have released hidden inflation and magnified the threat of unemployment. In January 1989 for example, the government announced further substantial price increases of 17% on food, 24% on cars and 60-80% on public transportation.[162] The standard of living is falling with a drop in real income in 1988 of 8 to 8.5% according to official figures (and down to the 1973 level).[163]

Price manipulation is not the same as allowing the market to determine the bulk of prices. In Hungary, so far the greater part of the economy is slated to remain in the hands of the government. Prices, capital allocation and the level of competitiveness are still determined at the center. Thus a "manipulative system" is much more prevalent than the market.[164]

Hungary's desperate economic condition ironically may either provide the impetus for a full scale movement to a market-based economy or act as a constraint to further significant economic reform. On the one hand, it would seem that if external constraints and domestic social peace would permit it, the logical road to economic recovery is the market. As noted, Pozsgay has spoken of the need for the market. On the other hand, the party's desire to survive in competitive elections may induce it to cynically adopt a populist platform that would mortgage the economic future of the country in exchange for maintaining temporary economic stability and political power. Whereas those who seek fundamental reform can only offer hardship and dislocation in the short term in exchange for a promise of long term improvement, the party can appeal to popular insecurity and historical etatism. The party could include in its platform measures to reduce the threat of unemployment, as well as assurances of wage indexation, the maintenance of social services and of the universality of education. These would represent a desperate and irresponsible approach by the regime but we have yet to see the limit of non-violent means that a ruling communist party will take when faced with the danger of political oblivion.

With the Soviet Union pushing for reform and with the East European states moving at varying paces, there are no uniform reform blueprints or agreed-upon reform strategies or principles of implementation in the socialist community. Yet as Carl McMillan states (Chapter 2), even though the Soviet Union allows each East European state to pursue its own path of economic reform, there must be sufficient regional homogeneity in the process of reform among the member countries to provide a common basis for the more decentralised interaction as envisaged by the Comprehensive Program formulated by the CMEA. And as will be shown there is considerable pressure for economic homogeneity or at least compatibility from reform leaders throughout the region.

Furthermore, for reform to succeed even in the best of circumstances, there must be credibility. The government in power must be able to convince the population that sacrifices are worthwhile and that there is thus a reasonable chance of success. The greater the degree of legitimacy that a government enjoys, the easier it is for it to maintain credibility and therefore induce people to cooperate effectively in a reform program. In the case of the socialist states though they all suffer from crises of legitimacy. Moreover, even in terms of the limited legitimacy that some of the regimes may enjoy, this is largely dependent on improving, or at least maintaining, the standard of living. Under current economic conditions this is exceedingly problematic. And, such difficulties are compounded by the fact that the populations in the East European states are pessimistic, with little faith in change. The regimes in some ways, therefore, are caught in a Catch-22 type of bind. If the reforms they have introduced are to have a chance of success, there is a need for popular optimism regarding the outcome. The preferred outcome for much of the population in the region is an improved standard of living. Yet, given the stagnant or declining standard of living in socialist societies, the population is naturally pessimistic about the future or at least highly skeptical of government reform programs. An official poll taken in 1988 in Poland, for instance, showed that only 7% of the respondents in the country believed that the reform program could succeed.[165]

To a significant degree, though, the various regimes in Eastern Europe bear direct responsibility for much of the lack of regime credibility. In

Poland, for instance, after the regime lost the fall 1987 referendum on the introduction of a variety of reform measures (which included sharp price increases), it brazenly proceeded to implement much of the program. Thus, as Jane Curry has stated, the Polish regime was basically sending out the message that rulers were different from the rest of the population and that they could not be challenged.[166] Moreover, the way in which the Polish regime handled the strikes in May 1988 again demonstrated the kind of contempt that it has toward the population. Its refusal to negotiate with Solidarity at the time and its use of force and of coercion brought about temporary industrial peace but at the cost of an even further demoralized population. It found out within a few months that it has no choice but to open lines of communication with Solidarity.

With a foreign debt which has risen to $39 billion,[167] with inflation growing to 100% per annum,[168] with acute shortages of materials, labor, machinery capital as well as of all types of consumer goods the regime has had to try to reestablish links with the people if it is to gain their cooperation in rebuilding the economy. Ironically for a socialist government which had tried to build its legitimacy on the basis of a social contract that was supposed to deliver economic security in exchange for the political acquiesce of the population, the Polish regime has had to make political concessions in order to compensate the population for massive economic failure.

Beyond Reform? But, ultimately, even if reforms were successful in terms of their current formulations in the Soviet Union and Eastern Europe, would they resolve the basic issues plaguing these societies, particularly in the economic realm? Effective reform produces synergy, that is, improvements in certain areas of the economy will help boost efficiency in others. Yet, as we have seen, reform in socialist states all too often has produced dysfunction rather than synergy. Measures to improve production in certain industries have led to shortages of materials in other areas. Attempts to rectify prices have resulted in huge rises in inflation in the states where reform has proceeded the furthest. Jan Vanous, for instance, has claimed that Eastern Europe is heading for hyperinflation and that the regimes would not be able to cut the inflationary spiral.[169]

In Poland the agreement in April 1989 for an indexing policy that will link wages (at 80%) to future price increases is likely to further fuel inflation according to many Polish economists.[170] The situation in Yugoslavia is not completely analogous but developments there are nevertheless disquieting for socialism. The government of Ante Markovic predicted in May 1989 that inflation for the year would reach 945%.[171] It is possible then that the East European states may be entering a *pre-Yugoslav* rather than a post-Communist stage.

Thus, there remains a fundamental issue. Is the socialist system really reformable in the sense that it could resolve the basic problems confronting it? There is considerable doubt among Western economists. Skepticism among dissidents and socialist workers at large may be even stronger. The very low turnout in the Polish vote in June 1989 is but an indication of a lack of faith in the system's reformability. Yet, as noted, available evidence in this work and elsewhere indicates that Gorbachev does not intend to bring about a systemic change. He is quite willing to push for further de-Stalinization but firmly rejects the de-Leninization of the Soviet system. Even in East European states where reform has progressed beyond that in the Soviet Union, de-Leninization has been largely rejected (with the possible exceptions of Poland and Hungary, and this is to be seen within the next few years). Even in Hungary Mihaly Bihari was expelled from the Communist party in April 1988 in large measure because he advocated the dismantling of parts of the Leninist structure.

Is there a means, then, of going beyond reform in a way in which this may be acceptable to the Communist regimes? The most crucial stumbling block is the role of the Party. If there is to be transcendence of the system, the role of the Party must change from one of dominance to that of influence. There is a subtle and intricate relationship between power and influence and perhaps this type of transcendence is not possible. There certainly is no historical precedent in socialist states. Nevertheless, this may be the only feasible way in the Soviet Union and in Eastern Europe. All societies have myths. In such a transformation the Party would need to accept a greatly diminished role and yet pretend that it still retained power. The population at large would need to defer to the Party in formal terms though it would know that the system had become essentially pluralistic. The Party would preserve its legitimizing ideological influence but it would allow the necessary autonomy of the economy, of technology and of science.[172] It would all require the kind of intricate political choreography that we witnessed in the last few years of Franco's rule in Spain. But "Francoization" would be even more difficult in Eastern Europe and the Soviet Union in view of the difficulties posed by their political cultures and enormous economic problems.

For such a solution compromise is necessary. This may be very difficult to attain, though, in socialist states. One of the leading intellectual supporters of Solidarity, in Poland, Adam Michnik, for instance, declared in 1988 that, "in Poland agreement is impossible and essential."[173] Some have been somewhat more optimistic. Zbigniew Brzezinski, a former national security adviser to the Carter White House seems to think that a solution in Poland (and elsewhere) is possible and obvious—the Communist rulers and the non-Communist ruled need to reach a compromise.[174] The June 1989 elections in Poland have been a step toward compromise though it remains to be seen whether a *workable* political compromise will be implemented. But even if such adaptation were to work at the domestic level in Eastern Europe it would ultimately require Soviet acquiescence and would also need to fuel a compromise at the interstate level—and thereby help effect a change in the Soviet-East European relationship itself.

The External Dimensions of Reform

The Soviet Union is yet to solve the dilemma that is has faced in Eastern Europe since the end of the Second World War—the inherent incompatibility of Soviet goals of cohesion and viability in the region.[175] Under Gorbachev, then, Soviet policy still has to cope with the dilemmas and paradoxes of the regional relationship. His reforms are intended to enhance not only the viability and thereby the stability of the Soviet system but also to ensure the stability of the East European states. In the past though the price of stability in East European states was high. The Soviet Union had to allow a greater degree of independence (that is, less regional cohesion). By all indications, though, Moscow still wants to promote both the primacy of the Communist party in the East European states and the unity of the socialist community, whether this is done bilaterally or through the instruments of the Warsaw Pact or the CMEA.

These are the broad goals though, and they may disguise flexibility and nuances. In terms of cohesion Moscow really has two concerns. One is cohesion under its tutelage, something that Moscow has found desirable but, as noted, often very costly. The second is autonomous regional cohesion in Eastern Europe. That has yet to recur although there is some movement in terms of culture and consciousness as Melvin Croan shows in Chapter 7. In the economic realm, however, bilateralism has been the predominant mode of economic interchange despite attempts at multilaterality within the CMEA.

The East European states could benefit from closer economic and even political cooperation among themselves. There are sound economic reasons for this and the problems of national minorities should reinforce the arguments for regional political cooperation. Such cohesion, moreover, need not be anti-Soviet. And, as J.F. Brown points out, Moscow may help the East European economies by encouraging East European cooperation[176] without necessarily having to fear its consequences.

There have been numerous indications, as we have seen, that Moscow may be more flexible in allowing the East European states the freedom to choose their mode of development under Gorbachev. And this can contribute to viability. There are, of course, intrinsic parameters and constraints on autonomy relating to asymmetries of size and long-term trade and investment commitments. But at least there appears to be a willingness to allow greater individual state decision-making on the part of the Soviet Union. (Ironically, in Czechoslovakia the regime has used such autonomy to reject reform.) Greater autonomy in Eastern Europe may mean that at least in the short run these countries will find it more difficult to achieve regional cohesion since they are unable to mesh even economic reforms. Left to their own devices, though, these countries may sooner rather than later discover both the benefits and viable means of multilateral cooperation.

Still, the Soviet Union has yet to indicate in any *unambiguous* fashion that it is prepared to accept East European multilateral cooperation without a controlling, or at least dominating, Soviet participation. It has ideological, strategic and economic fears that are difficult to alleviate. Moscow is especially concerned by the development of a pan-European consciousness in Eastern Europe that is exclusionary—that is one that further segregates the Soviet Union from Europe.

Therefore, the paradoxical aspects of the Soviet-East European relationship persist. The indirect method[177] seems to hold the best promise for achieving some of the key Soviet goals in Eastern Europe. In order for the East European regimes to become more viable they must be able to perform better economically. Better economic performance in turn is likely to occur only if reforms are introduced. The best way for the Soviet Union to encourage the introduction of reforms seems to be a hands-off approach which gives more leeway to the East European states to formulate their programs in order to cope with local needs. It is unlikely that if the Soviet Union attempted to impose perestroika on East European states from the outside that it would work. Thus although linear logic would suggest that the simplest way for the Soviet Union to achieve its goal of cohesion in Eastern Europe is to impose measures from the outside, this could be counterproductive. Cohesion achieved in this manner would merely aggravate long-term instability in the region. Therefore, the Soviet Union must continue to cope with the old dilemma of cohesion and viability and reforms must address Soviet and East European political, economic and military concerns.

Socialist internationalism

Under Gorbachev there has been a reexamination of the political and ideological relationship with Eastern Europe. As Karen Dawisha shows (Chapter 1), changes in the Soviet-East European relationship are part of the larger reform efforts of the Gorbachev regime. Pereotsenka (or reappraisal) has led to a Soviet reexamination and reappraisal of the nature of the international system and a redefinition of the correlation of forces and more specifically to the restructuring (or perestroika) of the ideological assumptions of Soviet-East Europeans relations. That in turn has meant, according to Dawisha (Chapter 1), a rejection of a single model of socialism and a greater stress on Europe as a "common home." Furthermore, perestroika has also created a need for a process of healing or bandaging of old wounds, perevyazka, which has further led to a rejection of formalism in relations among the socialist states and the promotion of indigenous reform as well as the reform of multilateral bloc mechanisms. All this then functions as part of a general effort to make the relationship more organic. These are significant shifts in policy and they have, moreover, considerable potential for bringing about additional major changes.

The promise of change, though, is not the same as actual transformation. Therefore, there is, as usual, reason for caution. Again it is important to retain a historical perspective of the evolution of the Soviet-East European relationship as Korbonski suggests in his contribution (Chapter 4). We should not minimize the salience of formulations such as Evgeny Primakov's "new philosophy of foreign policy."[178] Nevertheless as Ivan Volgyes points out, a "new philosophy" regarding foreign affairs does not necessarily amount to a new "foreign policy" (Chapter 6).

Certainly the emphasis on qualitative indicators in Soviet reform, whether it is at the domestic level or in evaluating the correlation of forces, is likely to play a vital role in the Soviet–East European relationship. It can potentially change priorities both for the Soviet Union and the East European states and provide a new sense of security. In what appears to be a rejection of the single model of socialism and the redefinition of socialist internationalism, Gorbachev as we shall see has set forth certain qualifiers. There can be various models of socialism as long as they are still Leninist.

The redefinition of socialist internationalism (under which the Brezhnev doctrine of limited sovereignty operated) then, has occurred within certain parameters. Reassurances in Moscow by Gorbachev, his proclamations in Soviet bloc capitals and the joint statement that he signed in Belgrade in March 1988 provide encouragement that substantive changes in the Soviet–East European relationship are taking place. (The ouster of such hardliners as Oleg Rakhmanin and the rise in influence of the advocates of greater flexibility such as Georgy Shakhnazarov, and Evgeny Primakov is also a hopeful sign). On his return from a visit to Moscow in March 1989, Karoly Grosz informed the Central Committee of the party that Gorbachev had told him that there should be maximum guarantees that force would not be used to interfere into the affairs of another socialist state.[179] The declaration in Yugoslavia contained the following clause: "Proceeding from the conviction that no-one has a monopoly over the truth, the two sides declare that they have no pretensions of imposing their concept of social development on anyone."[180] The latter was also a major step towards abandoning the Brezhnev doctrine, it seemed. It should be noted, though, that this was a bilateral agreement between the Soviet Union and an East European state that is not a member of the Warsaw Pact. Nevertheless, it is perhaps a reflection of the "new thinking" that Moscow had expressed elsewhere in Eastern Europe.

Moreover, recent reassurances appear to be part of a trend. In his visit to Prague in April 1987 Gorbachev declared that, "no one has the right to claim a special position in the socialist world. The independence of each party, its responsibility to its people, the right to resolve question of the country's development in a sovereign way—for us, these are indisputable principles."[181] In May of the same year, when he visited Bucharest, Gorbachev stated that "we are studying with close interest the experience of our friends and their explorations in the field of the theory and practice of socialist construction and we are trying to make broad use of everything that suits our conditions. In turn we are happy if the fraternal countries find something useful for themselves in the creative work that is under way in our country. I think that is the only way in which relations among Socialist states can and should be built: with full autonomy in defining a state's political course...."[182]

These statements certainly point to greater flexibility. We must also take into account, though, the qualifiers that Gorbachev added in each instance. During the Moscow meeting Gorbachev who tried to lay the Brezhnev doctrine to rest, also cautioned Grosz and the Hungarians against allowing events in the country to give rise to conditions like those in Czechoslovakia in 1968.[183] Furthermore, the next week the Soviet party paper *Pravda*, criticized the "deviation from socialism" in Hungary and warned of a rise of nationalism and "anti-socialist" feelings in that state.[184] It is true that the *Pravda* statement came while Gorbachev was out of the country but the Soviet leader himself has always sent out ambiguous signals. In Prague in April 1987, for instance, he also said that "at the same time we are profoundly convinced that the successes of the socialist commonwealth are impossible without concern on the part of each party and country not only for its own interests *but for the general interest and a respectful attitude towards friends and allies and the mandatory consideration of their interests* . . ."[185] (emphasis added). And, in his statement in Bucharest, Gorbachev added the phrase "and collective responsibility for the fate of world socialism."[186] Thus the general interest, the mandatory consideration of the interests of allies and the overall responsibility to socialism remain part of Gorbachev's reformulation of the Soviet position on socialist internationalism.

It is certainly possible that the evolution of the Soviet position will involve the elimination of these qualifiers. Still, in an interview with two American publications in May 1988, Gorbachev reaffirmed his policy that East European states should be free to choose their own political systems but he would not criticize the Soviet military interventions in Hungary in 1956 and Czechoslovakia in 1968. He argued instead that before the Soviet actions occurred "there was interference of a different kind."[187]

There are also ambiguities and contradictions in the positions of lesser ranking officials and academics. At a July 1988 meeting in Alexandria, Virginia of Soviet and American specialists, on the topic of the role of Eastern Europe in the evolution of East-West relations, the Soviet delegation led by Oleg T. Bogomolov, Director of the Institute of the Economics of the World Socialist System, significantly did not dispute the American view that Stalin had imposed communist hegemony on Eastern Europe in the post-war period.[188] But they adamantly refused to admit that since these governments in Eastern Europe were not freely chosen by the people, the legitimacy of the communist regimes is in question. Thus a challenge to a fundamental assumption of communist rule in Eastern Europe was not tolerated even by those who are at the leading edge of reform in the Soviet Union. What they appeared willing to contemplate thus was reform but not systemic change.

Yet, several months later Bogomolov expressed the view that a neutral Hungary, governed by a bourgeois democracy would not be a threat to Soviet security.[189] This would indeed represent a fundamental change in the socialist interstate system. True, those were the opinions of an "academic."

No one, so far, who has some degree of official policy responsibility has, however, supported Bogomolov's view. On the contrary, although reformers such as Shakhnazarov and Primakov have been willing to entertain a broad definition of socialism when it comes to the East European states, their baseline view is that these states can choose their own path only within the following parameters: the path must be "socialist" and the reform process must be orderly and non-extremist.[190] Rafael Fyodorov, first deputy chief, International Department of the Central Committee (which now subsumes the Liaison with Socialist Countries Department) characterized Bogomolov's view as harmful.[191] Shakhnazarov has contended that the East European states are "organically linked" to the Soviet Union (politically, ideologically, etc.), and that the Soviets are trying on the one hand to encourage effective reform in the region but on the other hand are concerned that if one or another state spinned out of control it would threaten Gorbachev's reforms at home.[192]

It does appear that the Soviet Union would be extremely reluctant to use force in Eastern Europe. But the Brezhnev doctrine must be also understood in the larger context of Soviet goals and perceptions which would condition the response of Soviet policymakers in a crisis situation. These involve not only matters of ideology, legitimacy and domestic stability, as seminal as those concerns are but, as Seweryn Bialer has observed, also Soviet aspirations as an influential global power.[193] Though military intervention would clearly extract a very heavy price in terms of East-West relations Bialer is very likely correct in his assessment that in its current circumstances the Soviet Union could ill afford to show itself to be so weak that it could not control a recalcitrant satellite on its European borders. Shakhnazarov, for instance, indicated in a meeting with Western scholars and policy advisors in March 1989 that although Soviet military intervention was highly unlikely in the future, it could not be excluded entirely. He stated that no one could be 100% sure and that the decision would be made by the Politburo in light of the prevailing situation.[194]

Lastly, whatever the ultimate Soviet intentions may be, assurances by Soviet and East European leaders have already had an impact on the perceptions of the populations of the East European states. Anecdotal evidence suggests that the populations of these states view such assurances as guarantees that there is no longer a threat of external military intervention. Reform in these states therefore becomes less of a controlled experiment. And in the states where reform is most advanced—Hungary and Poland— there is little in their political culture and history that suggests restraint and hard political realism. Ironically, despite the Soviet goal of greater regional stability, a growing belief in these states and elsewhere that the threat of Soviet military intervention has disappeared completely might well fuel the kind of demands that increase domestic instability to a level that would make Soviet intervention more likely.

Economic changes

Despite significant political changes, the main thrust of Gorbachev's reforms within the Soviet Union, as noted, appears to be economic. And in key respects, in the Soviet-East European relationship, economic considerations also seem to predominate. In particular if the Soviet Union is to view Eastern Europe more as a sphere of influence than one of dominance, then it may indeed be logical that economic relations should acquire greater importance.

The Instruments and Problems of Regional Cooperation. Moscow stresses interdependence in its external relations with Eastern Europe and this is best achieved through a restructuring or at least enhancing of economic linkages. The ambitious character of Soviet domestic economic initiatives and the comprehensive approach that Gorbachev has sought to take to domestic economic reform, including the emphasis on the qualitative factors, also would necessitate a reexamination of external economic relations. And, as Carl McMillan shows (Chapter 2), Eastern Europe is the Soviet Union's major economic partner. Nevertheless, Soviet goals are multifold and include political and economic considerations. It is thus not merely a matter of the Soviet Union trying to diminish its economic burden in Eastern Europe. Undoubtedly this is a consideration but Gorbachev's plans go well beyond that and ultimately they are part of his vision of the socialist community as expressed in economic terms.

At the December 1985 meeting of the CMEA which bore his imprint, Gorbachev gave a good indication of his vision and intentions for relations with the East European states. As McMillan shows, the importance of the new "Comprehensive Program to Promote the Scientific and Technical Progress of the Member-Countries of the Council for Mutual Economic Assistance up to the year 2,000"[195] derives not merely from its scope but also the proposed method of implementation. The scope itself is significant for it shows the internal/external linkages in Soviet policies. It, in effect, substitutes technical progress for resource development as the focus of CMEA activities. Furthermore, the proposed acceleration of technical progress in the region as a whole ties in well with Soviet domestic reform.

The method of implementation, though, is particularly important for Eastern Europe. Although inter-enterprise linkages had been proposed before and was one of the several concepts that were included in the 1971 CMEA program (which never really moved beyond the predominant bilateralism in the bloc), now it has top priority. Enterprises in member countries will be encouraged to engage in a variety of direct contacts on a more decentralised basis. This, as McMillan suggests, implies the strengthening of market instruments in intra-CMEA relations (Chapter 2). But, as McMillan adds, in order for this more decentralized interaction (as envisaged in the Comprehensive Program) to work, there must be a sufficient homogeneity in the process of reform in the member-countries so as to provide a common basis for interaction (Chapter 2).

Raymond Aron had suggested that in general a degree of homogeneity among states is required for effective interchange, in the sense that other societies should be similarly organized.[196] This quest for homogeneity further illustrates the need to integrate our understanding of the regional interstate system with an analysis of the internal politics and economics of the nations that make up that system. For neither endogenous system analysis nor a study of the external factors exclusively, can adequately explain the processes or policies in the region. And subsequent decisions in the CMEA show both the pursuit of homogeneity and the interdependence of domestic and external factors.

At the 43rd session of the CMEA in October 1987 the communique significantly emphasized "the necessity of a *restructuring* (perestroika) of the mechanism of collaboration and socialist economic integration"[197] (emphasis added). Furthermore, in July 1988 at the Prague meeting of the CMEA, nine out of the ten members (Romania abstained) issued a communique which stated that they had reached an "understanding on gradually creating conditions for the mutual free movement of goods, services, and other production factors with the aim of creating an integrated market in the future."[198] (The communique also called for an overhaul of the CMEA and stated that unanimous agreement had been reached on a collective production strategy for the years 1991–2005). Though much of this may be more hope than policy it is difficult to see how it could be realized even in part without a greater degree of homogeneity. Oleg Bogomolov, who has often expressed the view that all socialist states have a right to shape their own policies, in February 1988 told participants to a world conference on the world economy, that the GDR and Romania will eventually have to follow with domestic changes like those in the Soviet Union and the reformist East European states.[199]

Therefore, the general thrust is toward homogenization. The 1985 Comprehensive Program and agreements that followed, moreover, should further the Soviet goal of pushing for reform in the bloc along certain lines and of doing so without *appearing* to impose it from the top. Furthermore, sub-projects or programs formulated under the five broad areas of the Comprehensive Program are to be directed by a Soviet "head" organization (McMillan, Chapter 2) and thus the Soviet Union would retain its leading role in key areas, which should also enhance its already preponderant position in the CMEA.

As McMillan points out (chapter 2), it is now discernible as well, that one of the key Soviet goals in the region is to develop an interdependent and prosperous group of socialist states headed by the Soviet Union. This goes to the heart of the Soviet dilemma in Eastern Europe, that we discussed earlier, namely that of seeking bloc cohesion in the sense of conformity with its own values, patterns and policies, and of trying to ensure the viability of the East European regimes and indeed of the stability of the region itself. Since stability in the East European states and therefore regime viability is very much dependent on economic progress, by ensuring that there is an improvement in economic performance and that there is a betterment of the standard of living, Moscow can increase the viability of the East European communist parties. On the other hand, by enhancing interdependence in a community where the Soviet Union, if nothing else through its sheer economic weight, enjoys primacy, it can also enhance bloc cohesion. *Thus, if successful, Gorbachev would manage to eliminate the contradictions in the pursuit of the traditional Soviet goals of cohesion and viability.*

It would appear that the possibilities of progress to a qualitatively higher level of integration as envisioned by the Soviet Union are greatly improved by Gorbachev's reforms and those taking place in some of the East European states. The push for enterprise-to-enterprise contact in the CMEA, the general attempt at decentralization and the move toward greater currency convertibility all militate towards further integration. It is also important that Soviet policymakers seem to be better aware of the requirements for effective integration than before.[200] What were radical ideas put forth several years ago by such reformers as Hungary's Rezso Nyers have now largely gained Soviet acceptance. The move from bilateralism to multilateralism, however, is an exceedingly difficult one and Soviet plans for the bloc are particularly daunting. For, they do not merely seek to increase the current level of interdependence but to transform it qualitatively. (And the term "interdependence" itself might be something of a misnomer for given the huge size and the relative self-sufficiency of the Soviet economy there is bound to be an asymmetry not only in vulnerability or susceptibility but also in the level of dependence—all very much favouring the Soviet Union).

There is yet little evidence to suggest that Moscow is succeeding in its goal of creating an interdependent and prosperous group of socialist states headed by the Soviet Union. But, such a process is a lengthy one and thus it takes considerable time for policies to show results. It is, therefore, particularly important to look for indicators in a sector of cooperation where there has been greater integrative experience. Developments in the energy area, where multilateral socialist cooperation has been going on for a long time and where the East European states have the greatest interest in economic linkages, provide a useful case study for the analysis of the nature and process of adaptation in the economic realm.

McMillan shows the difficulties (Chapter 2) of *intensifikatsiia* (intensive development) in the area of energy cooperation. In order to achieve a viable regional energy program, there has to be a substitution of policy coordination for plan coordination. Yet the signals that have emerged after many years of cooperation in the energy area are mixed. Although high-level state-to-state approaches are ill suited to the process of intensive integration this approach continues and the energy sector retains the mixed character of the CMEA system. The East European states remain concerned about their fuel and other resource requirements and are seeking resolution through the CMEA mechanism even though previous arrangements may not have been entirely satisfactory.

Although there has been a decline in East European reliance on Soviet oil (with the exception of Romania) through a substitution of domestic energy sources, there has been an increasing dependence on the Soviet Union for natural gas. The Progress (Yamburg) natural gas pipeline is a major joint program that has had to be dealt with at the highest levels. Furthermore, as McMillan writes, the Soviet commitment at the 1986 session of the CMEA to the East European states to continue to increase Soviet energy shipments in the 1986-90 plan period implied joint planning at high official levels. Hungary, for example, is especially dependent on the Soviet Union for energy supplies. It imports 30% of its electricity.[201] At the 42nd Session of the CMEA Council, then Hungarian Prime Minister, Gyorgy Lazar complained that problems with the CMEA's "Mir" electrical power grid system had caused "extremely serious harm to the Hungarian economy."[202] The expansion of the unified power grid ("Mir") and the commitment to the development of nuclear power also involves high level joint planning rather than policy coordination. Such developments are far more closely associated with the previous pattern of extensive growth and "extensive integration" than the "intensive type of integration" which the Soviet Union seeks. Thus as McMillan writes, the Soviet Union and the East European states are involved in a difficult transition period in the energy sector where new Soviet thinking and policy initiatives have yielded some positive results but where the outcome is far from certain.

The causes for the mixed signals and the uncertainty in the energy sector, though, speak also of the problems facing domestic and regional reform. The strong interdependence of domestic and external change, as noted, are evident not only in the energy sector but in other areas as well. It is hardly accidental that even the language of reform employed in the CMEA, as we have seen, is similar to that used by Gorbachev domestically. First of all, then, the tensions and the contradictions between joint planning at high official levels and enterprise-to-enterprise relations in the CMEA reflect the domestic difficulties of perestroika. Despite some decentralization the very presence of the ministries in the Soviet Union continues to reinforce the centralizing bias of the system. More private enterprise would help. But in the Soviet Union the private sector and cooperatives account for only a small fraction of the Soviet economy as Marer shows (Chapter 5). Restrictions on the role of Soviet cooperatives, particularly in the areas of foreign trade, place an additional constraint on enterprise-to-enterprise contacts. Even in Hungary where reforms have advanced beyond those in the Soviet Union, the private and the cooperative sector is and for the foreseeable future will remain far smaller than the public one. Furthermore, neither in the Soviet Union nor in most of Eastern Europe is the move toward greater market determination through the encouragement of the private sector likely to progress rapidly because of severe constraints in terms of access to inputs, imports, finance, labor and markets (Marer, Chapter 5). Therefore, the domestic and external benefits of reform may not be fully realized and even limited yields may take a long time to achieve.

The shortage of consumer goods, especially in the Soviet Union, has placed new constraints even on the lively and substantial trade in goods conducted by tourists among socialist states—shoes from Czechoslovakia, for instance, foodstuffs from Hungary, and appliances from the Soviet Union. The magnitude of this trade was revealed by the Soviet deputy chief of customs control who stated that in 1988 more than 400,000 television sets, 200,000 refrigerators, and 50,000 washing machines were taken out of the Soviet Union by visitors.[203] Virtually all the goods were taken to Eastern Europe. In response to dire domestic shortages Soviet authorities in February 1989 decided to ban the export by tourists of television sets, refrigerators, washing machines, coffee, caviar, children's clothing, and shoes.[204]

Secondly, the continuing lack of homogeneity in the approach to reform and adaptation to changing conditions in the bloc inhibits cooperation. Attitudes to perestroika differ sharply for there is considerable diversity in Eastern Europe. There are common basic problems, though, as we have seen, for no East European state has resolved either the issue of legitimacy or fundamental economic questions. In the latter realm East European performance ranges from low-grade to catastrophic mismanagement. In the case of the GDR and Romania, the two East European states which are respectively best and worst off economically there is no admission that there are problems. Since Gorbachev has come to power the Honecker leadership has repeatedly stated that it did not intend to follow the Soviet lead on reforms. It is to be "socialism in GDR colors," as an editorial in the party daily put it in February 1989 and this includes maintaining the party's leading role, the state-run industries, with only a limited measure of private enterprise, and subsidized prices.[205] East Berlin's local party paper has been even more critical of reform. On February 27, 1989 it declared that "the threat of unemployment in Poland, Hungary, and the USSR is not compatible with socialism," because it violated the right to work.[206]

The GDR, under Erich Honecker seems to operate under the assumption that its approach is superior to that of the Soviet Union. And it is true that the GDR economy has performed somewhat better than the other socialist economies in the 1980s but it is slowing down and the era of easy growth appears to be over.[207] But not only is the GDR facing increasing internal economic difficulties, it is also bound to be affected by economic problems elsewhere in the bloc. Forty percent of its trade is with the Soviet Union and another one quarter is with the CMEA states.[208] Furthermore, the GDR may be under pressure not only from the East but also from the West since the domestic culture must contend on a daily basis with the penetration of the Western media, especially that of the Federal Republic of Germany. Honecker is 76 but he is in good health. A change in succession may lead to only a "half-generational" change, though, since those waiting in the wings are around 60, with relatively similar outlooks although they may be willing to adopt at least the forms of perestroika and glasnost. Still, there are reasons for caution, in part because of the exposed position of the GDR and the low level of legitimacy of the political system. The margin of error for the GDR regime therefore is much smaller than for the Soviet Union.

In the case of Romania, Ceausescu is pursuing a bizarre economic policy that is increasingly detached from economic rationality and everyday reality. Paradoxically, though, Romania's obsession with maintaining its independence or at least autonomy[209] has led it to become more dependent on the Soviet Union. Its dire economic conditions and its attempts to repay its hard-currency indebtedness have forced it to sharply augment its trade with the CMEA and the Soviet Union in particular. It also dramatically increased its imports of oil from the Soviet Union.[210]

Yet there has been no domestic economic relief since Romania announced in April 1989,[211] that it had paid off its foreign debts. Nor has it shifted its trade away from the CMEA. On the contrary, Romania remains a pariah nation as far as the West is concerned with Western capitals condemning one after the other, Ceausescu's gross violation of human rights.[212] The European Community also suspended negotiations for a trade and cooperation agreement with Romania in the spring of 1989 as a protest against the country's poor record on human rights.[213]

Elsewhere in the bloc, Czechoslovakia and Bulgaria have been reluctant to pursue reforms. Prague continues to persecute dissidents and maintains its centralized system. Bulgaria, which seemed to move towards adopting Gorbachev's reform measures reversed course in mid-1988. Reformers such as Chudomir Alexandrov were removed from the center of power. New repressive measures against the Turkish minority are symptomatic of the shift back toward economic and political orthodoxy.

In the case of Poland and Hungary, as noted, reforms are further advanced than in the Soviet Union. And, given recent developments, the pace of change is likely to accelerate. In Hungary, for instance, the Gorbachev reforms represent far more of an enabling factor than inspiration. Yet, if the reforms move too quickly, they may engender not only domestic dangers to the central role of the communist party but may also place Hungary so far out of sync with change in the Soviet Union and the bloc that regional homogeneity or even cooperation becomes more difficult to achieve. For example, in May 1989, Hungary under pressure from environmentalists decided unilaterally to suspend work on a large controversial joint dam project with Czechoslovakia.[214] Czechoslovakia, which has been increasingly critical of Hungarian reforms, reacted angrily and threatened to launch a $1.7 billion law suit against Budapest for breach of contract.[215]

Thirdly, multilateral and even bilateral economic cooperation in the region is inhibited by the paucity of the kind of new thinking that would help the states adapt to changing conditions. No conceptual framework has been developed, for instance, that would help facilitate cooperation among economies that have not only reached different levels of development but also take different approaches to reform. There is considerable frustration in the CMEA, especially among reformers. At a meeting on CMEA reform in the fall of 1988, in Sopron, Hungary, the chairman Kalman Pecsi decried the lack of new thinking. He contended that "If we scratch the surface we find everything is old" and that there was not a single document on which "radical reform" could be based.[216] Reszo Nyers, reflected on the consequences of this and stated in January 1989 that a reform of the CMEA was proving impossible because countries such as the GDR and Romania were actively attempting to stall such reform.[217]

Despite the preponderance of its political, economic and military power, the Soviet Union cannot enforce its will consistently or uniformly in Eastern Europe. As McMillan has stated (Chapter 2), Soviet economic imperatives in Eastern Europe are not simply policy choices but evolve under the force of circumstances which Moscow can only *partially* control. More decentralization and greater market orientation may make control, or at the very least predictability, considerably more difficult. Certainly, linear logic may not be an adequate analytical tool not only for Western analysts in predicting the future course of reform but also for Soviet and East European policymakers formulating new plans. The built-in contradictions and tensions both at the domestic and at the intra-bloc level ensure that there will be a great many unintended or unexpected consequences arising from current policies.

Marer (Chapter 5) makes a noteworthy point in contending that the Soviet decision to make it more difficult for the East European states to acquire Soviet energy goods, far from imposing a serious economic constraint on East European long-term development as planners in the region believe, may prove to be a blessing in disguise. That is, by forcing the East Europeans to become more efficient this will induce them to become more competitive on the world market. Whereas Marer is rather pessimistic about changes in the CMEA in the near future, he suggests that Soviet toughness with the East Europeans on energy and raw materials will likely be the only external factor that will in the long run yield substantial benefits to these states.

As persuasive as this argument is there are dangers in overstating it. Although it is clearly essential for the East European states (as well as for the Soviet Union) to become more competitive in international markets, there is no assurance that by implementing domestic reform and by distancing themselves from the Soviet Union economically they will be able to compete internationally. The world market has become extraordinarily competitive and the newly industrialized nations of the Pacific rim, particularly the four "little dragons" (South Korea, Hong Kong, Taiwan and Singapore) have become exporters with whom the East European states would have enormous difficulty in competing. The Soviet Union has conveniently played the role of "customer of last resort" for low quality goods that the East European states could not sell on the world market. Moreover, the difficulties that the socialist states have had in keeping up with the intense international economic competition of the 1980s could help create the kind of a centripedal economic force which is manifested in a regional market for states that have fallen behind.

Furthermore, there are rational reasons including geography, ease of transportation, and historical evolution, that suggest certain benefits in a regional, socialist market that functions on a more decentralized and equitable basis. A revitalized Soviet economy especially, should be quite a desirable export market for the East European states. And, even central planning, as Edward Hewett has written, can provide benefits in certain areas.[218] This is not to suggest that the need for drastic reform, as argued by the contributors to this volume, are not necessary. Rather, there is a need for some balance between continuity and change in order to adapt to evolving conditions and to create a more organic Soviet–East European relationship.

The Spectre of 1992. It is through the creation of such an organic economic relationship that the Soviet bloc may be able to cope with the more immediate potential external economic danger, namely the plans of the European Community to create a true common market by 1992.[219] Such an entity, will constitute by far the largest internal market in the world with over 320 million prosperous consumers. As barriers among the Community members disappear, greater barriers against external states are likely to come into being. For the East European states in particular this can present great economic dangers unless they manage to become more competitive. It is little wonder, therefore, that Hungarian economists who have had the longest experience with reform are especially worried about the prospects of "1992."[220]

Gorbachev has also expressed grave concerns about West European plans for economic integration. He has put his objectives in the context of the need to build a common "European home," a concept that calls on East and West Europeans (in a geographic area stretching from the Atlantic to the Ural Mountains) to cooperate politically and economically. In a meeting with the West German Foreign Minister, Hans-Dietrich Genscher in the Kremlin on July 30, 1988, Gorbachev warned that West European politicians would have to bear the responsibility for any damage that "1992" would cause to improving East-West relations.[221]

At an October 1988 meeting in Moscow with Chancellor Franz Vranitzky of Austria, he again warned that the political and economic integration of Western Europe, at the cost of the exclusion of its Eastern neighbours, would make it impossible to build a common European home. He asked, "But on the other hand what awaits the all-European process if the Western part of Europe cruelly closes itself off in a new formation?"[222]

In the long term the West European economic integration could lead to political unification. This certainly had been the intent of the founders of the European Community. The emergence of a second Western superpower is hardly a reassuring prospect for the Soviet Union unless it can ensure that this entity will not be hostile. For the East Europeans there are political and cultural concerns. An exclusionary West European political entity could help perpetuate Soviet domination of the region. Furthermore, it could delay the reestablishment not only of political but also of cultural links with the West that were severed by Soviet occupation. In a sense the East European states have been victims of *interrupted Europeanization*, politically and culturally. Certainly opposition groups in Poland and Hungary are hoping that after more than 40 years the process of Europeanization, characterized by political pluralism and cultural diversity, can be resumed.

Nevertheless, Moscow's and in many ways even Eastern Europe's concerns with "1992" are largely economic. For, West European political integration is unlikely in the near future if, indeed, it is feasible at all given British and French concerns in particular with national sovereignty. Economic integration though, represents an imminent threat. Western Europe is a crucial source of technology and capital as well as the world's largest market. Neither the East Europeans nor the Soviets can afford to be locked out especially at a time when they most need economic access.

Therefore, Moscow's diplomatic offensive in Western Europe may be driven in large part by economic considerations. It seems that Gorbachev has concluded that increased trade, hard-currency credits and Western technology can help stimulate the stagnant Soviet economy. Consequently, in 1988 the Soviet Union decided to borrow massively from the West European states. By October 1988 it had made arrangements with banks in West Germany, Italy and Great Britain for credits worth almost $5 billion.[223] Moreover, French banks have also become involved in discussing prospects for additional loans. Thus the Soviet Union is engaging in a significant import drive and West European nations want to participate in a major way in Soviet efforts to upgrade their industry. And with the fall of oil prices—oil being the Soviet Union's main source of hard currency—West European credit is most welcome.

Moscow, though, has also attempted to ensure that both it and the CMEA could deal with the European Community directly. In June 1988 the CMEA signed an agreement to establish official relations with the European Community.[224] The Soviet Union has since sought to negotiate its own trade agreement with the Community. The East European links with the European Community can benefit the Soviet Union in two ways. First, West European credits, technology and markets can help stimulate the economies of the East European states. This in turn would not only improve the prospects for political stability in these states, thereby reducing the potential need for Soviet political coercion or military intervention, but would also make them less burdensome trading partners. The Soviet Union has largely eliminated subsidies to its partners, but as Kazimierz Poznanski shows, the Soviet-East European trade relationship has been characterized by cyclical time patterns with each side periodically losing to the other.[225] Among the key causal factors for this, he cites are non-economic considerations (such as political stability) and the fact that prices have been determined arbitrarily.[226] The Soviet Union, given its current economic difficulties, therefore, would wish to minimize actual and potential external burdens.

Secondly, the Soviet Union may be able to use the East European states as a useful bridge to the Community. The GDR enjoys a special relationship with West Germany and this facilitates the flow of technology from the West. Improved relations between the East European CMEA states and Western Europe would help further unplug bottlenecks to Western high technology and credits. And given the CMEA emphasis on integration in the techno-scientific area, it is difficult to see how East European technology and technical know-how would not be transferred to the Soviet Union.

There are some problems though, in the expansion of East-West trade and flow of capital. In March 1989 the Organization for Economic Cooperation and Development (OECD) warned that increasing debt by the Soviet bloc could create payment problems, particularly if interest rates continued to rise.[227] East bloc hard-currency debts, according to the OECD increased to $129 billion by the end of 1988.[228] The Soviet trade deficit with the West, as noted, has been increasing. Nikolai Ryzhkov, the Soviet Prime Minister, revealed to the Congress of People's Deputies in June 1989 that the Soviet foreign debt stood at $53 billion.[229] Thus there are impediments to a dramatic shift in economic relations with the West but all parties may nevertheless find it beneficial to seek improvement.

The military dimension

Significantly, there is consensus, in a way, among the three contributors, Edward Luttwak, Ivan Volgyes and Karen Dawisha, who have dealt more extensively with the military dimensions of Soviet–East European relations. And the consensus is that there has been no change in the military relationship, or more precisely, that no change has yet occurred. All three perspectives are especially important for they provide examinations from somewhat different directions. With Dawisha the military concern is peripheral in the analysis of the Soviet–East European relationship. She demonstrates, though, that for the time being at least, politics have remained prime in that relationship. She also shows that reform in the Soviet Union, both in domestic and in foreign policy, can move at a different pace among the various sectors. Volgyes, in analyzing the East European perspective of the military dimension of the relationship, provides a very lucid appraisal of the East European frustrations and of wounded pride, all resulting from their inability to have a significant input in bloc military policy formulation.

The Soviet Union though is a unique member of the socialist military organization—the Warsaw Pact. It is the only superpower member. And it has a global vision as well as global strategic concerns. Furthermore, it is the sole nuclear power and thus the only member with a nuclear strategy. The Soviet Union, therefore, has certain military interests not only as a socialist power but also as a global and nuclear state. Seweryn Bialer has written about the difficulties of separating Soviet ideological and nationalistic motivations. He put it succinctly, "to distinguish analytically between the various elements of ideology and the many dimensions of Soviet nationalism is in essence to separate artificially factors that are not separate, distinct or counterposed to one another but inseparable, intertwined, Soviet in form and Russian in content."[230] Therefore, one cannot make a clean analytic distinction. Yet especially for analytic purposes one may need to at least temporarily separate the combination of ideology and nationalism, of ideology and *Realpolitik*, that represents the Soviet Union's view of the world. Soviet leaders have always been good Clausewitzians for whom politics have been prime, but Soviet grand strategy must be understood also in global, historical and military terms. It is important, therefore, to bring to this issue a perspective which examines Soviet military concerns in Eastern Europe not only from a Sovietological point of view but also from a grand strategic perspective which highlights the role of military technology and doctrine in shaping strategy.

Nuclear Weapons and Territory. Edward Luttwak (Chapter 3) emphasizes the role of nuclear weapons in shaping Soviet concerns and military doctrine as applied to Eastern Europe. Soviet understanding of the role of nuclear weapons as well as its response to American nuclear strategy, greatly influenced their perception of the importance of territory and thus the military significance of Eastern Europe, according to Luttwak. Though, as Ivan Volgyes contends, the Soviet Union has always sought to control the East European militaries both for strategic reasons and as a matter of internal policing (Chapter 6), and has done so with considerable success (as Kuklinski's revelations show), much of the Soviet strategy has been driven by the Kremlin's perception of the role of nuclear weapons. A decline in the role of nuclear weapons increases the significance of territory and of Eastern Europe as a defensive or offensive glacis. The Soviet–East European military relationship, therefore, is full of paradoxes for the political relationship is not always synchronized with Soviet military concerns. Luttwak, thus, points to the irony of a situation where the Soviet Union may pursue a more flexible political policy towards the East European states but strategic concerns arising out of its perception of the role of nuclear weapons and forces versus conventional ones, leads it to greater military inflexibility.

It may be possible that the Soviet leadership under Gorbachev does not adequately appreciate the implications of the type of trends identified by Luttwak and that they are less than adequately concerned with the consequences for Eastern Europe of their current military policies. This may be occurring not because of a lack of military representation in the Politburo but as a result of several broader determinants. First, there is no longer a sense of an East-West crisis and therefore Gorbachev can afford to shift Soviet focus away from military matters. Secondly, this relaxation of tension affords the opportunity for, and can be furthered by, arms reduction programs in Europe which de-emphasize nuclear weapons. Thirdly, Gorbachev's concentration on the economy rather than the military is a logical policy given the enormous economic difficulties that the country is facing and his belief that socialism cannot be revitalized without economic progress. And, fourthly, Gorbachev's overall approach to reform, with its lack of a clear blueprint and an adequate theoretical formulation, can lead to unexpected or perhaps even unintended consequences for current Soviet military policy.

This is not to suggest that there is not a great deal of thinking on and re-examination of key military/strategic problems in the Soviet Union. Soviet works, for instance by Vitaly Zhurkin and by M.A. Gareev on military doctrine, show a considerable sophistication but fall short of formulating a broad theory that incorporates the implications of a shift from nuclear to conventional weapons on East-West and on East-East political relations.

Luttwak, therefore, raises a vital issue and his arguments regarding the general effects of a shift away from nuclear weapons and the implications for Eastern Europe, are very persuasive. Yet it is not a matter of simply standing Moscow's traditional Clausewitzian approach to policy on its head. In relations with Eastern Europe it is unlikely that military considerations will simply drive political policy. This is not what Luttwak suggests. But it is entirely possible that military considerations will play a far larger role in Soviet policy toward Eastern Europe in the future than Gorbachev intends or expects. And this influence, as Luttwak suggests, is likely to manifest itself as a brake on Soviet political flexibility toward Eastern Europe.

For the time being there is considerable continuity between Gorbachev's military policies and that of his predecessors (going back to the 1970s), although there may be important changes about to take place. A crucial variable again is the Soviet attitude to the role of nuclear weapons in military strategy. Gorbachev's attempt to diminish and eventually eliminate the role of nuclear weapons is not entirely new. One can go back at least to January 1977 when Leonid Brezhnev laid down what became known as the "Tula line" in a speech that he made in the city of that name, south of Moscow.[231] Brezhnev disputed the utility of nuclear superiority and contended that the Soviet Union needed only nuclear weapons that were "sufficient" to deter those of the United States. This represented a shift in emphasis to conventional weapons which though perceptible even earlier was now made explicit. Moreover, in the same month, Brezhnev appointed as Chief of the Soviet General Staff, Marshal N. Ogarkov, a controversial officer who had wanted to shift spending from nuclear weapons to advanced conventional ones (though Ogarkov has been moved out of that post he retained a very powerful position within the Soviet military hierarchy until his retirement). Thus there has been an evolution of Soviet military thinking which has led it away from the emphasis on nuclear weapons.

This trend has been reinforced under Gorbachev. At the 27th Congress of the CPSU in February–March 1986 Gorbachev, though, emphasized what appears to be changes in the military doctrine.[232] The destructiveness of nuclear weapons, he contended, necessitated the creation of new forms in relations among states with different social systems. He also spoke of the impossibility of winning a nuclear war. He saw little if any utility for nuclear weapons. Therefore he appeared to be pushing hard toward what Edward Luttwak has called "the post-nuclear era."[233] He reinforced this impression at the October 1986 Reykjavik summit with Ronald Reagan.

The Soviet leader thus seems reluctant to admit any stabilizing role for nuclear weapons. Yet as Joseph Nye and other analysts have suggested, nuclear weapons have played an important stabilizing role, one that conventional weapons have not been able to perform as effectively in the past.[234] Such instability may place greater pressure on the East European states both in terms of having to demonstrate their reliability to the Soviet Union and by increasing their burden within the alliance (in order to improve Warsaw Pact capabilities).

But, in de-emphasizing nuclear weapons, and in signing the INF Agreement with the United States on the elimination of intermediate-range nuclear weapons Gorbachev did not merely reduce, or claim to reduce, the chances for nuclear conflict but in essence also reemphasized Soviet/Warsaw Pact conventional military superiority. For the West, a diminished nuclear deterrent in itself would magnify the conventional threat. A Western response, to redress the conventional imbalance however, could stimulate an expensive new arms race. Consequently to succeed on nuclear weapons Gorbachev has had to address the issue of conventional forces as well. This is in addition to his general concern with reducing military expenditures. For the Soviet Union but perhaps even more for the East European states, matters of military doctrine, alliance decision-making and modernization all operating within the larger political context, will determine whether Gorbachev's military policies will enhance their security.

Conventional Arms Reductions and Changes in Military Doctrine. Measures to reduce the danger of nuclear war are a welcome development for all states. But the East European countries would likely benefit from a change in military Soviet doctrine only if new thinking is also applied to conventional weapons, and leads to a diminution of the importance of territory and a reduction in the defense burden. Despite Gorbachev's early emphasis on nuclear policy there is now at least the appearance of some movement in this direction. At the May 1987 meeting of the Warsaw Pact in East Berlin the organization issued not only a communique but also a statement, "On the Military Doctrine of the Warsaw Treaty Member States."[235] The doctrine emphasized the "defensive nature" of the Pact. It stated that the organization would never be the first to use nuclear weapons or begin nuclear action against any state or alliance if it were not the subject of an armed attack itself. The document also declared that the Pact doctrine was based on the necessity of maintaining the balance of military power at the lowest possible level and on the expediency of reducing military potential to the level "sufficient to defence and for repelling any possible aggression."[236] Furthermore it outlined as one of the fundamental Pact objectives, the reduction of the armed forces and conventional armaments to "a level where neither side, maintaining its defense capacity, would have the means to stage a surprise attack against the other or (engage in) offensive operations in general."[237]

How radical a departure is this from past policy? In the early 1960s under Khrushchev the Soviet military developed a concept which was closer to *coalition warfare*[238] than before by assigning a greater role to East European forces. Though Khrushchev was only partially successful and the East European forces continued to play a relatively marginal role, often being the "hewers of wood and drawers of water", the integration of these forces in Soviet strategy gained momentum. And as Volgyes shows (in Chapter 6) that integrative momentum has not slackened. The only exception is Romania which pursues an autonomous military policy and has formulated its own military strategy based on a "people's war" doctrine.[239] None of the other non-Soviet Warsaw Pact (NSWP) states in Eastern Europe can formulate their own military doctrine or mount a coordinated national defense. As far as Romania is concerned the Soviet Union has managed to compartmentalize that challenge. In part this is due to Romania's military weakness and its inability to deny territory in case of Soviet need and also because of that Balkan state's relatively lesser strategic importance given its location in the Southern Tier of the Pact.

Gorbachev's push for higher levels of socialist integration also applies to the Warsaw Pact though there may be considerable difficulties in this area as well. Still, there is continuity. Moreover Khrushchev's decision to make greater use of the East European forces was in large part motivated by a desire to reduce Soviet military spending and transfer investments to the civilian sector. He also wanted to cut sharply the size of the Soviet military forces. But unlike Gorbachev he intended to (and did) shift emphasis to nuclear weapons in part as a cost cutting measure. Like Gorbachev, though, he wanted to enhance Soviet and Warsaw Pact security (and stability) at a drastically reduced military cost.

Khrushchev's efforts to reduce spending ultimately failed as did most of his attempts at reform. The East European states paid a particularly heavy price as they found themselves carrying a heavier military burden without an improvement in their security. In the Gorbachev era, a meaningful, positive change in the military realm for the East European states would involve, as noted, a reduction of the military burden they carry, a greater input in policy formulation and a diminution of the strategic value of their territory. All these are intertwined and, of course, depend on Soviet strategy and military doctrine, for ultimately, Warsaw Pact doctrine is formulated by the Kremlin.

As Luttwak shows (Chapter 3) reducing nuclear weapons will not yield great savings. He points out that the ground and tactical-air forces as a whole account for not less than 70% of Soviet military expenditures, excluding central overheads; and not less than 60% of those forces are assigned to the European theatre.[240] In the unlikely event that the Soviet Union would eliminate all of its strategic nuclear forces, this according to Luttwak would generate only a saving of 20%. Therefore, if the Soviet Union and the East European states are to benefit economically from reductions these would need to come in the conventional forces.

Yet, even if the Soviet Union were to make a decision on a massive reduction in conventional force expenditures, the benefits would not be immediately available. The momentum of weapons acquisition cannot be reversed suddenly either in the Soviet Union or the Warsaw Pact. Soviet force modernization has been proceeding at a strong (even if slightly reduced) pace, despite arms control talks and the INF Agreement. There have been significant increases in the delivery of the T-80 tanks (which can carry reactive armour), armoured personnel carriers, reconnaissance vehicles, TU-26 *Backfire* medium-range bombers, MiG-29 *Fulcrum*, and MiG-31 *Foxhound* A fighters, Su-24 *Fencer*, ground support aircraft and Mi-8 *Hip* E combat helicopters.[241] According to British Prime Minister Margaret Thatcher, the Soviet Union still produces 3000 tanks a year.[242] Furthermore, a study by the United States Joint Economic Committee has concluded that "in view of the immense sunk costs for plant and installed equipment in the defense production facilities and the fact that these cannot be readily converted to civilian use, the industrial modernization goals are unlikely significantly to impede the completion of the major strategic weapons that the Soviets have programmed through the 1980s."[243]

There has been some progress towards the reduction of armaments and forces. In part, the Soviet Union has embarked on certain unilateral measures. Its pullout from Afghanistan (which according to Nikolai Ryzhkov had cost it $70 billion)[244] provided a reassuring signal to the West of Gorbachev's intention to reduce confrontation and military expenditures. The Soviet Union and the Warsaw Pact states have also announced (and commenced) unilateral troop and military budget reductions. On December 7, 1989 at the United Nations Gorbachev stated that the Soviet Union would be cutting its conventional military strength in Europe by 500,000 troops, 10,000 tanks, 8,500 artillery pieces and 800 combat aircraft by 1991.[245] They would include front line units and the removal of 5,000 tanks from the Northern Tier states of the Warsaw Pact (and Hungary), Moscow subsequently announced that it would be reducing the military budget by 14.2% and would slash another 19.5% from spending on arms production.[246] Following the Soviet announcement, the East European states also proclaimed their intention to cut troops and military budgets.[247]

Moscow has commenced its troop reductions in Eastern Europe. In May 1989 it invited Western reporters to witness some of the withdrawals from the GDR. Furthermore, in June 1989 Ryzhkov informed the Congress of People's Deputies that the Soviet government intended to proceed further with cuts in the military budget at least until 1995, thereby slashing annual expenditures by up to one-third.[248] Moreover, Gorbachev had revealed a week earlier that Soviet defense expenditures (at 77.3 billion rubles or $128 billion) were several times the official figures that the Soviet Union had published for decades.[249] Though these figures are still well below Western estimates, at least projected reductions of a significant percentage of the budget have become somewhat more meaningful.

Nevertheless, although these unilateral cuts in conventional forces and military expenditures by the Warsaw Pact are positive steps, they have not reassured the NATO states. First, even when fully implemented, the Warsaw

Pact will enjoy considerable superiority in conventional forces. NATO will be outnumbered in manpower, and outmassed by 1.9 to 1 in tanks, 2.3 to 1 in artillery, and 1.4 to 1 in combat aircraft.[250] Secondly, the Warsaw Pact forces have the geographic advantage of a quick land route reinforcement capacity from the Soviet Union. Thirdly, Warsaw Pact figures on expenditures still do not represent actual outlays. The revised Soviet figures still fall far short of most Western estimates and clearly do not include such matters as expenditures for military space research. According to some Western figures Soviet defense spending in 1988 for instance was up 3% though Moscow had claimed that there was no increase.[251] Fourthly, unilateral cuts make no provision for proper verification measures. Nor do they prevent a buildup in some other areas. For instance, at the end of December 1988, Norway claimed that the Soviet Union had strengthened considerably its mammoth northern fleet based at the Kola Peninsula.[252] Thus the substantial reduction in conventional forces that the West seeks (and Soviet economic conditions argue for) are likely to come only through mutual verified agreement.

There have been encouraging developments in East-West talks on conventional forces. In January 1989 the Warsaw Pact and NATO states agreed to new comprehensive conventional stability talks as negotiations on Conventional Armed Forces in Europe (CFE). These talks replace the fruitless negotiations on Mutual and Balanced Force Reductions (MBFR) which were held in Vienna from 1973 until February 1989. CFE looks much more encouraging because East and West have come closer in their positions on conventional arms. In particular the Soviet Union has become more ready to acknowledge the existence of asymmetries and the need to address them. Moreover, both the Warsaw Pact and NATO have agreed that sharp cuts in conventional strength are needed.

Warsaw Pact proposals under Gorbachev have increased the scope and depth of potential cutbacks to which the East would agree. Questions relating not only to asymmetries but also to surprise attack and verification, have been more readily addressed.[253] In May 1989 the Warsaw Pact states offered to cut by about half its troops and conventional armaments (including aircraft) stationed in Central Europe.[254] For its part NATO has also moved towards deep asymmetrical conventional force reductions. In December 1988 for instance it called for radical cuts that would produce parity of ground forces at drastically reduced levels.[255] Moreover, in calling for *inter alia* the reduction of tank forces by both sides to 20,000 (from a Pact high of 51,500) and ceilings for any state in Europe to 12,000 tanks, NATO in essence was asking for an alteration of the Pact's military doctrine.

President George Bush's proposals at the end of May 1989 have gone even further in situating arms reductions within the context of overall defense planning.[256] He acquiesced to a long-standing Soviet demand that aircraft and helicopters should be included in conventional force reductions. But in proposing that there should be a ceiling of 275,000 each on Soviet and American ground and airforce personnel stationed outside of national

On Reform

territory in the Atlantic-to-Urals zone, he was asking for dramatic asymmetrical reductions. According to Bush, the Soviet forces would be reduced from 600,000 (that is by 325,000) and American forces by 30,000 (which would involve a 20% cut in combat forces).[257] The reduction of combat helicopters and aircraft in this zone to 15% below NATO levels would also impose heavily asymmetrical cuts on the Warsaw Pact.

Furthermore Bush set a very short timetable for those reductions. He asked that agreement should be reached within six months to a year and that the reductions should be accomplished by 1992 or 1993 at the latest. He also declared that his aim was "to achieve a less militarized Europe."[258] The latter is a goal that the East Europeans in particular should find most attractive.

An East-West agreement may indeed be in the works but the time frame may well prove to be overly optimistic. Several issues remain to be resolved. First, although the essence of the proposed agreement involves overall military capabilities rather than aggregate numbers of weapons and troops, the numbers' issue remains to be resolved. Figures published by the Warsaw Pact[259] and by NATO[260] differ sharply. There are, of course, different counting rules, but Warsaw Pact figures still appear rather skewered when compared to independent assessments, such as those by the International Institute for Strategic Studies. In February 1989, for example, the Warsaw Pact rejected assertions that it significantly outnumbered NATO.[261]

One of the major sticking points may turn out to be the problem of counting aircraft. According to NATO it has 3977 aircraft to 8250 for the Pact. Moscow strongly differs. It claims that it has only 7876 aircraft compared to 7130 for the Western alliance. The figures for helicopters differ even more sharply. NATO counts 2600 for itself versus 3800 for the Warsaw Pact. The East bloc asserts that it has only 2785 helicopters in comparison with 5270 for NATO.[262] Clearly reductions based on the figures of either party will lead to a radically different conventional balance.

Secondly, the Soviet Union and United States must find ways to effectively verify the cuts. The mandatory on-site inspection requirements of the INF and the "transparency" measures agreed to at Stockholm in 1986 provide important precedents. But monitoring compliance of conventional weapons on a large scale, especially aircraft, which can be moved easily, is a monumental task. It requires the kind of intrusiveness that could well raise political questions in the Soviet Union and Eastern Europe.

Thirdly, the Bush proposals do not include the British and French forces stationed in West Germany. The Soviet Foreign Minister Eduard A. Shevardnadze, has already objected that the highly trained 100,000 men were not included.[263] But the problem of including these forces reflects the heart of the difference between the two military organizations. Britain and France as independent (nuclear) powers can veto any inclusion of their forces. The East European states can oppose the Soviet Union at best on marginal issues.

Fourthly and most importantly, for such a proposal to succeed in truly diminishing tensions it must operate within a different strategic/doctrinal environment. Given Soviet/Warsaw Pact offensive capabilities and Soviet dominance over Eastern Europe, changes will have to be made largely (though not exclusively) in the East. Soviet concepts of security and military doctrine, Pact decision-making and approaches to matters such as modernization, must evolve.

Under Gorbachev Soviet concepts of security have begun to change. He has concluded, as noted, that the military danger from the Western alliance has diminished. For instance, he was emphatic in his contention before the all-Union Communist Party Conference in June 1988 that the danger of war had been pushed back.[264] Thus he brought Soviet views more in line with that of some of the East European leaders and certainly closer to the views of the East European populations.

Perhaps even more importantly, though, Gorbachev has placed a greater emphasis than his predecessors on the political dimensions of security. (Soviet military doctrine has operated traditionally both at the socio-political and at the military technical level.) In stressing politics, the Soviet Union has also engaged in greater self-examination. Gorbachev told the party conference in 1988 that "we did not (also) make use of the political opportunities opened up by the fundamental changes in the world in our efforts to assure the security of our state, to scale down tensions and promote mutual understanding between nations."[265] And thus we also see an increasing Soviet recognition that its security is linked to the security of other states. That is, it cannot enhance its own security by diminishing that of the other. It is not possible to know how deeply ingrained this view has become and to what extent the new position is merely tactical but at least it allows for greater changes in Soviet (and Warsaw Pact) military doctrine by shifting more emphasis to the political elements.

In terms of doctrinal changes the Soviet Union claims that a new defensive doctrine is already in force. What may also be interesting, at least in terms of potential changes in the military decision-making process in the Soviet Union, (and therefore by extension in the Warsaw Pact) is that civilian theoreticians have begun extensive discussions about military doctrine.[266] They have dealt with such matters as the nature of a defensive doctrine and the concepts of "reasonable sufficiency" and "defensive defense."

Unfortunately, a good deal of what has been written is conceptually muddled.[267] L. Semeiko of the Institute for USA and Canada for instance has argued strongly for "reasonable sufficiency." On the one hand he contended that there must not be an unreasonable excess of military potential and that the very structure and deployment of the armed forces must be shaped so as to diminish the possibilities of surprise attack.[268] Soviet civilian analysts such as Vitaly Zhurkin have argued quite logically, that it is possible to have "reasonable sufficiency" without parity.[269] But Semeiko argued, on the other hand, that "reasonable sufficiency" *presupposes* parity. Furthermore, he contended that in order for "reasonable sufficiency" to work the Soviet Union would have to be able to deliver "a crushing rebuff to the aggressor."[270]

The latter assertion also indicates the complications with the concept of "defensive defense." Though it may be significant in the longer term what influential military leaders such as Colonel-General M.A. Gareev have asserted that the basic method of action of the Soviet forces for repelling aggression will be defensive operations,[271] this does not necessarily exclude what the West may view as offensive tactics. The Soviet military in fact continues to call for "counter-offensive" capabilities within the framework of defense. General A.I. Gribkov, for instance, has claimed that "counter-offensive" actions not only do not contradict a defensive strategy but in fact are necessary "within the framework of defensive operations and engagements on axes."[272] And the Soviet Defense Minister D.T. Yazov, has contended that it was impossible to defeat an aggressor through defense alone.[273]

Perhaps somewhat ominously for the East European states Soviet discussions of "defensive defense" and "reasonable sufficiency" have also emphasized the defense of the socialist community. Yazov has contended that a defensive posture also meant that Moscow had to have the "quantity and quality of forces so as to reliably assure the *collective security of the socialist community*"[274] (emphasis added). And the former chief of staff of the Soviet Armed forces (until December 1988) and currently military adviser to Gorbachev, has spoken of "sufficiency" in terms of a "reliable defense of the Soviet Union and the countries of the Warsaw Pact."[275]

Thus although there is "new thinking" in Soviet strategy many of the old concepts remain. Though the unilateral Soviet and Warsaw Pact reductions are encouraging, they have not yet altered the basic posture and doctrine of the Soviet and allied forces. And what adds to the considerable Western skepticism regarding the actuality or prospects for the formulation of a new "defensive" doctrine are such assertions as those made by the new Soviet Defense Minister, D.T. Yazov, when he declared in June 1987 that the Warsaw Pact doctrine was *already* defensive.[276]

Decision-making and Reliability. In terms of decision-making within the Warsaw Pact there has been no substantive change. With the exception of Romania the East European forces remain under the tight Soviet control that Kuklinski described.[277] East European decision (except Romania) to unilaterally cut their forces and expenditures came after the Soviet decision and were clearly mandated by Moscow. Moreover, even a switch to a defensive posture does not necessarily mean a change in Pact decision-making. On the contrary, the need for coordinating defense may involve a strengthening of centralized command. This is the current case with Pact air defenses which are tightly controlled by Moscow. Perhaps, the best hope for a "substantive increase in input from the East European states comes from possible change in civil-military relations in the Soviet Union. If there is greater civilian input then Soviet and subsequently Warsaw Pact decision-making could be further decentralized.

Nevertheless, if a truly defensive doctrine is eventually implemented, then large-scale savings and even the withdrawal of Soviet troops from

Eastern Europe are possible, at least in the longer term. Still, even under the best of circumstances, these would be dependent on such factors as the resolution of the question of the reliability of the East European forces, and modernization of forces.

A change to a defensive doctrine may also raise particular questions regarding the reliability of the East European states. Ironically a defensive doctrine may increase rather than diminish the value of the East European territory. With a defensive doctrine the Soviet Union would need to forego its strategy of rapid offense (onto enemy territory). And a reduction in the size of its forces would also mean that it would need to increase its mobilization capabilities in order to ensure its security. In the case of Eastern Europe even if the Warsaw Pact could be dissolved, bilateral military relations, very likely, would have to be maintained. In order to ensure or to increase its mobilization potential, the Soviet Union would need to preposition huge quantities of weapons in Eastern Europe and to safeguard its lines of communication along potential axes of defensive and offensive operations. Deprived of the *surprise factor* which as John Erickson has written,[278] is a primary element of current Soviet military doctrine, Moscow would need to make certain that it in turn would not have to face surprises. And it would not be just the West that would have to provide this assurance (through treaties and confidence building measures) but Eastern Europe would have to reassure the Soviet Union that it remained a reliable buffer zone. The NSWP states, thus, might need to increase their military efficiency and expenditures in order to convince the Soviet Union that they were providing reliable buffer zones. They might also need to build and maintain a large military infrastructure, which would include airports, supply depots, roads and railways that would allow Soviet forces to quickly reestablish themselves in forward positions in case of danger. This would have to be done in addition to a variety of political measures, also designed to provide reassurance.

The Conundrum of Modernization. Waste in the Soviet military and throughout the Warsaw Pact has been of concern to Gorbachev who rightly holds that various military tasks could be performed more efficiently. It is not illogical to assume that modernization can increase efficiency and cut costs in certain areas. Furthermore, if it can be accompanied by a reduction in the size of the armed forces, then savings could be substantial. And, as noted, savings would need to come from economizing on the conventional forces. Gorbachev, therefore, seems to have concluded that one of the best routes to savings and greater military efficiency is through modernization. This involves changes in the management of military personnel and training as well as the introduction of more modern technology. Soviet proponents of reform, such as A.P. Alexandrov have emphasized that defense strength depends on technological progress.[279] The military has certainly jumped on the bandwagon of modernization.[280] They may indeed see a trade-off between force reductions and the acquisition of more sophisticated weapons. A leaner but more effective and powerful military force is not inconceivable.

Unfortunately, modernization is a complex phenomenon. Linear logic does not always bring about the desired results. The consequences of modernization may differ significantly from what was intended. Furthermore, modernization of the Soviet forces poses problems particularly for the East European states. There has always been a generational gap between the weapons that the Soviet Union and the East Europeans states deploy. But, in order to prevent this gap from growing wider, the East Europeans will also have to keep pace with the Soviet modernization program. Although none of the East European states have the latest Soviet weapons[281] Poland, the GDR and Czechoslovakia in particular have already increased their inventories of more modern and costly weapons.[282] Moreover, as the American experience under Secretary of Defense Robert McNamara in particular showed, linear logic in modernization can create false efficiencies and ultimately tremendous waste.[283] Reducing the quantity of weapons produced greatly increased their unit cost. A "technological fix" did not resolve budgetary (or strategic) problems.

Unfortunately "new thinking" at the Pentagon also emphasizes high technology weaponry. This is part of a general approach labelled "competitive strategies" (CS), which was mentioned by George Bush in the first presidential debates in 1988.[284] It had the support of the powerful chairman of the Joint Chiefs of Staff, Admiral William Crowe, who saw it as a promising technique for using high technology and advanced tactics to meet American military commitments worldwide with a shrinking military budget. It calls for a form of high technology, non-nuclear warfare that would be extremely swift, confusing and destructive. CS emphasizes speed, deception and unconventional weaponry in an all-out attempt to disrupt invading armies.[285] It is also an attempt to fuse strategy with the power of the latest industrial revolution—cybernetics.

If implemented CS would certainly complicate Soviet plans for "defensive defense." Furthermore, CS is a strategy that would likely stimulate a qualitative arms competition that the Soviet Union and the East European states can ill afford. It is ironic then that (unless there is a dramatic shift in their political relationship) as both superpowers seek to reduce military expenditures they may find themselves in a technological race that would eliminate the savings derived even from large-scale reduction of forces.

Yet whatever scenarios we formulate the Soviet Union could improve certain aspects of its military relationship with Eastern Europe. We are really speaking of small improvements rather than dramatic shifts, for the prospects of a fundamental change in Soviet–East European military relations are remote unless there is a dramatic alteration in the political configuration of the region and the continent. Nevertheless, petty frictions and humiliations that contribute to an East European sense of "wounded pride" can be alleviated. Though the Soviet Union is unlikely to allow a significant East European input in decision-making (because ultimately it considers itself exclusively responsible for its core security interests which are global as well as regional), Moscow can do a great deal more at least to give the appearance that the East European views are taken into account. To an extent this has indeed been happening under the process of perevyazka commenced by Gorbachev. After summits with Ronald Reagan, for example, Gorbachev took care to meet with the heads of the Warsaw Pact and to inform them about what had occurred. Unfortunately, though, Gorbachev's other goals of a qualitatively higher level of economic integration and of acceleration of domestic and external reforms could further stimulate the military integrative forces rather than decentralize military decision-making. Still, a Soviet willingness to consult should improve the "atmospherics" of Soviet-East European military relations.

* * *

Overall, though, the picture of external reform and regional change that emerges is only partially encouraging in terms of adaptation and the creation of a more organic relationship. It is not that there are no sectoral improvements or that there is no potential for significant beneficial changes. Rather it is a case where a series of negative developments can aggravate already poor relations. And the process itself is highly unpredictable with the potential for unintended and unexpected consequences. Yet a relationship among political entities does not operate on the basis of objective reality alone since perception, as we have noted, plays a crucial role. And in Eastern Europe there are, at least among reformers, great expectations of the Gorbachev regime. These relate not only to domestic but also to beneficial external changes. A positive image can help generate momentum for change. But if the perception and the image are too far removed from reality, then the lack of progress eventually creates bitterness and disillusionment. The consequent malaise and pessimism then negate the credibility that in turn is essential for the restructuring of the relationship.

Perceptions and Misperceptions

As we have noted the actions of states as well as individuals hinge to a significant degree on the perception of threat, opportunity and power. And, as Korbonski (Chapter 4) for instance, points out there are differences between elite and mass perceptions. In this case we are dealing largely, though not exclusively, with elite perceptions. In interstate relations the problems of perception for decisionmakers are intrinsic. There may be even differences in perception if the decisionmakers deal with issues in peacetime as compared to conflict.[286] And, as Robert Jervis points out, nearly all global issues depend, to a considerable extent, on the accuracy of the actors' perceptions for their resolution.[287] Yet the propensity of national decisionmakers to misperceive the motives of their adversaries or even the process that is unfolding before them in their external relations is not particularly encouraging in terms of the resolution or avoidance of conflict or in terms of the effective adaptation of regional relations. This problem, moreover, is often compounded by the existence of ideological screens which prevent an accurate assessment of the other side's intentions or policies.

Whereas in the case of the Soviet-East European relationship we are also dealing with the general problems of perception there may be significant facilitating factors such as the commonality of ideology. Is it possible then that East European and Soviet elites and in certain instances those sections of the population that have some indirect influence, have a more accurate understanding of policies and processes in the region than external (including Western) observers? This becomes a particularly salient question in the Gorbachev period because current and prospective reforms are in turn affected by domestic and regional perceptions. Recent statements by two well-known individuals in Eastern Europe are intriguing and help illustrate the problems of perception. Though neither holds power, they may reflect to a significant extent, some of the general perceptions of change in the region. Karen Dawisha cites Alexander Dubcek, the deposed head of the Czechoslovak party, who declared in a January 1988 interview, "I can say that if the CPSU had then (in 1968) had the leadership it now has, the armed intervention in Czechoslovakia by the five armies would have been unthinkable."[288] And Lech Walesa, the leader of the Solidarity union in Poland remarked in early May 1988, as strikes continued in the country, that "our tragedy, our problem . . . is that Brezhnev lived two years too long."[289] How accurate then are East-East perceptions?

Misperception can be particularly dangerous in Soviet-East European relations. In 1968, before the Soviet-Warsaw Pact invasion, most Czechoslovak leaders were under the strong impression that they had or could gain Soviet approval for their effort to build "socialism with a human face."[290] There are risks in misperception for the Soviet Union itself. Moscow needs to try to defuse crises in Eastern Europe before they explode. Perhaps Solidarity activist, Jacek Kuron, overstated the case somewhat when he declared that a new explosion in Poland "could destroy Gorbachev."[291] But, crises in Eastern Europe as noted, can badly damage Gorbachev domestically and multiple failures in the bloc would certainly help his opponents and may indeed allow them to topple him.

Elites in Eastern Europe moreover, are under pressure from the population at large which seems to believe that external restraints are disappearing. The East European people, however, have a history of misperceiving Soviet intentions and at times, the level of tolerance of their own regimes. In Hungary in 1956, Czechoslovakia, in 1968 and Poland in 1981 the people in particular, misperceived how far they could go. Perhaps the gulf between the people and the regime in socialist states is part of the problem. For instance, in 1989 millions of people in China underestimated the willpower of a totalizing regime to brutally enforce its rule.

There are, though, a number of significant advantages that the Soviet Union and the East European states have over the West in accurately perceiving developments and intentions in the region. They are perhaps at their best in assessing completed developments. For example, Romania was among the first to understand both the depth of the Sino-Soviet split in 1960 and its implications. The advantages include not only ideological commonality but also geography and a system of trans-national contacts. With greater decentralization as part of domestic and external reforms, these trans-national contacts should multiply and further aid decision-makers in correctly perceiving intentions and policies.

In the case of the Soviet Union, the generational change under Gorbachev has also aided that state in developing a greater understanding of developments in Eastern Europe. The current Soviet leadership is better informed and advised about Eastern Europe. As Paul Marer shows in his contribution, Gorbachev has surrounded himself with very knowledgeable advisers. Individuals such as Abel Aganbegyan and Oleg Bogomolov are knowledgeable about conditions in Eastern Europe. Furthermore, Gorbachev has been willing to take an activist role in Eastern Europe and this, in turn, forces on him a more consistent and nuanced reading of developments in that region.

Yet, the Soviet Union and the East European states do face enormous problems in correctly perceiving regional as well as domestic developments. In all cases of reform there are problems of perception due to the intrinsic uncertainties of such change. The reform process in the Soviet Union, in particular, is complex and the outcome appears to be indeterminate. Moreover, it may be inadequately understood by the Soviet leadership itself. Prudent decision-makers in Eastern Europe, however, need to make contingency plans for unexpected developments.

In Eastern Europe this is further complicated by inadequate information. As Korbonski shows (Chapter 4) the absence of basic information is endemic in Eastern Europe and it represents a major bottleneck which tends greatly to slow down progress in Soviet–East European relations. The increase in glasnost in the Soviet Union and at least in some of the East European states should facilitate matters. But since glasnost functions within certain parameters, and in only two out of the six East European allied states, the benefits in this area may be limited.

Perhaps one of the most important screens contributing to misperception in the Soviet–East European relationship occurs in the broad cultural realm which includes political culture. In the case of the Soviet Union it has been more than just a matter of ideological rigidity which led Moscow in the past to perceive certain changes in Eastern Europe as threatening or induced it to employ coercion when other measures may have been more appropriate. The Soviet Union is not merely a regional hegemon but, as one of the two superpowers, it has a unique self-image, perhaps historically and culturally rooted, but one that at least on occasion has led it to behave with considerable "superpower arrogance." That is, as a superpower it has been particularly insensitive to the small states in the region and this is why the process of perevyazka is potentially so important.

In the case of the East European states, their relation with the Soviet Union bears some resemblance to that of the Balkan states with the Ottoman Empire in its latter years. They respect Soviet military power but do not hold in high regard Soviet political, economic, intellectual and cultural endeavours. Quite often one finds a strong streak of elitism in East European culture combined not only with anti-Soviet but also with anti-Russian attitudes. Elements of the East European intelligentsia certainly display a very strong anti-Soviet and anti-Russian attitude as Melvin Croan shows (Chapter 7). Such intellectual and cultural over-confidence or arrogance, though, can only contribute to misperception.

Even geography is a source of controversy and cultural clash in this region. "Dissident" intellectuals have spoken increasingly of a need to think in terms of a "central Europe" or Mitteleuropa rather than Eastern Europe. It is true that several of these states have been traditionally much closer to Western Europe and the imposition of socialism, therefore, severed historical/cultural links. Dissident historicism, therefore, attempts to make an important point in attempting to re-label the region. On the one hand, it is an effort to re-establish links but on the other it is perhaps an even stronger attempt to decouple the region from the Soviet Union. The latter is part of a long-term move to differentiate between this region and the Soviet Union by using such labels as "Asiatic" at times, going as far as to call the Soviet bloc itself "Western Asia."[292] The idea of Central Europe can be viewed in certain respects then as part of the desire for independence from the Soviet Union. And, as Croan writes (Chapter 7), there is the impression that at least for some of the East European intelligentsia this amounts to a transcendental *Heilslehre*.

To an extent some of these feelings are understandable given past Soviet oppression in Eastern Europe and hurt national pride. Nevertheless, some of the dissidents display an anti-Russianism that prevents rational cultural interchange or basic understanding. Eminent dissident writers and intellectuals (some exiled in the West) like Milan Kundera take such positions quite frequently. Croan presents an excellent example of this in quoting Gyorgy Konrad, a brilliant Hungarian writer who does not have the slightest doubt about the superiority of East European culture (Chapter 7). He defiantly posits the notion that in a free exchange of ideas Eastern Europe would surely "colonize" the Soviet Union.

This may be an extreme form of cultural arrogance but a sense of cultural superiority permeates much of the thinking in Eastern Europe. Though East European officials are far more circumspect in their statements, a sense of cultural superiority is often evident. One can see this in the GDR's smug rejection of Soviet reform and even in the attitude of the Czechoslovak leadership in 1968. Among the more significant dangers engendered by this attitude is, then, that a cultural screen, just as an ideological one, can lead to misperception.

It would be a mistake, of course, to suggest that there is uniform cultural enmity toward the Soviet Union throughout Eastern Europe and among all writers of East European origin. As Croan shows (Chapter 7), some like Czeslaw Milosz would be quite willing to accept Russian culture in Central Europe. Others such as the Hungarian philosopher Ferenc Feher (who now resides in the United States) deplores cultural anti-Russian manifestations for he suggests that it is counterproductive. He contends that people in the USSR who could otherwise be sensitive to East European grievances will gather around the imperial banner if they feel themselves attacked in their "ethnic substance."[293] Nevertheless, in Eastern Europe the sense of cultural superiority remains pervasive.

As Croan suggests, Gorbachev is playing a helpful role in alleviating cultural confrontation. A well-educated, energetic individual with a sharp mind, and a stylish wife, Gorbachev contradicts the image of the low-brow, bullying and slow-witted Soviet leader that the East Europeans held and which Brezhnev so typified. Moreover, as noted, there is much that Gorbachev can do through a process of perevyazka, for old wounds in Eastern Europe do need healing. Furthermore, "the idea of Europe" can be a cultural unifying factor for the Soviet Union and Eastern Europe. And Gorbachev, as Dawisha (Chapter 1) shows, has spoken of Europe as a "common home". In June 1989 during his visit to West Germany, Gorbachev, reiterated this theme. Furthermore, he signed a joint "Declaration of Principles," the first such agreement the Soviet Union made with a West European state, committing both sides to "overcoming the division of Europe."[294] Though Gorbachev's primary interest is to improve Soviet–West European relations this should also help foster a general improvement in European relations. Combined with positive cultural tendencies in the Soviet–East European relationship and working under the umbrella of a Europe as a "common home," the growth of a regional, cultural identity in Eastern Europe could therefore be a truly healthy development.

In the case of Eastern Europe there is a need, though, for Gorbachev to be more forthcoming than to merely speak of Europe as a "common home" if he is to help improve Soviet–East European relations. As a perceptive analyst of communist affairs has pointed out, although the Soviet Union has its place in Europe, it is only partly European, for as a global power it has global interests.[295] By contrast, the East European states, he argues are wholly European. Eastern Europe needs closer relations with the western part of the continent more than the Soviet Union. This distinction must be reflected in the Soviet approach to East-West European relations. It should tolerate closer relations between the East European states and Western Europe not solely in the hope of economic gain or an enhanced ability to exercise political pressure on the Western Alliance but as a recognition that the cultural reunification of the continent is an instrumental factor in the normalization of Soviet–East European relations.

Such reunification need not threaten the Soviet Union for it can be compatible with respect for Soviet culture and Soviet political and military concerns. The notion of Mitteleuropa that Croan discusses, this sense of regional cultural identity, can function as a bridge between the Soviet Union and Western Europe rather than as an East European attempt at cultural (and political) secession. But Moscow must thus recognize that the East European states have different needs and that culturally secure nations that have re-established their historical links with their continental neighbours will make better partners for a reformed Soviet Union.

In terms of concrete Soviet measures that would offer proof of Moscow's willingness to allow the "Europeanization" of Eastern Europe even symbolic acts could have a great impact. The razing of the Berlin Wall would be quite a risky step for Gorbachev to take given domestic uncertainties, objections from the GDR, the sensitivity to the prospect of German unification both in East and West Europe and the dangers of exaggerated expectations in the Soviet bloc. Therefore, this may not be a very likely measure. During his visit to West Germany, in June 1989, Gorbachev was deliberately vague on the future of the Wall. Yet such a step, taken with the clear understanding that it was not (or at least not yet) part of a policy of allowing German reunification, would have enormous symbolic value in terms of signalling the cultural reunification of the continent and would represent a dramatic improvement in both East-West and East-East relations in Europe.

Risks and Risk-Taking

There is considerable fluidity both in the Soviet Union and in much of Eastern Europe where reform is being pursued. Yet change here needs to take place within certain parameters for the limits of Soviet-style socialism and Soviet flexibility in Eastern Europe remain to be defined. The Soviet Union as we have seen, is yet to show unequivocally that it is prepared to accept a radical transformation of the socialist inter-state system in Europe to one where it exercises no more than influence.

There are, therefore, a variety of risks in domestic and external reform and in attempting to adapt to changing conditions. There is a very real danger that economic reform can spill-over into demands for unacceptable political change. Potentially, reform can undermine the existing power structures in the Soviet Union and Eastern Europe. Since penalties for failure have been so severe in the past, it is little wonder that the political leadership and, for that matter, society at large in the region tend to be risk-averse. Yet the basic economic and political difficulties facing all the socialist societies and the binding forces in intra-socialist relations impel them to change even though such regimes as those as Ceausescu, Honecker and, to a lesser extent, that of Milos Jakes try to resist reform. Still, even in the most reformist East European states uncertainties regarding the Gorbachev regime must make ruling elites cautious. Attaching themselves to Gorbachev and his reform program may well make good economic and political sense but could create difficulties should the Soviet leader lose power. There are bureaucratic struggles in the Soviet Union and Gorbachev himself has admitted that there is significant resistance to his reforms. Although what he has proposed are not basic systemic changes they can be quite disruptive to the old order and a prolonged period of sacrifice without visible benefits could force either the replacement of the leadership or a drastic revision of Gorbachev's plans whereby he might settle for merely muddling through, à la Brezhnev.

Gorbachev, though, has consolidated his power and his chances of retaining it are quite good. Jerry F. Hough, a veteran observer of Soviet politics, has argued that the General Secretary is likely to be around for a long time and will continue to be in a position to pursue his policies of reform.[296] And the Soviet Union has attempted to convince the East European states that reform is being institutionalized. Yegor Ligachev, who is generally viewed in the West as an opponent of Gorbachev and of his reformism, for example, praised effusively Hungarian reforms during his April 1987 visit to Budapest.[297] He stressed their fundamentally socialist character and their ability to serve as a model for all who experiment with innovation. The message was fairly obvious. Even someone who is viewed as Gorbachev's chief opponent in the Politburo and a skeptic of certain elements of restructuring, supported the broad aspects of reform. Such reassurances may indeed be comforting in Eastern Europe. But in terms of institutionalizing reforms in the Soviet Union a basic problem remains unresolved. Reform has been instituted from the top and popular reaction, especially in the longer term is unpredictable. The outcome thus remains indeterminate domestically and therefore externally.

There are other risks as well both in the Soviet Union and in Eastern Europe. Perestroika and glasnost are at least in part responsible for the more open nationalistic manifestations in Soviet Armenia, Georgia, Uzbekistan, the Baltic republics, and in Azerbaijan. Ethnic discontent has been formenting under the surface for a long time but greater openness and flexibility allowed it to come into the open. In the first half of 1989 in Uzbekistan and Georgia alone well over 100 people were killed by police and troops or by gangs, in outbursts of ethnic violence.[298]

Nationalism and especially the question of national minorities poses the potential for tremendous destructiveness and instability in the Soviet bloc. Historic enmities and various forms of revanchism and irredentism in Eastern Europe have been kept in check to a significant degree by Soviet regional hegemony. This may, indeed, be one of the least attractive ways of bringing about regional peace but the Soviet Union has played a stabilizing role. With a restructuring of relations, and domestic reform old regional antagonisms are likely to come to the fore more easily. The problem of national minorities remain unresolved in Eastern Europe. Several of the East European states have significant ethnic minorities. The ill treatment of national minorities results not only from a general denial of individual human rights but also from that of collective ones. As Mary Ellen Fischer has put it "nationality rights are essentially collective rights since nationality is a form of communal existence."[299] Thus the denial of communal activities even if they are not specifically directed at certain ethnic groups have a very negative domestic impact. Moreover, the mistreatment of these national minorities raises the concern of co-nationals across borders.

As long as multi-ethnic countries in Eastern Europe continue to masquerade as unitary states, the problem of nationalities will remain unresolved. We are already witnessing a drastic deterioration of relations between

Hungary and Romania centering largely on the problems of the large (1.7-2 million) ethnic Hungarians living in Romania. The government-controlled press in Hungary, as noted, has become highly critical of what it claims to be the persecution of the Hungarian minority.[300] Tens of thousand ethnic Hungarians from Romania have sought refuge in Hungary.[301] The Hungarian government and the press continue to criticize the Romanian decisions to deny language rights, to reduce cultural programs and to consolidate Hungarian and Romanian villages in Transylvania. For Hungary, the treatment of ethnic Hungarians in Romania has become one of the most important and explosive external concerns. And Hungary is also concerned about the treatment of the sizable Hungarian minority in Czechoslovakia.

In Bulgaria where over 10% of the population is made up of ethnic Turks sporadic violence and expulsions have characterized the regime's response to this minority's aspirations to preserve its culture. Poland and Czechoslovakia, as well, have unresolved border and ethnic concerns. And should external constraints be lifted completely in the future, it is not inconceivable that the GDR and Poland would also need to conform to a number of ethnic and border disputes. Thus the problem of nationalities is very much part of a disquieting trend in domestic and regional restructuring.

Conclusion

Although what emerges in this collective study is not a particularly or uniformly optimistic picture, there are positive trends and tendencies regarding the resolution of key issues. There are no quick or easy solutions and clearly the states in the region are in for a painful adjustment period and one of difficult domestic and regional adaptation to changing conditions. But there is, at least, the possibility of the alleviation of some problems. It is not a case of crisis resolution for the proposed changes do not involve systemic transformations or transcendence with the possible exceptions of Hungary and Poland. Rather, what may be achieved is crisis diminution.

What we have also seen is that linear logic is not always adequate either in predicting outcomes or in understanding current processes. At times it is paradoxical logic that best explains developments and we are dealing with unintended or unexpected consequences. There are significant risks in reform both domestically and in the regional relationship. Yet there is a need to balance risk and this is particularly difficult to do in risk-averse societies. Nevertheless, the fundamental problems confronting the states in the region are such that without significant reform, political, economic and social crises may prove to be more dangerous than the dislocations engendered by restructuring.

Without restructuring the Soviet Union is likely to find it increasingly more difficult to retain its superpower status as it is left behind by the technological revolution that is sweeping the Western industrialized world. As such its economy could become incapable of supporting a military effort that allows it to cling to superpower status. In the case of the East European states, a failure to restructure would make them sink, perhaps irreversibly to Third World status. Some of the East European states, specifically Romania and Poland, may have already declined to underdeveloped-nation status and in such conditions the possibilities for domestic and regional instability, and perhaps violence, increase. Consequently, it would seem that the Soviet Union and Eastern Europe have little choice but to try to pursue internal reforms and attempt to create a more organic relationship in the region.

If the Soviet Union on the one hand and the East European states on the other are to change their relationship they must each adapt. For Moscow this would involve alterations in its ideology, in its view of the world, of security, of economic relations with the other socialist states and of the role of nationalities. Ultimately, though, Soviet political culture itself must change. But this may be one of the most difficult tasks facing the Soviet Union. As Walter Laqueur has written, "cultural revolutions involve not just the replacement of one political elite by another but lasting and radical change in the mentality of a nation."[302]

Nor is the task of the East European states an easy one. They need to exhibit a good deal of patience, political maturity, and this should include a commitment to gradualism and the resolution of the problem of national minorities. And as part of the transformation of their political culture they need to freely accept the Soviet Union as a fellow European state. The tasks of the East Europeans are further complicated by the remarkably strong linkages not only between Soviet domestic developments and foreign policy but also between Soviet and East European policy changes. Despite considerably greater Soviet flexibility in dealing with Eastern Europe, in many respects, perestroika itself, in the whole region, is indivisible. And because the Soviet Union remains the preponderant force in the area so much hinges on the success of change inside the communist superpower.

Reform in the Soviet Union under Gorbachev though has highlighted the internal contradictions of the socialist system. The centralizing impulse of the ideology, of the vanguard party and the accumulation of increasing power in the hands of the leader are in contrast to the need for economic decentralization and individual initiative. Soviet reforms have often created dysfunction rather than stimulated synergy. They have brought to the fore hidden inflation, unemployment, budget deficits and growing trade deficits. Though Gorbachev has encouraged discussion and even criticism he has also shown considerable distrust of spontaneity. Although he apparently wants to change the psychology of the people by shaking both the top and the bottom of society he has pushed reform from the top. At the meeting of the Congress of People's Deputies in June 1989 for instance, delegates could speak with unprecedented candor but when it came to substantive decisions it was clear that true power remained in the hands of Gorbachev and his compliant majority.[303]

Moreover, Gorbachev continues to hold to the traditional Marxist-Leninist belief in "scientific" solutions to social problems. Therefore we need to look cautiously at the process of adaptation in the Soviet Union. The language of democracy should not be confused with the substance. Adoption of democratic forms does not necessarily signal the emergence of civil society. Market-style reforms should not be mistaken for the acceptance of the ideology of the market. What Gorbachev has pursued is a kind of "scientific" Leninism, not Western liberalism, not a systemic change.

This is not to minimize the significance of Gorbachev's reforms or to dismiss the potential for unexpected changes. Rather, it is vital to keep in mind the context of these changes. For Gorbachev has not managed to eliminate the domestic contradictions. His policies on alcoholism, agriculture and cooperatives illustrate this. Failure to resolve the domestic contradictions, moreover, makes it more difficult for Gorbachev to deal with the contradictions in relation with Eastern Europe as reflected in the operations of the CMEA and the Warsaw Pact.

Furthermore, the failure to resolve these contradictions is part of and adds to the difficulty of meshing the pace of developments in the Soviet Union and in Eastern Europe. First, in the Soviet Union, at the time of this writing, glasnost has far outpaced perestroika. This is creating a potentially volatile situation where raised expectations and economic failure can lead to political instability. Secondly, developments in the Soviet Union and Eastern Europe are out of sync. Hungary and Poland are moving far ahead of the Soviet Union both on the political and economic fronts. The GDR, Romania, Czechoslovakia and even Bulgaria are rapidly lagging behind. Therefore, it is no longer a matter of regional homogeneity but increasingly a question of economic compatibility that is confronting these states. This does not necessarily eliminate the centripedal forces of ideology, geographic convenience or inability to compete on the world market but makes it far more difficult for the Soviet Union to resolve the seemingly contradictory goals of cohesion and viability in the bloc.

In the Warsaw Pact the Soviet Union has also instituted policies that may produce contradictory results. On the one hand, in pursuing a policy of denuclearization, in reducing some of the Soviet conventional forces unilaterally, in commencing to change the Warsaw Pact doctrine to what may turn out to be a more defensive strategy and in agreeing to a whole range of arms reduction talks, Gorbachev has fulfilled some important Western expectations of progress. Therefore he has made the Soviet Union a less menacing power and has diminished the Western impulse to counter a Warsaw Pact threat (certainly in West Germany and in much of Western Europe). This fits in with his notion that the Soviet Union can enhance its security by political means and by not threatening the security of others. It is also part of his linkage of security and international economic cooperation. During his visit to West Germany, in June 1989, for example, he declared, "We associate our policy of economic openness with the problem of universal security."[304] On the other hand his emphasis on efficiency and modernization, as noted, may turn out to be a trap—one of escalating costs (despite reduction of forces) and a qualitative arms competition with the West. In the case of the East Europeans, denuclearization, troop reductions and withdrawals may produce positive results but can also lead to greater instability, enhanced Soviet military control, magnified concern with reliability, greater emphasis on territory and relatively heavier military burdens.

There is then a cacophony of centripetal and centrifugal forces at work in the region. Despite attempts at a controlled experiment the policies of the reformist Soviet and East European leaders may well produce a whole range of unexpected results domestically and in socialist interstate relations. As Polish dissident Jacek Kuron has said, "Gorbachev has set the social forces in motion, and neither he nor anyone else can know what the consequences will be."[305] There are expectations of change both among some leaders and especially among the populations of several of the states. As well, there is resistance. Uncertainty is intermingled with hope. Cynicism, a pervasive malaise and anger also characterize the region. And the close intertwining of domestic and external factors adds to the regional turbulence.

Yet despite the enormous difficulties these states confront, it is not inconceivable that this turbulence will lead to the creation of a dramatically new, organic relationship between the Soviet Union and Eastern Europe. Nikolai Shmelev in projecting an optimistic, long-term outcome for Gorbachev's 1989 agricultural reforms suggested that the Soviet leader had deliberately initiated a "creative mess"—one that will lead to the necessary transformation.[306] Perhaps this is an apt description of the changes that Gorbachev has brought to the Soviet-East European relationship. In the next few years though we should be in a better position to assess whether the adjective is justified.

Notes

1. Harold and Margaret Sprout, "Environmental Factors in the Study of International Politics," *Journal of Conflict Resolution*, Vol. 1 (December 1957), pp. 309-28.

2. Rezso Nyers, "Hagyomony es ujitas a KGST—egyuttmukovesben" (continuity and change in CMEA cooperation) *Koszgazdasagi szemle*, (Budapest) 1982, No. 4 pp. 385-403.

3. Hélène Carrère d'Encausse, *Big Brother: The Soviet Union and Soviet Europe*, New York: Holmes and Meier, 1987, pp. 304-5.

4. K.W. Deutsch, "Kontinuitäten and Veränderungen in den internationalen Beziehungen bis zur Jahrhundertwenden," in *Osterreichisches Jahrbuch fur Internationale Politik*, 1985, p. 147, cited in Boris Meissner, "Gorbachev's *Perestroika*: Reform or Revolution." *Aussenpolitik*, No. 3, 1987, p. 213.

5. A. Korbonski, "Ideology Disabused: Communism Without a Face in Eastern Europe" in N. Kittrie and I. Volgyes, eds., *The Uncertain Future: Gorbachev's Eastern Bloc*, New York: Paragon House, 1988, p. 43.

6. Nish Jamgotch, Jr., *Soviet-East European Dialogue: International Relations of a New Type?* Stanford University Press, 1968, pp. 105 and 108.

On Reform

7. Cited in Michel J. Crozier, Samuel P. Huntington, and Joji Watunaki, *The Crisis of Democracy*, New York: Free Press, 1975, p. 187.

8. Z.Y. Gitelman, *The Diffusion of Political Innovation: From Eastern Europe to the Soviet Union*, Beverly Hills, CA: Sage Publications, 1972, p. 44.

9. Sarah M. Terry, ed., *Soviet Policy in Eastern Europe*, New Haven: Yale University Press, 1984, pp. 237-8.

10. See, for instance, Fyodor Burlatsky, "Karl Marx and Our Times" *New Times*, No. 23, 1983, pp. 18-20 or A. Aganbegyan, "Incentives and Reserves: Implement the Decisions of the November Plenary Sessions of the CPSU Central Committee," *Trud*, December 12, 1982.

11. Charles Gati, *Hungary and the Soviet Bloc*, Durham: Duke University Press, 1986, p. 128.

12. *Ibid.*, p. 149.

13. *Ibid.*, p. 137.

14. *New York Times*, October 2, 1988.

15. *Pravda*, February 25, 1986.

16. *Pravda*, January 28 and 29, 1987.

17. Gail W. Lapidus, "The Changing Relationship Between State and Society" Paper and roundtable address delivered at the "German-American Conference on the Gorbachev Reform Program: Its Impact on Soviet and East European Policies," Washington, D.C., March 20-22, 1988.

18. *New York Times*, January 8, 1989.

19. Paul Marer, *Dollar GNPs of the USSR and Eastern Europe*, Baltimore: The Johns Hopkins University Press, for the World Bank, 1985, pp. 1-15.

20. Abel Aganbegyan, "The Economics of Perestroika," *International Affairs*, (London), Vol. 64, No. 2, Spring 1988, p. 177.

21. *Ibid*, pp. 177-8.

22. Georg Brunner, "Reform Policies in South-East Europe: Political Aspects." Paper delivered at the "German-American Conference on the Gorbachev Reform Program: Its Impact on Soviet and East European Policies," Washington, D.C., March 20-22, 1988, pp. 1-12.

23. *Ibid.*, pp. 2-3.

24. Carrére d'Encausse, *op. cit.*, p. 314.

25. Gail W. Lapidus, "State and Society: Toward the Emergency of Civil Society in the Soviet Union," in Seweryn Bialer, ed., *Politics, Society and Nationality Inside Gorbachev's Russia*, Boulder, Colo., Westview Press, 1989, pp. 121-149.

26. Mikhail Gorbachev, *Perestroika*, New York, Harper and Row, 1987, p. 82.

27. Carrére d'Encausse, *op. cit.*, p. 314.

28. See Bennett Kovrig, "Political Reform in Eastern Europe" in N. Kittrie and I. Volgyes, eds., *The Uncertain Future: Gorbachev's Eastern Bloc*, New York: Paragon House, 1988, pp. 9-39.

29. Gorbachev, *op. cit.*,, p. 57.

30. *Globe and Mail*, Toronto, May 27, 1988.

31. *New York Times*, April 30, 1989.

32. *Toronto Star*, April 26, 1989.

33. *New York Times*, April 30, 1989.

34. *Ibid.*

35. *Globe and Mail*, May 22, 1989.

36. *Globe and Mail*, May 23, 1989; *New York Times*, May 21, 1989.

37. *Globe and Mail*, May 26, 1989.
38. *The Washington Post*, May 21, 1989.
39. *Toronto Star*, May 21, 1989.
40. *Globe and Mail*, May 26, 1989.
41. *New York Times*, May 8, 1988.
42. *Globe and Mail*, May 11, 1988.
43. *Globe and Mail*, March 17, 1989.
44. *New York Times*, May 28, 1989.
45. Ibid.
46. Ibid.
47. Ibid.
48. *Globe and Mail*, May 29, 1989, and CBC Television News, May 30, 1989, 10:00 p.m. EDT.
49. *New York Times*, May 28, 1989.
50. Ibid.
51. Ibid.
52. Report on NBC T.V. News, May 28, 1989, 7:00 EDT.
53. *New York Times*, May 28, 1989.
54. As cited by J. Sallot, *Globe and Mail*, March 13, 1989.
55. Ibid.
56. As cited by Bill Keller in "A Little Bit of Party Disunity Suits Gorbachev Just Fine," *New York Times*, April 30, 1989.
57. *Toronto Star*, January 8, 1989.
58. Walter Laqueur, *The Long Road to Freedom*, New York: Charles Scribner's & Sons, 1989.
59. *Globe and Mail*, May 26, 1989.
60. *Toronto Star*, May 24, 1989.
61. *New York Times*, May 28, 1989.
62. *Toronto Star*, April 1, 1989.
63. *The Globe and Mail*, May 23, 1989.
64. *New York Times*, April 9, 1989.
65. *Newsweek*, April 13, 1989, p. 34.
66. Ibid, p. 36.
67. *Globe and Mail*, May 19, 1989.
68. Ibid.
69. Ibid.
70. *Globe and Mail*, May 26, 1989.
71. *Globe and Mail*, May 29, 1989.
72. "Meetings of Europe Working Group of the Mutual Security Project: Moscow, March 28-30, 1989 Summary Report," Providence, R.I.: Brown University Center for Foreign Policy Development, April 11, 1989, p. 3.
73. Ibid, p. 2.
74. Ibid.
75. *Globe and Mail*, May 23, 1988.
76. *Toronto Star*, May 22, 1988.
77. *Eastern Europe Newsletter*, (London), Vol. 2, No. 9, May 9, 1988, p. 3.
78. Ibid, p. 4.
79. They were Zoltan Kiraly, member of parliament for Szeget; Mihaly Bihari, deputy director of the Institute of sociology; Laszlo Lengyel, a reform economist

On Reform

and one of the authors of the PPF's "Change and Reform" program in 1987; and Zoltan Biro, a writer and chairman of the HDF.

80. *Nepszabadsag* (Budapest), May 22, 1988.
81. Kalmar Kulcsar, "Emberi jogok: deklaraciok es valosag" (Human rights: Declarations and Reality), *Valosag*, (Budapest), Vol. XXXI, No. 4, 1988, pp. 1-12.
82. *Globe and Mail*, November 11, 1988.
83. *Globe and Mail*, January 12, 1989.
84. *Nepszabadsag*, February 13, 1989.
85. *Globe and Mail*, February 14, 1989.
86. *Globe and Mail*, February 13 and 21, 1989.
87. *Eastern Europe Newsletter*, Vol. 3, No. 4, February 22, 1989, pp. 4-5.
88. *Toronto Star*, May 29, 1989.
89. *Globe and Mail*, May 31, 1989.
90. *Globe and Mail*, April 13, 1989.
91. *Toronto Star*, May 21, 1989.
92. *Eastern Europe Newsletter*, Vol. 3, No. 4, February 22, 1989, p. 4.
93. *Budapester Rundschau*, as cited in the *Toronto Star*, May 27, 1987.
94. *New York Times*, April 12, 1989.
95. *Toronto Star*, May 29, 1989.
96. Gati, op. cit., p. 162.
97. *Globe and Mail*, March 16, 1989.
98. Alan Riding, "Italy's Communists Try Not to Be Ideologues," *New York Times*, May 7, 1989.
99. Ibid.
100. Aurel Braun, *Romanian Foreign Policy Since 1965: The Political and Military Limits of Autonomy*, New York: Praeger, 1978.
101. Western Nations including Canada criticized Romania harshly for violating the undertakings it made to respect human rights in Vienna in 1988 CBC News T.V., 10:00 E.D.T., May 30, 1989.
102. *Globe and Mail*, (London), June 3, 1987.
103. *Toronto Star*, July 9, 1988.
104. *New York Times*, September 4, 1988.
105. *Toronto Star*, April 22, 1989.
106. *New York Times*, May 28, 1989.
107. *Toronto Star*, April 22, 1989.
108. See, Henry Kamm, "In a Pro-Solidarity City, Poland's Coming Vote Is Stirring Little Excitement" *New York Times*, June 1, 1989; in the June 4, 1989, election only 62% of the electorate voted compared to 79% in the 1985 elections. *Newsweek* June 19, 1989, p. 43.
109. *Globe and Mail*, April 4, 1988.
110. *Toronto Star*, April 23, 1989.
111. *Globe and Mail*, June 3, 1989.
112. *New York Times*, June 1, 1989.
113. *Globe and Mail*, June 3, 1989; *New York Times*, June 1, 1989.
114. *Globe and Mail*, June 3, 1989.
115. *Globe and Mail*, June 6, 1989; CBC Radio News, June 6, 1989 7:00 a.m. EDT; CKO Radio News June 7, 1989, 7:30 a.m. EDT; *Globe and Mail*, June 20, 1989.
116. *New York Times*, April 12, 1989.

117. *International Herald Tribune*, May 25, 1988.
118. *Ibid.*
119. *Newsweek*, October 10, 1988, p. 49.
120. *Tass*, Moscow, October 1, 1988.
121. *Pravda*, October 5, 1988.
122. *Ibid.*
123. As quoted in the *New York Times*, November 6, 1988.
124. Alec Nove, *Socialism, Economics and Development*, London: Allen and Unwin, 1986.
125. Janos Kornai, *Growth, Shortage and Efficiency*, Berkeley: University of California Press, 1982, and "The Hungarian Reform Process," *Journal of Economic Literature*, Vol. XXIV, No. 4, December 1986, pp. 1687-1737.
126. S. Rosefielde, "The Soviet Economy in Crisis: Birman's Cumulative Disequilibrium Hypothesis," *Soviet Studies*, Vol. XL, No. 2, April 1988, p. 235.
127. *Business Week*, January 30, 1989, p. 50.
128. *Globe and Mail*, March 27, 1989.
129. *Toronto Star*, April 1, 1989.
130. *Globe and Mail*, March 27, 1989.
131. *Ibid.*
132. *Toronto Star*, April 1, 1989.
133. *Globe and Mail*, March 27, 1989.
134. *Business Week*, January 30, 1989, p. 50.
135. *Globe and Mail*, June 2, 1989.
136. *Globe and Mail*, March 27, 1989.
137. *Business Week*, January 30, 1989, p. 50.
138. *New York Times*, January 29, 1989.
139. *Vechernyaya Moskva* (Moscow), December 30, 1988, as cited in the *New York Times*, January 1, 1989.
140. Officially, the poverty level in the Soviet Union for an urban family of four is 205.6 rubles a month ($339.24 US) which works out to about 51 rubles ($85) a person. *New York Times*, January 29, 1989.
141. *Pravda*, March 30, 1989.
142. *Toronto Star*, March 16, 1989.
143. *Toronto Star*, March 17, 1989.
144. *New York Times*, April 30, 1989.
145. Judy Shelton, *The Coming Soviet Crash*, New York: The Free Press, 1988.
146. *Globe and Mail*, January 27, 1989.
147. The Central Intelligence Agency estimated that the Soviet economy grew by only 1.5% in 1988 and agricultural production fell by 2%, *New York Times*, April 23, 1989.
148. Abel Aganbegyan, "The Economics of Perestroika" *International Affairs* (London) Vol. 64, No. 2, Spring 1988, p. 181.
149. *Pravda*, February 6, 1989.
150. *Globe and Mail*, May 16, 1988.
151. Interview in *New York Times*, April 30, 1989.
152. *Ibid.*
153. *Ibid.*
154. *New York Times*, April 30, 1989.
155. *Globe and Mail*, March 30, 1989.

156. William E. Odom, "How Far Can Soviet Reform Go?" *Problems of Communism*, Vol. XXXVI, November-December 1987, pp. 23-7. Also see *Introduction* in this volume.

157. *Globe and Mail*, December 28, 1988.

158. *Globe and Mail*, May 6, 1989.

159. Jan Adam, "The Economic Reform in Industry: Is There Hope?" paper presented at the conference on "Before the Storm Breaks: The Extent, Limits and Dangers of Reform in Communist Hungary," Pennsylvania State University, April 14-17, 1988.

160. For further discussion on this issue see the excellent paper by Ivan Volgyes, "Class Struggle Revisited: The Problems of Class and Equality in Contemporary Hungary," at the conference on "Before the Storm Breaks: The Extent, Limits and Dangers of Reform in Communist Hungary," Pennsylvania State University, April 14-17, 1988, pp. 27-33.

161. *Ibid.* pp. 31-33.

162. *Globe and Mail*, January 9, 1989.

163. *Nepszabadsag* cited in the *Globe and Mail*, January 4, 1989.

164. Zbigniew Fallenbuchl, "Economic Restructuring in the Soviet Union and the World Economy" paper delivered at the conference on "Perestroika, Glasnost and International Security," University of Manitoba, February 2-4, 1989, p. 7.

165. *Newsweek*, May 9, 1988, p. 26.

166. Jane L. Curry, "*Glasnost*: Words Spoken and Words Heard" paper at "German-American Conference on the Gorbachev Reform Program: Its Impact on Soviet-East European Policies," March 10-11, 1988, Kennan Institute, Washington, D.C.

167. *New York Times*, April 23, 1989.

168. J.F. Brown, "Poland Since Martial Law," *Rand Note N-2822-RC*, December 1988, p. 26.

169. As quoted in *Newsweek*, October 24, 1988, p. 30.

170. John Tagliabue, "Hardship Ahead: Poland Can Exercise Political Will But There's No Way Out of Austerity," *New York Times*, April 23, 1989.

171. *Globe and Mail*, June 3, 1989.

172. Radoslav Selucky, for instance, outlined some aspects of such a transformation in his address at the "Conference on the Soviet-East European Relationship in the Gorbachev Era," University of Toronto, October 16-17, 1987.

173. *New York Times*, May 1, 1988.

174. *Newsweek*, May 2, 1988, p. 26.

175. See also J. F. Brown, "Relations Between the Soviet Union and Its East European Allies: A Survey," *Rand Report R-1742*, 1975.

176. J. F. Brown, "A Western Overview" in "East-West Relations and Eastern Europe," *Problems of Communism*, May-August 1988, pp. 57-60.

177. Edward Luttwak has written in relation to strategy that it operates on the basis of paradoxical rather than linear logic. This perceptive analysis seems to apply also to the Soviet-East European relationship. See *The Paradoxical Logic of Strategy*, Berkeley: Institute of International Studies, 1987.

178. E. Primakov, "Kapitalizm vo vzaimosvyazannom mire," *Kommunist*, No. 13, September 1987, pp. 102-10.

179. *Financial Times*, (London) March 30, 1989.

180. *Globe and Mail*, March 19, 1988.

181. *Pravda,* April 11, 1987.
182. *Pravda,* May 27, 1987.
183. *New York Times,* April 9, 1989.
184. *Pravda,* April 4, 1989.
185. *Pravda,* May 11, 1987.
186. *Pravda,* May 27, 1987.
187. *The Washington Post,* May 22, 1988.
188. As reported in the *Los Angeles Times,* July 10, 1988, by Robert C. Toth.
189. Brown University, Center for Foreign Policy Development, "Summary Report of Meetings of Europe Working Group of the Mutual Security Project, Moscow, March 28-30, 1989," Providence, R.I., April 11, 1989.
190. *Ibid,* p. 5.
191. *Ibid,* p. 3.
192. *Ibid,* p. 2.
193. Seweryn Bialer, "Central and Eastern Europe, *Perestroika,* and the Future of the Cold War," in William E. Griffith, ed., *Central and Eastern Europe: The Opening Curtain?* Boulder Colo.: Westview Press, 1989, p. 420.
194. Center for Foreign Policy Development, "Summary Report . . ." *loc. cit.,* p. 4.
195. Program passed in Moscow, December 1985. Text *Ekonomicheskoe Sotrudnichestvo Stran-Chlenov SEV,* Moscow, 1, 1986, pp. 1-13.
196. Raymond Aron, *Peace and War,* London: Weidenfeld and Nicholson, 1966, pp. 373-81.
197. Tass International Service, October 13, 1987.
198. *Pravda,* July 8, 1988.
199. Radio Budapest, February 21, 1988, 10:05 a.m. as reported in Radio Free Europe, *Background Report,* No. 60, April 6, 1988.
200. Aurel Braun, "Economic Developments in the Eastern Bloc: Is the Soviet Web of Control Tightening?" *Parameters,* Vol. IX, No. 3, 1979, pp. 46-55.
201. Bennett Kovrig, "Hungary," *Yearbook on International Communist Affairs 1987,* Stanford, Calif.: Hoover Institutional Press, 1987, p. 306.
202. Radio Free Europe, *Research,* November 21, 1986 (hereinafter cited as RFE).
203. *Globe and Mail,* January 4, 1989.
204. *Ibid.*
205. *Neues Deutschland* (Berlin), February 27, 1989 cited in *RFE Research,* No. 34, March 1, 1989, p. 1.
206. *Berliner Zeitung,* February 27, 1989 cited in RFE *Research,* No. 34, March 1, 1989, p. 1.
207. East European Program Meeting Report, "East Germany and the Current East European Crisis," No. 27, European Institute, The Wilson Center, Washington, D.C., 1988.
208. *Ibid.*
209. See Aurel Braun, *Romanian Foreign Policy Since 1965: The Political and Military Limits of Autonomy,* New York: Praeger, 1978.
210. *Financial Times,* London, April 28, 1987.
211. *Globe and Mail,* April 24, 1989.
212. *Toronto Star,* February 26, 1989; *Globe and Mail,* June 6, 1989.
213. *Toronto Star,* April 25, 1989.
214. *Globe and Mail,* May 16, 1989.

215. *The Economist*, May 20–26, 1989.
216. *Globe and Mail*, October 18, 1988.
217. *Nepszabadsag*, January 21, 1989.
218. For an interesting appraisal see Edward A. Hewett, *Reforming the Soviet Economy: Equality Versus Efficiency*, Washington: The Brookings Institution, 1988.
219. *New York Times*, May 22, 1988.
220. See especially, Bela Csikos-Nagy, "New Aspects of East-West Trade," *Hungarian Business Herald*, Budapest, No. 1, 1988, pp. 2-7.
221. *New York Times*, July 31, 1988.
222. *Tass*, Moscow, October 12, 1988, and *New York Times*, October 16, 1988.
223. Britain $1.6 billion, West Germany $1.6 billion and Italy $775 million, *Globe and Mail*, Toronto, October 19, 1988. Together with loans from Japanese banks, the total comes to about $9 billion. According to John Hardt this tops the combined total (of $8 billion) of the three previous years. *New York Times*, October 23, 1988.
224. *New York Times*, October 16, 1988.
225. K. Z. Poznanski, "Opportunity Cost in Soviet Trade with Eastern Europe: Discussion of Methodology and New Evidence," *Soviet Studies*,, Vol. XL, No. 2, April 1988, pp. 299-307.
226. Ibid, p. 305.
227. *Globe and Mail*, March 2, 1989.
228. It amounted to $2.6 billion in 1988 and $1.1 billion in the first quarter of 1989. *Globe and Mail*, March 30, 1989, and April 26, 1989.
229. *Toronto Star*, June 10, 1989.
230. Seweryn Bialer, "The Political System," in Robert F. Byrnes ed., *After Brezhnev: Sources of Soviet Conduct in the 1980s*, Bloomington: Indiana University Press, 1983, p. 10.
231. See Strobe Talbott, "The Road to Zero," *Time*, December 14, 1987, pp. 22-23.
232. See the excellent article by Dale R. Herspring, "On Perestroika, Gorbachev, Yazov and the Military," *Problems of Communism*, July–August 1987, pp. 99-107.
233. Edward N. Luttwak, *op. cit.*, 1987, p. 46.
234. James A. Schear and Joseph S. Nye, Jr., "Addressing Europe's Conventional Instabilities," *The Washington Quarterly*, Summer 1988, pp. 45-47.
235. *Pravda*, May 30, 1987.
236. Ibid.
237. Ibid.
238. A. Ross Johnson, "The Warsaw Pact: Soviet Military Policy in Eastern Europe," Santa Monica: Rand Report, P-6583, July 1981.
239. Aurel Braun, "The Yugoslav-Romanian Concept of People's War," *Canadian Defense Quarterly*, Summer 1977, Vol. 7, No. 1, pp. 39-43.
240. See also, International Institute for Strategic Studies, *The Military Balance 1987-1988*, London: International Institute for Strategic Studies, 1988, pp. 29-31 (henceforth, *The Military Balance*).
241. *The Military Balance*, 1987-1988, pp. 27-29.
242. *Globe and Mail*, May 30, 1989.
243. As quoted in *The Military Balance 1987-1988*, p. 32.
244. *New York Times*, June 8, 1989.

245. "Strategic Datalink," The Canadian Institute of Strategic Studies, December 1988, Datalink No. 11.
246. *Toronto Star*, January 22, 1989.
247. For instance, the GDR will be cutting its armed forces by 10,000 soldiers, 600 tanks and 50 warplanes and will reduce its military spending by 10% within a two-year period. *Globe and Mail*, January 24, 1989; Hungary announced cuts in defense of 17% a manpower reduction of 9,300 and a withdrawal of 251 tanks, 30 armoured personnel carriers, 43o artillery pieces, 6 tactical rocket launchers and an aircraft during a two-year period. *Globe and Mail*, January 31, 1989.
248. *New York Times*, June 8, 1989.
249. *Ibid.*
250. "Strategic Link," loc. cit.; *Military Balance 1988-1989*, pp. 15-46.
251. U. S. government figures as cited by CBS News 6:30 EDT, April 22, 1989.
252. *Globe and Mail*, December 28, 1988.
253. See *Documents of the Meeting of the Political Consultative Committee of the Warsaw Treaty Member States, Warsaw, July 15-16, 1988*, Moscow: Novosti Press 1988.
254. *Globe and Mail*, May 31, 1989.
255. *Globe and Mail*, December 9, 1988; *Newsweek*, December 19, 1988; *New York Times* December 4, 1988.
256. *New York Times*, May 30, 1989 and June 1, 1989.
257. *New York Times*, June 1, 1989.
258. *Ibid.*
259. See "Warsaw Treaty Organization and North Atlantic Treaty Organization: Correlation of Forces in Europe," Moscow: Novosti Press, 1989.
260. See "Conventional Forces in Europe: The Facts," Brussels, NATO, November 1988.
261. *New York Times*, February 5, 1989.
262. *New York Times*, May 30, 1989.
263. *New York Times*, June 1, 1989.
264. *Pravda*, June 29, 1980.
265. *Ibid.*
266. One of the more prolific civilian writers is L. Semeiko of the USSR Academy of Science's Institute of the USA and Canada. See in particular his "Instead of Mountains of Weapons," *Izvestiia*, August 13, 1987.
267. See Aurel Braun, "Whither the Warsaw Pact in the Gorbachev Era?" *International Journal*, Winter 1987-1988, Vol. XLIII, No. 1, pp. 63-105.
268. Semeiko, loc. cit.
269. V. Zhurkin, S. A. Karaganov and A. V. Kortunov, "Old and New Challenges to Security," *Kommunist* (Moscow), No. 1, January 1988, pp. 46-50.
270. Semeiko, loc. cit.
271. *Krasnaya Zvezda*, June 23, 1987.
272. *Krasnaya Zvezda*, September 23, 1987.
273. D. T. Yazov, *Na strazhe sotsializma i mira*, Moscow: Voenizdat, 1987, p. 33.
274. *Pravda*, June 27, 1987.
275. *Krasnaya Zvezda*, May 9, 1987.
276. *Pravda*, June 27, 1987.
277. "Documentation," *Orbis*, Winter 1988, pp. 28-29.

278. John Erickson, "The Warsaw Pact—The Shape of Things to Come?" in K. Dawisha and P. Hanson, eds., *Soviet-East European Dilemmas*, New York: Holmes and Meier, 1981, p. 166.
279. *Izvestiia*, June 10, 1985.
280. See, for instance, Colonel-General E. Kolibernov, *Krasnaya Zvezda*, November 21, 1985.
281. *The Military Balance, 1987-1988*, pp. 47-52.
282. *Ibid.*
283. See A. Braun *"Whither the Warsaw Pact . . . ,"* loc. cit.
284. *Newsweek*, November 14, 1988, pp. 24-25.
285. *Ibid.* 24.
286. Norman Z. Alcock and Alan C. Newcombe, "The Perception of National Power," *Journal of Conflict Resolution* Vol. XIV, No. 3, September 1970, p. 342.
287. Robert Jervis, *Perception and Misperception in International Politics*, Princeton, N.J.: Princeton University Press, 1976, pp. 58-76.
288. *L'Unita*, January 10, 1988, FBIS-EEU, January 19, 1988.
289. *New York Times*, May 8, 1988.
290. See Zdenek Mlynar, *Nightfrost in Prague*, New York: Karz, 1980.
291. *Newsweek*, May 4, 1988.
292. Josef Brodsky, cited in T. Judt et al., eds., *Debating the Nature of Dissent in Eastern Europe*, Washington, D.C.: The Wilson Center, 1987, p. 75.
293. Ferenc Feher, "Comments" in Tony Judt et al. *Debating the Nature of Dissent in Eastern Europe*, Washington, D.C., Occasional Paper no. 9, The Wilson Center, pp. 75-76.
294. *Toronto Star*, June 14, 1989.
295. J. F. Brown, loc. cit., p. 60.
296. Jerry F. Hough, "Gorbachev Consolidating Power," *Problems of Communism*, Vol. XXXV, July-August 1987, pp. 21-44.
297. *Nepszabadsag*, (Budapest), April 27, 1987.
298. *New York Times*, June 8, 1989; *Toronto Star*, April 15, 1989.
299. M. E. Fischer, "The Politics of Inequality in Romania," in D. N. Nelson (ed.), *Communism and the Politics of Inequality*, Lexington, Mass.: Lexington Books, 1983, pp. 192-119.
300. *New York Times*, May 29, 1988.
301. *Ibid.*
302. Walter Laqueur, *The Long Road to Freedom*, New York: Charles Scribner's & Sons, 1989.
303. See Bill Keller, "Congress failed main task, Sakharov rages," *Globe and Mail*, June 10, 1989. *Ibid.*
304. *Toronto Star*, June 17, 1989.
305. "Gorbachev: The View from Warsaw," *Harpers*, July 1987, p. 27.
306. As quoted by Michael Kramer, "Can Gorbachev Feed Russia?" *New York Times Magazine*. April 9, 1989, p. 92.

Epilogue

Aurel Braun

Spectacular developments have been taking place in the eastern part of the European continent during the summer and early fall of 1989. Turmoil, foment and radical change would only partially describe the almost daily political and economic shifts as I write this Epilogue in October. Reforms in Hungary and Poland seem to be moving at breakneck speed. In the Soviet Union domestic changes have been accompanied by dramatic announcements on relations with Eastern Europe. The past few months thus seem to have been among the most eventful in the post-war history of the region.

First, in the realm of Soviet-East European relations, Moscow appears to have formally abandoned the Brezhnev doctrine. In October 1989, the seven Warsaw Pact Foreign Ministers, meeting in Poland, affirmed a policy of non-interference in each other's affairs.[1] Even more importantly, during his visit to Finland, Mikhail Gorbachev is reported to have declared that in the case of the East European States, "We [the Soviet Union] have no right, moral or political right, to interfere in events happening there."[2] And the spokesman for the Soviet Foreign Ministry, Gennadi Gerasimov, told western reporters that the Brezhnev doctrine was dead, and added jokingly that Moscow has adopted the "Sinatra doctrine" in Eastern Europe. He referred to the Frank Sinatra song "I did it my way" [sic] and added that "Hungary and Poland are doing it their way."[3] Furthermore, Soviet Communist Party spokesman Nikolai Shishlin asserted that the Soviet Union would not object to Hungary's leaving the Warsaw Pact and becoming neutral.[4] Moreover, in the second half of 1989, Soviet proposals, for arms reductions and for the elimination of the Warsaw Pact and NATO, reinforced the impression that the Soviet Union may indeed be more flexible, even in the military area, in its relations with the East European states.

Secondly, changes within the Soviet Union itself suggest that domestic, political and economic restructuring should help in the transformation of the Soviet-East European relationship. The Soviet Foreign Minister Eduard Shevardnadze declared before the Supreme Soviet that the intervention in Afghanistan had been illegal.[5] Furthermore, Evgeny Primakov, now the chairman of the Council of the Union, the upper chamber of the new Supreme Soviet and a candidate member of the Politburo, stated during a visit to the United States that the Soviet legislature was drafting legislation that will establish a requirement for the Soviet President to consult with and involve the Supreme Soviet before he could order military intervention in another country.[6] And in many instances, Moscow also appeared to exhibit greater tolerance towards the nationalities in the Soviet Union. For example, in September 1989 the legislature of Lithuania declared the 1940 Soviet annexation of the republic invalid.[7]

Furthermore Soviet political and economic changes seemed to support movement in the same direction as reforms in Eastern Europe. The Supreme Soviet in October 1989 voted to eliminate special seats for the Communist Party and other official organizations in national and local elections.[8] The press in the Soviet Union also became far more critical of the failures of government. And Gorbachev decided to settle major strikes by the miners during the summer of 1989, not through confrontation but through compromise and concessions. Extensive discussions have begun in the Soviet Union on the issues of property rights and the growing cooperative movement. And the Soviet Union decided to drastically devalue the ruble (in the case of tourist exchange rates).

Thirdly, there has been a dramatic acceleration of reform in the two East European states where *perestroika* and *glasnost* have been most advanced—Poland and Hungary. In Poland the Communists, unable to form a government, gave way to a Solidarity-led government. Moreover, the latter has decided to embark on radical economic change to create a free-market economy in Poland. In Hungary, the ruling Hungarian Socialist Workers' Party transformed itself into the Hungarian Socialist Party and changed the name of the country to the Republic of Hungary. Furthermore, they committed themselves to building a multiparty "parliamentary democracy" and a market-style economy.[9] Moreover, the speaker of the Hungarian parliament, Matyas Szuros, suggested that under certain circumstances Hungary would like to become a neutral state.[10] And in October 1989 the new Socialist Party of Hungary condemned the 1956 Hungarian invasion.[11]

Fourthly, changes have taken place even among the most hard-line states in Eastern Europe. Following Gorbachev's visit to the German Democratic Republic (GDR), mass defections of tens of thousands of GDR citizens to the West through Hungary, and massive street demonstrations, Erich Honecker was forced to resign in October 1989. His replacement, Egon Krenz, 52, though widely perceived also as a hard-liner, has opened up a dialogue with demonstrators, has refrained from employing massive force against them and has expressed a willingness to discuss reform. In Bulgaria, perhaps shaken by the events in the GDR, the hard-line Communist leadership under Todor Zhivkov has admitted to problems in implementing perestroika and pledged that it would increase efforts to implement reforms.[12] In Czechoslovakia, although the leadership of Milos Jakes has shown itself to be quite willing to use massive repression against dissidents, large-scale demonstrations for reform broke out in October 1989.

Thus the whole region seems to be not only in foment but also alive with possibilities. Clearly a great deal of what has happened is positive in terms of allowing greater internal freedom and in improving relations between the Soviet Union on the one hand and Eastern Europe on the other. Yet the euphoria over these developments ought to be balanced with some caution. A number of relevant questions ought to be asked in analyzing the developments of the past several months. Is the Soviet–East European relationship changing fundamentally, wholly or just in part? Are previous trends being reversed or strengthened and accelerated? And are current trends and tendencies in the relationship as determined by domestic and external factors, irreversible?

Soviet–East European Relations

A closer examination of Soviet statements shows that in the case of Soviet and East European relations, Moscow has not eliminated all the qualifiers. It should be noteworthy that Gorbachev's statement in Finland on non-interference in Eastern Europe included the following sentence: "We assume others will not interfere either".[13] Given that the claims of external (Western) interference were used in part as justification for the Soviet invasions of Hungary, Czechoslovakia and Afghanistan, such a qualifier cannot be dismissed entirely. This is not to suggest that Gorbachev was being disingenuous in his statement but rather that as a good lawyer he pays attention to the "fine print" and does not wish to foreclose his options.

Furthermore, Gorbachev's encouragement of the Polish Communists to enter into a coalition government with Solidarity, his support for the transformation of Hungarian Socialist Workers' Party and his measured advocacy of reform in the GDR were not only positive acts in helping improve the lot of the people of Eastern Europe but represent a continuing interest and constitute at least subtle interference in the affairs of the East European states.

Gorbachev may also have provided some hints that his support of the new Hungarian Socialist Party might not be completely open-ended. In his congratulatory message to the head of the new party, Rezso Nyers, he expressed confidence that relations between the Soviet Communist Party and the Hungarian Socialist Party "will rest on the experience of interaction, which has always played an important role in Soviet-Hungarian relations, and will serve the cause of peace and *socialism* and the interest of the people of the two countries"[14] (emphasis added).

In the case of Gerasimov's proclamation of the "Sinatra doctrine" (ironically the song has dark overtones, mentioning that the "end" is near and that the singer is facing "the final curtain"), the qualifiers were quite evident. In the same interview Gerasimov stated that both Hungary and Poland still had obligations as members of economic and military alliances with the Soviet Union, "We may witness a change in government in Warsaw or Budapest, but international obligations do not necessarily go away with a change in government".[15] Furthermore, Nikolai Shishlin bracketed his remarks about Hungary's right to leave the Warsaw Pact by declaring that, "But you know that Hungarian officials declared that they are ready to be in the Warsaw Pact, until now".[16] And finally, though Shevardnadze has been willing to denounce the Soviet invasion of Afghanistan (although according to the Western sources the Soviet Union had been supplying the Kabul regime massively with armaments[17]), he has refused to denounce the Soviet invasion of Czechoslovakia.[18] His claim that he was not free to make a pronouncement on the matter since the invasion had been a joint decision with other members of the Warsaw Pact seems particularly disingenuous in light of the fact that both the governments of Poland and Hungary have denounced the invasion as illegal.

All this is not meant to suggest that the Soviet Union is not moving towards greater flexibility in dealing with Eastern Europe or that no encouragement should be drawn from the statements made by various Soviet leaders. Indeed, it does appear that Soviet military intervention in Eastern Europe is becoming increasingly less likely. Yet the continuation of the use of qualifiers by Soviet leaders should provide some *caveats* against the conclusion that the Soviet Union has abandoned its interests in Eastern Europe altogether. Indeed it seems that Gorbachev has signalled the United States in particular that he was prepared to allow a great deal of leeway in Poland and Hungary as long as their allegiance to the Warsaw Pact or to the Council for Mutual Economic Assistance (CMEA) was not threatened.[19]

Indeed Soviet concern with the Warsaw Pact should not be forgotten despite all of the positive steps that the Soviet Union has taken towards reducing armaments and military tensions. And there have been encouraging signals in the past few months. Moscow has altered its stance on the American Strategic Defense Initiative (SDI), opening the way for an early conclusion of a treaty cutting the superpower strategic inventories. It has been far more cooperative than expected at the talks on conventional forces in Europe (CFE). Warsaw Pact proposals for new ceilings on combat aircraft have brought it far closer to NATO's position, thereby greatly enhancing the chances for an early agreement on conventional forces. The Soviet Union and her allies have also continued the unilateral cuts first announced by Moscow in December 1988. These reductions have included first line forces that would be essential to surprise attack. Indeed, the International Institute for Strategic Studies may be correct in its assessment that by 1991, "the unilateral reductions, once complete, will *virtually* eliminate the surprise-attack threats which has so long concerned NATO planners"[20] (emphasis added). Soviet moves towards a doctrine of "defensive defence" and "reasonable sufficiency" may also provide reassurances for Eastern Europe (except for the additional demands based on territory as nuclear weapons are downgraded and as defensive postures require the protection of strategic depth).

All these shifts, however, are subject to a certain time lag since even the changes in Soviet/Warsaw Pact surprise-attack capacity are dependent on the completion of current discernable trends in Soviet and Warsaw Pact military reductions. And despite the developments of the past several months the Soviet–East European relationship still needs to be viewed through the prism of the Warsaw Pact and of Soviet input in that organization. For, Soviet changes in the Warsaw Pact would be symptomatic of alterations in that relationship. Military reductions and purported changes in Soviet/Warsaw Pact doctrine, however, have yet to yield changes in the crucial decision-making structure of the Warsaw Pact. Though such changes may take place in the future, the meetings of the Warsaw Pact such as that in October 1989 indicate that the Soviet controlled decision-making process and the integrative process have remained unaltered. This involves not only such matters as Soviet command over the entire air defence system of the bloc (except that of Romania) but also control over the training, indoctrination and promotion of high ranking officers in the armed forces of the East European states. Changes in these areas are essential, especially if for instance the Hungarian attempt at depoliticizing the armed forces is to be successfully implemented.

Soviet military relations with the East European states, as noted, will also be affected by Moscow's changes in military doctrine (which in effect is Warsaw Pact doctrine) and by Soviet military modernization. First, Soviet doctrinal ambiguities have not yet been resolved, and there are still valid questions as to whether the Soviet Union envisions an "offensive-oriented" defense. Overall though, the tendency seems to be greater emphasis on a "defensive defense." Secondly, however, even a truly defensive doctrine does not necessarily lead to savings, though the potential for reductions in the military budget may seem to be greater. If we accept that the NATO doctrine has been largely defensive then one can see that military costs can escalate wildly even with a smaller number of troops and reductions in equipment acquisition. The crucial variable seems to be that of modernization.

Modernization includes not only the acquisition of new and more advanced equipment but also the upgrading of military management and training. In both these areas, at least over the past several months, the Soviet Union has moved along rather disquieting trends. The American Secretary of Defense Richard Cheney claimed in September 1989 that the Soviet Union was placing modern tanks into service at such a high rate that in less than two years they would more than offset Soviet announced tank reductions from Eastern Europe.[21] The Soviet Union has been fitting out two new 65,000-ton Tbilisi-class aircraft carriers.[22] Moscow has also continued research and development of systems that are at the cutting-edge of military technology, such as the new supersonic vertical-take off-fighter, the Yak-41.[23] And in October 1989 U.S. officials claimed that the Soviet Union began updating its anti-missile system around Moscow.[24] These modern high-technology systems are precisely the type that can lead to the kind of cost escalations that result in higher expenditures despite a reduction in the number of weapons produced. It is possible, though and perhaps even likely, that Gorbachev will restrain or reduce this qualitative competition, either through unilateral action or by agreement with the United States. The other element of modernization, though, might be more difficult to control.

Soviet changes in military management and training had been proceeding at full stream despite reductions in the size of the armed forces. Enhanced training, as the Western forces have learned, can be extremely expensive. Furthermore, in order to achieve better management the Soviet Union needs to deal with the issues of morale and initiative. Reductions in the size of the Soviet armed forces have caused significant problems of morale. These have been compounded by poor living standards for officers and enlisted men. The level of discontent, especially among the officer corps, has been growing dramatically. An opinion poll published in October 1989 in the Soviet government's newspaper showed that, "the mood of a significant part of the officer corps is creating a crisis situation in the army".[25] A dissident group of Soviet officers formed an organization called *Shield* to press for improved conditions and political changes in the armed forces.[26]

Gorbachev's reaction has been interesting, for in many respects it mirrored his approach to pressures in the economic sector (for example in his dealings with the miners). In a meeting with military leaders on October 18, 1989, he reportedly proposed a sharp increase in military pay.[27] Thus, savings from the reduction of personnel could be offset by increases in salary, benefits and training costs. There is consequently a good likelihood that the anticipated savings in military expenditures will not (or at least not fully) materialize given current trends. And this in turn would put additional pressure not only on the Soviet economy but also on Soviet-East European relations in the military and the economic realm as the Soviet Union would seek to share burdens in both areas.

Domestic Factors

Gorbachev's attempts to restructure the economy have been failing in large part. Figures released by the state statistics committee *Goskomstat* in October 1989 revealed that production slumped since July 1989 and that despite the rise in food imports the food supply to many areas actually worsened.[28] Furthermore, an opinion poll published in the Soviet weekly *Ogonyok* in October 1989 showed that the Soviet population had very little faith in *perestroika*.[29] Only 12 percent believed that it would lead to significant improvement. Pessimism regarding reform is also a reflection of the difficulty of changing the political culture in the country which, in turn, is essential to a true transformation of the political and the economic system.

Though specific reform measures may produce benefits in the long run, developments in the past several months give little cause for optimism— at least in the short term. In September 1989, for instance, Vladimir Filanovsky-Zenkov, the first deputy minister for oil and gas in the Soviet Union, stated that reorganization had brought about chaos in the oil industry and that output would be at least 10–12 million tons lower than planned (and below the level of the previous year).[30] Furthermore, the package of wage hikes and consumer goods that Gorbachev promised striking miners in the summer of 1989 also came at a damagingly high cost to the Soviet economy. In September 1989 Soviet Prime Minister Nikolai Ryzhkov estimated the cost at 3 billion rubles (about $4.8 billion). Given the huge Soviet budget deficit, the strain is enormous. Ryzhkov declared that "our country will not survive another strike like that."[31] Yet new, though smaller, miner strikes have broken out in October 1989. Agriculture has remained a disaster area for the Soviet Union, with huge losses in production as halfway and contradictory measures are introduced and implemented. Egor Ligachev, the Politburo member in charge of agriculture, complained publicly in October 1989 that there was no systemic approach to limiting losses.[32] And he projected that it will take 5 to 7 years to ease chronic food shortages in the Soviet Union.

Crucial price reforms have been put off and discussions of property rights have fallen far behind those in Poland and Hungary in terms of creating the necessary individual rights. Furthermore, the Gorbachev regime has not only not resolved economic contradictions but its mixed signals have created further confusion. Although cooperatives have been encouraged and have grown considerably in number and scope of activity, popular envy and even outrage at "profiteering" (and Gorbachev's own ambivalence) have led to the introduction of highly restrictive legislation and taxation in the fall of 1989 that could well stifle a good deal of the cooperative movement.[33]

In political terms, the Gorbachev regime has made it evident that the movement towards greater freedom is not necessarily a linear development. The Soviet leader has continued to oppose the creation of alternate parties and has discouraged the radicals in the Supreme Soviets who have congregated around individuals such as Boris Yeltsin in the Inter-regional Deputies group. Furthermore, in October 1989 Gorbachev has come down very heavily against press coverage that he considered excessively critical. In a series of dismissals of editors and harsh attacks he has shown that he has a very strong authoritarian streak. Furthermore, the attacks on the press by various members of Gorbachev's regime also demonstrated the problems of attitude. Notions of freedom of the press, so common in Western culture, have yet to take root in the Soviet Union. And, finally, restrictive legislation on strikes in October 1989, which forbids strikes in all vital industries, is a further indication that Gorbachev certainly intends to place parameters on political and economic freedoms within the Soviet Union.

These parameters are also reflected in Gorbachev's dealings with ethnic minorities in the Soviet Union during the past few months. Dialogue and some concessions have been accompanied by some very harsh statements and threats. For instance, protests in the Baltic states in August 1989 brought very harsh condemnations from the Soviet party's Central Committee. It labelled Baltic nationalists, extremists and warned of disastrous consequences.[34] This harsh condemnation, it then became known, had been fully endorsed by Gorbachev. Moreover, they had some impact. The Latvian Popular Front, for instance, toned down its demands for independence at its congress in October 1989.[35] Nevertheless ethnic strife has continued to grow throughout the Soviet Union, and Gorbachev may indeed be forced into more repressive measures. Still, by indicating that there are limits to his tolerance of nationalist dissent, he has sent signals not only inside the Soviet Union but may well have suggested that his in-state measures could have implications for Soviet–East European relations.

Domestic economic developments certainly have had an impact, as noted, on the Soviet Union's bilateral and multilateral external economic relations. Moscow continues to encourage multilateral cooperation through the framework of the CMEA. Despite changes in Eastern Europe, the East European states are still highly dependent on the Soviet Union for fuel and raw materials and will continue to be so in the near future. The Soviet Union, on the one hand, and Eastern Europe on the other, continue to be each others' largest trading partners with more than 50 percent of their total exchange (with the exception of Poland and Hungary) conducted in intra-CMEA trade.[36] Nevertheless the different pace of reform can create problems of synchronization. As Soviet *perestroika* falls further behind changes in parts of Eastern Europe, intra-bloc trade difficulties will magnify. There may be hopes for a CMEA *a deux vitesse* (two speed). But, as economic decentralization proceeds at increasingly different speeds, centrifugal forces are likely to greatly damage even a "multi-speed" organization.

But all these issues are also affected by the prospects for Gorbachev's own political survival. So far he continues to prove himself to be a superb politician. Economic difficulties have not prevented him from strengthening his own position. He not only has built himself an alternative power base in the Supreme Soviet that makes him less dependent on the Party but in September he strengthened his position in the Party itself. He dismissed three members of the Politburo and brought in a key supporter, the KGB chief Vladimir Kryuchkov.[37] Therefore, he has likely extended the timeframe within which he has to produce positive results in his attempts to reform the Soviet system. Furthermore, since a great deal of reform in Eastern Europe is dependent on his political survival, this strengthening of his position should encourage reformers in Eastern Europe as long as they understand that there are limits to Gorbachev's tolerance.

The Acceleration of Change

Dramatic changes in Poland have created the potential for a radical transformation of the domestic system and of Polish-Soviet relations. Nevertheless, it should be noted that with the powerful office of the Presidency in the hands of the Communists, together with the Ministries of the Interior, Defense and Foreign Trade, at least so far, developments in Poland, as spectacular as they may seem, may still be viewed as a controlled experiment. But as economic conditions continue to deteriorate and Poland is experiencing hyper-inflation, drastic measures introduced by the Solidarity-supported government of Tadeusz Mazowiecki could bring about profound change. In October 1989 the government put forth a far-reaching program aimed at introducing free-market mechanisms and capitalist institutions "in the swiftest possible way."[38] This seems quite similar to the "Sachs plan" proposed by Jeffrey Sachs, a Harvard economist who is a specialist on hyper-inflation.[39] It involves *inter alia* the lifting of price controls, the elimination of state subsidies and the sell-off of state industries. At least in the short term, it would result in massive unemployment and further steep price increases. If successful, such a plan would create a capitalist economy in Poland, making it difficult for that state to continue to participate in the CMEA despite the government's promises that membership of both that organization and the Warsaw Pact would be preserved.

Failure of the plan, however, would discredit Solidarity and could lead to a takeover by the Communist Party or even civil war. The problem with the introduction of such a radical reform plan in part involves Polish-political culture. The four decades of socialism have created not only economic mismanagement but a social safety net on which millions of Poles depend and thus a mentality of dependence. Even with the promised massive Western help, the implementation of the proposed measures would still create enormous disruptions and unemployment. The Polish communists have already begun to try to capitalize on the fears of the population. They have commenced small demonstrations and questioned the mandate of the government to introduce such radical changes.[40] Though the credibility of the communists is extremely low, they are trying hard to improve their image and have voted to transform and rename their party.[41] Therefore, the Polish party, which over four decades in power has virtually destroyed all of its credibility, might be able to resuscitate itself as a legitimate political force if it can take advantage of Solidarity's mistakes and portray itself as the true protector of the working class. Thus Solidarity has taken a tremendous risk in assuming power in a coalition government at a time when the country faces the most disastrous economic conditions in the post-war period. Still, in Poland, the transition in power to date has been relatively gradual. We could say that there has been political transcendence, and this may continue if political (and economic) compromises can be continued in the future.

In the case of Hungary, political changes may turn out to be more abrupt. They involve not merely the transformation of the Hungarian party into the Socialist Party and profound changes in its structure. The proposal for completely free elections in 1990 could sweep even this "new" party into political oblivion.

There is widespread skepticism in Hungary about the transformation of the Hungarian communists even among the more radical reformers in the party itself. For example, some have attacked the party programs designed to encourage market forces as a means of granting advantages to party members. Lajos Bokros, a reformist communist, who is a Managing Director of the Hungarian Bank, said in an interview, "this is not privatization or a democratization of ownership, but a transformation of what was called administrative ownership by the state into private ownership by the old managerial class and nomenklatura."[42] Nevertheless, the movement has been away from Marxism-Leninism towards Social Democracy as the Leninist structure is being dismantled. And, one of the fundamental questions in Soviet–East European relations will be whether Soviet Marxism-Leninism is compatible with East European Social Democracy. Moreover, in Hungary, the subsidiary question may be whether this will involve a Marxist-style Social Democracy or whether Marxism itself would be abandoned and a non-Marxist Social Democratic system instituted.

Hungarian reassurances that they will remain in the CMEA and the Warsaw Pact might help. It is interesting that Matyas Szuros himself, at the October 1989 celebrations of the 1956 revolution, declared to the assembled crowds that Hungary wanted to maintain "undisturbed and balanced relations with the Soviet Union."[43] But this would be extremely difficult to do, for a radical transformation of the Hungarian economy will make it increasingly more difficult for it to function within the CMEA framework. Indeed, Hungary's tremendous interest in the European Community and its obsession with 1992 indicates that the Hungarians see their future more with the West than with the East.

Hungary, though, may have the best chance to "leap into the future" as Hungarians like to say. It is in the strategically less significant southern tier of the Warsaw Pact, it has redirected a good deal of its trade to the West, it has a small population and territory and it is likely to get considerable Western aid. Yet, it is still dependent for energy and raw materials on the Soviet Union, and it does have continuing long-term commitments to the Soviet Union and to the CMEA. Moreover, given military threats from Romania (made quite explicit in this summer of 1989) and the growing dispute over ethnic problems in the latter state, Hungary might find it advantageous to remain a member of the Warsaw Pact as a means of protecting itself from its eastern neighbor.

The Reluctant Reformers

Among the "non-reformist" states in Eastern Europe some changes are taking place, but it is difficult to identify trends or tendencies. It is possible that in the GDR Egon Krenz will prove to be a true reformer. There are, however, limits in the GDR on reform due to the very nature of the state. The GDR is an artificial construct where the regime's legitimacy cannot be based on nationalism. Thus it needs to rely on ideology. It is not surprising therefore that Krenz, despite proclaiming his readiness to engage in reform, has vowed to preserve the Communist Party's hold on political power.[44]

In Bulgaria promises of greater reform should be viewed with some skepticism. Todor Zhivkov has a history of making promises under pressure and then retracting them as soon as the right opportunity arises. The nature and pace of Bulgarian reforms, therefore, will depend in part on the continuation of internal and external pressures and, of course, on the physical and political health of Zhivkov. In Czechoslovakia the regime is standing fast with conservative policies, but if reforms spread further in the bloc and begin to enjoy a degree of success, it will be increasingly more difficult for Prague to resist change. Lastly, in Romania there has been no change in the past several months and the bizarre domestic, political and economic policies of the Ceausescu regime are likely to continue as long as that leader remains in power.

* * *

In sum, the dramatic changes in parts of Eastern Europe and even in the Soviet Union raise at least as many questions as they provide answers. Changes are so numerous that it is difficult to exclude any possibilities. But in terms of trends and tendencies, most of the fundamental dilemmas and contradictions in the Soviet Union, in much of the East European states and in Soviet-East European relations remain unresolved. Though certain developments in the past few months are most encouraging, it is premature to speak of irreversible trends. Certainly there has been an acceleration of certain trends. Reform in Poland and Hungary has taken off, and especially the latter may be able to perform a successful "leap into the future," perhaps through a form of "Finlandization."

But in the Soviet Union there is still no systemic change domestically, and this is bound to have an impact on their relations with their fellow socialist states. The doctrine of socialism though is increasingly tested and concepts will need to be redefined. De-Leninization has begun in Poland and Hungary. What is "socialist" and what is acceptable "socialism" in Eastern Europe are increasingly more relevant questions. Hungary and Poland (or any other East European state that should engage in fundamental restructuring) also face a great dilemma. Should they accelerate reform so that they could "lock in" the changes against possible external shifts in Soviet policy? Or are they likely, by moving too quickly, to precipitate precisely the kind of Soviet clampdown that they fear? For, despite all the positive Soviet signals, Soviet-East European relations are still in a state of flux. And although the Soviet Union may be a tired superpower, it would be a mistake—especially for the East Europeans—to view it as a spent force. Moreover, change even within certain parameters is still highly dependent on the survival of Gorbachev and Gorbachevism.

Notes

1. *Globe and Mail*, Toronto, October 28, 1989.
2. *New York Times*, October 26, 1989.
3. *Ibid.*

Epilogue

4. *Globe and Mail*, October 30, 1989, and ABC T.V. interview on "This Week with David Brinkley," October 29, 1989, 10:30 A.M. E.D.T.
5. *Globe and Mail*, October 24, 1989.
6. *New York Times*, October 28, 1989.
7. *New York Times*, October 24, 1989.
8. *New York Times*, October 25, 1989.
9. *Newsweek*, October 23, 1989, p. 36.
10. *Toronto Star*, September 29, 1989.
11. *Globe and Mail*, October 21, 1989.
12. *Globe and Mail*, October 30, 1989.
13. *New York Times*, October 26, 1989.
14. *Globe and Mail*, October 10, 1989.
15. *New York Times*, October 26, 1989.
16. *Globe and Mail*, October 30, 1989.
17. *Globe and Mail*, October 4, 1989.
18. *New York Times*, October 28, 1989.
19. See Thomas L. Friedman, "How Washington Shifted to Embracing Gorbachev," *New York Times*, October 22, 1989.
20. *Globe and Mail*, October 6, 1989.
21. Richard B. Cheney, "Preface" in Department of Defense, *Soviet Military Power 1989*, Washington, D.C.: Department of Defense, 1980, p. 6.
22. *Ibid*.
23. *Newsweek*, October 30, 1989, p. 54.
24. *Globe and Mail*, October 27, 1989.
25. *Izvestiia*, Moscow, October 20, 1989.
26. *New York Times*, October 22, 1989.
27. *Globe and Mail*, October 23, 1989.
28. *Globe and Mail*, October 30, 1989.
29. As cited in the *Globe and Mail*, October 23, 1989.
30. *Globe and Mail*, September 28, 1989.
31. *New York Times*, September 17, 1989.
32. *Globe and Mail*, October 10, 1989.
33. *Globe and Mail*, September 27, 1989.
34. *New York Times*, August 27, 1989.
35. *Globe and Mail*, October 10, 1989.
36. United Nations Economic Commission for Europe, *Economic Survey of Europe in 1988-89*, New York, United Nations Publication, 1989, pp. 159-165.
37. *Newsweek*, October 2, 1989, pp. 22-3.
38. *Globe and Mail*, October 13, 1989.
39. See Leslie Wayne, "A Doctor for Struggling Economics," *New York Times*, October 1, 1989.
40. *New York Times*, October 21, 1989.
41. *Globe and Mail*, October 4, 1989.
42. Cited in the *Toronto Star*, October 14, 1989.
43. *Globe and Mail*, October 24, 1989.
44. *Globe and Mail*, October 31, 1989.

Bibliography

"A Blueprint for Gorbachev's Integration Strategy?" *PlanEcon Report*, Vol. 11, No. 36 (September 4, 1986).

Abramov, L.G. *SEV: Kapital'nye vlozheniia—perspektivnaia sfera strodnichestva*. Moscow: Nauka, 1987.

Abstracts of Hungarian Economic Literature, Vol. 16, No. 6 (1986), and Vol. 17, No. 1 (1987).

Adam, Jan. "The Economic Reform in Industry: Is There Hope?" Paper presented at the conference on "Before the Storm Breaks: The Extent, Limits and Dangers of Reform in Communist Hungary," Pennsylvania State University (April 14–17, 1988).

Aganbegyan, A. "Incentives and Reserves: Implement the Decisions of the November Plenary Sessions of the CPSU Central Committee." *Trud* (December 12, 1982).

_____. "Problems in the Radical Restructuring of Economic Management in the USSR." Unpublished, in English translation (August 1987).

_____. *The Economic Challenge of Perestroika*. Bloomington: Indiana University Press (1987).

_____. "The Economics of Perestroika." *International Affairs* (London), Vol. 64, No. 2 (Spring 1988).

Alcock, Norman Z., and Alan C. Newcombe. "The Perception of National Power." *Journal of Conflict Resolution*, Vol. XIV, No. 3 (September 1970).

Alton, T., et al. "Money Income of the Population and the Standard of Living in Eastern Europe." Research Project on National Income in Eastern Europe, Occasional Paper No. 98. New York: L.W. International Financial Research, Inc. (1987).

Amalrik, Andrei. *Will the Soviet Union Survive Until 1984?* New York and Evanston: Harper and Row (1970).

Angelov, Ivan. "Driving Forces and Resistance." *Sofia News* (July 29, 1987).

Aron, Raymond. *Peace and War*. London: Weidenfeld and Nicholson (1966).

Ash, Timothy Garton. "Does Central Europe Exist?" *New York Review of Books*, Vol. XXXIII, No. 15 (October 9, 1986).

Aslund, Anders. "Who Are Gorbachev's Economic Advisers?" Unpublished paper. Washington, D.C.: Kennan Institute, Wilson Center (September 16, 1987).

Asmus, Ronald D. "The National and the International: Harmony or Discord." Radio Free Europe Research. *RAD Background Report/144 (Eastern Europe)* (December 10, 1985).

Aspaturian, Vernon V. "Eastern Europe in World Perspective." In Teresa Rakowska-Harmstone, ed., *Communism in Eastern Europe*. Bloomington: Indiana University Press (1984).

Berend, Ivan. "The Role of Cultural Identity in Eastern Europe." In Ivan Berend, Josef Brada, Charles Gati, and Peter Sugar, eds., *Eastern Europe: A Question of Identity*. Occasional Paper No. 2. Washington, D.C.: East European Program, Wilson Center (1985).

Berliner Zeitung (February 27, 1989). Cited in Radio Free Europe, *Research*, No. 34 (March 1, 1989).

Bialer, Seweryn. "The Political System." In Robert F. Byrnes, ed., *After Brezhnev: Sources of Soviet Conduct in the 1980s*. Bloomington: Indiana University Press (1983).

———. "Central and Eastern Europe, Perestroika, and the Future of the Cold War." In William E. Griffith, *Central and Eastern Europe: The Opening Curtain*. Boulder, Colo.: Westview Press (1989).

Bialer, Seweryn, ed. *Politics, Society and Nationality Inside Gorbachev's Russia*. Boulder, Colo.: Westview Press (1989).

Bilak, Vasil. "Unser Löwe is noch immer ein Löwe." *Der Spiegel*, No. 44 (October 28, 1985).

Bogomolov, O.T. "CMEA Economic Strategy in the 1980s." *The World Socialist Economy*. Moscow: Nauka (1986).

Bourne, Eric. "May East-Bloc States Now Chart Their Own Socialist Paths?" *Christian Science Monitor* (April 18, 1988).

Bovin, A. "Perestroika i sud'by sotsializma." *Izvestiia* (July 11, 1987).

———. *SSSR v Sisteme Sotsialisticheskoi Ekonomicheskoi Integratsii*. Moscow: CMEA Secretariat (1986).

———. "Sotsialisticheskiye strany na perelomnon etape mirovogo ekonomicheskogo razvitiya." *Kommunist*, No. 8 (May 1987).

Brada, Josef C. "Sartor Resartus? Gorbachev and Prospects for Economic Reform in Czechoslovakia." *Harvard International Review* (November 1987).

Braun, Aurel. "The Yugoslav-Romanian Concept of People's War." *Canadian Defense Quarterly*, Vol. 7, No. 1 (Summer 1977).

———. "Soviet Naval Policy in the Mediterranean: The Sonnenfeld Doctrine and Yugoslavia." *Orbis*, Vol. 22, No. 1 (Spring 1978).

———. *Romanian Foreign Policy Since 1965: The Political and Military Limits of Autonomy*. New York: Praeger (1978).

———. "Economic Developments in the Eastern Bloc: Is the Soviet Web of Control Tightening?" *Parameters*, Vol. IX, No. 3 (1979).

———. "Whither the Warsaw Pact in the Gorbachev Era?" *International Journal* (Winter 1987–1988).

Brown, James F. "Relations Between the Soviet Union and Its East European Allies: A Survey." *Rand Report R-1742-PR* (1975).

———. "A Western Overview," in "East-West Relations and Eastern Europe." *Problems of Communism* (May–August 1988).

———. "Poland Since Martial Law." *Rand Note N-2822-RC* (December 1988).

———. *Eastern Europe and Communist Rule*. Durham and London: Duke University Press (1988).

Brunner, Georg. "Reform Policies in South-East Europe: Political Aspects." Paper delivered at the "German-American Conference on the Gorbachev Reform Program: Its Impact on Soviet and East European Policies." Washington, D.C. (March 20–22, 1988).

Buchan, Alistair. "The Future of NATO." *International Conciliation*, No. 565 (November 1967).
Budapest Television Service in Hungarian (January 25, 1987). In Foreign Broadcast Information Service, *Daily Report: Eastern Europe*. Washington, D.C. (January 30, 1987).
———. (April 26, 1987). In Foreign Broadcast Information Service, *Daily Report: Soviet Union*. Washington, D.C. (April 27, 1987).
Bulgarian Foreign Trade, No. 4 (1986).
Bunce, Valerie. "The Empire Strikes Back: The Evolution of the Eastern Bloc from a Soviet Asset to a Soviet Liability." *International Organization*, Vol. 39, No. 1 (Winter 1985).
Burlatsky, Fyodor. "Karl Marx and Our Times." *New Times*, No. 23 (1984).
Business Week (January 30, 1989).
Byrnes, Robert F. *After Brezhnev: Sources of Soviet Conduct in the 1980s*. Bloomington: Indiana University Press (1983).
Canadian Institute of Strategic Studies. "Strategic Datalink," Datalink No. 11 (December 1988).
Carlisle, Olga. "A Talk with Milan Kundera." *New York Times Magazine* (May 19, 1987).
Chazanov, Mathis. "Gorbachev's Reforms Draw Mixed East Bloc Reaction." *Los Angeles Times* (April 9, 1987).
Chebrikov, V.M. Speech on the occasion of the 110th anniversary of F.E. Dzerzhinskiy's birth. *Pravda* (September 11, 1987).
Chrzova, Jana. *Newsweek* (April 25, 1988).
Croan, Melvin. "The Politics of Division and Detente in East Germany." *Current History*, Vol. 84, No. 505 (November 1985).
Crozier, J., Samuel P. Huntington, and Joji Watunaki. *The Crisis of Democracy*. New York: Free Press (1975).
Csaba, L. "CMEA and East-West Trade." *Comparative Economic Studies*, Vol. XXVIII, No. 3 (Fall 1986).
———. "Le CAEM sous le signe de la restructuration." *Le Courrier des Pays de l'Est*, No. 313 (December 1986).
———. "The Council for Mutual Economic Assistance and the Challenge of the Eighties." *Külpolitika*, Vol. 13, No. 5 (1986), and Vol. 14, No. 1 (1987).
Csikos-Nagy, Bela. "New Aspects of East-West Trade." *Hungarian Business Herald* (Budapest), No. 1 (1988).
Curry, Jane L. "*Glasnost*: Words Spoken and Words Heard." Paper delivered at "German-American conference on the Gorbachev Reform Program: Its Impact on Soviet–East European Policies." Washington, D.C.: Kennan Institute (March 10–11, 1988).
"Czechoslovakia's Husak Backs Soviet Reforms and Hints He May Follow Suit." *Los Angeles Times* (March 21, 1987).
Dawisha, Karen. "Gorbachev and Eastern Europe: A New Challenge for the West." *World Policy Journal* (Spring 1986).
———. *Eastern Europe, Gorbachev, and Reform: The Great Challenge*. Cambridge University Press (1988).
Dawisha, Karen, and P. Hanson, eds. *Soviet–East European Dilemmas*. New York: Holmes and Meier (1981).

Dawisha, Karen, and Jonathon Valdez. "Socialist Internationalism in Eastern Europe." *Problems of Communism*, Vol. 36, No. 2 (March-April 1987).

"Declaration on Soviet-Polish Cooperation in Ideology, Science and Culture." *Pravda* (April 22, 1987).

D'Encausse, Hélène Carrère. *Big Brother: The Soviet Union and Soviet Europe*. New York: Holmes and Meier (1987).

Deutsch, K.W. "Kontinuitäten and Veränderungen in den internationalen Beziehungen bis zur Jahrhundertwenden." In *Osterreichisches Jahrbuch fur Internationale Politik* (1985).

Devlin, Kevin. "PCI Scholar Assesses Impact of Soviet Changes on East European Regimes." *Radio Free Europe Research*. RAD Background Report, No. 83 (May 21, 1987).

———. "Italian Communist on Contradictions and Crisis in Eastern Europe." *Radio Free Europe Research*. RAD Background Report, No. 91 (June 5, 1987).

Diehl, Jackson. "Bulgaria, Once a Soviet Favorite, Faces a Squeeze." *New York Herald Tribune* (May 9-10, 1985).

———. "Gorbachev Calls on Eastern Europe to Change But Not to Mimic." *Washington Post* (April 13, 1987).

"Documentation." *Orbis* (Winter 1988).

Documents of the Meeting of the Political Consultative Committee of the Warsaw Treaty Member States, Warsaw, July 15-16, 1988. Moscow: Novosti Press (1988).

Drewnowski, J., ed. *Crisis in the East European Economy: The Spread of the Polish Disease*. London: Croom Helm (1982).

Eastern Europe Newsletter (London), Vol. 2, No. 9 (May 9, 1988), and Vol. 3, No. 4 (February 22, 1989).

East European Economies: Slow Growth in the 1980s, 3 vols. A compendium of papers submitted to the Joint Economic Committee, Congress of the United States, 99th Congress, 1st Session. Washington, D.C.: U.S. Government Printing Office (1985-1986).

East European Program Meeting Report. "East Germany and the Current East European Crisis," No. 27. Washington, D.C.: European Institute, Wilson Center (1988).

Economist (December 26, 1987; April 9, 1988; May 20-26, 1989).

Ekonomicheskoe Sotrudnichestvo Stran-Chlenov SEV, Vol. 1. Moscow (1986).

Erickson, John. "The Warsaw Pact—The Shape of Things to Come?" In K. Dawisha and P. Hanson, eds., *Soviet-East European Dilemmas*. New York: Holmes and Meier (1981).

Falk, Richard, and Mary Kaldor. "The Post-Yalta Debate." *World Policy Journal*, Vol. 2, No. 3 (Summer 1985).

Fallenbuchl, Zbigniew. "Economic Restructuring in the Soviet Union and the World Economy." Paper delivered at the conference on "Perestroika, Glasnost and International Security." University of Manitoba (February 2-4, 1989).

Feher, Ferenc. "Comments." In Tony Judt et al., eds., *Debating the Nature of Dissent in Eastern Europe*. Washington, D.C.: Wilson Center (1987).

———. "Eastern Europe's Long Revolution Against Yalta." *Eastern European Politics and Societies*, Vol. 2, No. 1 (Winter 1988).

Financial Times (London) (April 28, 1987).

Bibliography

Fischer, M.E. "The Politics of Inequality in Romania." In D.N. Nelson, ed., *Communism and the Politics of Inequality.* Lexington, Mass.: Lexington Books (1983).

Foreign Broadcast Information Service. *Daily Report: Eastern Europe* (January 19, 1988).

_____. *Daily Report: Soviet Union* (October 14, 1987).

Foreign Trade (Moscow), Vol. 3 (1987).

Garthoff, R.L. *Soviet Military Policy: A Historical Analysis.* London (1966).

Gati, Charles. "The Soviet Empire: Alive But Not Well." *Problems of Communism,* Vol. XXXIV, No. 2 (March–April 1985).

_____. *Hungary and the Soviet Bloc.* Durham, N.C.: Duke University Press (1986).

_____. "Gorbachev and Eastern Europe." *Foreign Affairs,* Vol. 65, No. 5 (July 1987).

Gitelman, Z.Y. *The Diffusion of Political Innovation: From Eastern Europe to the Soviet Union.* Beverly Hills, Calif.: Sage Publications (1972).

Globe and Mail (June 3, 1987; March 19, 1988; April 4, 1988; May 11, 1988; May 16, 1988; May 23, 1988; May 27, 1988; October 18, 1988; November 11, 1988; December 9, 1988; December 28, 1988; January 4, 1989; January 9, 1989; January 12, 1989; January 24, 1989; January 27, 1989; January 31, 1989; February 13, 1989; February 14, 1989; February 21, 1989; March 2, 1989; March 16, 1989; March 17, 1989; March 27, 1989; March 30, 1989; April 13, 1989; April 24, 1989; April 26, 1989; May 6, 1989; May 16, 1989; May 19, 1989; May 22, 1989; May 23, 1989; May 26, 1989; May 29, 1989; May 30, 1989; May 31, 1989; June 2, 1989; June 3, 1989; June 6, 1989; June 20, 1989).

Gorbachev, Mikhail. *Political Report of the CPSU Central Committee to the 27th Party Congress* (February 25, 1986). Moscow: Novosti Press Agency Publishing House (1986).

_____. Speech to 27th Party Congress. *Pravda* (February 1986).

_____. *Perestroika: New Thinking for Our Country and the World.* New York: Harper and Row (1987).

"Gorbachev: The View from Warsaw." *Harper's* (July 1987).

Griffith, William E., ed. *Central and Eastern Europe: The Opening Curtain?* Boulder, Colo.: Westview Press (1989).

Guerra, Adriano. *Rinascita* (April 11, 18, and 25, 1987).

Hannigan, J., and C. McMillan. "The Energy Factor in Soviet–East European Energy Relations," Research Report No. 18. *East-West Commercial Relations Series.* Ottawa: Institute of Soviet and East European Studies, Carleton University (1981).

_____. "Joint Investment in Resource Development: Sectoral Approaches to Socialist Integration." *East European Economic Assessment, Part 2–Regional Assessments.* A Compendium of papers submitted to the Joint Economic Committee, Congress of the United States, 99th Congress, 1st Session. Washington, D.C.: U.S. Government Printing Office (1981).

Hanson, Philip. "The Soviet Twelfth Five Year Plan." In R. Weichhardt, ed., *The Soviet Economy: A New Course?* Brussels: NATO (1987).

Hatschikjan, Magarditsch. "Der Ostblock und Gorbačov 1986," Konrad-Adenauer-Stiftung Forschungsinstitut. *Interne Studien,* No. 7 (1987).

Havel, Vaclav. "The Power of the Powerless." *Cross Currents,* Vol. 2 (1983).

_____. "Anatomy of Reticence." *Cross Currents,* Vol. 6 (1986).

Herspring, Dale R. "On Perestroika, Gorbachev, Yazov and the Military." *Problems of Communism* (July–August 1987).

———. "The Soviets, the Warsaw Pact, and the East European Militaries." In William E. Griffith, ed., *Central and Eastern Europe: The Opening Curtain?* Boulder, Colo.: Westview Press (1989).

Hewett, Edward A. "The June 1987 Plenum and Economic Reform." *PlanEcon Report*, Vol. 111, No. 30 (July 23, 1987).

———. *Reforming the Soviet Economy: Equality Versus Efficiency.* Washington, D.C.: Brookings Institution (1988).

Honecker, Erich. Speech in Moscow commemorating the Great October Socialist Revolution. East Berlin ADN International Service in German (November 2, 1987). In Foreign Broadcast Information Service, *Daily Report: Soviet Union*. Washington, D.C. (November 3, 1987).

Hough, Jerry F. "Gorbachev Consolidating Power." *Problems of Communism*, Vol. XXXV (July–August 1987).

Hungaropress (various issues).

Huntington, Samuel P. "Social and Institutional Dynamics of One Party Systems." In Samuel P. Huntington and Clement H. Moore, *Authoritarian Politics in Modern Society*. New York: Basic Books (1970).

Huntington, Samuel P., and Clement H. Moore. *Authoritarian Politics in Modern Society*. New York: Basic Books (1970).

Institute of International Strategic Studies. *Military Balance* (1968/1969, 1978/1979, 1987/1988). Washington, D.C.: IISS (1969, 1979, 1988).

International Herald Tribune (May 25, 1988).

Izvestiia (June 10, 1985; October 10, 1987).

Jackson, Marvin. "Bulgaria's Economic Reforms—How Long Is the Road Ahead?" *PlanEcon Report*, Vol. III, Nos. 34–35 (August 27, 1987).

Jamgotch, Jr., Nish. *Soviet–East European Dialogue: International Relations of a New Type?* Stanford: Stanford University Press (1968).

Jervis, Robert. "Hypotheses on Misperception." *World Politics*, Vol. XX, No. 3 (April 1968).

———. *Perception and Misperception in International Politics*. Princeton, N.J.: Princeton University Press (1976).

Johnson, A. Ross. "The Warsaw Pact: Soviet Military Policy in Eastern Europe." Santa Monica, Calif.: Rand Report, P-6583 (July 1981).

Judt, T., et al. *Debating the Nature of Dissent in Eastern Europe*. Washington, D.C.: Wilson Center (1987).

Kamm, Henry. "Russians Extend Call for Candor to Relations with East Bloc." *New York Times* (April 23, 1987).

———. "In a Pro-Solidarity City, Poland's Coming Vote Is Stirring Little Excitement." *New York Times* (June 1, 1989).

Kaufman, Michael T. "Gorbachev Draws a Mixed Reaction from Soviet Bloc." *New York Times* (February 12, 1987).

———. "Poles Show Weariness of Gorbachev's Policies." *New York Times* (March 27, 1987).

———. "Glasnost Upsetting to Soviet Allies." *New York Times* (April 5, 1987).

Keller, Bill. "Soviet Bloc Feels the Reins Loosening." *New York Times* (January 3, 1988).

———. "A Little Bit of Party Disunity Suits Gorbachev Just Fine." *New York Times* (April 30, 1989).
———. "Congress Failed Main Task, Sakharov Rages." *Globe and Mail* (June 10, 1989).
———. "Eastern Europe: Soviet Asset or Burden? The Political Dimension." In Ronald H. Linden, ed., *Studies in East European Foreign Policy*. New York: Praeger (1980).
———. "Eastern Europe." In Robert F. Byrnes, ed., *After Brezhnev: Sources of Soviet Conduct in the 1980s*. Bloomington: Indiana University Press (1983).
Kis, Janos. "Das Jalta-Dilemma in der achtziger Jahren." *Kursbuch*, Vol. 81 (September 1985).
Kittrie, N., and I. Volgyes, eds., *The Uncertain Future: Gorbachev's Eastern Bloc*. New York: Paragon House (1988).
Klaus, Vaclav. "Socialist Economies, Economic Reforms and Economist: Reflections of a Czechoslovak Economist." Paper presented at the Conference on Alternative Models of Socialist Economic Systems, Gyor, Hungary (March 18–22, 1988).
Kolibernov, E. *Krasnaya Zvezda* (November 21, 1985).
Konrad, Gyorgy. *Antipolitics*. New York and London: Harcourt Brace Jovanovich (1984).
———. "Is the Dream of Central Europe Still Alive?" *Cross Currents*, Vol. 5 (1986).
Korbonski, A. "Ideology Disabused: Communism Without a Face in Eastern Europe." In N. Kittrie and I. Volgyes, eds., *The Uncertain Future: Gorbachev's Eastern Bloc*. New York: Paragon House (1988).
Kornai, Janos. *Growth, Shortage and Efficiency*. Berkeley: University of California (1982).
———. "The Hungarian Reform Process." *Journal of Economic Literature*, Vol. XXIV, No. 4 (December 1986).
Köves, A. *The CMEA Countries in the World Economy: Turning Inwards or Turning Outwards*. Budapest: Akad. Kiado (1985).
Kovrig, Bennett. "Hungary." *Yearbook on International Communist Affairs*. Stanford, Calif.: Hoover International Press (1987).
———. "Political Reform in Eastern Europe." In N. Kittrie and I. Volgyes, eds., *The Uncertain Future: Gorbachev's Eastern Bloc*. New York: Paragon House (1988).
Kramer, John M. "Chernobyl and Eastern Europe." *Problems of Communism* (November–December 1986).
———. "Can Gorbachev Feed Russia?" *New York Times Magazine* (April 9, 1989).
Krasnaya Zvezda (June 23, 1987; September 23, 1987).
Kuklinski, Ryszard. "Wojna z narodem Widziana od srodka." *Kultura* (Paris), No. 4/475 (April 1987).
Kulcsar, Kalmar. "Emberi jogok: deklaraciok es valosag" (Human rights: declarations and reality). *Valosag* (Budapest), Vol. XXXI, No. 4 (1988).
Kundera, Milan. "The Tragedy of Central Europe." *New York Review of Books*, Vol. XXXI, No. 7 (April 26, 1984).
———. "Prague: A Disappearing Poem." *Granta*, Vol. 17 (1985).
———. "Man Thinks, God Laughs." *New York Review of Books* (June 13, 1985).
Kusin, Vladimir V. "Gorbachev and Eastern Europe." *Problems of Communism*, Vol. XXXV, No. 1 (January–February 1986).
———. "Brezhnev Doctrine Rejected in Stockholm Agreement?" Radio Free Europe Research, *RAD Background Report/138 (East-West Relations)* (September 29, 1986).

———. "The 'Yugoslavization' of Soviet-East European Relations?" Radio Free Europe, RAD Background Report, No. 57 (March 29, 1988).

Lapidus, Gail W. "The Changing Relationship Between State and Society." Paper and roundtable address delivered at the *German-American Conference on the Gorbachev Reform Program: Its Impact on Soviet and East European Policies.* Washington, D.C. (March 20–22, 1988).

———. "State and Society: Toward the Emergence of Civil Society in the Soviet Union." In Seweryn Bialer, ed., *Politics, Society and Nationality Inside Gorbachev's Russia.* Boulder, Colo.: Westview Press (1989).

Laqueur, Walter. *The Long Road to Freedom.* New York: Charles Scribner's and Sons (1989).

Lavigne, M. "Problématique de l'enterprise multinationale socialiste." *Economies et Sociétés,* Vol. XI, Nos. 1–2 (1977).

———. "The Evolution of CMEA Institutions and Policies and the Need for Structural Adjustment." Paper presented at the conference on the Soviet Union and Eastern Europe in the World Economy. Washington, D.C.: Kennan Institute (October 1984).

Lenin, V.I. *Sochineniya,* 2nd ed., Vol. 22. Moscow (1929).

Levin, Viktor. Moscow Domestic Service in Russian (August 13, 1987). In Foreign Broadcast Information Service, *Daily Report: Soviet Union.* Washington, D.C. (August 14, 1987).

Lewis, Flora. "Gorbachev's Messages." *New York Times* (October 14, 1987).

Linden, Ronald H. *Studies in East European Foreign Policy.* New York: Praeger (1980).

Lukes, Igor. "To Reform or Not to Reform: Gorbachev's Initiatives and Their Impact on Czechoslovakia." *Harvard International Review* (November 1987).

L'Unita (January 10, 1988).

Luttwak, Edward. *The Paradoxical Logic of Strategy.* Berkeley: Institute of International Studies (1987).

Marer, Paul. *Dollar GNPs of the USSR and Eastern Europe.* Baltimore: Johns Hopkins University Press, for the World Bank (1985).

Marer, Paul, and Wlodzimierz Siwinski, eds. *Creditworthiness and Reform in Poland: Western and Polish Perspectives.* Bloomington: Indiana University Press (1987).

Markham, James M. "Sovereignty Made Soviet Bloc Issue." *New York Times* (March 7, 1985).

———. "East Trade Bloc Seeks Tie to West." *New York Times* (December 2, 1987).

Marrese, M., and Vanous, J. *Soviet Subsidization of Trade with Eastern Europe.* Berkeley: Institute of International Studies, University of California (1983).

Mason, David S. "Soviet Reforms and Eastern Europe: Implications for Poland." Paper prepared for delivery at a conference on "New Dimensions of the Polish Economy." Wichita State University, Kansas (October 6, 1987).

Matejka, Harriet. "Déséquilibres, endettement et ajustement au sein du CAEM." *Etudes Internationales,* Vol. 19, No. 2 (June 1988).

McAdams, A. James. *East Germany and Detente.* Cambridge: Cambridge University Press (1985).

"Meetings of Europe Working Group of the Mutual Security Project: Moscow, March 28–30, 1989 Summary Report." Providence, R.I.: Brown University Center for Foreign Policy Development (April 11, 1989).

Meissner, Boris. "Gorbachev's Perestroika: Reform or Revolution?" *Aussenpolitik*, Vol. 38, No. 3 (1987).
Meyer, Henry Cord. *Mitteleuropa in German Thought and Action*. The Hague: Martinus Nijhoff (1955).
Milosz, Czeslaw. "Central European Attitudes." *Cross Currents*, Vol. 5 (1986).
Mlynar, Zdenek. *Nightfrost in Prague*. New York: Karz (1980).
MTI in English (October 13, 1987). In Foreign Broadcast Information Service, *Daily Report: Soviet Union*. Washington, D.C. (October 14, 1987).
Nagorski, Andrew. "The Rebirth of an Idea." *Newsweek* (March 30, 1987).
NBC Television News. 7:00 EDT (May 28, 1989).
Nepszabadsag (Budapest) (April 27, 1987; May 22, 1988; January 21, 1989; February 13, 1989).
Neues Deutschland (Berlin) (February 27, 1989). Cited in Radio Free Europe, *Research*, No. 34 (March 1, 1989).
Newsweek (May 9, 1985; May 2, 1988; May 4, 1988; October 24, 1988; November 14, 1988; April 13, 1989).
New York Times (May 1, 1988; May 8, 1988; May 22, 1988; May 29, 1988; July 31, 1988; September 4, 1988; October 2, 1988; October 16, 1988; November 6, 1988; January 1, 1989; January 8, 1989; January 29, 1989; February 5, 1989; April 9, 1989; April 12, 1989; April 23, 1989; April 30, 1989; May 8, 1989; May 21, 1989; May 28, 1989; May 30, 1989; June 1, 1989; June 8, 1989).
North Atlantic Treaty Organization. "Conventional Forces in Europe: The Facts." Brussels: NATO (November 1988).
"Novaia myshlenie i perspektivy sotsial'nogo obnovleniia mira." *Voprosy Filosofii*, No. 6 (1987).
Nove, Alec. *Socialism, Economics and Development*. London: Allen and Unwin (1986).
Novopashin, Yu. S. "Political Relations of Socialist Countries." *Rabochiy Klass i Sovremennyy Mir*, Moscow (September–October 1985).
Nyers, Rezso. "Hagyomony es ujitas a KGST—egyuttmukovesben" (Continuity and change in Cmea cooperation). *Koszgazdasagi szemle* (Budapest), No. 4 (1982).
Odom, William E. "How Far Can Soviet Reform Go?" *Problems of Communism*, Vol. XXXVI (November–December 1987).
Oldenburg, Fred. "Osteuropa-Basis or Bürde für die Weltmacht UdSSR." Berichte des Bundesinstituts für die ostwissenschaftliche und internationale Studien, No. 29 (1987).
Overy, R.J. *The Air War 1939–1945*. London: Europa (1980).
Parry, Geraint. *Political Elites*. London: Allen and Unwin (1969).
PlanEcon Report, Vol. 111, No. 1 (January 7, 1987).
Pond, Elizabeth. "Pursuing the Ideal of a Central Europe." *Christian Science Monitor* (March 6, 1987).
Pravda (September 26, 1968; June 29, 1980; March 12, 1985; February 25, 1986; February 26, 1986; September 24, 1986; January 28, 1987; January 29, 1987; April 11, 1987; May 11, 1987; May 27, 1987; May 30, 1987; June 27, 1987; August 12, 1987; October 15, 1987; June 29, 1988; July 8, 1988; October 5, 1988; February 6, 1989; March 30, 1989; April 4, 1989).
Primakov, E. "Novaia filosopfii vneshei politiki." *Pravda* (July 10, 1987).
———. "Kapitalizm vo vzaimosvyazannom mire." *Kommunist*, No. 13 (September 1987).

Radio Budapest. 10:05 A.M. (February 21, 1988). As reported in Radio Free Europe, *Background Report*, No. 60 (April 6, 1988).

Radio Free Europe. *Research* (November 21, 1986).

Reiman, Michal. "Die 'Sowjetisierung' Mittel- und Sudosteuropa." *Kursbuch*, Vol. 81 (September 1985).

Reuters dispatch from Budapest (September 24, 1987).

Riding, Alan. "Italy's Communists Try Not to Be Ideologues." *New York Times* (May 7, 1989).

Rosefielde, S. "The Soviet Economy in Crisis: Birman's Cumulative Disequilibrium Hypothesis." *Soviet Studies*, Vol. XL, No. 2 (April 1988).

Sallot, J. *Globe and Mail* (March 13, 1989).

Schear, James A., and Joseph S. Nye, Jr. "Addressing Europe's Conventional Instabilities." *Washington Quarterly* (Summer 1988).

Schopflin, George. "Central Europe: A New Political Identity." *Meeting Report*, No. 21. Washington, D.C.: East European Program, Wilson Center (May 1987).

Scott, Harriet Fast, and William F. Scott. *Armed Forces of the USSR*, 2nd ed. Boulder, Colo.: Westview Press (1981).

Selucky, Radoslav. Address at *Conference on the Soviet-East European Relationship in the Gorbachev Era*. University of Toronto (October 16-17, 1987).

Semeiko, L. *Izvestiia* (August 13, 1987).

Seton-Watson, Hugh. *The "Sick Heart" of Modern Europe*. Seattle and London: University of Washington Press (1975).

Shelton, Judy. *The Coming Soviet Crash*. New York: Free Press (1988).

Shipler, David K. "U.S. Applauds (Softly) at Changes in Eastern Europe." *New York Times* (January 3, 1988).

Shiriaev, Iu. "Problems in the Development of Direct Relationships Among Economic Organizations of CMEA Member Countries." *Zahranicni obchod*, No. 1 (1982). English version in *Soviet and East European Foreign Trade*, Vol. 18 (Fall 1982).

Shishlin, Nikolay. Moscow Domestic Service in Russian (May 15, 1987). In Foreign Broadcast Information Service, *Daily Report: Soviet Union*. Washington, D.C. (May 18, 1987).

Simecka, Milan. *The Restoration of Order*. London: Verso Press (1984).

Sinanian, Sylvia, Istvan Deak, and Peter C. Ludz, eds. *Eastern Europe in the 1970s*. New York: Praeger (1972).

Skilling, H. Gordon. "Independent Communications in Communist East Europe." *Cross Currents*, Vol. 5 (1986).

———. "Independent Currents in Czechoslovakia." *Problems of Communism*, Vol. XXXIV, No. 1 (January-February 1985).

Sophia News (August 26, 1987).

Sprout, Harold and Margaret. "Environmental Factors in the Study of International Politics." *Journal of Conflict Resolution*, Vol. 1 (December 1957).

Stalin, Joseph. Call for rearmament. *Pravda* (February 10, 1946).

Szporluk, Roman. "Defining 'Central Europe': Power, Politics, and Culture." *Cross Currents*, Vol. 1 (1982).

Szulc, Tad. "Perestroika Gets Mixed Reviews in East Europe." *Los Angeles Times* (July 19, 1987).

Szűrös, Mátyás. "Wir sind inzwischen erwachsen geworden." *Der Spiegel*, No. 37 (September 8, 1986).

Bibliography

Tagliabue, John. "East Bloc Seems Divided on Speech." *New York Times* (November 4, 1987).

———. "Rumania, Ever the Maverick, Resists Soviet Spirit of Change." *New York Times* (December 2, 1987).

———. "Austerity and Unrest on Rise in Eastern Bloc." *New York Times* (December 6, 1987).

———. "Husak Steps Down as Prague Leader." *New York Times* (December 18, 1987).

———. "Soviets Letting Trade Partners Shop Around in Hard Times." *New York Times* (January 4, 1988).

———. "Hardship Ahead: Poland Can Exercise Political Will But There's No Way Out of Austerity." *New York Times* (April 23, 1989).

Talbott, Strobe. "The Road to Zero." *Time* (December 14, 1987).

Tass (June 17, 1987; October 13, 1987; October 1, 1988; October 12, 1988).

Tass International Service (November 3, 1986; October 13, 1987).

Taubman, Philip. "Soviets Won't Push Policy on Allies, Gorbachev Says." *New York Times* (November 5, 1987).

Teague, Elizabeth. "Gorbachev Addresses Prague Rally," Radio Liberty. *Research Bulletin*, No. 16 (April 22, 1987).

———. "Ligachev Endorses Hungarian Reforms," Radio Liberty. *Research Bulletin*, No. 18 (May 6, 1987).

Terry, Sarah M., ed. *Soviet Policy in Eastern Europe*. New Haven: Yale University Press (1984).

Tiraspolsky, A. "Le Sommet du CAEM: Vers un Politique Economique Commune." *Le Courrier des Pays de l'Est*, No. 289 (November 1984).

Toronto Star (May 22, 1988; July 9, 1988; January 8, 1989; January 22, 1989; February 26, 1989; March 16, 1989; March 17, 1989; April 1, 1989; April 22, 1989; April 23, 1989; April 25, 1989; April 26, 1989; April 24, 1989; May 21, 1989; May 29, 1989; June 10, 1989; June 14, 1989; June 17, 1989).

Toth, Robert C. "Soviets Appear to Soften Policy on Intervention." *Los Angeles Times* (December 28, 1987).

———. *Los Angeles Times* (July 10, 1988).

Tuohy, William. "East German Official Says No to Soviet Style Reforms." *Los Angeles Times* (April 9, 1987).

USSR Council of Ministers. Resolution. "On the Procedure for the Creation on USSR Territory and the Activity of Joint Enterprises and International Associations and Organizations of the USSR and Other CMEA Countries" (January 13, 1987).

USSR Supreme Soviet, Decree of the Presidium. "On the Procedure Governing the Activity of Joint Economic Organizations of the USSR and Other CMEA Countries on USSR Territory" (May 26, 1983).

———. "On Matters Concerning the Establishment on USSR Territory and the Activity of Joint Enterprises and International Associations and Organizations with the Participation of Soviet and Foreign Organizations, Firms and Management Organs" (January 13, 1987).

van Brabant, J. "Recent Growth Performance, Economic Reform, and the Future of Integration in Eastern Europe," Working Paper No. 5. Department of International Economic and Social Affairs, United Nations (July 1987).

———. "The CMEA Summit and Socialist Economic Integration: A Perspective." *Jahrbuch der Wirtschaft Osteuropas*, Vol. 12 (1987).

Vanous, Jan. "East European Economic Slowdown." *Problems of Communism* (July-August 1982).

Vechernyaya Moskva (Moscow) (December 30, 1988).

Vladimirov, O. *Pravda* (June 21, 1985).

Vlasin, H., and N. Alekhin. "Scientific and Technological Cooperation." *The World Socialist Economy*. Moscow: Nauka (1986).

Volgyes, Ivan. "Between the Devil and the Deep Blue Sea: Gorbachev and Eastern Europe." *International Journal*, Vol. XLIII, No. 1 (Winter 1987-1988).

Warnock, J. "The Soviet Union's Role as an International Supplier of Nuclear Technology, Equipment and Materials." M.A. thesis, Institute of Soviet and East European Studies, Carleton University, Ottawa (1986).

"Warsaw Treaty Organization and North Atlantic Treaty Organization: Correlation of Forces in Europe." Moscow: Novosti Press (1989).

Washington Post (May 22, 1988; May 21, 1989).

Wiesel, I. "K.G.S.T." *Figyelö*, Vol. 31, No. 7 (1987).

Wolfe, Thomas W. *Soviet Power and Europe 1945-1970*. Baltimore: Johns Hopkins University Press (1970).

Yazov, D.T. *Na strazhe sotsializma i mira*. Moscow: Voenizdat (1987).

———. Meeting between Yazov and writers. Moscow Television Service in Russian (January 16, 1988). In Foreign Broadcast Information Service, *Daily Report: Soviet Union*. Washington, D.C. (January 22, 1988).

Zhikov, Todor. "Todor Zhikov's Report to the BCP National Conference." *Embassy of the People's Republic of Bulgaria, Press release: BTA Report No. 103, January 28, 1988.* Washington, D.C.

Zhurkin, V., S.A. Karaganov, and A.V. Kortunov. "Old and New Challengers to Security." *Kommunist* (Moscow), No. 1 (January 1988).

Zoubek, John. "EEC-CMEA Relations," Radio Free Europe Research. *RAD Background Report/98 (Economics)* (June 16, 1987).

———. "Recent Moves in EEC-CMEA Relations," Radio Free Europe Research. *RAD Background Report/191 (Economics)* (October 21, 1987).

Zubkov, A. "CMEA Energy Supply." *The World Socialist Economy*. Moscow: Nauka (1986).

About the Editor and Contributors

About the Editor

Aurel Braun is Professor of International Relations at the University of Toronto. He received his Ph.D. from the London School of Economics. His works include *The Warsaw Pact: Change and Modernization* (forthcoming, Westview), *Small-State Security in the Balkans* (1983); *Romanian Foreign Policy Since 1965: The Political Military Limits of Autonomy* (1978); *The Middle East in Global Strategy* (editor) (Westview, 1987); and *Ceausescu: The Problems of Power* (1980). He is the author of numerous articles and chapters on Soviet-East European relations, the Warsaw Pact, the CMEA, and strategic issues. His articles have appeared in *Orbis, Problems of Communism, The International Journal, Millennium,* and *Sudosteuropa*.

About the Contributors

Melvin Croan is Professor of Political Science and Chairman of the Russian Area Studies Program at the University of Wisconsin, Madison. He is the author of *East Germany: The Soviet Connection* (1976), and has published extensively in such journals as *Survey* and *Problems of Communism*, and contributed to major volumes on communist and international affairs, including *U.S. Troops in Europe* (1971).

Karen Dawisha is Professor of Government at the University of Maryland, College Park. Her latest book is *Eastern Europe, Gorbachev, and Reform: The Great Challenge* (1988). Among her other recent works are *The Kremlin and the Prague Spring* (1984); *The Soviet Union in the Middle East: Policies and Perspectives* (co-editor) (1982); *Soviet-East European Dilemmas: Coercion, Competition, and Consent* (co-editor) (1981); and *Soviet Foreign Policy Towards Egypt* (1979).

Andrzej Korbonski is Professor of Political Science at the University of California, Los Angeles, Co-director of the RAND/UCLA Center for the Study of Soviet International Behavior, and Director of the UCLA Center for Russian & East European Studies. His most recent works include *The Soviet Union and the Third World: The Last Three Decades* (co-editor) (1987); and *Soldiers, Peasants, and Bureaucrats: Civil-Military Relations in Communist and Modernizing Societies* (co-editor) (1982).

Edward N. Luttwak is holder of Arleigh A. Burke Chair in Strategy, Center for Strategic and International Studies, Washington, D.C., and consultant to the National Security Council, Department of Defense, and Department of State. He is the author of *Strategy: The Logic of War and Peace* (1987), *On the Meaning of Victory* (1986); *The Israeli Army* (with D. Horowitz) (1986); *The Pentagon and the Art of War* (1985); *The Grand Strategy of the Soviet Union* (1984); *The Grand Strategy of the Roman Empire* (1976); and other books also published in fifteen other languages.

Paul Marer is Professor and Chairperson of International Business at the School of Business, Indiana University. He is the author of *Soviet and East European Foreign Trade* (1973); and editor of *U.S. Financing of East-West Trade* (1975); *East European Integration and East-West Trade* (with J.M. Montias) (1980); *Polish-U.S. Industrial Cooperation* (with E. Tabacynski) (1981). Professor Marer is the author of more than fifty articles and chapters on centrally planned economies and East-West trade and visited China three times during 1982–83. He has served as consultant to the World Bank on centrally planned economies, to the International Monetary Fund on Hungary, to the OECD and the UN on East-West trade and technology transfer, and to various Congressional committees on Eastern Europe.

Carl H. McMillan is Professor of Economics at Carleton University, Ottawa, Canada. He is the author of more than a dozen books. Some of his most recent books include *Multinationals from the Second World War: Growth of Foreign Investment by Soviet and East European Enterprises* (1987); *The Soviet–West European Relationship: Implications of the Shift from Oil to Gas* (with John Hannigan) (1983); *The Economic Dimension of Canadian-Hungarian Relations: Achievements, Problems and Prospects* (with Istvan Doboszi) (1982); *Export Diversification: The Case of Canadian Trade with the USSR and Eastern Europe* (1981); and *The Soviet Energy Stake in Afghanistan and Iran: Rationale and Risk of Natural Gas Imports* (with John Hannigan) (1981).

Ivan Volgyes is Professor of Political Science at the University of Nebraska, Lincoln. He is the author or editor of more than twenty-four books. His most recent works include *After the Fall: Romania at the End of the Ceausescu Era* (forthcoming); *The Uncertain Future: Gorbachev's Eastern Bloc* (1988) (editor with N. Kittrie); *Guns and Butter: An Analysis of the Defense Expenditures of the Eastern European Warsaw Pact States, 1979–1985* (Prepared for the National Council on Soviet and East European Studies, 1986); *Politics in Eastern Europe* (1986); and *Europe and the Superpowers* (editor with Steven Bethlen) (Westview, 1985). He has published numerous articles and chapters on Eastern Europe.

Index

Aganbegyan, Abel, 85-86, 93
Agriculture, 164-165, 224
Amalrik, Andrei, 127, 132(n58)
Andropov, Yuri, 69, 73, 139
Arms control, 59, 73, 113, 187, 189, 190-194, 216(n247), 221-223
Austria, 53, 56, 118, 130(n16)

Baltic states, 149-150, 163, 204, 224-225
Bovin, Aleksandr, 102-103
Brezhnev, Leonid, 68-69, 73, 139, 188
Brezhnev Doctrine, 75, 128(n3), 176, 218. *See also* Ideology; Socialist internationalism
Bulgaria, 205
   and reform, 20, 48, 90, 182, 219, 228
   Soviet Union and, 67, 70, 81(n10), 116-117
Bush, George, 192-193

Ceausescu, Nicolae, 75, 155
   and reform, 19, 23, 92, 104, 182
   Warsaw Pact and, 108, 109
Central Europe, 118-128, 201. *See also* Ideology
Chernenko, Konstantin, 69, 73, 139
CMEA. *See* Council for Mutual Economic Assistance
Cooperatives, 163-164, 180, 224
Council for Mutual Economic Assistance (CMEA), 44(nn 17, 18), 72, 185, 227
   and economic reform, 21-22, 26-33, 40-42, 44(nn 20, 22), 45(n25), 46(n46), 76, 98-100, 177-180, 182-183, 225
   and energy, 33-40, 41-42, 46(nn 39, 47)
   See also Economics
Culture
   and East European identity, 116-128, 129(n6), 181, 184-185
   East European political, 5, 153-154, 156-157, 171, 176, 200-203, 206, 226
   Soviet political, 142, 147-148, 149, 164, 171, 203, 206, 223
Czechoslovakia, 69-70
   1968 invasion of, 56, 67, 107, 199, 221
   and reform, 23, 91-92, 182, 219, 228

Debt
   East European, 34, 43(n4), 95
   Soviet, 165, 166, 185, 186, 215(nn 223, 228)
Defense, 60(nn 2, 3, 4, 6), 61(nn 7, 8, 10, 11, 12, 15)
   and modernization, 196-198, 207. *See also* Technology, military
   Soviet Union and, 10, 17-18, 49-59. *See also* Soviet Union, and defense
   and Warsaw Pact, 20-21, 23-24, 104-114, 186-196, 207-208, 221-223. *See also* Warsaw Pact
   See also Arms control; Eastern Europe, and stability
Dubcek, Alexander, 18, 24, 199

Eastern Europe, 115-116

245

and cultural identity, 116-128, 129(n6), 184-185
and defense, 17-18, 51, 52-53, 56-57, 58-59, 104-114, 187-189, 190, 195-196, 197, 208. *See also* Warsaw Pact
economies of, 28-29, 43(n7), 71, 76, 78, 172, 181-182, 226-227. *See also* Economics
and politics, 47-48, 59-60, 70-71, 75-77, 78-79, 80, 90. *See also* Politics
and reform, 2, 5, 23-24, 76-77, 78, 79-80, 84-85, 89-100, 104, 126-128, 138-139, 150-160, 167-171, 206, 225-228. *See also* Reform
and stability, 28, 43(n5), 70-71, 76, 91, 104, 107-108, 113, 127, 159, 172, 176, 178-179, 185, 204-205, 206. *See also* Nationalism
See also Bulgaria; Council for Mutual Economic Assistance; Culture, East European political; Czechoslovakia; German Democratic Republic; Hungary; Poland; Romania; Soviet-East European relationship
East Germany. *See* German Democratic Republic
East-West relations
and Eastern Europe, 71-72, 73, 77-78, 203
and ideological change, 12, 207-208
and military strategy, 187, 192-194
and trade, 32-33, 39, 45(n27), 78, 183, 184-186
Economics
and CMEA, 29-42, 98-100, 177-180, 182-183, 225
East European, 28-29, 43(n7), 71, 72, 89-95, 111-112, 152, 167-170, 172, 181-182
and East-West relations, 32-33, 78, 182, 184-186
and reform, 3-4, 5, 19, 21, 26-28, 76, 79, 84-100, 149, 160, 161-171, 173, 177-184, 219. *See also* Reform, economic
Soviet, 29, 84-89, 141, 162-167, 212(nn 140, 147), 223-224
See also Debt; Marketization; Trade
Elitism, 119-121, 130(n20), 201. *See also* Intelligentsia
Energy
and CMEA, 27, 29, 30, 33-40, 41-42, 46(nn 39, 47), 98, 179-180, 183
and reform, 5, 223-224
Ethnic groups. *See* Nationalism
European Community. *See* Western Europe

Feher, Ferenc, 201-202

GDR. *See* German Democratic Republic
German Democratic Republic (GDR), 67, 69, 110, 116
and reform, 23, 48, 91, 181-182, 219, 227
Glasnost. See Reform
Gorbachev, Mikhail
and East-West relations, 184-185, 207
economy and, 26, 41, 164-165
ideology and, 11-24, 206-207
military policies of, 188-189, 194, 223
reform and, 1-2, 3, 101, 139-141, 143-148, 150, 159-161, 171, 203-204, 206, 224-225
and Soviet-East European relationship, ix, 3, 4, 5, 9-10, 41, 69, 74-80, 126, 127, 136-137, 174-175, 177, 198, 199, 200, 202-203, 218, 220. *See also* Council for Mutual Economic Assistance
See also Soviet Union
Grosz, Karoly, 104, 151, 152, 154, 155, 174

Havel, Vaclav, 123, 129(n6), 130(n21)
Honecker, Erich, 75, 104, 181, 219

Index

Hungary, 205
  1956 revolution, 107, 152-153
  politics in, 48, 168-169
  reform in, 5, 77, 79, 90, 93-97, 139, 142-143, 150-155, 159, 167-169, 182, 210-211(n79), 219, 226-227, 228
  and Soviet Union, 69, 180, 220
  and Warsaw Pact, 110, 227
Husak, Gustav, 75, 91-92, 104

Ideology
  and cultural identities, 117
  East European, 23-24, 69, 103-104, 227, 228
  Soviet, 10-19, 22-23, 71, 102-103, 138-139, 161-162, 173-176, 186-187, 194-195, 206-207
  See also Culture; Reform, ideological
INF Agreement, 77-78, 111, 189, 193. *See also* Arms control
Information, 65-66, 200
Intelligentsia, 119-123, 125-126, 129(n12), 130(n17), 144-149, 201
Italian Communist Party, 154-155

Jakes, Milos, 23, 75, 91-92, 219
Jaruzelski, Wojciech, 75, 77, 104, 156, 157

Kadar, Janos, 75, 152
Khrushchev, Nikita
  and defense, 53, 55, 189-190
  and Eastern Europe, 67, 68, 73
  and reform, 137-138, 143
Konrad, Gyrogy, 120-121, 122-123, 126, 131(n55), 201
Kundera, Milan, 121-122, 125-126, 130(nn 18, 19), 201

Liberalization. *See* Reform
Ligachev, Yegor, 14, 144, 161, 165, 204

Marketization, 95-97, 160, 162, 167-168, 177, 180
  regulators on, 87, 89, 93, 163-164

See also Cooperatives; Prices; Reform, economic
Marxism-Leninism
  East bloc and, 10, 11, 138, 227
  and Soviet Union, 102-103
  See also Ideology
Masaryk, Thomas, 118
Medvedev, Vadim, 161-162
Military. *See* Defense
Milosz, Czeslaw, 122, 131(n35), 201
Mitteleuropa. *See* Central Europe

Nagy, Imre, 152-153
Nationalism, 110, 117, 149, 150, 155, 186-187, 204-205
NATO. *See* North Atlantic Treaty Organization
Nemeth, Miklos, 151, 152, 153
North Atlantic Treaty Organization (NATO), 58, 192-193
Novopashin, Yuriy, 16
Nuclear energy, 36-38, 43(n13), 46(n37), 180. *See also* Energy
Nuclear weapons, 49, 52-59, 60(n6), 61(n11), 186, 187-189, 190. *See also* Defense
Nyers, Rezso, 136, 151, 153, 183

Pereotsenka, 11-13, 143, 173
Perestroika
  effects of, 3-4, 102, 160, 207, 219, 223
  and Soviet-East European relations, 11, 13-18, 79, 173, 181
  See also Reform
Perevyazka, 11, 18-23, 143, 173, 198, 200, 202
Poland, 48, 69, 122, 171, 226
  1980-1981 Solidarity movement, 67, 70, 72, 107, 108-109
  reform in, 90, 142-143, 150, 151, 156-159, 170, 182, 211(n108), 219, 225-226, 228
Politics
  and cultural identity, 116-117, 122-123, 127-128

East European, 70-71, 75-77, 80, 103-104, 109, 150-160. *See also* Culture, East European political
and reform, 1-4, 5, 19-20, 28, 47-48, 78-79, 88, 90, 96, 136-137, 141-160, 168-169, 170-171, 203, 219
Soviet, 12, 68-70, 73, 74-75, 142-150, 160-161, 194, 204, 219, 224-225. *See also* Culture, Soviet political
See also Ideology; Reform, political
Pozsgay, Imre, 151, 153
Prices
energy, 34-35, 36, 42, 43(n10)
reform and, 21-22, 32, 41, 87, 88, 89, 94, 95, 165-166, 168, 170, 224. *See also* Marketization
Primakov, Evgeny, 102, 218-219
Progress pipeline, 35-36, 45(n31), 180

Rakhmanin, Oleg, 15, 16
Reform, 136-141, 150, 187, 203-208
economic, 3-4, 5, 19, 21-22, 26-28, 32, 41-42, 76, 79, 84-100, 141, 160-171, 173, 177-184, 219, 223-224. *See also* Marketization
ideological, 11-19, 22-24, 101-104, 173-176, 227, 228
political, 1-4, 5, 19-20, 47-48, 76-77, 78-79, 80, 88, 141-160, 171, 219, 224-228
See also Eastern Europe, and reform; Soviet-East European relationship, reform and
Research and development, 91, 138
and CMEA, 30-32, 38, 39-40, 98
See also Technology
Romania, 69, 109-110, 190
energy and, 40, 46(n40)
human rights and, 155, 182, 211(n101)
reform and, 19, 23, 48, 92, 181, 182, 228
Ryzhkov, Nikolai, 160

Sakharov, Andrei, 144, 147

Shmelev, Nikolai, 165-166
Socialism. *See* Ideology; Marxism-Leninism
Socialist internationalism, 14-16, 174-176. *See also* Brezhnev Doctrine; Ideology
Solidarity, 156-159, 170, 226
Soviet-East European relationship
defense and, 10-11, 104-114, 186-198, 221-223
and economic reform, 26-28, 177-186, 225
and economics, 28-42, 76
and ideological reform, 11-24, 103-104, 173-176
perceptions of, ix, 2-3, 4-5, 9-11, 65-81, 112, 125-127, 135, 198-203
reform and, 4, 5, 47-48, 76-77, 78-80, 135-137, 138-139, 150-151, 172-173, 200, 203-204, 205-208, 213(n177), 218-221, 228
See also Eastern Europe; Soviet Union
Soviet Union, 137-141
and defense, 10, 17-18, 49-59, 60(nn 2, 3, 4), 61(nn 7, 8, 10, 12, 15), 186-198, 207, 221-223. *See also* Defense
and economics, 26-29, 84-89, 91, 98-100, 141, 160-167, 170-171, 177, 212(nn 140, 147), 223-224. *See also* Economics
foreign policy, 3, 16-18, 32, 45(n25), 102-103, 218
ideology, 11-24, 71, 102-103, 161-162, 173-176, 206. *See also* Ideology
and politics, 47-48, 68-70, 73, 74-75, 141-150, 160-161, 204, 219, 224-225. *See also* Politics
republics within, 149-150, 204, 219, 224-225
See also Council for Mutual Economic Assistance; Culture, Soviet political; East-West relations; Gorbachev, Mikhail; Soviet-East European relationship

Index

Stalin, Joseph, 49-51, 66-67, 68

Technology
  military, 196-197, 222-223
  and Soviet Union, 86, 166
  See also Research and development
Trade, 91, 163
  East-West, 32-33, 183, 184-186
  Soviet-East European, 27-28, 29, 32, 42(n1), 44(n19), 95, 98-100, 136, 181, 183-184, 185, 225
  See also Economics

Union of Soviet Socialist Republics (USSR). *See* Soviet Union
United States, 49-59, 79-80, 192-193, 197. *See also* East-West relations

Walesa, Lech, 156, 157, 199
Warsaw Pact (WTO), 72, 105-114, 186, 189-198, 207-208
  stability of, 20-21, 23-24, 218, 221-222, 227
  See also Defense
Western Europe, 78, 80, 184-186, 202
World War II, 49
WTO. *See* Warsaw Pact

Yeltsin, Boris, 144-145, 146, 148
Yugoslavia, 66-67, 170

Zhivkov, Todor, 75-76, 90, 104, 219, 228

Augsburg College
George Sverdrup Library
Minneapolis, MN 55454